Practical Psychology in Construction Management

TOM MELVIN, P.E.

Engineering/Management Consultant
Stoughton, Massachusetts

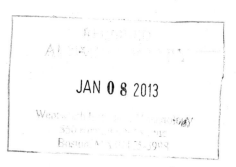

VAN NOSTRAND REINHOLD COMPANY

NEW YORK   CINCINNATI   ATLANTA   DALLAS   SAN FRANCISCO
LONDON   TORONTO   MELBOURNE

Van Nostrand Reinhold Company Regional Offices:
New York   Cincinnati   Atlanta   Dallas   San Francisco

Van Nostrand Reinhold Company International Offices:
London   Toronto   Melbourne

Copyright © 1979 by Litton Educational Publishing, Inc.

Library of Congress Catalog Card Number: 79-1009
ISBN: 0-442-25298-6

Manufactured in the United States of America

Published by Van Nostrand Reinhold Company
135 West 50th Street, New York, N.Y. 10020

Published simultaneously in Canada by Van Nostrand Reinhold Ltd.

15 14 13 12 11 10 9 8 7 6 5 4 3 2 1

Library of Congress Cataloging in Publication Data

Melvin, Tom, 1935–
    Practical psychology in construction management.

    Includes bibliographies and index.
    1. Construction industry—Management—Psycholog-
ical aspects.   2. Psychology, Industrial.
I. Title.
HD9715.A2M39   658'.92'4   79-1009
ISBN 0-442-25298-6

To
Helen, Jackie, Brian, Janet
and Timmy; my father, John J. Walsh; and
especially the memory of my mother, Mary M. Walsh.

About the author . . .

A registered professional engineer, Tom Melvin has advanced degrees in both psychology (M.Ed.) and mechanical engineering (MS).
During the last seventeen years, working in private industry and
in government, he has held numerous construction related positions including project engineer, consultant, instructor, designer,
clerk of the works, inspector and research analyst. In addition to
teaching courses in construction management and psychology at
Boston State College, he has presented seminars on problem solv-
ing/creativity techniques to a variety of industrial groups. He has
also designed a series of data guides which are used by technical
personnel around the country.

   Other endeavors have included: roofer, factory worker, tugboat
deckhand, and paratrooper. He resides in Stoughton, Mass. with
his wife and four children.

Acknowledgment

Time and space limit giving adequate recognition to the many individuals who generously contributed background material for this book. To all, my thanks. However, I would like to single out a few, and convey my gratitude to the following:

Bill Morrissey, Dean at Boston State College, who was a vital link in the complex chain of events which led to the concepts of the book.

Gene Falken, Vice President at Van Nostrand Reinhold Company, who gave me the opportunity to transform the concept into a reality.

Paul Melvin, Melvin Engineering Consultants of Weymouth, Mass., who meticulously reviewed the draft, and who advised me, both as a brother and a designer.

Steve McCarthy, S. L. McCarthy and Associates of Boston, Mass., who provided me with many professional insights into the somewhat unpredictable world of construction.

Alberta Gordon, Managing Editor, and all the staff at Van Nostrand Reinhold Company, for their dedication and cooperation in bringing this text to fruition. No author could ask for more.

And finally last, but certainly not least, my family and friends who cheerfully bore the inconveniences associated with this project.

Again, my thanks to all.

Tom Melvin
Stoughton, Mass.

Contents

Chapter 1

Introduction: Psychology and Construction Management

Abstract

This chapter begins by stating the major premise of the text: *the psychological aspects of construction management may well spell the difference between the success and failure of a project.*

The text here answers the who, what, and how questions, and outlines the material to be discussed. Overall, the volume, after analyzing the basics of construction and psychology, focuses on the individual, the group, and fundamentals of meetings. The last chapter analyzes problem-solving and creativity.

This introduction ends by identifying three broad categories of project problems: common, psychological, and inherent.

CONTENTS OF CHAPTER 1

QUESTIONS AND PREVIEW

1. How can one relate psychology to construction management?
2. Identify the three groups that comprise the construction team.
3. List 10 common problems that occur on most projects.
4. Identify at least five psychological problems that affect many projects.
5. Name three inherent problems found peculiar to the construction industry.

INTRODUCTION: THE PSYCHOLOGICAL SIDE
OF CONSTRUCTION

> *A new principle is an inexhaustible*
> *source of new views*
>
> Vauvenargues

Generally, construction is classified into the overlapping categories explained below.

1. Building Construction, Private or Public

Based upon need or a wish to expand, an institution decides to launch a building program; a bank speculates on a shopping center; or a government agency requires a new hospital or school. After establishing preliminary functional and budgetary criteria, the owner subsequently retains an architect who designs the structure with special emphasis on occupant comfort and special needs (i.e., esthetics, air conditioning, elevators, sound control, kitchen facilities). By public advertising, contractors competitively bid; usually the lowest responsible bidder receives the contract.

2. Home Construction

This classification primarily includes individual homes and small apartment complexes. Often the owner (contractor/developer) provides all designing and building services.

3. Highway Construction

Commonly used to stimulate the economy, the owners, usually the government (local, state, or federal) finance highway projects. These agencies sometimes provide the design services with their in-house staff. Contractors competitively bid, often on a unit cost basis, and the lowest responsible bidder wins the project.

4. Heavy Construction

This classification includes the larger projects (i.e., dams, tunnels, and harbors) that cost millions of dollars. Because of these large expenditures, the federal agencies often finance these projects. Large, specialized engineering firms provide the design, while the larger contractors, with their unique staff capabilities and heavy equipment, handle the brunt of construction.

5. Industrial Construction

One finds in this category such extremely complicated projects as process plants, utility plants, mills, and refineries. Usually privately funded by the larger corporations (i.e., oil companies and utilities), these projects demand the utmost in expertise and ingenuity from engineers and contractors alike (consider a nuclear plant!). Due to the nature and cost of these imposing projects, only a relatively small number of engineering firms and contractors qualify to meet the criteria set forth by the owners.

As diverse as these classifications seem, all types of construction follow the same general sequence: the owner conceives, the designer plans, the contractor builds. This construction team,* consisting of the owner, archi-

---

*Intending no irony, we use "construction team" throughout this text. The term, especially "team," carries a connotation of fellowship and harmony—a condition not necessarily enjoyed on every project. For lack of a better term, however, we use it, but in the neutral sense. Construction calls for collective effort by three groups, and how well these groups communicate, cooperate, and coordinate determines the outcome of the job.

Similarly, we use "problem" throughout to describe generally any technical or personal condition that requires correction, improvement, or modification.

tect, and contractor, works together to achieve the common goal: a successful project.

Another common feature of the construction classifications concerns the costs. Even the most modest building involves relatively large expenditures for the owner. Construction costs are so high that, collectively, the construction industry serves as an indicator of the nation's economy, accounting for yearly expenditures of over a billion dollars, greater than 10 percent of our gross national product. Small contracting firms number over three-quarters of a million, with individual proprietors totaling nearly 80 percent. The large construction firms (approximately 10 percent) account for over 75 percent of the annual dollar volume of construction. Each year, thousands of new construction teams launch various ventures. Each and every project calls for financial speculation, intricate planning and scheduling, mobilization of an army of men, machines, and material, and, finally, a complex weaving of communication, coordination, and cooperation. Few technical details are overlooked.

When it comes to interactions within the construction team, however, the heart of any project—*people* build, not plans and specs—too often the project is casually left to fate, success and satisfaction dependent on how smoothly (or abrasively) a certain personality meshes with a random combination of other personalities. Little consideration is given to the individuals that make up the team, each with an exclusive personality, ability, and "roles" to play, each speaking his own unique language. It is no small wonder that so many projects fail, not only in terms of money, but psychologically as well. Sometimes the two failures merge and, to one's dismay, an adversary created on today's project may well hold tomorrow's purse strings.

Regardless of what team a person belongs on—owner, contractor, or architect—he must work effectively with people. To do so successfully certainly improves productivity and efficiency, as well as saving time and money and, of course, reducing headaches. Every project encounters technical difficulties (interpretations, errors and omissions, noncompliances, and unforeseen circumstances beyond human control). Not only do these physical problems originate in all phases of a project, they simultaneously run a race with time and schedules. Stoically all construction people learn to live with these dilemmas.

To these physical obstacles, why add people problems to aggravate the friction? For example, at a progress meeting an architect informs the mechanical subcontractor that he has installed the wrong size duct. They check the plans, and find there, in a small detail buried in the maze of lines, the correct duct size. This is a definite noncompliance, but now emotions begin to emerge. The boss tin-knocker shouts: "Stupid design! Why the hell didn't you show it more clearly! Every other branch is a different size!" The designer caustically replies, "Can't you read plans and specs? Are you blind?" Red faces, swearing, and threatening ensue. The sub antagonizes the designer and vice versa. Each side builds enemies, possibly for a duration long after the final completion date. Who wins? No one. Closer to home, for another example, a supervisor saddles an individual with an unreasonable workload, or fails to reward his efforts, especially at review time; or worse, he criticizes the subordinate in public. The worker naturally feels hurt and hostile, so he stomps into the boss's office and angrily sounds off. Who wins? No one. Sure, at the explosive moment, the individual may feel relieved by blowing his safety valve, but after the anger dissipates, what result remains? More than likely, hard emotions.

On a more general level, how would a manager (or, for that matter, an architect or an owner) handle the following nontechnical predicaments, all of which undeniably affect the outcome of a project:

- a project directed by inadequate or incompetent leadership
- a project charged with emotion: mistrust, hostility, and prejudice
- a project staffed with problem people: the aggressor, the introvert, the crusader, the liar, the shiftless, etc.
- a project perplexed with erratic lines of communication: inaccuracies, rumors, secrets, absence of documentation, etc.
- in short, a project overburdened with people problems: personality clashes, prejudices, blind spots, back-biting and bickering

One needs no crystal ball to predict the outcome. Everybody loses something: the owner, the designer, the contractor.

This book proposes to discuss many similar (and typical) situations that commonly confront construction personnel. Equipped with a few basics of psychology and a few practical suggestions, one may remedy or alleviate the resulting friction. There are no magic formulas, no promise of absolute success. In fact, psychologists are the first to acknowledge that because the study of a single individual encompasses such a vast array of complex factors, they never can hope to predict behavior with certainty. Instead they settle for probabilities. Yet probabilities prove more useful than blind guesses. Therefore, a few practical tools are offered, to be utilized according to an individual's style and status.

A. Introduction

Without further preliminaries, we offer the following questions and answers to show the reader the total framework and major premises of this text.

1. What is the Intent of the Book?

First and foremost, the book is a highly practical, technically limited, presentation of principles of construction management and applied psychology—a blend of basic psychology/industrial psychology/Dale Carnegie/construction management.

By judicious application of these principles one may more effectively handle interpersonal problems, thereby saving time and money. Suppose a salesman or a consultant offered to sell a plan guaranteed to cut time, shave costs, and improve production. Furthermore, he claims to have developed a proven package of techniques and tips that demonstrate how to: (1) improve one's understanding of human behavior, especially that of ourselves and those we deal with; (2) maximize one's potential to grow, both personally and professionally; and (3) solve problems (technical or personal), especially those that require unique solutions.

Most assuredly, any normal manager would be interested. He recognizes the potential of greater profits, in terms of time, money, and satisfaction. In fact, certain plans and techniques already exist, the results of research and study in applied psychology. Therefore, it would seem reasonable to channel a portion of one's energies into learning how to work with people more efficiently. Improvement in this area can readily convert into dollars and cents; certainly it can never penalize the project. As stated at the outset, applied psychology promises no guarantee of 100 percent payback, but successful application of a few psychological techniques may well decide the outcome of the bottom line: profit or loss.

2. To Whom is this Book Directed?

Any practitioner in the construction field should find this material highly useful, and should be exposed to an innovative view of the important, and often overlooked, psychological side of construction management.

For expediency, this presentation skims over the vast amount of technical data; therefore, students and laymen should easily understand the contents. It is assumed, however, that the reader possesses a basic background, or keen interest, in some discipline of construction (i.e., own, design, or build). It is suggested that anyone who wishes a deeper coverage of the scientific data refer to the bibliographies for a compilation of many excellent books. Regarding psychology, any attempt at a notable dissertation is left to the academics and researchers who live in this intricate world of behavior. As with the construction data, only the highlights from prominent research studies and investigations are presented. We urge you again realize that psychology deals with probabilities, not absolutes. About one *particular* individual or one *specific* situation, you can predict nothing with certainty, only a probability. Therefore, proceed accordingly.

On a broad scale, psychology is defined as the study of behavior. It investigates behavior, stripping away the veneer of myth and irrational beliefs, so that one may more realistically comprehend why people act in certain ways. With this background, one can somewhat predict human behavior—an extremely difficult task at best. Granted that psychology lacks the precision of physics, but it certainly exceeds the accuracy and perception of a rigid personality cemented together with prejudgment and prejudice.

In passing, we propose that the applicability and efficiency of any tool, physical or psychological, rests with the operator. Each individual remains the best judge of himself and his environment. Consequently, he alone must select the proper techniques to suit his lifestyle.

3. How is this Text Unique?

Most texts on construction management approach the subject from a point of view external to the individual; i.e., contracts, duties, responsibilities, building methods and procedures—the nuts and bolts. This text, however, concentrates primarily on the internal processes—those interpersonal relations between members of the construction team that invariably affect the success or failure of any project. From carefully researched scientific investigations, a number of psychological results are applied to overall construction management problems. Some topics to be covered are: personality, needs, interests, values, attitudes, abilities, motivation, self-assessment and evaluation, assertion, group interactions, meetings, problem-solving and creativity.

B. Outline of Book

As the title implies, the subject matter encompasses three vast fields: construction, management, and psychology. Therefore, to resolve the expanse of material content, logic, and sequence, the presentation all too briefly covers construction management through the artificial device of a typical project—government agency as owner, architect as designer, and general contractor as the lowest responsible bidder.

The remaining sections identify circumstances of conflict and tips and techniques to remedy the frictions. One can relate the given examples to actual conflicts as seen on the project site. Each chapter begins with a brief abstract and a series of questions. We suggest that the reader ponder these questions diligently before reading the chapter. This device (an applied psychology technique) improves the process of learning and understanding.

A list of the topics to be discussed follows:

Chapter 1. Introduction: Psychology and Construction Management—typical problems: technical, psychological, inherent

Chapter 2. Basics of Construction Management—contracts, the construction team

Chapter 3. Basics of Psychology—conceptions of man, learning, attitudes, motivation, personality, psychology of occupations.

Chapter 4. The Individual—self-assessment, worker traits of architects, engineers, administrators, contractors, project managers, superintendents, and tradesmen, assertion and aggression, assertive training techniques

Chapter 5. Group Dynamics—group pressures, leadership, communication, cohesiveness, intergroup conflict and resolution

Chapter 6. Communications and Meetings—forms of communication, listening and speaking, nonverbal language, meeting preparation and conduction

Chapter 7. Problem-Solving and Creativity—basics of problem-solving, definition and nature of creativity, conducive traits, techniques: Osborn, Synectics, and Parnes

---

Box 1.1. COMMON SENSE AND PERCEPTION

Most people believe themselves to be street psychologists of the first order. After all, so goes the rational, after surviving a number of years on this planet, with all its hassles and crises, and its catalog of characters and weirdos roaming the streets, one must surely know about himself and his fellow man. Furthermore, the argument claims, psychology involves little more than plain old common sense. And construction people by the nature of their work, pride themselves on their common sense and their ability to overcome obstacles. To some extent, this is true, for without practical ingenuity, few projects would be successfully built.

Sometimes "common sense" leads to erroneous conclusions (is the earth really round?). As an illustration, consider the two building details in (a) and (b).

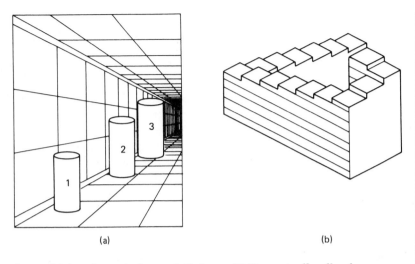

(a)   (b)

In a which column is largest? Column 3? No, actually all columns are of equal size. How would one design, bid, or build the staircase shown in b? But, one argues, these figures are only visual illusions, similar to illusions of touch (one hand in ice water, the other in hot water), temperature (in the middle of a harsh winter, a 50° day seems warm), and time (in boring meetings, time seems to drag interminably). All these perceptual and cognitive illusions bear little relevance to construction management. Although that argument is somewhat true, these perceptions demonstrate an extremely important psychological point. Many times, an individual's common sense blinds him to an obvious reality. How often does an individual mistakenly "see" what is in front of his nose because of common sense—his attitudes, values, preconceptions, and prejudices, in short: his definition of "common sense." One should keep in mind one man's common sense may be considered utter stupidity by another.

CONSTRUCTION PROBLEMS

Life isn't all beer and skittles

T. Hughes

Every project precipitates a legion of frustrations of one sort or another. Many are dispatched easily; others require concerted effort and expertise.

On the day the owner first conceives the idea, he figuratively lifts the lid of Pandora's box. Problems are part and parcel of construction management, in fact, part and parcel of any engineering endeavor. Construction being an expensive and risky venture at best, however, it embraces a cluster of problems, some peculiar to itself.

Arbitrarily, we divide these problems into three types: common (technical/legal)—these garden variety issues usually occur on most projects; psychological (people/management/supervisory)—these, often subtle but nevertheless insidious, all too frequently intensify common problems; and inherent (communication/personality differences/time)—this particular triad is an inherent part of any construction project, unlike other industries. For the present, the common and psychological problems are listed only for introductory purposes. In later chapters they will be discussed in detail.

A. Common Problems

Each problem, varying in both depth and diversity, appears in reasonable order of frequency:

- Change orders (necessity or request)
- Differing site conditions (ledge, water, soil)
- Noncompliances (intentional and otherwise)
- Errors and omissions
- Weather (acts of God)
- Interpretation of plans and specs
- Delays in work and scheduling
- Claims and pricing of claims
- "Or equal" interpretations
- Payment requisitions (general contractor/subs)
- Punch lists
- Labor problems and strikes (trades and/or factories)
- Guarantee items
- Retainage
- Safety, accidents
- Payment for stored materials
- Theft, vandalism, protection of equipment
- Suspension of work (reasonable and unreasonable)
- Acceleration of work
- Legal problems (codes, permits, government agencies, litigation)

On any particular project one usually experiences some of these common problems that, depending on the cost and the people involved, range from the ridiculous to the catastrophic. For example, an owner dislikes the color of the floor tile in a mop closet so he condemns the workmanship or, at the other extreme, the outer walls crack due to settling of the building, and the case goes to court.

B. Psychological Problems

The following types of behavior sometimes cause, and most certainly aggravate, the common problems:

- Poor leadership and supervision in direction, decisions, confidence, dedication, planning and execution, and assertiveness
- Breakdown of communication
- Confusion concerning each person's role, responsibility, and duties
- Mistrust and dishonesty
- Unrealistic definition of problems
- Inefficient approach to problem-solving
- Lack of motivation
- Disrespect of others
- Hostility and prejudice
- Poor discipline

All human beings, being imperfect mortals, exhibit several of these deficiencies to some extent. Every thermometer reads something on the scale. Still, by honestly evaluating one's shortcomings, educating oneself to proven techniques, motivating oneself to persevere (and sometimes falling short of the mark), an individual may grow both personally and professionally. This text concentrates on identifying and possibly preventing or tempering these types of people problems.

C. Inherent Problems

Economic statisticians often list construction companies high on the list of annual business failures. Based on the disproportionate number of contractor bankruptcies, one must accept their findings as indicative of the capriciousness of the industry. Every project adopts an exclusive identity and confronts the construction team with a panorama of unpredictables. Who can predict weather, factory shutdowns, strikes, poor leadership, owner vacillation, and misunderstanding—all within the confines of a time schedule? To make matters worse, picture a contractor bidding a typical job on a lump-sum basis (low bidder wins)—a before-the-fact estimate of the costs of a paper project. Most industries (i.e., auto, aircraft, and capital equipment) build a prototype, compile costs on the labor, research the materials involved, and then price the product accordingly. With their own staff they iron out the bugs in the laboratory. A construction team debugs in the field with *three* different groups: owner, designer, and contractor, each group having various values, goals, and norms—"identity." Under these nebulous conditions, one can well understand why so many contractors fails—the amazing fact is that so many survive.

Every technical industry, especially those that research and develop products, face many similar imponderables. Yet, very few industries face a combination of these inherent difficulties that penalize construction.

1. Communication

Without delving into the intricacies of semantics and linguistics, we can see that communications, even on the most fundamental level, poses certain issues. A sends a simple message to B. Did B understand A? If not, does A realize B misinterpreted the message? How often does an individual, especially in nonverbal communication, read a message incorrectly. All too often when both A and B witness the same thing, they see it differently—a result of personalities (needs, interests, values, etc.) As a simplistic example, consider the shade of floor tile in the mop closet, as mentioned above. The color, in effect, sends a message with the following conceivable results. The tile sub sees a perfectly good floor. The architect perceives it as an insult to his esthetic sensitivity. The same floor tile, but two interpretations, and indicative of a very serious practical difficulty peculiar to construction. Contractually we communicate (and interpret) via written words and diagrams. During the design stage the specification (spec) writer translates his ideas into words and phrases, adds a word here, deletes a word there, maybe punctuates loosely—often sufficient but never perfect. But in the trailer, when the fur flies over an interpretation, everyone rushes to the specifications and quotes every word with the confidence and certainty of an evangelist preaching the Bible.

In construction, specs are written in a logical, orderly manner to describe the quality of workmanship, the quality of the materials, and the descriptive features of the project. Essentially the specs communicate those aspects of the job best described with words. In the plans, the diagrams portray the physical details, locations, and dimensions, those items best described with diagrams. Due to the technical complexity of the message, undoubtedly communication of the highest form, one finds a sort of modern hieroglyphics not unlike translating a foreign language. Yet, because a "word" can never absolutely describe the actual "thing," something is inherently lost in the process of translation. Of course, even with this deficiency, contractors still erect great structures via the plans-and-specs method.

Another obstacle to be overcome involves the relative values and abilities of the construction team. Because the owner often knows little about the technical language, he relies solely on the architect or engineer to reflect his requirements adequately. Consequently, at one end of the communication spectrum, the sender of the message (the architect or engineer), limited by semantics, time, and practicability, strives to describe the project adequately so that the contractor can bid and successfully build. Meanwhile, at the other end of the spectrum, the receiver (general contractor and subcontractors) must accurately interpret the message, often second-guessing the architects and engineers. Many shades of gray exist; when one includes the personalities, goals, attitudes, and values of each construction group, the potential communication gaps multiply.

2. Personality Differences

In most industries, one group (the company) researches, designs, builds, and essentially "owns" the product. The company team consists of various personalities, of course, but company rules, philosophies, and norms tend to minimize these differences for the common goal, the product. Mavericks are unappreciated, and are sometimes fired, because conformity, to some extent, is necessary for group survival. Each member works for the same company.

In construction, at least three groups must produce the final result, each contributing a specific component. The owner group supplies the finances; the architect and engineer group supplies the design; the contractor group supplies the actual construction. In general, one common goal bonds these groups together—the final product, say, a building. A contract binds the architect to the owner; a contract binds the general contractor to the owner; contractually nothing joins the architect to the general contractor—a highly unusual predicament. One expects that owners, architects, and contractors view the project from different vantage points, based on such factors as values and motives. For instance, an owner, usually a business manager or government administrator, may stress economic austerity. He may try to wring blood out of every brick. An architect, however, possibly a sensitive artist, may emphasize esthetics as his top priority. The general contractor, possibly robust and aggressive may push practicability in order to maximize his profit. Alluding again to our mop closet floor tile, a contractor sees no reason to replace the tile (money lost) for such a stupid reason; the architect, for esthetic reasons, perceives the situation differently, and, a problem results. In addition, consider that within the construction team, not only do individuals differ, but each group also differs in values, attitudes, motives, norms, and goals—another seed of friction and disagreement. For example, an owner bases an architect's fee on a percentage of the total project cost. Consequently, if an architect (an imperfect mortal like any human) increases the project cost by unrealistically tightening the plans and specs, or by adding unnecessary frills, his fee increases accordingly. This leads to an intrinsic conflict: the architect's gain versus the owner's loss. Furthermore, with respect to the owner and the general contractor being bound together under a lump-sum contract, the probability of conflict increases. Obviously, any corner that a contractor cuts means higher profits (i.e., marginal workmanship and materials; unequals for "or equal"; out-and-out noncompliances). One group's loss may spell another group's gain.

We note another important psychological fact concerning any conflict, not only in construction, but personal as well. How one perceives a conflict by far overshadows the actual conflict itself. Imagine this situation at an incomplete high-rise building: a floor slab begins to sag occasioning these plausible reactions: Chicken Little dashes to the phone to call his attorney; The Inquisitionist blames the designer (contractor, clerk of works, a passing motorist); Mr. Cool takes the necessary safety measures, and prepares to shore up. The same situation yields three perceptions and three responses. Fundamentally, an individual would do well to examine his reaction to conflicts and friction: Moan and groan? Push the panic button? CYA? Or fight the urge to freeze, collect the pertinent facts, cross his fingers, and make a decision?

Concerning most obstacles, this book offers little solace. On each and every project one will encounter numerous sources of frustration as a fact of life: interpretations, delays, coordination impasses over late deliveries, and the spectrum of personalities. But possibly some basics of psychology may assist an individual in perceiving himself and others realistically, with all the contingent assets and deficits. With such understanding and comprehension a fair, equitable, respectful interaction for all members may occur in the imperfect world of construction.

3. Time

Invariably construction contracts specify a duration; most contracts include a liquidated damage clause, which allows the owner to assess the general contractor a certain amount (say, $100 per day) for each day beyond the contract completion date. (In settlement the owner receives only that amount which represents the actual damage.)

Economically, to all groups in the construction team, time converts into money. To an owner, time lost translates into lost revenue or services. To a designer, time lost means wasted design effort. To a contractor, particularly, time remains critical from contract start to final acceptance; it is a race with escalation, inflation, wages, and liquidated damages.

Furthermore, every project forces upon each member of the construction team everyday pressures, obstacles, tasks, and responsibilities, ensuring that everyone race just to keep pace, let alone move ahead of schedule. One jumps here; drives there; does this, does that; calls him, writes them. Construction management calls for an all-out effort, often extracting a mental and physical toll. Repeatedly a conflict arises and, if not resolved within a very short time, causes subsequent delays in the sequence of operations. Progress stops, but wages, damages, inflation losses, and frustration plod along. Time, a stoic adversary, ticks away. The duct runs into a column—what to do? Meanwhile the insulator and the accoustical tile subcontractor wait impatiently in the wings.

Figure 1.1.

Many problems demand immediate resolution. Consequently, the need for a quick response forces a supervisor to make hurried judgments based on sometimes incomplete or controversial information. But he charges ahead, reasonably chooses the best of his alternatives, and moves on to the next obstacle. Unfortunately, sometimes today's hurried decisions haunt one tomorrow. Or as so aptly phrased in that common wall sign: "When you're up to your ass in alligators, you find it hard to explain you intended only to drain the swamp." But, gamble or not, decisions must be made; indecision may prove worse. In fact, most disagreements emerge in shades of gray, seldom in neat black or white. Therefore, capable managers assemble all reasonably available facts, weigh the alternatives, gamble judiciously, and then take a stand. Who could ask for more?

Bibliography

Bonny, J., and J. Frien, eds. *Handbook of Construction Management and Oranization*. New York: Van Nostrand Reinhold Co., 1973.

Bush, Vincent G. *Construction Management*. Reston, Virginia: Reston Publishing Co., 1973.

Clough, Richard H. *Construction Contracting*, 3 ed. New York: John Wiley & Sons, 1975.

Goldenson, Robert M. *The Encyclopedia of Human Behavior*. Volumes I and II. New York: Doubleday and Co., 1970.

Wheeler, Ladd, Robert A. Goodale, and James Deese. *General Psychology*. Boston: Allyn and Bacon, Inc., 1975.

Chapter 2

Basics of Construction Management

Abstract

Chapter 2 commences with a brief review of the various types of design and construction contracts. Next is a discussion of the typical organization of those groups that join together to form the construction team: owner, architect, and contractor. After analyzing the rights and responsibilities of each group, the text examines common problems and disputes, along with the methods by which these issues are resolved (usually via meetings). Finally, the chapter concludes with a number of techniques and tips that will assist in either preventing or most certainly alleviating the impact of typical construction problems.

CONTENTS OF CHAPTER 2

CONSIDERATIONS AND CONTRACTS
A. Design Agreements
  1. Architectural Services
  2. Design–Build
  3. Construction Management
B. Construction Contracts
  1. Lump Sum
  2. Cost Plus Fee
  3. Guaranteed Upset Cost Plus Fee

GROUPS IN CONSTRUCTION MANAGEMENT
A. Owner
  1. Typical Organization
  2. Responsibilities of the Owner
  3. Rights of the Owner
  4. Contractual Limitations
B. Architect
  1. Typical Organization
  2. Responsibilities of the Architect
  3. Rights of the Architect
  4. Contractual Limitations
C. General Contractor
  1. Typical Organization
  2. Responsibilities of the General Contractor
  3. Rights of the General Contractor
  4. Contractual Limitations
D. The Construction Team
  1. Predesign Phase
  2. Design Phase
  3. Construction Phase

PROBLEM, DISPUTES, DIFFICULTIES
A. Common Problems
  1. Change Orders
  2. Payments
  3. Delays

RESOLVING PROBLEMS
A. Meetings
B. Arbitration
C. Courts

PROBLEM PREVENTION

A. Prevention for the Owner
  1. Predesign Phase
  2. Design Phase
  3. Construction Phase
B. Prevention for the Architect
  1. Design Phase
  2. Construction Phase
C. Prevention for the Contractor
  1. Bid Phase
  2. Construction Phase

QUESTIONS AND PREVIEW

1. Explain the highlights of a standard agreement between an owner and an architect (i.e., services rendered, design phases, roles of the architect and owner).
2. Name three types of construction contract. Give advantages, disadvantages, and appropriateness of each.
3. Review the standard contracts (see Appendix I). What provisions cause most disputes?
4. Describe the typical organization of each construction group: owner, architect, and contractor.
5. Identify the most important rights, responsibilities, and contractual limitations of each group.
6. List causes of change orders, payment disputes, and delays. How can they be prevented?
7. By what means are disputes usually resolved? What factors determine whether or not a dispute ends in arbitration or in court. Explain the arbitration procedure.
8. Name five preventive measures that an owner, an architect, and a contractor can adopt to minimize conflicts during the various contract phases.

CONSIDERATIONS AND CONTRACTS

Even thieves have a code of laws

Cicero

The dictionary defines management as "1. Act or art of managing; conduct; control; direction. 2. Judicious use of means to accomplish an end." Obviously, in construction the means of money, men, and materials is used to accomplish an end, the final project. Traditionally the term "construction management" (CM) applied to the contractor, who, in the course of prosecuting his work, controlled and directed all operations. In recent years, however, with the necessity of multiphase contracts and the "fast-track" dictates, the term has often been attributed to professional consultants. Usually these consultants, under a separate contract with the owner, provide overall advisory and supervisory services in coordinating several independent contracts.

For our purposes, construction management is arbitrarily designated to include a team* that consists of three groups: owner; architect and engineer; and general contractor and subcontractor. Each group, in fact, contributes a share of the duties and responsibilities as the means to accomplish the end. The owner conceives; the architect or engineer designs; the general contractor and subcontractor build.

Fundamental to any project, the owner first identifies a particular need, either in terms of shelter or utilization. A corporation may require a plant modernized or facilities expanded. A bank or realtor may deem a new apartment complex a lucrative investment. A mayor or governor, confronted with population shifts, urban blight, or public pressure, may need a hospital built or a school renovated. Needs constantly arise for building and plants. Even communities, like all living things, grow old and must be replaced. This evolution may occur quickly (a fire) or slowly through years of long-range, urban redevelopment. These owners take many shapes and forms, but all possess one thing in common—a need. (In fact, all human beings have needs, a hierarchy of needs that, each and every day, they faithfully strive to satisfy, each in his own peculiar fashion and style, as will be discussed in the following chapter.) For now, our owner, in order to satisfy a particular want, conceives of an idea—the project. Possibly the project originates with only vague conceptions, but as he mulls it over, definitions and limitations begin to take form. Naturally he checks his available finances; otherwise, with insufficient funds, he rejects the idea, and must try less expensive avenues or compromises to satisfy his needs.

If sufficient funds can be committed, the owner begins to formulate a plan to study such other requirements as the manpower, knowledge, and expertise necessary to get underway. He investigates the potential return on his investment (money or services) and, because construction involves large expenditures, he approaches this commitment cautiously. Theoretically, all executives and public officials spend wisely. He consults with his own group, reassesses and refines the needs and costs until the idea evolves into an outline and then into an initial commitment, which is commonly recognized

*We stress again the neutral meaning of "team."

as the predesign phase. Often in this stage an owner elects to retain an architect for predesign review and recommendations concerning site locations, schedules, and, of course, budget estimates. Other owners choose to perform the predesign services with their own staff.

Let us assume that the owner's staff performs the predesign tasks for a building; these may include:

- Selection and cost of a site
- Determination of preliminary requirements, such as useful area/total area; office space; square feet per person; orientation of building; climatic needs; location; transportation facilities and materials handling; types of construction (height, size, interior and interior finish, fire resistance); equipment (elevators, air conditioning, security, communication); and flexibility for future expansion.
- Compilation of cost estimates, to cover total project cost; cost of land; site improvement cost; building cost/land cost; cost per square foot, cost per cubic foot, cost per (student, patient, apartment); and resale value.

With the predesign study concluded, the owner again compares the costs against his needs and available budget. If the comparison proves favorable, he must engage a group of experts to carry the project further. Like anyone who spends, he wants the maximum benefit for the least cost. Therefore, he engages the experts. He contracts an architect to advise and design and a contractor to implement the design. The owner selects an architect by either of two methods: by direct selection or by AIA—approved competition. This leads us into design agreements.

A. Design Agreements

Generally an owner retains an architect to provide professional services; however, design-build corporations and construction management firms offer various options discussed below.

1. Architectural Services

The owner may engage an architect: as a specialized consultant for a particular project or problem; as an expert witness; as an arbitrator; or as a construction manager. In most projects, especially public work, the owner engages the architect to provide the basic services below.

Phase I—Preliminary Plans and Specifications.   The architect (with his engineer consultants) discusses and investigates the owner's requirements.

He prepares master plans, sketches, and studies. He offers advice and recommendations. He resolves with the owner compromises to fit the budget. After this initial work, he proposes a written preliminary program that should satisfy the need within the financial restrictions. From this foundation he develops preliminary plans, specifications, and cost estimates, which he submits to the owner for review and approval.

Phase II—Working Plans and Specifications. In this phase, the architect and engineers prepare the completed working drawings and specifications in detail sufficient to be bid. Additionally, the architect may assist in packaging the contract documents, evaluating bids, and in awarding the contract.

Phase III—Supervision of Work. During construction the architect inspects the work for conformance to contractual documents. Typically, he provides general administration of the project:

- He reviews the progress of the job, checks contractor's payment requisitions, and acts accordingly.
- He inspects for noncompliances, interprets the contract documents, and makes recommendations regarding change orders and claims.
- He checks shop drawings, samples, and schedules.
- He conducts final inspections.

Overall, the architect serves the owner in the capacity of advisor, agent, and judge.

2. Design-Build

In this type of arrangement the owner contracts with a single organization, usually a large contractor who furnishes both design and construction services. This turnkey approach yields a number of distinct advantages to the owner. During the design phase, the contractor applies his practical construction experience to reduce, at least potentially, the costs of unnecessary quality of workmanship and materials (and also change orders).

Another advantage concerns time. Often the actual construction can commence before the development of final plans and specs. For instance the design-builder could plan and begin the foundation work before finishing the final design.

In design-build, however, the owner must weigh the disadvantages: he loses the benefits of open competitive bids; he also loses the advice and judgment of an objective party (the architect) who has no stake in the profits of the contractor.

3. Construction Management

In this category the owner finds several variations of services rendered. The choice depends on the particular situation. In times of rapid inflation or necessity, the owner commonly decides to cut the design and construction time. Therefore, construction commences before the completion of the working documents—referred to as "fast-track." Sometimes the government, for economic reasons, decides to spread the wealth by awarding a number of smaller, more manageable contracts to local firms, instead of one expensive contract to a large international contractor. Usually the time restrictions or the magnitude of the project determines the final choice of construction management. Because an owner finances several simultaneous contracts in lieu of one vast project, or fast-tracks, he creates a number of coordination difficulties. As a consequence, he contracts a construction manager (either an architect, a large contractor, or a construction management specialist) to oversee all the projects. Essentially the owner establishes a team comprising himself, the construction manager, and the architect or engineer (O-CM-A/E),* who work from the project's inception, through planning, to completion.

During the predesign phase, the CM contributes to the general planning of the total complex. He places special emphasis on optimizing efficient methods and procedures when integrating the individual projects. In the design stage the CM advises and coordinates the various consultants (A/E's) in the consequences of their designs; the CM reviews the plans and specs; he prepares total cost estimates; and, if required, he recommends the purchase of long-lead items. In general he reduces the probability of conflict and confusion among the several contracts. Before and during the prosecution of the contracts, he acts as an agent, advisor, and arbitrator, performing duties similar to those of an architect, but in an overall supervisory capacity, encompassing a number of projects.

As stated previously, in the typical project assumed here, the owner usually selects an architect to design the project. With a completed design, the owner must then address himself to the choice of bid proposal.

B. Construction Contracts

1. Lump Sum

Under this form of contract, the owner, with a complete set of working plans and specs, advertises for bid. For private work, an owner may in-

---

*Henceforth, we shall use the following designations: O, owner; A, architect; E, engineer; A/E, architect-engineer; GC, general contractor; S, subcontractor; C/W, clerk of the works; CM, construction management or construction manager.

vite only select contractors to bid; for public work, the owner settles for any qualified bidder. The contractors estimate the cost of the work, add their profit margin plus a little to offset contingencies, and submit their bids. The owner analyzes the proposals and awards the contract to the lowest responsible bidder. Basically, the owner agrees to pay the contractor the proposed bid amount, assuming the contractor fulfills his contractual obligations. Lump-sum contracts benefit the owner in that, theoretically, competition yields the lowest cost, and, therefore, the best buy. Sometimes a contractor may bid too low, and he may resort to sacrificing the quality of materials and workmanship or to generating change orders and claims to avoid taking a loss. Other disadvantages of lump-sum contracts involve the long period of time. While the A/E completes the design, costs and wages may rise. Also, if all bid proposals exceed the budget, the owner must commit additional financing or request design deletions, both of which add to the time period.

2. Cost Plus Fee

This type of contract provides that the owner pay to the contractor the cost of the project plus a fee (either negotiated with a single contractor, or on a competitive-fee basis). Under this agreement, the project time can be reduced considerably if the owner agrees to begin construction with partially complete plans and specs, and to pay for premium time, double shifts, and special equipment.

Obviously, these contracts present some glaring dangers: the owner must wait until project completion before actual costs can be determined. Also, the incentive of the contractor to stress efficiency and frugality may be somewhat tempered. Because overhead expenses subtract from his fixed fee, however, he usually expedites the project.

3. Guaranteed Upset Cost Plus Fee

In order to set a limit on his construction costs, an owner may prefer this type of contract. The contractor, usually after competitively bidding, agrees to perform the work as stipulated in the contract documents for a fixed fee and a cost not to exceed the prescribed budget. If he exceeds the budget, he pays the excess costs. To encourage economy, the owner often provides an incentive clause, under which both owner and contractor share in the cost savings.

Box 2.1. CONSTRUCTION WORKER REQUIREMENTS

Irrespective of the type of contract, to build even the simplest structure requires a number of workers, each with his specific career skills. From vocational research, psychologists have correlated certain traits with specific careers. For example, according to some common stereotypes, architects are creative, engineers prefer dealing with things and concepts rather than with people, and tradesmen are robust and aggressive. Collectively, many such stereotypes prove true; on the individual level, however, no absolutes can be stated. With this caution in mind, note that scientists have assembled overall qualification profiles for particular careers to describe those components required for adequate job performance. Some of these components are psychological in nature, such as interest, temperaments, attitudes—those factors that combine to form one's personality. Consequently, on any given project site, one may predict that there will be differences of perspectives and opinions between the various members. This premise will be examined later in the text, but for the present, we quote a number of worker requirements associated with specific construction careers.*

ENGINEERING, SCIENTIFIC, AND TECHNICAL COORDINATION
Work Requirements
    An occupationally significant combination of: Intellectual capacity to comprehend and apply engineering, scientific, or technical principles and methods; organizational ability to plan, formulate, and carry out programs and policies; verbal facility to deal effectively with personnel; and mathematical ability.

ADMINISTRATION
Worker Requirements
    An occupationally significant combination of: Organizational ability to plan, formulate, and execute policies and programs; capacity to acquire knowledge of various administrative concepts and practices and successfully apply them to different organizational environments; verbal facility to deal effectively with persons at all levels; facility with numbers to prepare and review various financial and material reports; ability to relate to people in a manner to win their confidence and establish rapport; flexibility to adjust to changing conditions; and an analytical mind to solve complex problems.

MANAGERIAL WORK
Worker Requirements
    An occupationally significant combination of: Ability to plan, initiate, and execute programs; ability to understand, interpret, and apply procedures

and directives; numerical facility to analyze and use statistics and maintain production and inventory controls and records; leadership qualities; verbal facility; and the ability to relate to people in order to motivate and direct employees and to maintain good employer-employee and customer relationships.

SUPERVISORY WORK (CONSTRUCTION)
Worker Requirements
   An occupationally significant combination of: Ability to understand, learn, and apply the techniques appropriate to the field of work supervised; ability to communicate this knowledge to the persons supervised; ability to demonstrate efficient technical "know-how" or work along with subordinates in difficult phases of a job; initiative and drive, and ability to maintain harmony in working relationships and among workers.

CRAFTSMANSHIP
Worker Requirements
   An occupationally significant combination of: Ability to learn and apply craft techniques, processes, and principles; ability to use independent judgment in planning sequence of operations and in selecting proper tools and materials; ability to assume responsibility for attainment of prescribed qualitative standards; ability to apply shop mathematics to practical problems, such as computing dimensions and locating reference points from specifications data when laying out work; spatial perception to visualize arrangement and relationships of static and moving parts and assemblies represented in blueprints and diagrams; form perception as required in such activities as inspecting finished work to verify acceptability of surface finish; and some combination of finger and manual dexterity and eye-hand coordination to use handtools and manually controlled power tools when executing work to close tolerances.

   In Appendix IV, the reader will find the complete occupational descriptions for each of the above fields.

*Dictionary of Occupational Titles, Volume II, U.S. Department of Labor, Bureau of Labor Statistics, 1965.

GROUPS IN CONSTRUCTION MANAGEMENT

> *True it is that politics makes strange bedfellows*
>
> Charles D. Warner

In a typical project, the owner (an agency) signs an agreement with an architect for full services (preliminary design phase, working design phase, and supervision phase). Subsequent to the working design, the agency awards a construction contract (lump sum, competitive bid) to the lowest responsible contractor. Legally, the procedure strikes one as extremely precise and professional—all in black and white so that, apparently, nothing can go amiss. Furthermore, all these contracts and agreements have weathered years of test and revision. Therefore, one may confidently acknowledge the legal consequences that obligate all parties to duly fulfill all terms of the contract.

Yet, people, not documents, build projects. For certain, the legal documents define duties and limitations, but, because of expense and time, few construction conflicts wind up in the courts. Instead, most problems are resolved in conference rooms, in the clerk's trailer on a quasi-legal level, or over the telephone. In accordance with the contracts, most construction personnel understand and acknowledge defined responsibilities and roles in the course of the project. And ideally (seldom an actuality), each individual strives to fulfill each and every obligation, dot every "i" and cross every "t"—thoroughly idealistic. Nevertheless, even under the best of conditions and intentions, serious conflicts still arise. Each project yields a unique mixture of obscurities and oversights, surprises and unpredictables, both in terms of personalities and events encountered. The construction team, not the judges, remedies these conflicts, usually on a face-to-face basis with team members. In fact, sometimes people outside of contractual obligations weasel into the picture. Even though not party to the contract during the project life, hundreds of individuals, who represent tens of groups, interact with the construction management team.

Here are some familiar groups one may encounter, a few of which compound the difficulties:

- Owner
- Architect
- Engineers
- General contractor
- Subcontractors
- Subsubcontractors
- Upper management (O, A, GC)
- Vendors
- Government inspectors (OSHA, Public Safety, Public Health)
- Local agencies (police, fire, housing)
- Local committees and neighborhood groups
- News media
- Politicians
- Insurance companies (O, A, GC)
- Lawyers (O, A, GC)

- Union organizations
- Contractor organizations
- Professional organizations
- Banks, realtors
- Future users, occupants

Calculated on a one-to-one basis, close to 400 combinations are possible; in other variations, the possibilities multiply astronomically. Fortunately, only a few groups interact in any particular meeting (O, A/E, GC, S). However, all the above-listed individuals or groups affect the project in some manner and measure. For instance, all projects require enforcement of codes and safety standards, usually performed by local inspectors. Every project needs financing; therefore, insurance companies, banks, and lawyers come into the total picture. Unfortunately, some projects collide with sensitive local and national issues, which breed staunch adversaries. One need not strain memories to recall daily news stories of groups protesting the construction of a nuclear plant, or a highway through an urban area, or a prison in the center of an affluent town.

Although contracts rarely bind the construction team to these groups, managers and owners often must deal, and deal satisfactorily, with them. At times an individual may find himself fenced on one side of a controversial issue. He stands with not only his legal obligations, but his personality, drives, fears, values, beliefs, group goals, and pressures as well. Meanwhile, on the other side, 10 or 100 people, each with his unique self, coalesce in a common front against him. This can engender a difficult public relations situation, but, at times, it is a fact of life in construction. Later chapters analyze group dynamics and intergroup conflicts, but our discussion here is limited to the three major groups of the construction team: the owner, the architect, and the general contractor.

A. Owner

As remarked in the beginning of the chapter, all owners possess one thing in common—a need. If the need demands urgent action or promise of profits, the owner finances the project. Other than this descriptive simplification, little can be said about a specific owner and his particular organization. In overall terms, however, construction classifies owners into four types:

- government agencies, which build and manage schools, highways, prisons, public health and mental health institutions, and other support services
- public service organizations, which provide utilities (e.g., electricity, gas, telephone) for public consumption

- corporations and manufacturers, which build to satisfy their own requirements (e.g., plants, mills, and factories), and
- developers and investors, who build for investment (e.g., apartment complexes, office buildings, shopping centers, etc.)

1. Typical Organization

Each type of owner specializes in a certain field. He staffs his organization accordingly with individuals who can best serve the goals and guidelines of management. In order to achieve efficient management, most organizations follow the pyramidal type of organization, the president or a board of directors at the apex, and the subordinates beneath, as illustrated in Fig. 2.1.

In most projects, designers and contractors would probably deal with several of the people described below.

a. Director/Administrator.   Usually the Director/Administrator prepares the outline of needs and cost requirements; he assists in planning and development inclusive of land purchases; he oversees design and construction; and he often supervises maintenance and security. During the project life, he draws upon his support staff for advice (in addition to consulting with the project architect).

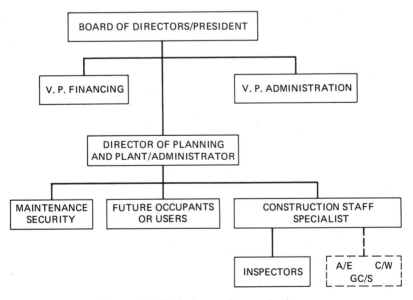

Figure 2.1. Typical owner's organization.

b. Construction Staff Specialist (i.e., Engineer, Manager). In order to communicate about construction knowledgeably, the owner assigns a qualified employee to act as construction staff specialist. Primarily he serves as a liaison between the owner's staff and the architect. Some owners retain a collaborative architect or construction manager who represents the owner in his interactions with the design architect. This staff specialist position calls for a good understanding of architecture and construction, building techniques and sequences, economical design, and, most importantly, the owner's needs. When the construction begins he usually represents the owner at the meetings. Therefore, he must have the ability to relate effectively and responsibly with all types of individuals.

c. Future Occupants. In the predesign and design phases of specialty projects such as schools, hospitals, or power plants, the owner's management should consult with the future occupants or users. They can offer valuable assistance regarding equipment, furnishings, communications, controls, and other specific necessities. As the result of their knowledge and experience, a higher initial cost of certain equipment and materials may repeatedly pay for itself over the years of use (in money, satisfactory service, or both). The owner should use these people to *develop* his program, not *design* the project.

d. Maintenance and Security. Often overlooked, this department can prevent serious future maintenance and security headaches that occur after the owner accepts the completed project. Through the years this department gains considerable practical experience in the owner's daily operation. Therefore, they, not the architect, may more accurately judge the relative costs of future maintenance and the quality and durability of materials, equipment, and finishes. During the construction phase, this department could double as construction inspectors. In general, however, the owner (especially a government agency), staffs a separate inspection team (i.e., general construction inspectors, mechanical inspectors, and electrical inspectors). These inspectors report directly to the construction staff specialist.

2. Responsibilities of the Owner

Obviously, the specific provisions and wording of a contract define the owner's responsibility. On every project one must carefully study the *actual* provisions in effect. Provisions that apply to project *A* may be deleted from the contract in project *B*. Still, most contracts contain a number of familiar duties for the owner to fulfill (see Appendix I for reproductions of standard AIA contracts).

In the design stage the owner shall provide the architect with the following:

1. A complete program explaining the owner's needs.

2. An authorized representative who acts on the owner's behalf in such an expeditious manner as to cause no delay in the progress of the architect's work.

3. All information, carefully researched and documented, describing the physical characteristics, the legal considerations, and the location of utilities. This includes:

- a certified land survey of the site
- borings and test pit data
- the rights-of-way and restrictions, easements, boundaries, and contours of the site
- service information regarding water, sewer, gas, electricity, and telephone lines
- necessary pertinent legal information

The design agreement provides for the owner to pay, usually by a certain method, the architect for the basic services and to pay extra compensation for additional services (such studies, designs, and services over and beyond the basic items).

In construction, the contract between the owner and general contractor generally includes these provisions:

1. The owner shall pay to the contractor the total amount (lump sum) for the performance of the work. The exact procedures for payment vary, but usually, as the job progresses, the owner will make periodic payments equitable with actual work, less a percentage of the retainage.

2. The owner shall pay the contractor for extra work (authorized change orders).

3. In justified delays that originate from causes other than contractor neglect (strikes, owner or architect neglect, unavoidable late delivery of equipment), the owner shall grant extensions of time.

4. The owner shall issue all instructions to the general contractor through the architect.

5. The owner shall furnish all surveys describing the site, the legal limits, the location and type of utilities, and all necessary information under the owner's control promptly so as not to delay the construction process.

6. The owner shall secure and pay for easements.

7. The owner shall purchase and maintain his own liability, property, and other specified insurances.

3. Rights of the Owner

Most contracts give the owner certain rights:

1. The right to award other contracts connected with the project. Coordination of these contracts lies with the owner, however.

2. The right to stop the work, and carry out the work. This would occur in a situation where a contractor fails to correct defective work or defaults.

3. The right to require bonds.

4. The right to inspect the work.

5. The right to withhold retainage from periodic payments.

6. The right to make changes in the work (and pay accordingly).

7. The right to withhold payments for a justified cause (e.g., a dispute concerning interpretation versus a claim).

8. The right to deduct from payments equitable amounts for faulty or incomplete work.

9. The right to use completed portions of the project before final acceptance of the total project.

10. The right to terminate the contract (and settle according to contract provisions).

4. Contractual Limitations

The contract legally limits those actions of the owner that unduly interfere with the contractor's responsibilities, viz, the owner cannot: interfere unreasonably with the prosecution, the direction, or the control of the construction work; or issue direct instructions or unduly assume control and direction concerning the construction means, methods, techniques, sequences, procedures, and coordination necessary to complete the work.

The owner and his representatives (in fact, every member of the construction team) must understand fully their rights, roles, and responsibilities so that conflicts in the construction trailer may at least be contained to a legal, factual basis. Otherwise many problems can explode into a medley of individual emotion and personalities. For example, a construction inspector requests that the project super change a detail in the masonry (or plumbing system, etc.). The contractor complies, only to find out later that the inspector had no authority to request such a change.

B. Architect

An idealist, encouraged by the AIA descriptions and the code of ethics, could envision architects dwelling in the heavens rubbing shoulders with the gods and holy men. Practically speaking though, architects, like tinkers and tailors and saints and sinners, differ in depths and dexterity like the rest of us mortals. Therefore, one describes the "typical" architect with no more precision than that applicable to a "typical" owner or contractor or any "typical" professional. Overall (and objectively), to design any building demands a person of many talents, interests, and skills compatible with a kaleidoscope of professions—artist, scientist, businessman, and psychologist to name a few.

Even with a well-prepared program from the owner, the architect still faces innumerable choices of substance and structure. With or without pencil and paper, his mind immediately begins to process the incoming data, and, like a computer, ciphers, compares, combines, coordinates, and rejects and revises based on his past experience and his personality. Simultaneously he integrates his design within the limits set by functions and finances—no simple proposition. As an artist, he translates words into spatial concepts in harmony with colors and textures and geometrical patterns. As a designer he empirically conceives and coordinates components of space and substances into a functional yet fulfilling totality. As a businessman, he researches the values of the property plus the probable costs—and advises on the integrity of the investment. And as a result, he applies his knowledge of methods, materials, and equipment to yield an acceptable compromise. Furthermore, architecture is itself a business, and, like all free enterprises, must profit or die. Finally, as an architect, he crowns his experience and expertise by melding these diverse traits into the final attainment—a unique blend of functions, esthetics, and cost efficiency. The result, hopefully, will be in conjunction with the owner's program, as well as the designer's profit motives.

In the construction phase, the architect assumes a new role, that of judge. Theoretically he favors neither the owner nor the contractor, but exerts his efforts to ensure that both parties meet their obligations. Nevertheless, as a practical observation, because the owner pays the architect to act as his agent and adviser, a more skeptical observer may expect the architect to side with the owner to some degree; after all he holds the purse strings. In any case, during construction the architect functions as the hub of the construction team. Responsible for general administration of the project, he usually schedules and chairs the meetings, processes all communication, and inspects, approves, and disapproves various requests and submissions. When problems (common/technical) arise, the disputes usually involve the architect, primarily because the contract authorizes that he, and he alone, decides the interpretation of the plans and specs. Psychologically, his discretion and the manner in which he performs these duties determine the social climate of the project. Without doubt, the success of the project depends in no small part upon his leadership and social skills. Of all members of the construction team, he deals with the many individuals over the longest period of time.

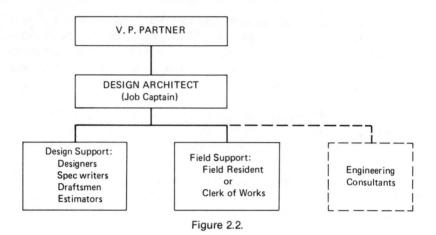

Figure 2.2.

1. Typical Organization

By arbitrary but realistic definition, the A/E group is illustrated in Fig. 2.2.

a. Design Architect.   Responsible for the overall project, he supervises his design staff until the award of the construction contract, after which he maintains the liaison between the owner group and the general contractor group. His specific duties include the day-to-day administration as the project progresses (e.g., communication, inspections, meetings, interpretations, approval, rejections). In the design stage, he allocates the needs of the owner to his support group: (1) architectural designers, who draw the architectural concepts and details; (2) spec writers, who specify the criteria for materials and the quality of the workmanship; (3) estimators, who prepare cost estimates; and (4) draftsmen, who, under supervision, draw the individual components.

b. Clerk of Works.   During construction the design architect relies on his field staff, provided by a field representative who makes periodic inspections on the job, or a clerk of works who resides at the site on a permanent basis. For our scheme of organization it is assumed a clerk of the works provides the field support (usually the owner pays the clerk's salary via the architect).

Daily the clerk monitors the job for conformance with the plans and specs. Obviously, this position requires not only a solid practical background in a number of construction specialties but, because the clerk deals directly with the daily conflicts and frustrations, firm but fair, diplomatic judgment. He checks and inspects all work performed and all materials incorporated into the project. If he discovers a noncompliance, he immediately notifies the architect. He prepares daily reports and maintains a diary; these are often regarded as a nuisance, but, in some crucial conflicts, they prove to be invaluable documents. In addition he typically processes information (e.g., shop drawings, correspondence, change order requests, and verification of change order work.)

c. Engineering Consultants. Some architectural firms maintain their own engineering staffs. More often than not, however, an architect contracts with engineering consultants to furnish the design of such project specialties as structural, mechanical (plumbing and HVAC), electrical, and landscape aspects.

In any case, the A/E relationship with respect to the owner contractually resembles that of the GC/S; the architect and the GC assume, respectively, the legal responsibilities of the engineers and subcontractors.

2. Responsibilities of the Architect

As can be examined in Appendix I, the standard contract between an owner and an architect provides that the architect render certain services (design and supervision), and that the owner pay a certain fee. Should the architect (or his consultants) fail to provide these services or lack diligence or skill in executing contractual obligations, the owner can hold the architect liable. (If the A/E commits an error in judgment, the owner may find himself in a less tenable legal position.) In general, the architect must prepare the contract documents carefully and accurately so that a contractor, skilled in his trade, can understand, within reason, the work involved. If a contractor completes the project in conformance with the plans and specs, and the final result proves faulty, the owner theoretically holds the architect liable, sometimes an allegation very difficult to prove. Unfortunately, at times the contractor unfairly takes the heat caused by a design deficiency. Depending on a typical contract (not necessarily the AIA agreement), and without precise distinction between "shall" and "will" we list familiar specific responsibilities below.

In the design phase, the architect:

1. Will be responsible for professional and technical accuracy and coordination of designs, drawings, specifications, estimates, and other work furnished by his consultants.

2. Will in the preliminary phases, prepare and submit preliminary reports, master plans, studies, sketches, and estimates pertinent to the development of the project. Upon approval he shall prepare and submit schematics and outline specs to describe the size and character of the entire project (e.g., floor plans, elevations and proposed structural, mechanical, and electrical systems) and preliminary cost estimates.

3. Will in the working design phase, prepare and submit complete working plans and specs in sufficient detail to permit the construction of the entire project.

In the construction phase, the architect:

1. Will provide general administration of the project through review and observation of construction.

2. Will visit the site periodically to inspect and to determine the progress and quality of the work. On the basis of his inspections, he will keep the owner informed. He will also require his consultants to visit periodically and inspect pertinent work.

3. Will conduct final inspections and report the results to the owner.

4. Will condemn all work that fails to conform to the contract documents.

5. Will in writing, render his decision concerning all questions regarding the interpretations of, or compliance with, the contract documents.

6. Will review and act on all requests for changes in the plans and specs in accordance with contract provisions.

7. Will, based on observation, take appropriate action on requisitions for periodic progress payments to the general contractor in accordance with contract provisions.

8. Will promptly check for compliance, shop drawings, samples, schedules, and other data submitted by the general contractor.

9. Will render in writing, with reasonable promptness, his decision concerning claims or disputes in question between the owner and contractor.

3. Rights of the Architect

We note at this point that the construction contract presents an unusual dilemma. Although the architect, in fact, plays an essential leadership role in the construction team, the construction contract embodies no provision that creates a contractual relationship between the architect and the contractor. Instead by virtue of the O/A agreement the architect derives his authority to represent the owner and to act as his agent. Nevertheless, the terms of the construction contract accord considerable authority to the architect in this role of agent/advisor.

Contingent upon the particular contract, the architect claims the:

1. Authority to act on behalf of the owner as provided by the provisions of the contract.

2. Authority to reject work that fails to conform to the contract documents.

3. Authority to require special inspection or testing of work whether fabricated, installed or completed (subject to contract provisions).

4. Right, at all times, to inspect the work whenever in preparation and progress.

5. Right to approve the quality of materials and workmanship.

6. Authority to reasonably instruct the contractor to improve his progress if the project lags behind schedule.

7. Right to interpret the requirements of the contract documents.

8. Authority to order (by written order) minor changes in the work not involving money or time extension, and consistent with the intent of the contract documents.

4. Contractual Limitations

Because the architect acts on behalf of the owner, the reader should note that the contractual limitation imposed on both parties relates to similar issues: neither party can unduly interfere with the contractor's responsibilities.

1. The architect cannot unreasonably interfere with the prosecution, the direction, or the control of the construction work.

2. The architect cannot issue direct instructions concerning the construction means, methods, techniques, sequences, procedures, and coordination necessary to complete the work. Note: the architect is not responsible for the above, nor is he responsible for the contractor's failure to carry out the work.

3. The architect cannot unduly assume control and direction of the construction work.

4. The architect cannot change the contract except as provided by the contract terms, which is usually by the written consent of owner, contractor, and architect.

5. The architect cannot deny the contractor the right to submit disputes involving legal issues to arbitration or to the courts. Delays, liquidated damages, and claims for extra work fall under this provision.

C. General Contractor

Simplistically, one may define a typical general contractor as an organization of technical personnel who possess the craft and capacity to bid and build a project in accordance with the contract documents. No less talented (or typical) than the architect, the contractor creates in a different medium. He works with things—the bricks and boards, the cement and steel, the paint and polish necessary to convert design concepts into actual constructs.

Of the contractor construction commands a skein of abilities that thread the range of human occupations: builder, businessman, lawyer, financier, army general, gambler, and last, expert in human and public relations.

As a builder, obviously, he must understand construction means, methods, techniques, sequences, etc. In addition, he must recognize what, when, and how to improve on each process so as to maximize his profits. Unfortunately, at times a few deadbeat contractors carry this to the extreme, overstepping contractual limits. Under a competitive lump-sum contract, the contractor essentially claims that he can complete the job at least cost to the owner, and still make a profit. How well he implements this claim determines his profits—a hard case of put up or shut up.

As a businessman, the successful contractor must effectively apply his knowledge of management skills, business techniques, and strategies, as well as accounting, taxes, sales, purchasing, etc. He either knows what to bid and when to bid, or sorely pays the penalty for his miscalculations, which, for small proprietorships, comes directly from their pockets.

As a lawyer, he must thoroughly understand contracts, legal and contractual problems, mediation, arbitration, litigation, warranties and guarantees, bonding, documentation, and any and all judicial matters. He must accurately determine when and where to seek professional legal counsel. Contractually, the contractor deals with the largest number of people on (and outside) the construction team, the owner for one, but also subcontractors, vendors, and suppliers under individual contracts. Should any of the subs or suppliers fail to uphold his contract, the general stands liable to the owner. Therefore, he may be forced into litigation twice—as a defendant against the owner, and as a plaintiff against his subs.

As a financier, he must manage the finances, cash flow, cost control, cost and corporate accounting, payrolls, insurances, and bonds. He must decide when to buy or to lease equipment. Most important, he must keep timely records of the running costs of the project. If, during the course of construction, actual costs far exceed the estimates, beware, something may be amiss.

As the army general, he must organize and mobilize men and equipment. He must purchase, expedite, and transport materials. He must plan and coordinate every sequence of the project from establishing the supply of deliveries on time in the right place to keeping open lines of communication and cooperation. And finally, he must approach the total project with the dedication, intensity, foresight (and unpredictability) of an army invading an island beachhead.

As the gambler, the contractor risks money to make money. In bidding, like a clairvoyant, he studies the plans and specs, estimates the costs, weighs the odds (bid too high or too low?), and places his bet. If he bids too low, or misses a certain phrase or detail in the contract, or fails to execute the project efficiently, or lucks out badly, he may bankrupt the business.

As the expert in human and public relations, he must interact with workers, his subgroups, agencies, the public, and the unions. He must remedy all disputes and disagreements ranging from labor/management to union/union, for all jeopardize the quality and reputation of the job. Therefore, he must offer assistance to alleviate, if not correct, any issues. Liable for his subs, he also stands liable for the actions of union tradesmen who owe primary allegiance to the union, not the company. A laborer, setting a water pipe in a trench is notified that he is laid off. Disgruntled he shovels a pile of gravel into the pipe. Consequently the flushometers hang up, with the final result that the plumbing sub pays the cost of cleaning out the total system.

With respect to government agencies, the general must abide by their rules and regulations, and must reasonably suffer the peeves and peculiarities of individual inspectors and officials.

Finally he must protect the worker and the public—in addition to human and legal consequences, serious accidents always damage the contractor's image, as well as his insurance premiums.

1. Typical Organization

Although some construction organizations consist of a number of separate departments (e.g., financial, accounting, purchasing, estimating, sales, engineering, mechanical, and special services), the typical organization sketched in Fig. 2.3 emphasizes the project manager and the project superintendent.

a. Project Manager.   Vested with considerable authority and responsibility, the project manager devotes his energies and expertise to completing

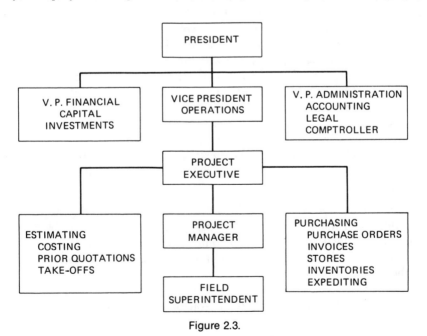

Figure 2.3.

the job within the contract time and the cost considerations. His efforts directly contribute to the project's success: ideally, maximum profits in minimum time. Psychologically and somewhat prejudicially, his performance and social behavior, in no small part, are used to measure the integrity and competence of the total organization.

As the contractor's project representative, he serves as a general liaison between the field staff and the architect and owner. He attends meetings, presents the contractor's position regarding conflicts and claims, and plays a vital part in the general planning, scheduling, and controlling of the construction. He prepares monthly budget statements. He checks subcontract payment requisitions. He submits contractor payment requisitions, and reviews change orders and claims and correspondence. He issues reports, and ensures that the daily, weekly, and monthly reports comply with company criteria. He enforces the project's safety standards. As a result of these tasks he closely associates with a large number of individual groups: architects, engineers, owners, staff, subs, subsubs, vendors, unions, officials, and the public. Therefore, in addition to his field duties, he must conduct himself with tact and diplomacy.

b. Project Superintendent. Allied tightly with the project manager, the project superintendent oversees the day-to-day field operations. He confers daily with the trade foremen, decides on details, resolves minor disputes, defines and submits major disputes for discussion at construction meetings. He inspects quantity and quality of the workmanship and materials. He reports any noncompliance. He schedules and coordinates the progress of the work. He forms a close alliance with his purchase agents and expediters to ensure prompt, accurate deliveries. He checks cost records and approves payrolls. He prepares the job records and reports, and maintains a daily diary documenting conditions, issues, and events that may later prove crucial.

Because he represents the owner on a personal, day-to-day basis, he reflects not only the technical competence of the company, but the public relations image as well. Therefore, he must be quite adept at working with various types of individuals.

c. Support Personnel. This category includes the purchasing agent, the expediter, and the scheduler. As the titles indicate, each specializes in certain critical functions necessary to complete the project in terms of lowest costs and time. In smaller organizations one individual may wear any or all of these hats.

2. Responsibilities of the General Contractor

As a consequence of the construction contract with the owner, the contractor burdens himself with a precarious situation that demands countless duties but confers few rights. Regardless of obstacles and difficulties, the owner expects the general to complete the project in accordance with the contract documents—so well expressed by "Don't tell me about the labor pains, just show me the baby." To accomplish this, the general contractor supervises all construction techniques, methods and means, sequences and schedules. He pays for all the labor, materials, equipment, and machinery necessary to complete the work. He employs a competent superintendent who resides at the site during the prosecution of the work. He complies with laws and ordinances, with union agreements and labor practices, with insurance and tax requirements. He stands responsible to the owner for all acts and omissions of his employees, his subs, and his agents.

Although construction contracts vary from project to project, the reader can identify common specific responsibilities below. As suggested by the AIA contract (Appendix I), the contractor is required to:

1. Study carefully the contract documents, and at once report to the architect, any error, inconsistency, or omission. Under such situations disreputable contractors sharpen their change order pencils.

2. Supervise and direct the work.

3. Be responsible for all construction means, methods, techniques, sequences, and procedures in fulfilling the work.

4. Be responsible for coordinating all portions of the work.

5. Provide and pay, unless otherwise specifically noted, for all labor, materials, equipment, tools, equipment and machinery, water, heat, utilities, transportation, and other facilities and services necessary for the proper execution of the work.

6. Warrant to the owner and the architect that all equipment and materials furnished will be new (unless otherwise noted), and that all the work will be of good quality and free from defects. If required by the architect, the contractor shall furnish satisfactory evidence as to the kind and quality of materials and equipment.

7. Pay all sales, consumer, and other taxes required by law.

8. Secure and pay for all necessary permits, fees and licenses legally required at the time bids are received.

9. Give all notices and comply with all laws, ordinances, rules, and orders of any public authority bearing on the project.

10. Employ a competent superintendent to be at the site full time during the progress of the work. The superintendent will represent the contractor, and all communication given to the superintendent is as binding as if given to the contractor.

11. Be responsible for all acts and omissions of his employees, and his subcontractor's employees and agents.

12. Prepare and submit for the approval of the architect, immediately after award of contract, an estimated progress schedule. In addition he will

promptly submit shop drawings and samples that illustrate some portion of the work.

13. Forward all communication to the owner through the architect.

14. Promptly pay each subcontractor an amount to which the subcontractor is entitled, less the applicable retainage, in accordance with the contract provisions, and upon payment from owner.

15. Be responsible for initiating, maintaining, and supervising all safety precautions and programs. He shall take all reasonable precautions for the safety and protection of all people, materials, equipment, and property. If, by contractor (or sub) negligence, an accident occurs, the contractor will make remedy.

16. Purchase and maintain all insurances specified in the terms of the contract.

17. Promptly correct, at his own expense, all work (fabricated, installed, or completed) rejected by the architect.

3. Rights of the General Contractor

The rights of the contractor are few, but these precious provisions generally address important issues related to progress payments, extra payment, termination of contract, courses of appeal, and methods and sequences used to prosecute the work.

1. Of utmost importance, the contractor has the right to expect payments from the owner. Therefore, depending upon the particular provisions, the contract specifies the contractor's rights concerning such issues as:

- the method and amount of progress payments,
- the conditions and payment for extra work (approved change orders),
- recourse, should the owner fail to pay or terminate the contract,
- justification for delays and extensions of time,

Usually, if the owner fails to pay, the contractor, upon written notice, can stop the work until payment is made.

2. The general contractor has the right to process the work by using any methods, means, techniques, sequences, and equipment that he chooses (assuming all conform with applicable laws and contracts).

3. The general contractor can purchase his materials, and contract his subcontractors (unless limited by the contract) wherever he sees fit to do so.

4. The general contractor has the right to appeal decisions of the owner and the architect. In public contracts, the contractor can appeal to a board

of appeals or a specified official. Ultimately, the contractor has the right to submit any legal dispute to the courts for resolution.

4. Contractual Limitations

The construction contract limits the owner and the architect from interfering with the rights and duties of the contractor. Reciprocally, the contractor must not infringe on the rights of these parties, such as inspection of work and award of other contracts.

In addition the contract frees the contractor from responsibility for damages caused by design error and omissions. Specifically, the general contractor:

1. Cannot interfere with the rights, nor with the responsibilities imposed upon the owner/agent in the prosecution of the contract.

2. Shall not do work without Contract Documents. He shall *not* deviate from the plans and specifications without proper documented authorization.

3. Shall *not* be liable to the owner or the architect for damages resulting from errors, inconsistencies, or omissions in the contract documents. From a public relations view, however, this divorce from design errors may be easier said than done.

4. Shall *not* be responsible to ensure that the plans and specifications are in accord with applicable laws, statutes, building codes, and regulations.

5. Will *not* be required to contract with any subcontractor or person or organization against whom he has a reasonable objection.

6. Shall *not* substitute any subcontractor, superintendent, person, or organization who has been accepted by the owner or architect unless the properly approved by such.

Box 2.2 CONTRACT PROVISIONS

"The owner shall pay . . ."

"The architect shall be responsible for the professional and technical accuracy . . ."

"The contractor shall be responsible for all construction means, methods, techniques . . ."

Gerry Fox

D. The Construction Team

This discussion of construction management concludes with a brief review of the groups that comprise the construction team, the time sequences involved in a normal project, and the fabrication of a "typical" project. Because building encompasses such a wide variety of projects, each unique, practicality limits the presentation to those aspects of the construction industry that best typify most projects. This "typical" project, like most projects, involves a general order and sequence, the three Cs (communication, coordination, cooperation), and, of course, common problems and procedures.

The construction team consists of three broad memberships: the owner (O), a government agency (say, state level); the architect (A/E) and his engineering consultants; and the contractor (GC/S), unionized, and the lowest responsible bidder.

The sequence from inception to completion follows:

1. Upon request from a state institution (say, a state college or institution), the agency establishes certain functional and budget requirements (say, a school building to cost several million dollars).

2. The agency selects an architect (A), who, in turn, contracts for the appropriate engineering (E) services.

3. The A/E prepares the plans, specs, and cost estimates. After review and revision by the agency, the contract documents proceed to the bid stage.

4. The agency advertises the project: open bids on a lump-sum basis.

5. General contractors and specialty subcontractors submit bids; generally the lowest responsible bidders win the job.

6. The project moves into the construction phase. The architect, who represents the owner, renders interpretations and ensures compliance with the contract documents. Various state officials and inspectors also represent the owner. Contractually the owner signs a contract with the architect and another with the general contractor, who signs contracts with consultants and subcontractors, respectively.

7. The general contractor mobilizes his forces, coordinates his subs, applies his expertise and equipment, and executes the project within a stipulated time period in accordance with the contract documents.

All this information is collected and presented in Fig. 2.4. Although each construction project varies somewhat from this fabrication, the typical project underscores two objectives:

1. In actuality, it closely represents a government-awarded construction project that joins the various groups contractually.

2. Psychologically, it shows the sequences and the circumstances under which these groups interact.

As can be seen from the schematic, the project process involves a time sequence not only in terms of total project life span, but contractually and psychologically as well. We divide this sequence into the following three phases.

1. Predesign Phase

In this phase the owner draws from his in-house staff to form a study group. On the basis of their investigation of needs and resources, the owner makes a financial commitment. At the end of the study phase, the owner group (O) establishes contact with the architect, psychologically and contractually.

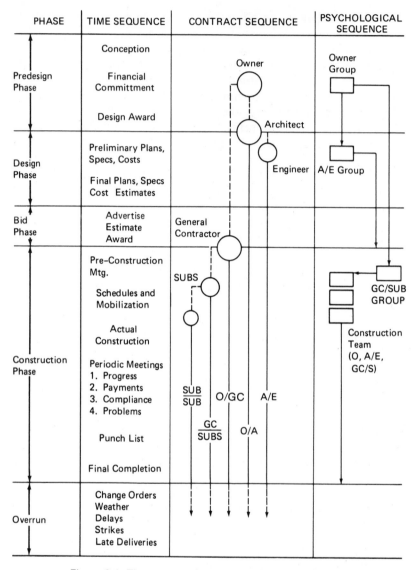

Figure 2.4. The construction process: A typical project.

2. Design Phase

Upon selection by the owner, the architect contracts with his engineers and consultants to create the architect/engineer (A/E) group. Initially the A/E group meets with the O group to discuss the general scope of the project, the budget limitations, and special features or needs. From this information, the A/E designs the plans and specifications, usually progressing through a preliminary submission to final bid documents.

Contractually, the owner signs an agreement with the architect to perform the design/administrative services. Generally this agreement runs for the duration of the project from the date of the design agreement to the final completion date of the construction project. The architect in turn contracts with consultants for essentially the same duration.

Psychologically, the architect first assembles the A/E group in the initial design phase. Throughout this phase the O group and A/E group interact in the more or less harmonious atmosphere of client-advisor.

3. Construction Phase

Following the successful bid of the project, the owner signs a contract with the general contractor, who, in turn, contracts with his subcontractors, vendors, and material suppliers. The duration of the contract essentially runs from date of receipt of the "notice to proceed" through a specified time. By virtue of change orders, disputes, and delays, the actual completion date often extends beyond the original contract date. Psychologically, the contractor, upon award of the contract, assembles his general contractor/subcontractor (GC/S) group, which unites with the O and A/E groups to form the construction team.

During a project, the majority of activities (and most of the interactions) occur during the construction period. Consequently, most of the problems and conflicts happen in this phase, and logically so, because the errors, oversights, and omissions that are missed in the study-design-bid phases all too readily surface in the actual building of the project. In a later section, some preventative techniques to minimize these errors, oversights, and omissions are reviewed, but, for the present, we will examine some of the major common problems.

First, a few additional justifications are submitted relative to the concept of the "typical" project. To the critical reader, this artificial concept may seem too far removed from contemporary construction, which, with its collage of people and events, defies "averages" or "typicals." True to some extent. Yet it does provide the microscope by which the reader can examine those psychological elements that pervade every project. In fact, even the ancients recorded some of these human elements and relationships to support the veracity of a "typical" project (see Box 2.3).

Box 2.3. PERCEPTION, PSYCHOLOGY, AND THE PARTHENON CONSTRUCTION TEAM

The Parthenon illustrates the relationship between construction and psychology. History identifies the following members of the construc-

tion team, organized not unlike contemporary teams:

- *Initiator—Pericles (Athenian commander and statesman)*
- *Financiers—the Athenians (and her allies)*
- *Project superintendent—Pheidias (great sculptor and friend of Pericles—patronage?)*
- *Architects—Ictinus and Callicrates*
- *Contractors—thousands of metrics (freeman of foreign birth), freedmen, and slaves who supplied, respectively, the professionals, contractors; artists, painters, goldsmiths, sculptors, veneerers, metalworkers, quarrymen, carters, stonecutters, carpenters, and masons; the laborers*
- *The inspectors—groups of diligent citizens who not only inspected the project, but exposed price gouging and payroll padding as well. They also assisted in coordinating job progress and expediting labor and materials. If a worker, so notes the chronicles, performed sloppily or incompetently, the Athenians fired him, or worse. This situation seldom occurred, however, because of high patriotism and piety (piety or punishment?)*

The project cost totaled $4.2 million over a 15-year span with the average worker earning 1½ to 2 drachmas (35¢) per day.

PARTHENON
(447–432 BC)

By virtue of optical illusions, the eye tends to perceive:

- *horizontal lines that appear to dip in the center*
- *straight columns that appear concave*
- *corner columns that appear thinner than the other columns, and appear to lean outward*

To counteract these optical illusions, Pericles's architects compensated by subtly curving the stones:

- *the floor and architraves arch slightly to offset the illusion of sag*

- *the columns swell ¾ of an inch in diameter from the base to the middle, then taper to the top to offset the appearance of concavity*
- *the thickness of the corner columns slightly exceeds the diameters of the inner columns to offset the appearance of thinness*
- *the columns lean slightly toward the center so as to appear straight*
- *the metopes, not actually square, appear square when viewed from below*

To add human interest to this great work of construction, and to illustrate that history repeats itself, we mention the job super, Pheidias. Painter, bronze designer, sculptor, he mastered every form of art to become the greatest sculptor in Greece. Already an old man, he not only superintended the whole Periclean building program (total project cost: $57 million) and designed the sculptured ornaments, he also created the statue of the goddess, Athene Parthenos. The statue stood 38 ft high, had a body sculpted from ivory and a robe made from gold (2545 lbs. of gold). Unfortunately, upon completion, the citizen-inspectors discovered that a portion of the gold and ivory reserved for the statue had suspiciously disappeared from Pheidias' studio. The political foes of Pericles, his friend, leaped at the opportunity to discredit the government. They charged Pheidias with theft and convicted him. Luckily the people of Olympia interceded, and bought his freedom (other than the names, it reads like yesterday's newspaper exposé). The price that Pheidias paid in return meant that he relocate to Olympia to make the chryselephantine statue for the temple of Zeus. Pheidias built a statue of such beauty and magnificence that history proudly lists it as one of the Seven Wonders of the Ancient World. Apparently in his final years, fate brought him only additional grief; one myth contends that he died in an Athenian jail; another claims that the citizens of Elis put him to death (432 BC). Such are the woes of the job superintendent.*

*Seven Wonders: (1) Pyramids of Egypt; (2) the Pharos at Alexandria; (3) the Hanging Gardens and Walls of Babylon; (4) the Temple of Artemis at Ephesis; (5) the statue of the Olympian Zeus (by Pheidias); (6) the Mausoleum at Halicarnassus; and (7) the Colossus of Rhodes.

PROBLEMS, DISPUTES, DIFFICULTIES

> *Anything that can go wrong*
> *will go wrong.*
>
> Murphy's First Law

The first chapter divided construction conflicts into common problems (technical/legal); psychological problems (people/management/supervisory); and inherent problems (communication/personality differences/time). From a semantic point of view, a problem is loosely defined to mean any situation that differs from the ideal and requires remedial action. Obviously, problems vary in depth in terms of cost and frustration. A major change order (i.e., an owner request for special equipment) may involve large expenditures and little frustration, whereas minor punch list items (e.g., a broken doorknob, a cracked window, or a holiday) may churn considerable hostility.

A. Common Problems

As emphasized, every construction project faces any number or combination of these difficulties, which the construction team must remedy. In fact, the origin and outcome of common problems depend directly on how skilled the construction group (and individuals) manage the psychological and inherent issues. This book concentrates on the psychological and inherent issues, but, because this chapter reviews the basics of construction management, it seems appropriate here to address some of the more fundamental technical and legal problems, too.

For completeness, we repeat the common problems in a reasonable order of frequency: (1) change orders; (2) different site conditions; (3) noncompliances; (4) errors and omissions; (5) weather; (6) interpretation of plans and specs; (7) delays; (8) claims; (9) "or equals"; (10) payment requisitions; (11) punch lists; (12) strikes; (13) guarantee items; (14) retainage; (15) safety, accidents; (16) payment for stored material; (17) theft, vandalism; (18) suspension of work; (19) acceleration of work; and (20) legal problems.

We notice that many of the items can (and do) overlap with several others. An interpretation may result in a claim-versus-change-order controversy, which may ultimately wind up in court. Severe weather may delay the progress of the job, therefore calling for a contract modification (change order) to grant an extension of contract time. Unfortunately, in many situations, even the most capable and conscientious can exert no control over weather, strikes, and acts of God, and little direct control over theft, safety, and the actions of others (acceleration or suspension of work). As discussed later, however, owners and architects can alleviate, if not prevent, many difficulties especially in the study-design phase.

Change orders, payments, and delays are three major problem areas in project after project.

1. Change Orders

As invariably stated in the construction contract, an owner may order changes (within the general scope of the work) consisting of additions, deletions, or other modifications. Of course, the owner adjusts the contract sum and time accordingly.

In practice, a project that requires no changes is rare. Only the most naive optimist would expect no contract modifications, even under the most ideal conditions—excellent design, capable people, and noble motives. In fact, so frequently do parties modify the contract that the budget generally provides a contingency, usually 5–15 percent of the total project cost, to absorb these extra costs. Why? The extras originate because of innumerable reasons, many of which cause considerable hard feelings among the groups. Frequently, an owner requests a number of changes that he could easily have anticipated in the study-design stage. Often the A/E group commits an error or fails to coordinate or describe the work adequately and a contractor, a businessman to the root, recognizes opportunity's knock (on a noncompetitive basis) with respect to change orders. The more frequent causes of change orders are discussed below.

a. Request. In time, functional needs change and oversights occur; therefore, an owner or architect, being frail humans, requests a modification. Each of us could unearth many mistakes the O-A/E group has buried via change orders.

b. Differing Site Conditions. This heading includes not only unanticipated subsoil conditions, such as rock, ledge, and water, but latent conditions uncovered in renovating buildings (i.e., condition of piping hidden in the chases or above the ceilings).

c. Inadequate Plans and Specifications. The term "inadequate" covers errors, omissions, oversights and lack of foresight, ineffective communication with the owner, and poor coordination between the consultant's specialty designs, resulting in interferences, and disputes over the scope of work. More often than not the owner pays for these corrective changes.

d. Delays. If the contract justifies the delay (typical reasons—unusually severe weather, acts of God, and strikes), the owner grants an extension of time. If, however, the contractor fails to provide solid justification, the owner may assess liquidated damages. Because this type of conflict involves legal matters (i.e., the contractor may claim that the O or A/E caused the delay), the court often decides the outcome.

e. Inspection and Acceptance. In order to verify alleged defects the O or A/E may order the contractor to perform special tests. If the results prove the work in compliance, the owner issues a change order.

f. Suspension of Work. Sometimes, by reason of a program change or late delivery of owner-furnished equipment, the owner suspends (or delays) the project. Therefore, he must consider paying the contractor for such standing costs as: costs attributed to nonproductive men and equipment; costs of stopping and remobilization; additional overhead costs.

g. Miscellaneous.   A few less frequent causes of change orders are mentioned for reference: termination of contract for convenience of owner; acceleration of work; escalation of labor and materials; ripple effect; possession prior to completion.

2. Payments

One may question the veracity of money being the root of all evil, but few can deny that money makes the project move. Without a repeated flow of sufficient cash, in time, all projects will stop. In fact, if a contractor undergoes intermittent difficulties with his cash flow, the effect spills over to his subs, vendors, and material suppliers; if not immediately righted, it adversely affects the quality and progress of the total project. We discuss a few familiar money problems below.

a. Periodic Payment Requests.   Most contracts specify certain routines for periodic payments. Usually on a monthly basis, the contractor requisitions a progress payment based upon the value of the work (less retainage) completed by him and his subcontractors. The architect checks the request for accuracy and compliance, and, depending upon the particular provisions of the contract, he submits his recommendation to the owner (or issues a "Certificate of Payment"). Within a stipulated time, the general contractor receives his payment, and, in turn, he pays his subcontractors accordingly.

Three frequent disputes erupt: (1) the architect (or owner) disagrees with the contractor over the dollar value of work completed; (2) the general neglects to pay the subcontractor an equitable amount, or the subcontractor, upon payment from the prime, neglects to meet his proper financial obligations; (3) the owner withholds payment because of a contractual controversy, such as defective work, or liquidated damages, or the (private) owner deliberately delays payments so he can utilize the funds elsewhere. As a final illustration, and actually a frequent occurrence the (public) owner, as a consequence of bureaucratic restrictions, processes payments all too slowly.

b. Retainage.   Typically a construction contract will provide that a percentage (as high as 10 percent) of each periodic payment be retained by the owner as a protection against defective work, claims by subcontractors and vendors, and liquidated damages. Many contractors claim that, because of performance and payment bond protection to the owner, this retainage unnecessarily forces them to work with only 90 percent funds, a serious issue, especially for a subcontractor who completes his work early in the project. He must wait until the job is completed before he receives his 10 percent.

c. Payment For Stored Material.   Few owners wish to pay for materials not yet installed because of theft, vandalism, and security requirements. Still fewer contractors want to purchase early only to be denied payment until actual installation. If a contractor delays purchase, however, inflation cuts into his lump-sum bid price—a potentially serious bind. Fortunately, certain contracts stipulate that upon acceptable proof of ownership, and under proper protection (in a bonded warehouse), the owner will pay for store material (less retainage).

d. Final Payment and Punch Lists.   At the end of a project, the contractor requests an inspection to determine a list of generally minor noncompliances—hence the "punch list." Subsequently, the contractor corrects this list of deficiencies. He asks for final inspection, after which he applies for final payment. Punch lists cause troubles in one major respect: several groups may punch out a project. The owner's inspectors, government inspectors, and the A/E inspectors may each compile separate lists, with many repetitive, minor items. Understandably, a contractor may consider the smaller items inconsequential (a stain on the rug, a broken window); however, the owner may perceive them as eyesores. In those cases where the contractor neglects to correct these minor deviations, an owner may perform the work and charge it against the contract price.

e. Guarantees.   The contract usually requires that the contractor correct all defects in his work during a warranty period, usually one year after the date of final acceptance. Several conflicts may occur. In cases of "use and occupancy acceptance," the owner may use the equipment (e.g., pumps, fans, and other mechanical and electrical equipment) for months. Naturally a contractor assumes that the guarantee begins on the date of use and occupancy acceptance, whereas the owner assumes the date of final acceptance. At times the owner and contractor may energetically disagree over where to draw the fine line between guarantee and regular maintenance. Some owners consider the one year as a free ride from maintenance. Another disagreement can occur because the owner may lack the manpower or experience to operate some of the more sophisticated equipment (especially the control systems). Therefore, what the owner considers a defective system, a guarantee item, may be in actuality the result of misoperation or incompetence (a control switched to "off" position).

3. Delays

Another troublesome area concerns delays and time adjustments. The contract obliges the prime to complete the project within a specified time. Because time converts into money, the sooner the contractor finishes the job, the sooner all groups realize the benefits. At times a contractor can attribute a delay to circumstances beyond his control. Such reasonable excuses a contractor accounts to extra work (change orders); acts of God (i.e., earthquakes, floods, tornadoes); labor strikes; factory strikes; late delivery of equipment; and owner-caused delays. In such cases the owner grants an extension of time. But in those situations where a contractor neglects to anticipate the requirements of the work with respect to the material, labor, or equipment, the contract holds him liable to the owner for damages incurred. Especially in private building, the speculated project promises an immediate return on investment in terms of money (e.g., apartments) or goods (e.g., factories). Consequently a postponed completion date causes not only additional expense due to inflation, but loss of revenue. In accord with the contract, the owner deducts liquidated damages (e.g., $100 per day beyond the project completion date). In those cases of severe loss that necessitate litigation, the courts enforce the liquidated damages only when the amounts withheld represent the actual damages sustained by the owner.

The remainder of this chapter examines the methods by which the construction team can attack these problem issues, and steps they can use to prevent or mitigate such frequent difficulties.

RESOLVING PROBLEMS

Either I will find a way, or I will make one.

Sir P. Sidney

Even under excellent conditions, controversial issues consistently crop up in construction management. How does the construction team resolve them? Usually by meetings, arbitration, and the courts, depending upon the severity of the problems. Ordinarily, meetings suffice for normal problems, but for contractual disputes that threaten large losses, the courts settle the matter. Other than inadequate mention of arbitration and the courts in this section, this book concentrates on the most inexpensive and direct approach, the meeting. Practically speaking, the legal and monetary consequences of the issue determine the route of resolution. Ranging in cost and consequences from a broken doorknob to an ominous cracked foundation wall, problems are normally ranked in various strata: minor, moderate, and serious.

Minor issues (e.g., cleanup, pesty punch-list items, and nuisances), contractors often remedy to the satisfaction of the majority, although sometimes owners wearily learn to live with them rather than waste time and effort haggling over nickels and dimes.

With respect to intermediate issues that foretell moderate costs and consequences (e.g., quality of work, interpretation of plans and specs, reasonable delays), the parties investigate the particulars and complexities of each case. As a result of conversing and corresponding, these problems are usually settled with varying degrees of success (as seen by who wins and who loses). Often a wise compromise is chosen, for rarely is anything settled that fulfills every contract provision with all "t's" crossed and all "i's" dotted. Perfection eludes mortals. Also, those inherent communication and personality difficulties force everyone to give and take to some extent. Psychologically individuals must reasonably trust and respect one another, except for cause. If not, the project bogs down in a hopeless quagmire of deceit and subterfuge and tiresome tugs of war. Everyone eventually loses.

Finally, ranked lowest, are those serious issues that plague hard luck projects and threaten legal disputes and potential high losses (e.g., costly errors and omissions, alleged damage caused by delays and interferences, expensive claims). In such a case the best one can do is to define the problem accurately, document his position, and pass these troubles to higher management or to counsel. Let the courts decide.

In addition to this loose ranking of technical problems, construction people must also consider the continuum of human nature. At the pessimistic extreme of human frailty, none of us, even if guilty (individual or a group), aspires to lose money, prestige, or status, to be labeled stupid or incompetent, or be held accountable at the risk of losing a job or a business. Therefore, one can anticipate being bombarded with diverse excuses, obscurities, smokescreens and coverups, and out-and-out lies and thievery. This would be especially true if the problem defied precise definition and responsibility. Lawyers defend the guilty as well as the innocent. At the other extreme of human nature, the optimistic end, one comfortably finds all the problems placed neatly into either black or white slots (never tinged with shades of gray), and the accused is unquestionably guilty. The hero, white hat and all, openly acknowledges his mistake, bites the bullet, and suffers the cost, regardless of the consequences.

Possibly most humans like to think of themselves in the white-hat category, but, realistically, most fall within the extremes, neither hero or rascal. Therefore, one must broadmindedly accept the differences among the personalities encountered, as well as understand one's own psyche. Conflicts should be tolerated, both technical and psychological, as well. In fact, conflict and differences, on an eyeball-to-eyeball level, can often strengthen an organization, as long as they contribute constructively and fail to consume the energies of the group. Since everyone lacks certain abilities, virtues, and insights, others have different complementary natures. If an individual can respond to issues honestly and maturely, and work with others adroitly, he can usually reconcile his differences. Even in those unfortunate situations where an honest difference of opinion cuts a cleft between the roles and responsibilities of the groups, neither party need feel personally offended if the other carries the issue to higher authorities. After all, everybody marches to different drummers.

A. Meetings

Fortunately, and contrary to the Chicken Littles of this world, not every issue portends a disaster. Few projects climax with a Tower of Pisa, or a Babel. Most conflicts are found to be the garden variety, which construction groups manage to solve in formal or informal meetings. Typically, per contract, they meet periodically: to review progress and compliance; to assess payments; to exchange information and clarify misunderstanding; to prevent errors; and to define and resolve a host of issues and irregularities. Arbitration and the courts, last resorts at best, cost money, and invariably create hard feelings, because few parties profit, lawyers excluded. Therefore, the meeting proves the easiest, cheapest, and quickest method to achieve solutions. Simple enough in concept, but in fact, too many meetings waste time, accomplish little, and test one's fortitude. Worse yet they degenerate into social events, focused on television sports and free lunches or Roman circuses, gladiators and all.

Why should this be so? It should not; this text asserts the point emphatically. Although meetings are mentioned only briefly in this section, they are analyzed in detail in Chapter 6—how to prepare and conduct meetings, how to handle problem people and problem situations and strategies. Before climbing to the vertex of that pyramid, however, first we must lay the foundation. In this chapter and the next the basics of construction management and the basics of psychology lay the ground tier. Chapters 4 and 5 build up the structure by analyzing the individual and the group, and, finally, Chapter 6 culminates with communication and meetings. For now, only a few general procedures are mentioned with respect to treating any trouble.

Commonly, those closest to the day-to-day operations, the clerk, super, or resident, first locates an alleged discrepancy (say, a scope-of-work issue).

He should check and verify the allegation by communicating with the responsible representatives on the site. If a problem, in fact, exists, he should promptly notify his superior. The architect being charged with administration of the project should be notified promptly, along with the owner and contractor. *Open, prompt communication rarely causes more hostility than whispered secrets.* Depending on the urgency and nature of the problem, the architect may elect to call an emergency meeting or to wait until the next scheduled meeting. Possibly via phone or informal conference, he can clear up the issue with the pertinent party. Say, in the initial stage, most parties attempt to resolve, or at least discuss, the issue. If the team documented *everything*, the mound of paperwork would surely bury them and their pocketbooks. The architect can verbally convince the general that the work in question falls within the scope of the work or vice versa.

If the problem creates an impasse, however, and no decision satisfactory to all parties can be reached, then each should document his position as dictated by the particular contract. The general contractor should prepare a protest in writing, stating his position and premises, and including documents, spec references, letters, and other supporting data. He should forward the protest to the proper officer in the company or agency or to the architect, whichever is designated by the contract. Also, if in accord with contract terms, the contractor must file his notification and continue his operations under protest; otherwise he breaches the contract.

If the proper official (owner or architect) refuses the appeal in writing, the contractor's top management and counsel must decide whether or not the dispute, in terms of money or legal consideration or possibly client/public relations, warrants further action, namely arbitration or the courts.

If the contractor decides to pursue the issue, he must thoroughly support his position. This includes a definitive statement of his position, and supporting data: documentation, reports, letters, shop drawings, photographs, diaries, minutes of meetings, and daily reports—whatever may be pertinent to fortify his claim. (See Appendix III for a review of documentation.)

B. Arbitration

When the problem becomes a contractual dispute, too costly for a party (say, a contractor) to absorb willingly, he more than likely submits the dispute to arbitration to be judged by experts in the construction field. Generally, because court action causes costs, not only in legal fees but in inconveniences and public relations as well, arbitration offers a less painful choice. In most public contracts, arbitration is not provided for, although the contract does provide for appeals to be submitted to officials of the awarding authority. Common disputes that usually end in arbitration include: quality of workmanship or materials; cost of change orders; poor supervision; errors and omission in design; delays alleged to be caused by indecision or interferences by the owner or his agent; and liquidated damages.

Following well-established procedures that comply with the construction industry rules of the American Arbitration Association, a party who wishes to initiate arbitration makes a written demand on the other. He states the nature of the disputes, the costs involved, and the remedy sought, and he requests that the dispute be submitted to arbitration. Upon agreement, each party sometimes selects an arbitrator (usually a construction expert), or they may additionally choose a third arbitrator. In any case the board consists of one to three persons, each a disinterested party known for his experience and knowledge. In the hearing, the board listens to the arguments on each side, after which it decides the outcome. Within a short period of time, it issues the award, enforceable by law.

C. Courts

Awarding a contract generally implies that it will terminate after both parties have reasonably fulfilled all contractual provisions and obligations in a satisfactory manner. Most contracts are so fulfilled. Sometimes, however, a party seriously breaches a contract, willfully or unintentionally. Depending on cost and consequence, the injured may, ultimately, bring the other party to court to compel compliance with the contract or to recover for damages he has sustained.

Common breaches of contract follow.

1. By owner:
   - failure to make prescribed payment
   - unreasonable delay
   - failure to pay for extra work (change order disputes)
   - undue interference with the control and direction of the work, both contractual responsibilities of the contractor
2. By contractor:
   - faulty performance
   - defaults; failure to complete or perform the work
   - unjustified delays
   - failure to honor financial obligations
3. By architect:
   - failure to complete or discharge duties
   - errors and omissions attributable to lack of diligence or skill

As mentioned earlier every project contract involves minor deviations, but the relatively small costs preclude the necessity of court action. With costly contract violations, however, the only recourse is to consult an attorney. On the basis of many precedent cases settled in court, he can guide management in terms of the cost/benefit ratio and, more important, the probable outcome of the dispute.

PROBLEM PREVENTION

An ounce of prevention is
worth a pound of cure

Proverb

The preceding sections examined construction management, defined a typical project, described design and construction contracts, analyzed the various component groups and their duties, and, last but certainly not least, reviewed common problems and difficulties encountered on most projects. We now add a few techniques and tips to moderate if not actually prevent, these conflicts.

First, however, we mention an important consideration that often entails dimensions other than monetary aspects—specifically, good will and public relations. Both are somewhat abstract concepts that are convertible into money, especially when one considers the opportunity for future work. Architects, contractors, and owners all live by their reputations, their past performances, their abilities, and their integrity. Therefore, a relatively minor conflict may cause a deep chasm between various groups. For example, suppose a contractor maintains a dirty job, a site cluttered with debris and nuisance traffic, or an architect submits sloppy reports to an owner. In both cases, these minor details convey an unfavorable impression to the owner, and possibly carry over to the public. Consequently, the owner, especially in private work, may opt to select others to perform future work. In fact, a dirty project reflects on everybody's reputation. Often the public sector, inclusive of future clients, measures one's performance by sometimes irrational standards. Do we not all form unfavorable judgments about another's abilities on the sole basis of sloppy correspondence or a peculiar mannerism or style of dress? As another example in this vein, consider minor punch-list items, say, a rug stain, inconsequential to a contractor, but an eyesore to an owner. Again recognize the effects of the relative values of each group: a contractor may readily shrug off these minor items with the reasonable statement, "Look, I've just completed a $2 million project— why the hassle over a $100 stain?" Meanwhile the owner fumes that after spending millions, he got a shabby job. Remember that word of mouth can be lethal.

Possibly, the project as designed leaves the owner with a minor but persistent maintenance problem (i.e., an exposed aggregate walkway, embedded with cigarette butts and traffic dirt, that defies conscientious cleaning). Therefore, in the future, the client will seek other architects. Pay attention to minor details. Always emphasize good will with all parties and especially the public. Reputations pass fast.

Another dimension concerns public relations, especially job safety. A serious accident damages the reputation of all. A child drowns; a workman falls to his death; everyone suffers. As with any trouble, major or minor, it would be well to remember Mark Antony's immortal words about Caesar, which apply equally in construction, "The evil that men do lives after them, the good is oft interred with their bones." Therefore, some suggestions for preventing problems follow.

The reasoning behind many of these measures will be explained in the course of this book. Some tips may strike one as obvious; many, however, result from acute observation and psychological studies.

A. Prevention for the Owner

The owner first conceives the project, determines his needs, invests large sums, and finally lives with the result long after the designer and builders depart. Therefore, active and diligent attention to all phases of the project, especially in the predesign phase, increases the probability of a maximum benefit/low cost ratio. Directly, the owner can prevent those costly change orders that originate with ill-defined or inaccurate programs concerning the specific goals of the project. Only in rare cases can one justify major program revisions in the working-plan stage or, worse, in construction. Major program revisions indicate a complete lack of communication either within the owner's group or between the owner and designer. Therefore, as a broad general deterrent, the owner must plan, and the more precise and detailed the planning, the fewer the headaches in the future.

1. Predesign Phase

Specifically, we suggest that the owner, or the individual in charge, should:

1. Staff his group with capable people, especially a construction expert who can knowledgeably act as the liaison between upper management and the architect and contractor group. Incorporate within the group, individuals, each with a particular background in areas such as financing, operations, planning, or maintenance, so that the group in totality has a wide

range of strengths. Each individual complements the group. Assign the responsibility of the program to one person along with the necessary authority to accomplish the task.

2. Define his present situation and his actual needs in line with available finances and future projections. Do his homework. He should encourage input from all departments so that he can accurately establish a list of priorities. Set up periodic brainstorming sessions for they develop good ideas and help to pinpoint areas of disagreement. Remember that the owner builds this project to satisfy certain needs. If he fails to identify these needs, he lives with the shortcomings or pays dearly via change orders or dissatisfaction in the future.

3. Research similar projects to inform himself of the results. Visit newly constructed projects and confer with the owners and users. They can assist the owner with a wealth of practical suggestions, as well as actual construction and operating costs that he can adapt to his requirements.

4. Determine reasonable budget commitments and time schedules. Stress simplicity, usage, and economy unless esthetics rate high on priorities (i.e., a memorial).

5. Carefully research the as-is conditions, legally as well as physically. In preparation for the architect, assemble all available support documentation, such as surveys, maintenance and operating data, utility and subsurface data. Far too many projects begin with substantial change orders for unanticipated ledge, water, or existing piping. The owner should be especially careful in researching the scope and accuracy of the legal requirements of the job. In fact, he may decide to delay the project at the inception, rather than to discover later that the contractual entanglement of an architect and contractor further complicates the legal issues (i.e., a factory in a snob-zone suburb, a nuclear plant near a city, an apartment building close to wet lands, or a massage parlor adjacent to a school).

2. Design Phase

With an accurate program, the owner should, in the design phase:

1. Choose an architect suitable to the project at hand. Like doctors, many architects specialize. Choose one adept in such projects as hospitals, schools, or industrial complexes as appropriate. (If your toe ached, would you visit a neurologist?)

2. Avoid choosing an architect on the premise that larger firms produce the best results, or on the basis of friendship or politics. Granted, this may be a very difficult suggestion to implement in public work especially, if the architect generously contributes to the campaign coffers. Nevertheless, accepting the imperfections of the world, the owner should stoically make

do with an architect of choice—along with the potpourri of contractors who assemble under the umbrella of "lowest responsible and eligible bidder."

3. Spell out his needs and priorities at the initial meeting with the architect. Candidly discuss the budget. Expect no architect to work miracles, for the equation reads:

$$\text{Budget} = \text{quality} + \text{quantity}$$

Within a fixed budget, the owner trades off one against the other. Be open and honest. Be concrete and specific about needs and expectations. Be respectful of the architect's position, advisor/agent—the expert in the art of architecture.

4. Communicate, communicate, and communicate. Submit a list of priorities, and ask the architect to respond to each. Assist him in every way possible. Other than the fact that the contract requires the owner to furnish him with surveys, boring test data, etc., the owner should urge his staff to assemble this information in a logical, useful manner. Conduct meetings between the owner's staff and the architect to explain clearly specific details and problems that may occur during and after construction (i.e., coordination, scheduling, maintenance, expansion, conversion). Emphasize strongly, in no uncertain words, that the architect designs, not the staff. Of primary importance, the owner's function concerns providing input and information to aid him in creating a project successful to all parties.

5. Set up realistic time schedules. Haste makes waste, and all too frequently a project designed expeditiously may collect dust on the shelf awaiting funding.

6. Schedule periodic meetings, say, at midpoint and completion of the preliminary and working stages. Review the general direction and scope of the project and the budget estimates. Because a picture is worth a thousand words, the owner may wish to consider a model or special drawings to aid his staff and occupants in spatially perceiving the total project. As noted previously, if an owner makes major design revisions at the working stage, it reflects a serious lack of communication, or worse, indecision and incompetence. Not only do such alterations cost money, they cause considerable frustration as well.

7. Review the plans and specifications relentlessly. An eraser today may preclude expenditure tomorrow. First check compliance to the most important criteria, then follow up with the minor items. Use checklists, either in-house, or those developed over the years and found in technical publications. If an owner objects to a certain detail, he should submit his objections to the architect and request that he provide reasons that satisfy the owner's staff.

8. Acknowledge that humans, because of multifaceted personality traits, differ with respect to their interpretation of beauty and esthetics—a highly individualistic matter. So the owner should, within reason, leave this decision to the architect. After all, the owner retains the designer to provide this service. With respect to function, the contract holds the architect responsible and liable for the design. Therefore, take steps to prevent confusion and conflict; avoid meddling.

3. Construction Phase

By this phase, the plans and specifications should reflect accurately the priorities of the owner. The following steps smooth the construction:

1. In addition to that of agent/advisor, the architect assumes a new duty, that of a judge, to ensure that both the owner and the contractor fulfill their obligations. Respect this dual role.

2. Two contracts bind the owner, respectively, to the designer and to the contractor—both experts in their fields. Respect this expertise. Make every possible effort to establish rapport within the construction team. Show respect by arranging conference areas conducive to a professional setting. A conference room in a dirty cellar with orange crates for chairs sends a very damaging nonverbal message. Supply proper facilities for storage, parking, and the like; doing so creates the impression that the owner is an asset to the team.

3. Identify the official who will represent the owner group. Explain the channels of authority, and explain the duties and legal limitations of the inspection team. Instruct the staff and inspectors to issue no direct orders to the contractor concerning means, methods, etc. necessary to complete the work.

4. If public law dictates that the owner follow certain bureaucratic procedures, then explain these procedures and policies fully at the initial meeting. A printed outline or an illustrative example (e.g., a copy of a previous change order or periodic payment) helps to clarify certain procedures. Again it creates a favorable impression.

5. Early in the project, assert the owner's position. Emphasize that the staff expects compliance with the plans and specifications. If an owner accepts shoddy work, it causes three problems:

- He suffers the consequences of this shoddy work.
- It reinforces the shady contractor who profits from the noncompliance.
- It penalizes the reputable contractor who tries to comply. He may adopt the attitude that on future work, he will emulate the rationale

of the rogues, and cut corners, too. His attitude is understandable because humans, like dynamic systems, tend to follow the path of least resistance.

6. By contract the owner has no right to interfere with the control and direction of the work. By interfering unduly, he may relieve the contractor of his obligation. Even on a minor scale, this provokes psychological conflicts. Therefore, leave the contractor to his duties.

7. Construction, being a very complex technical endeavor, can do without the burden of personality clashes. Be fair, reasonable, and always tactful. Inform your group, especially the inspectors, that their specific duties serve two purposes: (1) to help the contractor avoid costly errors; and (2) to check that the contractor complies with the plans and specs. Therefore no Gestapo tactics; they cause untold grief. If the staff includes a socially deficient member, transfer him away from the interactions.

8. Request change orders judiciously; accept change proposals cautiously—few contractors suggest alterations out of benevolence. Refrain from inundating the project with changes; they not only drain your pockets, but erode morale.

9. If a contractor encounters difficulties or delays, work with him to remedy the conflict instead of drawing up battle lines.

B. Prevention for the Architect

Many of the preventive measures below integrate with those for the owner. Besides money considerations, however, a problem-free project benefits the architect in another respect—his reputation. In an AIA study (1967) clients ranked architectural services in the following order:

- adequate and functional planning
- checking for contractor compliance to the plans and specs
- aesthetic design
- developing plans
- acting as an agent for the owner

Therefore, a design that falls short (or appears to fall short) of adequate and functional planning, or a project fraught with change orders, errors, omission, overruns, lawsuits, and maintenance headaches can cripple, particularly, the architect's reputation. Subsequently, it may cost him future clients. Good business sense, in fact survival, demands that designers seriously attend to these measures.

1. Design Phase

Of primary importance, the A/E group must meet the owner's requirements within budget limitations. Of equal importance, the A/E group must satisfy its own needs, psychological and renumerative. Therefore, we suggest that an architect:

1. Choose reputable owners and projects consistent with his abilities, experience, and interests. Either commit oneself 100 percent or decline an agreement.

2. Select consultants prudently, for the contract holds the architect liable for their work. Any error that they commit reflects on the architect's reputation. Certainly their past performance, talents, and fees will influence the choice, but consider also the compatibility of the working relationship. Poor rapport can cost money also.

3. Communicate, communicate, and communicate with the owner and the consultants. Accurately analyze the owner's total program, particularly in the initial phases. The architect should meet with his staff, the future occupants, and, if possible, the operations personnel so that a satisfactory combination of needs, esthetics, quality, quantity, and costs may be effectively defined. With his advice the architect should be open and candid, and totally realistic. Request documented priorities and financial data. Explain the plan to approach various details. Keep the owner informed verbally and with correspondence as to progress and intent.

4. Schedule periodic meetings during the initial design stages, and submit minutes of these meetings noting important decisions and revisions agreed upon. Thoroughly justify any deviations from the owner's original program. Often a personnel replacement in the owner's staff will try to change previous decisions or institute a new program, thereby forcing the A/E group to alter or scrap a design—definitely a source of friction.

5. Be economical and esthetic in the design, but never saddle the owner with a future maintenance and operational headache. Positively ensure (via documentation) that the owner knows what he buys. An irate owner can irreparably damage potential for future services.

6. Be aware that most change orders occur because of ill-defined owner programs, unknown site conditions, and confusion over scope of work between the contractors and his specialty subcontractors. Strive to clarify all questions. If the owner submits an obscure or unrealistic program, work with him until both agree on all the major requirements. Then follow through with the minor details. If the site conditions or documentation of tests and services leave questions as to their veracity or thoroughness, take additional tests, or research as-is conditions. Explain to the owner that these additional costs will prevent future changes. Insist that the consultants coordinate properly. In fact, utilize published checklist procedures to verify the coordination systematically (i.e., interferences, equipment fits, vague scope of work at the interfaces). Take the time to verify such commonly used references as "as shown on the plans"—too often nothing shows. Explicitly

state the proper sub who performs what task—too often a conflict arises over who "hooks up," or "tests," or who provides temporary heat or security, or who supplies power. Never use "by others"—specify. Always flag special items such as security police, premium times, scheduled shutdowns. Never use zero tolerance words (straight, square, level)—give limits. Undoubtedly one could generate a list of thousands of dos and don'ts. Compile a checklist that best suits the particular needs.

7. Remind his group of the fundamental intent of the plans and specs: a message to the contractor describing in sufficient detail what the owner wishes built. Place oneself in the role of the contractor, the estimator, the job super, the fabricator. Try to imagine how each accomplishes his job. Ease his task. Present the information in a clear legible manner, not a cryptic code cramped on one page. Follow standard formats used in the industry; use universal symbols—they offer less chance for misunderstanding. Be conservative in the use of revolutionary materials or design concepts. Some people tend to be pioneers, courageous and tenacious, but discretion remains the better part of valor in construction.

8. If a problem or unique situation occurs on a particular project, capitalize on mistakes; educate the in-house staff and consultants to prevent reoccurrence.

2. Construction Phase

The contract charges the architect with the general administration of the project. Therefore, his leadership abilities definitely affect the psychological performance of the construction team (e.g., communication, coordination, cooperation, dedication, motivation, discipline, respect, problem definition, interpretation, and decision). Below, we offer a few suggestions:

1. Conduct all meetings on a professional level. Prepare for meetings appropriately (i.e., an agenda outlining topics and situations to be discussed) and request that others prepare as well. At the preconstruction meeting, clarify the roles and authority of the group representatives; establish lines of communication; schedule conference and inspection dates and times. Review the important provisions of the contract, and the special items (e.g., shutdowns and/or coordination with owner, pertinent administrative policies and procedures, storage areas, parking facilities, nuisance factors). Explain that during the progress of the work, disagreements and conflicts, technical and personal, will require cooperation and consideration on everyone's part. Therefore, at this meeting try to set an environment of rapport and respect. First impressions last.

2. In the exceptional role of advisor/agent/judge, and the noncontractual relationship with the contractor, the architect should endeavor to be firm

but fair. When dealing with minor conflicts, especially those shaded in gray, be flexible. Give and take, for life seldom blesses us with all wins, nor curses us with all losses. Such an approach forms an excellent basis for co-operation. When confronted with serious issues, however, be totally consistent, and assert oneself appropriately.

3. Psychologically, the architect sets the pace for the team. If he conducts himself professionally, asserts himself accordingly, and works with his intellect, in all probability, the others will follow suit.

4. Select a competent, honest, diplomatic C/W. As the day-to-day eyes and ears of the project, he can amplify or attenuate the conflicts.

5. Be proud and confident of the design; it shows. Respect the expertise of the contractor and subs. If they forward suggestions, listen courteously—one can always learn, and possibly profit from the discussion. The final evaluation lies, of course, with the architect.

6. Stop serious personality clashes before they evolve into out-and-out warfare. If need be, appeal to higher management. Possibly a transfer will correct the situation.

7. In small matters make decisions promptly; in serious situations, be immediately visible and attentive. Define the problems, collect the facts, and document the findings. With regard to major legal conflicts, refer the issue to higher authority and instruct the others to do likewise.

8. Keep all correspondence and minutes accurate, punctual, and thorough. Never write anything insulting in a letter. A person may shrug off a verbal insult spoken in the heat of a disagreement, but not so with the written word. This point is explained in Appendix III.

9. Inform the owner regarding job progress (per contract), but also update him on all problems and potential delays. It is better that he hear of misadventures from the architect than from a third party.

C. Prevention for the Contractor

Recognizing that a disproportionate number of contracting businesses end in bankruptcy, economists list some major reasons why a project may lose money:

- poor estimating, resulting in unrealistically low bidding, or intentional low bidding in hope of anticipated change orders
- lack of proper investigation concerning labor and site conditions (e.g., labor supply, transportation facilities, and local laws)
- adverse weather, strikes, acts of God, and other unpredictable circumstances
- inflation

- inefficient management and supervision of the project, or inadequate technical expertise

Obviously, many of these causes depend on the whims of fate; others depend on the application of sound business and technical techniques. Although the majority of causes fall outside the scope of this book, we ask again: why add psychological problems to the existing list of woes?

1. Bid Phase

Nothing can replace technical expertise in properly estimating a job: diligent study of the plans and specs; past cost records; available men and equipment; site visits; finances involved; and, of course, the impositions of the bonding company. This section offers a few techniques concerning psychological factors.

1. First and foremost, the contractor should learn the reputation of the architect and the owner. Are they considered to be fair, secure, and reasonable or are they pegged as hardnosed, financially unstable, and possibly incompetent? A few phone calls today to trustworthy sources (previous contractors, agencies, and financial institutions) may provide the contractor with some pertinent insights to assist in his decision. This consideration may appear Borgia-like, but such factors certainly influence the profit margin.

2. Set up a systematic procedure to check estimates. Recheck estimates independently. Utilize updated cost records from previous projects. Try to formalize and refine this procedure, for it reduces chances for error. Tailor the many published charts to best suit the particular organization.

3. Wherever possible the contractor should brainstorm with the staff to solve particular technical problems and to discover new, more efficient approaches or applications to cut time and costs (but, of course, in compliance with the contract). Chapter 7 presents a few researched systems that can generate creative solutions.

2. Construction Phase

Being the last group to join the construction team, and being involved in the somewhat competitive nature of a lump-sum bid, places the contractor at a psychological disadvantage. Additionally, in the execution of an untested design, and because of the vast unpredictable technical unknowns, most conflicts manifest themselves in the construction stage. A latent defect in the design becomes readily obvious in construction. Also, many owners change horses and philosophies midstream. In either case, most troubles entangle the contractor to one degree or another, whether he actually causes the problem or not. All too often a marginal design or an obscure program unjustly penalizes the contractor. Especially in those gray problems some people tend to rationalize that the contractor should remedy the deficits—after all he stands guilty until proved innocent. "He installed it, didn't he?" The contract harnesses him with many responsibilities and few rights. Therefore, any methods to prevent pitfalls, especially in the psychological area, should be implemented. During construction the contractor may wish to consider the following ideas.

1. At the outset, the contractor group should project a professional image. Take pains to establish a sincere working relationship with all other groups of the construction team. Even under serious conditions, good rapport and mutual trust go a long way to lessen the impact for all. Unless absolutely necessary, avoid submitting a claim at the first conference. It starts a project on the wrong foot.

2. Abide by the bureaucratic policies of the owner (submission of progress schedules, correct formats for change orders, claims, periodic payments, and other special documents). To shrug off the paper work as inconsequential implies that the GC/S group considers another's job as less worthy. Submit shop drawings and samples promptly.

3. Prepare for conferences. An agenda requires only an hour's preparation, but it demonstrates that the prime has prepared; also, it reminds one of topics to discuss, and it eases taking of notes.

4. The general should make every possible effort to communicate, coordinate, and cooperate with his subs, the architect, and the owner's representatives. Follow through on all correspondence—it protects the contractor, too. Keep accurate records. Cost records lay the basis for future bids, while job records may prove crucial to future conflicts (litigation or arbitration).

5. If a contractor discovers or anticipates a problem or delay, he should bring it to the forefront immediately before time worsens the consequences. If a claim is felt justifiable, then notify the owner in writing. If the dispute persists, then, in accordance with the contract, file the claim and continue the work.

6. The GC/S group should perform no work unless properly authorized in writing. Verbal directives or agreements sometimes become forgotten, unintentionally and otherwise, leaving the contractor holding the bag.

7. The general should never flood the owner with change order requests spurred by ulterior motives or minor claims This approach causes a number of potential effects: (1) they may threaten the architect's integrity because they imply a questionable design; (2) they may convince an owner that the prime plans to bleed him dry. Everyone accepts the fact that builders construct with the hope of maximizing profits, but not to the detriment of

another's wallet. Sometimes, in retaliation, an endless punch list becomes a weapon of revenge. Try a smoother approach—when a contractor encounters minor extra work items that involve little costs, he should perform the work in the interest of public relations and good will, and tactfully publicize his philanthropic gesture. As long as these freebies stay within reason, the good will investment pays back handily. When the pipe shown on the plans runs smack through the center of a window, redirect the piping without glowing about how stupid all designers are.

8. If the GC/S group observes a design oversight, an error, or omission, handle the situation diplomatically: no profuse criticism for the plans and specs; no sighs of despair, nor chuckles of glee. Everyone lives in glass houses, and only masochists enjoy committing errors. Therefore, let the designer save face. Present the observations discreetly and stand by for correction.

9. As the job progresses, immediately remedy any nuisance items that crop up—trash, debris, cleanup. Restrict the operations and storage areas to the designated locations. Thoroughly coordinate all shutdowns and necessary inconveniences. Instruct workers not to steal the owner's parking places, tie up his elevators or traffic, or dirty his existing buildings—all minor items in themselves but sources of aggravation to the owner.

10. The GC/S group should maintain a clean job. No project need resemble a battlefield. Right or wrong, it reflects on one's technical ability. More important, enforce a rigid safety program. Construction workers all appreciate the hazards of construction, but many accidents can be prevented. In addition to human suffering, accidents cost money and muddy reputations. Psychologically, active participation on management's behalf concerning safety raises worker morale.

11. The general and his subs should always be reasonable and fair. To requisition for 60 percent payment with only 30 percent of work complete demonstrates little respect for the designer or owner. Never try to push off Volkswagen caliber equipment as an "or equal" to a Cadillac—for the same reasons.

If an inspector or a clerk harrasses a GC or a sub, the issue should be taken to the architect. If the harrassment continues, appeal to higher management.

BIBLIOGRAPHY

AIA Document A201. "General Conditions of the Contract for Construction." Washington: The American Institute of Architects, 1976.

AIA Document B141. "Standard Form of Agreement Between Owner and Architect." Washington: The American Institute of Architects, 1977.

Bonny, J., and J. Frien, eds. *Handbook of Construction Management and Organization*. New York: Van Nostrand Reinhold Co., 1973.

Bush, Vincent G. *Construction Management*. Reston, Virginia: Reston Publishing Co., 1973.

Clough, Richard H. *Construction Contracting*. 3 ed. New York: John Wiley & Sons, 1975.

Cowgill, Clinton H. *Building For Investment*. New York: Reinhold Publishing Corp., 1951.

Coxe, Weld. *Marketing Architectural and Engineering Services*. New York: Van Nostrand Reinhold Co., 1971.

Durant, Will. *The Life of Greece*. New York: Simon and Schuster, 1966.

Goldenson, Robert M. *The Encyclopedia of Human Behavior*, Vol. I and II. New York: Doubleday and Co., 1970.

Merritt, Frederick S. *Building Construction Handbook*, 2 ed. New York: McGraw-Hill Book Co., 1965.

National Geographic Society. *Greece and Rome, Builders of our World*. 1968.

Dictionary of Occupational Titles, Vol. II, U.S. Department of Labor Bureau of Labor Statistics, 1965.

Wheeler, Ladd, Robert A. Goodale, and James Deese. *General Psychology*. Boston: Allyn and Bacon, Inc., 1975.

Chapter 3

Basics of Psychology

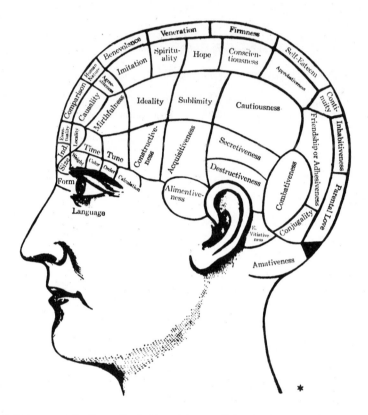

Phrenology, an early, theoretical attempt to map behavioral locations in the brain.

Abstract

Psychology, the study of behavior, yields some valuable and practical insights into the management of construction. Within this context, the discussion begins with our overview of man as perceived by the psychologist. Next are presented those methods used by scientists to measure and assess behavior.

Primarily, the dominant theme of the chapter centers around some of the building blocks that make up the personality. This unique "identity," which distinguishes one person from another, is the sum of varied complex traits—many of which are learned, not inherited.

In sequence, the topics covered include: learning; attitudes and values; motivation and needs; personality theories and concepts; and, finally, the interesting relationship between personality and career.

CONTENTS OF CHAPTER 3

VIEWPOINTS AND METHODS
  A. Psychological Conceptions of Man
    1. Neurobiological
    2. Behavioral
    3. Cognitive
    4. Psychoanalytic
    5. Humanistic
  B. Methods of Psychology
    1. Experiment
    2. Observation
    3. Survey
    4. Test
    5. Case Study

LEARNING
  A. Definition of Learning
  B. Techniques for Learning
    1. Motivation
    2. Instruction
    3. Participation
    4. Knowledge of Results
    5. Practice
    6. Whole versus Part
    7. Overlearning
    8. Environment

ATTITUDES
  A. Formation of Attitudes and Prejudices
  B. Persuasion and Propaganda
    1. Persuasion
    2. Propaganda

MOTIVATION
  A. Theories of Motivation
    1. The Behavior Theory
    2. The Unconscious Motivation Theory

3. The Cognitive Theory of Motivation
4. Maslow's Theory of Motivation and Needs
B. Maslow's Theory of Human Motivation
1. Physiological Needs
2. Safety Needs
3. Love and Belonging Needs
4. Self-Esteem Needs
5. Cognitive Needs
6. Esthetic Needs
7. Self-Actualizing Needs
C. Motivation, Needs, and Occupation

PERSONALITY

A. Definitions and Difficulties
B. Theories of Personality
1. Type
2. Trait
3. Developmental
4. Dynamic

OCCUPATIONS AND PERSONALITY

A. Maslow's Hierarchy and Occupations
B. Determinants of Occupation
1. Personal Characteristics
2. Job Characteristics

QUESTIONS AND PREVIEW

1. Explain how the different conceptions of man could influence the method of psychological investigation?
2. What is learning? Are traits learned or inherited?
3. How are attitudes formed? Prejudices?
4. Name commonly held attitudes (and prejudices) relative to architects, contractors, administrators, civil servants, and tradesmen. Explain the consequences of such stereotypes.
5. What motivates human beings? Identify some basic needs that all humans attempt to satisfy. What is self-actualization?
6. What is personality? How is it measured? Can it be changed?
7. How does one's personality affect the choice of vocation?
8. What determinants are involved in choosing an occupation?

VIEWPOINTS AND METHODS

All looks yellow
to the jaundiced eye

Pope

Appropriate for contemporary fashion, psychology is defined as the scientific study of the behavior of man and other animals. "Behavior" means those actions of an organism that can be observed directly or indirectly, or can be measured by instruments. This book limits the discussion to the behavior of man. Even with this limitation, however, man's behavior, like the tip of the iceberg, entails an awesomely complex and often incomprehensible study. Therefore, a further restriction confines the discussion to a very modest coverage of a few select topics with particular emphasis on their applicability to the management of construction. The coverage includes: learning; attitudes; motivation; personality; group dynamics; and creativity.

In that psychology attempts to understand, predict, and, at times, influence behavior, this coverage should yield partial understanding and insight into the most important of creatures—ourselves and those we interact with. Undoubtedly, the ability to answer any of the questions below should certainly lead to an improved understanding of our behavior and that of our fellow humans.

How can humans learn more efficiently? How can they foster creativity in solving problems and overcoming obstacles?

What motivates people? Why do they strive to satisfy their needs? How can we motivate ourselves and others? What factors determine the type and quality of leadership?

Where do we acquire values, attitudes, and prejudices? How do they affect our behavior and our choice of occupation? By what techniques do others try to persuade us? How can one detect (and nullify) propaganda? How can people communicate (speak, listen, and write) more effectively? What is meant by personality? How do scientists assess traits? What factors determine whether we like or dislike another person (and vice versa)?

What processes occur when individuals join to form a group? How and why do group pressures influence (and sometimes frustrate) us? How do groups develop to form trust and cohesiveness? How do groups behave when interacting with another group, especially in adverse situations?

Each and every question is important and the subject of continuing investigations. Fundamentally, all the answers relate intimately to our very lives, and, consequently, spill over into the mainstream of our occupations, in this instance, that of construction management. In no small way, each of us stakes a claim in this fascinating subject. As a pragmatic consideration, every person can improve his level of competence in a particular task, say, in developing his social or communication skills, in correcting a bad habit, or in learning an innovative technique. Whatever the reason, a basic appreciation of psychology will enhance the chance for success. But equally, if not more important, the individual can gain insight into his own behavior. Where or in what manner do we acquire our personality—our interests, abilities, attitudes, and even our prejudices? Psychology attempts to weed the fiction from the fact. It is not uncommon for a person to discover that a dearly cherished belief is false, the result of a prejudice transmitted by a parent, a peer, or a group to which he belongs. Falsehoods are learned as easily as facts. Furthermore, many people are so inclined to generalize from a single person or experience as to stereotype the total population.

Construction exposes an individual to various characters, many of whom think and act in various ways, and value goals other than his own. Therefore, following an especially painful experience or severe confrontation, there exists the strong tendency to generalize from one particular individual or specific group to "all owners" or "all architects" or "all contractors." For instance, a tradesman may label "all" owners as technical illiterates or "all" architects as prima donnas or "all" contractors as ruthless businessmen. (On a more personal level, he may generalize his relationship with his parents to include all parents. He perceives all mothers to be kind, gentle, and wise—a perception contrary to fact.) In fact, throughout life, on the basis of experiences, heredity, and the external processes, human beings perceive and "see" things in highly individualistic ways. Box 3.1 illustrates this point.

Box 3.1. PERSPECTIVES AND PERSONALITY

For years, psychologists have used projective tests to obtain some insight into how a person "emotionally reacts" to an ambiguous object. One of the more famous tests is the Rorschach ink blot. Although some scientists question their validity, the ink blots underscore the multifaceted responses from person to person.

What do you see?

Different people will report seeing different shapes as they look at the object from their unique vantage. Because of experiences, training, personality, a person may see any or all of the shapes below:

| Two Statues | Two Birds Pecking Food | Butterfly |

Possibly you could return to the original ink blot and discover other configurations. In any case, the point to remember is that when you are communicating with another person, it is well to keep in mind that they may have learned to experience different emotions or to see differently from you. Each of us, in a highly individualistic way, "reads" or "projects" his own interpretation and feelings into ambiguous situations and stimuli. Therefore, difficulty in recognizing this fact of life could lead to confusion. For example, imagine how a new power plant "looks" to various individuals, and consider the consequences of intermeshing these perspectives:

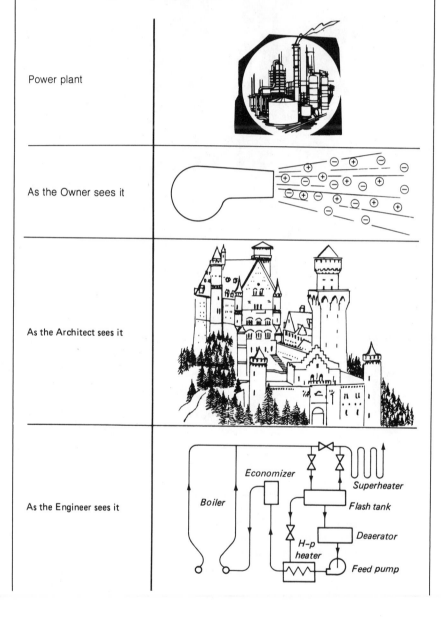

Power plant	
As the Owner sees it	
As the Architect sees it	
As the Engineer sees it	Economizer, Superheater, Boiler, Flash tank, H-p heater, Deaerator, Feed pump

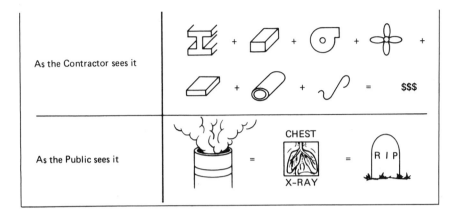

| As the Contractor sees it | (shapes) |
| As the Public sees it | (illustration) |

Researching topics ranging from prejudice to personality assessment, from learning to problem-solving procedures, the psychologist uses more accurate, statistical methods than laymen's common overgeneralizations. Following established scientific methods, he first recognizes a situation and defines its parameters. Next, he embraces a certain postulate, which he then validates (or invalidates) by applying tests and measurements. The final outcome proves or disproves his hypothesis. In any event, new questions and ideas may be raised that generate more investigation until, ultimately, the psychologist better understands the behavior of man. This process is oversimplified. In actuality, the procedure requires considerable time, money, and dedication. Frequently, too, the interpretation of the results depends on the viewpoint (paradigm) of the observer, which we now examine.

A. Psychological Conceptions of Man

As discussed in the introductory chapter, personality influences how a person perceives, interprets, and evaluates what he observes. In construction, a particular building may generate totally different perceptions depending on the personality or interests of the observer, as demonstrated in the power plant example.

An architect examines the lines, the shadings, and the blending of shapes and concepts. The owner pragmatically concentrates on the usage, the income and services derived, or the maintenance and operational factors. The contractor, in turn, mentally pieces the structure together in a logical sequence, probably noting how he could revise or circumvent expensive, but artistic details of the designer. The same building affords three possible perceptions. Psychologists, like construction personnel, act similarly. Depending upon his paradigm, his conceptions of man, the psychologist describes human behavior from a number of vantage points. For example, suppose you scratch your ear; your actions could be explained from several points of view: neurobiological; behavioral; cognitive; psychoanalytic; or humanistic.

1. Neurobiological

A psychologist, neurobiologically inclined, would explain that somewhere within the twelve billion nerve cells of your brain, certain actions between the brain and the nervous system defined the itch and initiated your overt act; the scratching.

2. Behavioral

The behaviorist would reduce your actions to an interaction of stimulus and response. Concerned little with what occurs within you (the black box approach used in engineering), he observes you scratching.

3. Cognitive

The cognitive psychologist would emphasize the mental processes that prompted your action.

4. Psychoanalytic

The psychoanalyst, adopting the Freudian conception of man, would stress the unconscious motives.

5. Humanistic

And finally, the humanist would claim that because of your freedom to choose, you determine your actions; to scratch or not to scratch.

Of course, in any given psychological investigation, the scientist may approach the issue from any number or combination of viewpoints. Depending upon the discussion at hand, this text utilizes the findings and adopts the paradigms from all of these approaches with special focus on the behavioristic, the cognitive, and the humanistic schools.

B. Methods of Psychology

1. Experiment

The experimental method, the basis of scientific knowledge, offers the most precise findings in behavioral investigations. In fact, being in construction, we all value the empirical methodology of science, which applies to all building projects: mechanics, heat, light, electricity—the range of physics and engineering. In laboratory tests, the experimenter stresses the beam, measures the deflection, and derives an equation to reflect the cause-effect relationship: the deflection is directly proportional to the load. In the study of behavior, the general restrictions and difficulties hinder the efforts. Behavior involves an infinite number of variables, many with unknown relationships. Therefore, the investigator must carefully control all conditions, virtually an impossibility. Accepting this, he manipulates certain variables that he believes have major consequence. Then he measures the dependent variable (that topic or event he wishes to study) and attempts to infer a cause-effect relationship. For example, suppose he wished to determine the effect of special training on the rate of learning a specific task. A psychologist would compare two groups, one that received no training and one that had. He would measure their performance, and infer whether or not the special training had an effect. Outwardly, it seems straightforward, but actually it is very difficult because the experiment itself often influences the behavior that he tries to measure. Like chameleons people display only favorable colors when others observe them. Another restriction concerns ethics; obviously, no experiment can be conducted that would even remotely injure a subject, mentally or physically. In construction, the completed structure proves (or disproves) the design. It is a one-shot test.

2. Observation

With the observational method, the investigator carefully and unobtrusively observes the behavior of focus; he records accurately and objectively without bias or manipulation. This procedure is utilized in our day-to-day dealings with others; of course, our yellow jaundice proverb often colors the observation. The construction inspection is no more than this technique.

3. Survey

When a psychologist wishes to assess causes of behavior without waiting for a result to occur naturally, or when the behavior essentially precludes observation, he may elect the survey method. He inquires directly by asking for the underlying reasons behind the behavior. Therefore, he can accumulate considerable data in a relatively short time. Under controlled, systematic circumstances, surveys provide surprisingly informative results (i.e., public opinions, election predictions, consumer surveys). In fact, politicians and union officials often determine policies based on survey findings. Two major deficiencies may possibly occur in the survey method: (1) the subjects may willingly or unconsciously distort the true causes of their behavior; and (2) a biased sample may result in an erroneous picture of the population segment that the investigator desires to study. Therefore, one must be cautious in drawing conclusions. When a manager or architect telephones a few colleagues to learn the reputation of a person or some equipment, he is, in effect, conducting a survey—a very small sample of dubious accuracy, but nevertheless a survey.

4. Test

With valid tests, a psychologist can measure a wide assortment of behavioral aspects ranging from achievement, aptitudes, interests, personality traits, memory, creativity, and accomplishments. Tests enable investigators to obtain a large amount of data from people without elaborate technical equipment and with only minor interference to their daily routines. From the analysis of results, the investigator relates variations in test scores to variations that exist between people. Unfortunately, to properly create a valid test involves considerable groundwork—preparing, scaling, and establishing norms. An examination for professional engineering registration falls into this category.

5. Case Study

For those psychologists who study specific individuals, case histories (scientific biographies) offer a wealth of important information. Utilizing a variety of sources (school records, vocational evaluations, tests—academic and psychological, and interviews), the investigator integrates this material to provide a "picture" of that person. By comparing several case histories related to a specific topic, he may develop hypotheses he can investigate further on a larger scale. For example, in researching personality traits and creativity, MacKinnon studied a number of creative architects. Anne Roe, in a vocational investigation, examined 64 eminent scientists. From the data, she drew a profile of an "average" eminent scientist.

In this text, a number of case studies, and all the other methods, will provide data and information from which we will sketch profiles of "typical" people and groups seen on the construction site. As with any small sample, the results gleaned from case studies are statistically insignificant. Therefore, one should avoid drawing false inferences or incorrect generalizations from such limited data.

LEARNING

Learning by study must be won;
'twas ne'er entailed from sire to son.

Gay

In everyday life as well as in construction, one can observe remarkable differences between the novice and the expert. The novice (at times awkward, unsure, and fumbling) contrasts acutely with the expert (often dextrous, confident, and skilled). Of course, given the inherent potential ability, the novice eventually, through effort and training, becomes adept and competent. Initially, all humans begin new tasks as novices, but somewhere during the training period, personal needs and talents join in varying degrees and combinations to attain a final level of expertise. Throughout our lives, the learning process continues because the future invariably brings new obstacles and difficulties that must be overcome. Biologically, the organism adapts to its changing environment; psychologically, a healthy individual adapts likewise, in the positive sense. Depending on the intensity of motives and learning techniques, and, of course, native potential, people can all learn excellence. By way of reference, the reader may ask what specific qualities other than genetic endowments distinguish the professionals from the ruck of practitioners? Investigators emphasize several qualities:

- dedication to purpose
- attention to detail
- ability to cope with mistakes
- perserverance in the face of disappointment

Such virtues are needed on any project.

In the following chapter, each of these characteristics will be examined in detail. For the present discussion we merely mention that each and every expert learns *all* these qualities. If, at times, we appreciate the dedication in terms of time and effort to achieve a "master" status, all too often we fail to realize our own enormous capacity to learn. Unfortunately, bad habits are acquired as readily as good ones.

So fundamental to understanding behavior, and because of the vast practicalities and social consequences, learning, and its governing principles, have been painstakingly researched by psychologists. In this section we present these research results as they concern the definition of learning, and techniques for learning.

A. Definition of Learning

Learning is defined as the process by which one acquires new information, habits, and abilities. Or, in the tradition of the behaviorists, some psychologists define learning as the essentially permanent modification of behavior that originates from interactions with surroundings. In order to refine and limit the definition, it is assumed that learning applies only when the following criteria are met:

1. The interaction between the individual and his environment causes a change in the way he thinks, perceives, or responds. A tragic accident may cause a "change of heart" about safety programs.

2. An activity, such as observation, practice, or study causes this change, exclusive of activities such as illness, maturation, or drugs. As a project manager assumes new responsibilities, he learns new approaches to grow professionally.

3. The change in behavior extends over a relatively long period. Illness or fatigue may produce changes, but these generally have only transitory effects. Training from college and apprentice programs are obvious examples.

A little reflection on this definition should convince the reader that learning encompasses more than a specific skill or a particular occupation. In fact, learning covers the alphabet of human behaviors:

- motor skills (learning to work with hand tools, operate equipment, use drafting instruments)
- complex activities (learning to read and to interpret plans and specs; to program computers; to survey with a transit; to apply science and mathematics)
- attitudes, prejudices, and beliefs (learning "feelings" toward people and issues—love and war being extreme consequences)
- social behavior (learning customs, and occupational and social roles; learning how to deal with people and peers, and supervisors and subordinates in social interactions)
- emotional responses (learning the acquisition of various emotional responses such as resentment, sympathy, fear, and anger)
- thinking and communication (learning how to think, how to solve problems; in fact, learning how to learn)

As a practitioner of construction, a person continually learns new tasks throughout his career. Commonly he gains his knowledge via formal study or on-the-job training. Sometimes, because of new situations and responsibilities, or an urge to improve himself with the possible hope of promotion, he updates his qualifications. Continuously the environment changes, and man adapts accordingly. Problem-solving is the vessel to an active productive life. Therefore, scientists judiciously ask how can people learn more efficiently?

B. Techniques for Learning

Generally, when learning occurs, behavior is modified in some manner. Therefore, psychologists observe and measure this overt change in performance. But what actually transpires within the person? Unfortunately the question begs for an absolute answer. The neurobiologist attacks the question by probing the firings of the neurons or the electrochemical change that occurs within the brain or nervous system. The behaviorist studies learning from the stimulus-response activity, whereas another scientist argues that the answers lie in the cognitive, as he examines the analytical and creative processes that occur within the mind. Even though fragmented by different paradigms, however, all agree on certain points. Animals, as well as man, learn, although society's demands force humans to utilize their intellect more than animals. Humans rely on learning to a greater degree and less on instincts, reflexes, and physiological drives. Essentially, when man enters the world, he finds himself less able to deal with immediate needs than an animal. Consequently, he passes through a prolonged maturation period (infancy, childhood, and adolescence) during which he acquires certain skills, complex habits, the ability to communicate and create—he learns. (In construction, experience, on-the-job training, and the school of hard knocks are occupational maturation periods.) Although psychologists have yet to discover one overriding principle of learning (if one indeed exists, other than innate ability) they agree that motivation lays the foundation. Driven by a need or faced with a situation that promises a reward (or reduction of punishment) an organism learns. If not properly motivated, an organism retains its status quo. Psychologists generally agree that practice and repetition advance this learning process. For example, the more projects a contractor (designer) builds (designs), the more he generally learns. Furthermore, research demonstrates that spaced sessions of review and practice usually produce improved results more than one massed session. Sometimes, but not always, more efficient learning is accomplished by breaking down a complex task into smaller units. In construction, the total project is divided into more manageable components (i.e., plans—L,A,S,P,H,E;* specs—approximately 25 sections or 16 divisions of the Construction Specifications Institute format).

*L—Site   P—Plumbing
 A—Architectural   H—Heating and Ventilating
 S—Structural   E—Electrical

On the basis of extensive experimentation, a number of factors and techniques have proved instrumental to effective learning, and we will discuss them now.

1. Motivation

Although motivation is not actually a technique, obviously little is learned unless one applies himself. Furthermore, the more motivated (by virtue of interest or anticipation of reward) the more improved the learning. Strong, internal incentives usually lead to self-actuation, which in turn proves to be superior to external motivation. In our society, people work for money; yet, as will be seen in the discussion of vocations, such other factors as self-esteem, creativity, self-satisfaction, and even the fear of failure, may compel individuals to excel in their jobs. With respect to supervisor-subordinate relations, psychologists emphasize that positive reinforcement surpasses criticism and punishment as motivational catalysts. People react more positively to approval than to disapproval; therefore, managers should recognize that the most effective technique for dealing with marginal performance of a task involves coupling constructive criticism with encouragement. Stated proverbially, "You catch more flies with honey than with vinegar." Caustic criticism and ridicule—a definite no-no for supervisors—reap tensions, hostility, and other negative factors that interfere with learning more acceptable behavior. If a person is barraged with insults or weighted under with pressure, more than likely his mind will not be fully on his job. Instead, much of his energy will be wasted in preoccupation, nervousness, or revenge.

If a supervisor shows confidence in his subordinates and vice versa, this confidence encourages the recipient to behave positively. The worker tends to fulfill this expectation because of raised self-esteem. Studies also show the reverse: the supervisor who expects poor performance from a worker may be creating such a defeatist attitude that the worker gravitates to poor execution of his job. This self-fulfilling prophecy applies also to groups. For example, if an owner totally mistrusts a contractor, then no matter what the contractor may offer—concessions or friendly gestures—in all probability the owner group will "see" a devious ulterior motive. "What has he got up his sleeve?" In response, the contractor may then be expected to behave in a retaliatory manner.

2. Instruction

Efficiency is greatly increased in learning by receiving (or giving) sufficient preliminary instructions. Such initial instructions establish a frame of reference and highlight the important features. Technically, before commencing a new project or examination of plans and specs, the reviewer should receive (or give) a thorough briefing and highlighting of the tasks at hand. The project manager or job captain, who thoroughly instructs his subordinates on the total scope, instead of fragmented tasks, greatly improves the chance of successful completion. If the subordinate can see the total picture, he is less likely to head down dead ends or retread old grounds.

On a managerial level, proper instruction and training provide the basis for the smooth transition in future promotions. As a supervisor or owner, it makes sense that subordinates be actively trained to be capable of assuming a key slot and new responsibilities. Interpersonally, it tends to motivate one to improve himself, thus self-fulfilling the expectation prophecy. Organizationally, it lessens the impact of a vacated position (via promotion, resignation, or expansion).

3. Participation

Closely related to motivation, active participation greatly improves the learning process, especially when comparing new information with what is already known and remembered. Participation retains attention so that new data are encoded in familiar terms and, therefore, the information is recovered more readily.

4. Knowledge of Results

Generally when one knows how well he performs, he learns faster and more efficiently. For example, suppose an individual performs a specific task incorrectly. Unless corrected, he continues to repeat the mistake until his maladaptive behavior becomes entrenched—a bad habit often very difficult to unlearn. Consequently, the situation forces him to undo the bad habit and learn the correct response. Frequent checks, especially in the embryo stages, preclude the formation of bad habits. From a supervisory viewpoint, a subordinate should be critiqued, especially when he functions dissatisfactorily. The manager should discuss the issues with him, tactfully point out the deficiencies, and suggest remedial action. Each worker deserves the opportunity to learn (correctly) and to grow and mature in his job. A manager who neglects his responsibility of pointing out weak areas (while rewarding strong points) shortchanges the worker, and suffers the result of his neglect.

5. Practice

The common proverb states that "practice makes perfect," and truthfully so. Nevertheless, psychologists have investigated beyond this proverb into another important area of practical consequences: the efficiency of a long learning period (massed practice) versus a number of short learning periods (spaced practices). Studies indicate that the most fruitful technique depends on the type of task. For complex material, which requires considerable effort for understanding, one should rely on massed practice because it takes time to acclimate himself—to get his feet wet. Once a person accomplishes this indoctrination, however, he peaks his interest, which tends to sustain his involvement. Reviewing a "scope of work" would be best handled by this massed practice approach. (Instead of first attacking a plumbing section, it may prove more productive to get the total scope first.)

For rote memory, detailed materials, or skills that require muscular coordination, tests show that distributed practice periods result in superior learning, as opposed to one long training period. Other studies indicate that for many tasks, people can learn more efficiently by judicious combinations of massed and spaced practice. For example, initially, a long period of study gives us the general structure; later, the distributed practice periods help us to master the details. With little stretch of the imagination, the reader should recognize the applicability of this technique to designing, examining, and estimating.

6. Whole versus Part

Similar to the questions posed in the practice technique, should one go through the material from stem to stern (the whole method) or break the material into the components? Again, tests show that the best approach depends on the task at hand.

For complex material that requires continuity for understanding, psychologists feel that the whole method results in more efficient learning. For example, before attacking the details, an architect should understand (learn) the owner's complete program. The same could be said for estimators and schedulers.

For unorganized material with little intrinsic meaning, generally the part method yields the best results. Still, the combination of both methods may yield better learning. One can sweep the totality of the material with the whole method, and, with the part method, can concentrate on difficult details. Again, we point out the applicability of these methods to planning and estimating.

7. Overlearning

If practice makes perfect, overlearning promotes lasting retention. Experiments indicate that the results of overlearning will justify the extra time and effort—up to the point of diminishing returns. Overlearning is easily identified as a form of experience. Through the years, after completing a number of projects, after repeatedly resolving common problems and adapting to new situations, constructioneers (managers, designers, tradesmen, etc.) expand their reservoir of knowledge.

8. Environment

In order to participate actively, an individual must minimize causes of interference and distraction by improving the conditions under which he works. Often construction personnel labor under various pressures, and shrinking time deadlines. Tension mounts. Efficiency drops. Consequently, errors are committed and propagated. Although little can be done about raw weather conditions, it is apparent that the tradesman who must work in severe cold or rain will certainly function less productively than his comfortable colleague. For intellectual tasks, distracting work areas take their toll. Loud voices, cluttered desks or drafting boards, constant traffic, all detract from a favorable learning condition. It would be well for supervisors to attend to these matters, on and off the site.

In Appendix II, a few learning strategies for improving memory are analyzed in detail.

ATTITUDES

When the judgment is weak, the prejudice is strong

O'Hara

An attitude can be defined as the predisposition to evaluate or respond to a person, a situation, or an event in a certain way, favorable or unfavorable. Psychologists find no sharp distinction between attitudes and beliefs (and opinions). Often a person tends to be more conscious (and sometimes verbal) of his beliefs and opinions although frequently his attitudes originate subtly on an unconscious level that may preclude verbalization. When someone makes a decision at a job site, get his specific concrete reasons. All too often decisions are made on the basis of a hazy justification—"I don't know—it seems ok."

Attitudes play a crucial role in how one feels about people, life, health, freedom, money, achievement, education, and his job—construction management. In fact, this enduring fabric of experiences, feelings, thoughts, and drives greatly influences the career a person chooses. Some respected scientists assert that they can adequately describe a person's personality (and possibly predict his behavior) by determining his predisposition toward persons, objects, concepts, and situations. Attitudes provide somewhat the plans and specs of our personalities and our life styles. They serve as guides to our behavior; they provide the standards and structure by which we judge ourselves, our colleagues, and the multitude of interactions that join us. It has been hypothesized that attitudes result from a complex combination of emotions, intellect, and motivational components, each in varying degrees. In situations involving sympathy and prejudice, by and large, emotions more than intellect determine the response. The opposite occurs when dealing with objective scientific matters. Few of us would argue over the results of a valid slump test, whereas the beauty of the concrete finish may welcome opposing opinions. With regard to the motivational components, although an individual's attitude may color his reaction to people and situations, their effect on his actual behavior depends on the strength of the predisposition. A sensitive architect, who places an ultimate premium on esthetics, may dogmatically and unjustifiably demand additional finish work on the concrete cited above, whereas a contractor, who blindly holds justice as a premium, may stubbornly bring the case to court, regardless of the cost. Sometimes, decisions in construction step beyond the money boundaries.

From experiences in life, as well as on the project, the reader certainly realizes that people possess various predispositions, preferences, and prejudices, all of which contribute to their "make-up." Because of these variations, both in diversity and degree, it can be anticipated that the probability of misunderstanding and disagreement grows in proportion. For example, the architect strives for creativity; the contractor drives toward maximum profits; the owner pursues simplicity and low costs. Each of these factors may be mutually exclusive: maximum profits may conflict with low costs or emphasis on creativity. In fact, each group in the construction team has differing attitudes, contractual and psychological, about what goals and methods are to be esteemed. Chapter 5 will examine this premise in detail. Fundamentally, human beings embrace literally thousands of attitudes that emanate from only a handful of values. Small in number, such values profoundly affect one's general outlook. Everyone clings tenaciously to certain beliefs about goals, desirable and undesirable, and how such goals may be obtained or avoided. When an individual prizes something highly, this intensity drives him vigorously. For example, if a manager places high marks on superior job performance, he will be strongly motivated to do well, by his everyday effort as well as by evening education, both formal and personal. In fact, he may well demand excellence, sometimes conflicting with another person's values, often in ways that cannot be easily resolved. As an illustration, the supervisor may cherish his career as his life's work. Meanwhile, the subordinate may be more interested in television. On any given project, there will be a wide difference of attitudes: a plumber may shrug, "It's just another job"; a small contractor, on the brink of bankruptcy, will be chopping and cutting to save the business; a civil service inspector may be indifferent to the sub's plight, "It's no money out of my pocket."

Psychologists classify two basic kinds of values. The first kind relates to present conduct: intelligence, wealth, honesty, courage. The second kind refers to end states of existence: equality, religious salvation, peace. Like the Pharaohs building the pyramid, each individual constructs his own characteristic hierarchy of values, some of which he cherishes more dearly than others. Therefore, like the tottering subcontractor, he may find himself in a conflict, such as having to choose between profits and honesty. Depending on the hierarchy and the pressures exerted by the group to which a person belongs, he usually expresses that attribute of highest strength. Unfortunately, one man's gold is another man's dust. The same is implied for groups as well. Hence: conflict.

On the basis of considerable psychological testing, via questionnaires, scientists conceptualize the following to be the basic six categories of values for the individual:

1. Theoretical. Values truth in the philosophical scientific sense; intellect; the rational (e.g., the pure scientist, the engineer)
2. Economic. Values the pragmatic and useful; money and material wealth (e.g., the contractor)
3. Esthetic. Values the artistic, both in form and grace (e.g., the architect)
4. Social. Values social considerations and interactions (e.g., the salesman)
5. Political. Values power, prestige, the opportunity to influence (e.g., the supervisor)
6. Religious. Values the religious aspects of the world (e.g., a clergyman)

These attributes seldom occur as isolated entities, but in combinations called value systems. Each person constructs his unique pyramid to form his particular psyche.

A. Formation of Attitudes and Prejudices

Just as humans learn to walk and talk and read and write, they also learn attitudes that once cemented, doggedly resist modification. At birth a baby holds no inherent or instinctive values (good or bad), but as he grows and matures and gains experience in life he acquires them. How? One psychologist breaks down the development into four broad processes:

1. The person gradually assimilates the beliefs and attitudes of those with whom he closely identifies (i.e., his parents, peers, teachers, and colleagues).

So strong is this assimilation that many sons choose careers similar to those of their fathers (see Box 4.1). As will be discussed, there are direct correlations between personality traits and occupation.

2. He frequently forms certain attitudes because of a dramatic, impressive experience that he may generalize to related situations (i.e., a gratifying summer job may lead into a particular career).

3. Daily experiences and observations may create or reinforce a prejudgment toward a specific group or situation. During the course of many construction meetings, for example, one may be inclined to mold specific impressions about certain people, groups, and ideas. All in all, this is how reputations are built. At the preconstruction meeting, strangers may be reluctant to actively engage in open communications. Instead, they feel their way around. After a few meetings, however, when the tempo and the climate have stabilized, each party begins to form opinions about people and conditions. After a number of projects together, people generally establish who are the "good guys" and "bad guys" in terms of competence, integrity, and rapport. Because of strong group associations, members often conform to collective standards, and adopt ready-made, packaged attitudes. A subordinate may parrot the preferences of his supervisor; a tradesman echoes the opinions of union leaders. If top administration takes a carefree or hard-line attitude toward a contractor, it can be assumed that the inspection force will follow in suit.

Other studies indicate that parents and highly regarded mentors provide models that are emulated, consciously and unconsciously. These models reward, overtly or subtly, attitudes considered to be of importance, and admonish those actions deemed to be incompatible with their cherished value system. Of course, other factors and experiences influence in no small measure: namely, friends who generally hold similar views and beliefs; educational systems that inculcate societal standards; communities that stress certain mores; and, finally, vocations that emphasize certain traits and deemphasize others. Unfortunately, not all attitudes rate high on a scale of intellect and justice. Humans also learn prejudices, generally acknowledged to imply an unfavorable tendency or prejudgment toward a particular idea or person solely on a foundation of stereotypes and emotion. Because this form of learning depends on close affiliations and personality structure, seldom can prejudices be readily modified. More often than not, they blind people to the realities of their environment so that, consequently, a person will accept without question specific attitudes that rest on a foundation of muck.

Therefore, as suggested by one prominent psychologist, and this is directly applicable to construction management, an individual should endeavor, as a minimum, to identify his prejudices—and strive to mitigate their impact on his overt actions. Everybody holds opinions and prejudices about members and groups of the construction team. (See Box 3.2 for common stereotypes.) To recognize these prejudgments for what they are is essential to effective interpersonal relations. One should always try to work with the intellect and the hard facts of the situation.

Box 3.2. CONSTRUCTION STEREOTYPES

The architect as seen by himself

The contractor as seen by the owner

The engineer as seen by the tradesman

The civil servant as seen by everyone

Gerry Fox

B. Persuasion and Propaganda

Although we concede that fused attitudes and prejudices can seldom be changed, we note that many are superficial in nature, and can be modified to some extent. Every day advertisements, actually methods of persuasion, and propaganda bombard the public through the media or by direct contact. These messages have one target: to influence people. In construction management, from project inception through completion, everyone attempts to persuade one another in some mode or manner. For example, with a favorable attitude and good rapport, a contractor may convince an owner of the necessity for a marginal change order, or the owner may sway the superintendent to grant him a small extra at no cost. At every meeting one can witness the "selling" of viewpoints and positions. Considerable research has been done in the areas of persuasion and propaganda.

1. Persuasion

Generally persuasive communication involves three key components. Evidently there must be: (1) a message; (2) a sender of the message; and (3) a recipient. In addition, the sequential responses to the message must be considered; attention, understanding, and acceptance. Obviously, if the recipient pays no attention to the communication, or misunderstands, then the desired goal of the persuader fails to materialize. Given attention and understanding, however, the effectiveness of the message rests upon whether the receiver accepts or rejects the contents.

The basics of communication will be analyzed in Chapter 6. Only a few results from the social research field will be examined here.

1. Scientists identify several factors that affect the persuasiveness of the sender: his credibility; his attractiveness; and his power. First, with regard to credibility, it appears that objectivity and expertise both directly favor his image. For example, if an eminent engineer condemns a concrete finish, in all probability most people would accept his judgment solely on the basis of his reputation, whereas if a grubby, illiterate cement finisher argued against the judgment, say in broken English, he would find few supporters. Secondly, if a sender is attractive in the sense of projecting a "likability" (charisma), and is identifiable to a recipient who feels both similarity and familiarity, he contributes positively to his persuasiveness. Third, the power of the sender often results in the swaying of the recipient's attitude. The influence will be in proportion to the sender's authority and the magnitude of the rewards and punishments he can deliver: "Do it my way or you're fired!"

At a construction conference, the speaker who may sway the most people (all other factors held equal) would be credible, charismatic, and powerful.

Remember, however, that truth arrives in all shapes, styles, and deliveries. It may well prove that the cement finisher is correct even in the face of eminence and expertise. Regardless of status, let each person have his say, and evaluate the contents of the message objectively.

2. Scientists postulate that the personality characteristics of the receiver, such as intelligence and ego, determine his receptivity to the message. Although far from conclusive, there seems to be a propensity that individuals with low self-esteem drift along with the tide of persuasion. Possibly this inclination originates with the fact that a low-esteem person places less credence on his own opinion than on that of the sender. To such an unfortunate, cohesive group norms can be overpowering sources of pressure. Consequently, he conforms, even to the point of sacrificing his own values and opinions. Finally, the reader could reasonably assume that highly intelligent people resist persuasiveness more consistently than less intelligent recipients. Research shows few consistent relationships, however.

2. Propaganda

Using typical persuasive techniques, the propagandist attempts to influence attitudes and behavior to line up with his goals (good or bad) by primarily appealing to emotions, not to reason or enlightenment. We list several techniques below, many of which are dubiously applied at construction meetings.

a. Loaded word.   This device uses emotionally charged words to create a prejudicial impression, favorable or unfavorable (i.e., an "inexpensive" product as opposed to a "cheap" product or a "thrifty" owner versus a "stingy" owner or a "competent" contractor versus a "sharp" contractor).

In Appendix III, we assert that a person must use extreme care in choosing the correct word, especially in framing a letter. To describe a piece of equipment as "inexpensive" will draw a different response than to refer to it as "cheap."

b. Transfer of Testimony.   Using this technique, the persuader tries to win over the recipient by associating his idea or intention with a prestigious person or accepted belief. "Frank Lloyd Wright invented this design!" or "This is the way Stone and Webster builds on a job, and they're recognized throughout the world!" or "M.I.T. uses this product!" So what? They can be wrong at times.

c. Bandwagon.   By using this device, the sender urges the recipient to behave in a particular fashion by group pressure. "Everybody does it this way, what's wrong with you?" Especially with noncompliances, the argument commonly revolves around the justification: "But that's the way I've always done it. Everybody does it this way!" The implication is that you are an odd ball.

d. Card-stacking. The propagandist deliberately distorts the message by emphasizing assets and good points while suppressing liabilities. He intricately manipulates "statistics," "research," and "science." For example, a salesman (designer) highlights the qualities of his system without mentioning future serious energy or maintenance requirements. "Here, look at this chart. Laboratory facts! This electrical heat system is a revolutionary concept—clean, dependable, and simple to control." True, but two years later the user almost goes bankrupt because of operating costs.

e. Arousal of Needs. The sender appeals to an actual need, but "hard-sells" the notion that the "solution" benefits the recipient more than the sender. A salesman stresses that your own best interest will be served, not his, if you purchase his product. "Look, my job is to help you. I'd feel remiss if you let this opportunity go by."

f. Appeal to Prejudice. This device appeals primarily to prejudices, hence, is essentially emotional. For example, a salesman determines a particular prejudice that you have, then proceeds to frame his pitch around your prejudgment. "Sure I know you've had a very unpleasant experience with *those* people. I don't blame you for feeling angry. But I've got a solution to your problem."

As with prejudice, the reader should assess propaganda for what it is—an appeal to emotion. It may be useful to know that "everybody does it that way," but deal with the objective merits of the current situation.

MOTIVATION

*It is motive alone that gives
character to the actions of men*

Bruyére

Motivation (also called drive, urge, and force) refers to behavior set into motion because of a need felt by the individual. This need indicates that the organism lacks a particular satisfaction, and, therefore, strives to achieve relief. If starving, a human does little except search for food. Psychologists usually view motivation as a dynamic process that initiates, sustains, and directs various activities. Obviously, this broad definition deals with all types of internal forces (conscious and unconscious, as well as physical and psychological) ranging from simplest wants to highest aspirations.

Technically the term motivation involves several aspects such as: "needs," which imply the element of want; "urges," which stress impelling forces; and finally "incentive," which suggests a reward. Humans, by necessity, must satisfy bodily needs—hunger, thirst, elimination; all are physiological aspects of motivation. On the psychological side are such needs as: self-esteem; recognition and acceptance; knowing and understanding; and maximizing one's potential. Above and beyond the necessity of a paycheck, which in turn purchases food, drink, and shelter, a career offers the avenues by which a person can satisfy his other needs. As a case in point, architecture provides the opportunity to satisfy an urge to create; contracting may be the route to achieve "success," independence, and recognition for the entrepreneur.

In broad terms motivation falls into either of two classifications: (1) organic; or (2) personal or social. Under the organic heading, the list includes basic drives that originate from bodily needs: hunger, thirst, pain, elimination, sex, as well as those that originate from unspecified physiological sources (manipulation, investigation, stimulation). Under the personal or social heading are those motives that a person acquires (learns) in the course of social experiences: affiliation, imitation, achievement, competition, cooperation, aversions, interests, levels of aspiration, and a matrix of others.

Obviously the sheer numbers of human motivation involve very complex factors and definition dilemmas. For example, a person may express the same motive in several ways. He may show antagonism to an opponent by fight or flight, say, walking off the job. Or a person may interpret (or misinterpret) motives in various ways. In a hostile team setting, a contractor's request for a change order may be construed as an underhanded attempt to bleed the owner dry. Likewise, a contractor may attribute a designer's lengthy punch list to ignoble roots, such as harassment. In another instance, a person may express several motives in a single action. A designer or manager may work relentlessly in order to capture both fame and fortune.

To compound the numerical and definitive woes, motivations vary in intensity and magnitude from completing a simple detail in two hours to pursuing a lifetime ambition with no regard to "blood, sweat, and tears." For example, outwardly one assumes that the more attractive the reward, the harder a person will strive to reach that goal. In fact, society overflows with certain individuals (artists, soldiers, scientists, Type A personalities) so strongly driven, that they sacrifice life, limb, and family in the course of their punishing pursuit. What catalysts drive such individuals? What principles govern the variations in these forces underlying overt behavior? Unfortunately, psychologists have failed to achieve (or agree upon) a simple and orderly theory of motivation. Nevertheless, over the years, several theories have emerged as the most promising.

A. Theories of Motivation

1. The Behavior Theory

The behavior theory emphasizes that needs spur activity. Therefore, humans learn habitual ways to satisfy these urges. Experiments demonstrate that actions that satisfy a need tend to be repeated. Stated in behavioral terms, an organism encounters a stimulus, responds in some manner, and, as a consequence, gets reinforced for his actions. Habits are learned (and extinguished) in this fashion. A hard-working manager who repeatedly gets merit raises, bonuses, and recognition will possibly develop a "workaholic" life style, whereas the hard worker who receives nothing for his extra efforts may be inclined to slack off. This very point has been argued by opponents to union and civil service systems. It has been alleged that both systems stifle superior effort. The rationale may be: "Why should I hustle when everybody else is covered with cobwebs and moss. We all get paid the same."

2. The Unconscious Motivation Theory

This theory focuses on unconscious impulses instead of overt behavior. According to the Freudians, much of human action originates from unconscious wishes and unrecognized feelings. Forgetting an appointment with a person repeatedly or forgetting his name may indicate an unconscious hostility toward that person. There have been numerous cases of people who seem to acquire neurotic ailments that "save" them from threatening situations, e.g., becoming too ill to attend a difficult meeting.

3. The Cognitive Theory of Motivation

According to this theory, besides the gravity of unconscious factors, a person usually motivates himself according to thought-out purposes and plans. For example, one chooses his occupation on an essentially conscious level. He weighs the pros and cons. He investigates the demands of the job. He assesses his abilities, interests, rewards, attitudes, personality characteristics, and life goals. If the demands match the personality traits, and fate smiles favorably, one finds a compatible career. It could be argued that each person in construction consciously gave thought to his career choice in accord with his abilities and the opportunities afforded by life. At least the text assumes this to be the case.

4. Maslow's Theory of Motivation and Needs

This system classifies a hierarchy of needs. The strongest needs obviously stem from the basic biological survival requirements, such as hunger, thirst,

Figure 3.1.   Maslow's Hierarchy of Needs.

and pain. Figuratively, they form the base of a pyramid. (See Fig. 3.1.) At the apex of this hierarchy, Maslow lists the need to create, the innate desire to maximize one's potential. Because this theory is so well acknowledged in managerial and vocational circles, and is readily appropriate to construction management, this text opts for this particular theory.

B. Maslow's Theory of Human Motivation

Why does a scientist (or manager or businessman) spend endless hours at work, forgoing other activities and pleasures? What drives an individual to amass a fortune at any cost, even health? What urges the artist to create or the businessman to succeed or the employee to excel? Biological wants alone fail to account for the passion and mystery of behavior; otherwise a person well fed and bed would cease to labor. Therefore, Abraham Maslow, a leader in humanistic psychology, proposed a novel way of classifying human needs. He assumed that each human had a hierarchy of motives ascending in potency from the basic biological needs (i.e., hunger, sex, and self-esteem) to more complicated psychological motives, such as the search for truth and beauty. According to Maslow, man must satisfy, at least partially, the needs at the lower levels before those at the apex become important enough to initiate action. For instance, under conditions of starvation or serious danger, satisfaction of these survival requirements dominates behavior. Under such adverse conditions, the prestige needs seem meaningless. The contractor confronted with bankruptcy cares little about the beauty of a concrete finish. Man seeks food and safety first; once these needs are satisfied, he proceeds up the pyramid to higher tiers.

Specifically, Maslow listed seven needs fundamental to human motivation, which we now examine.

1. Physiological Needs.

This category includes the requirements for survival: hunger, thirst, air, elimination, fatigue, temperature regulation, avoidance of pain. Failure to satisfy these necessities usually results in termination of life. In any case, when humans experience hunger, thirst, pain or extreme fatigue, they concentrate on little else except gratification.

Although not generally required for survival, deprivation of sex activity causes physical and emotional discomfort. It is true that a few individuals create and develop under the burden of unfulfilled physiological wants, but they are exceptions rather than rules.

2. Safety Needs

When a person, as is commonly the case in this society, gratifies his physiological requirements, he then turns his attention to achieving equilibrium with respect to safety needs. Under normal conditions (exclusive of daredevils with their unique value systems) human beings want to feel safe, out of harm's way, and protected from threats of violence. In a collapsing building, all else seems trivial in comparison: a surveyor drops a delicate transit, a glazier smashes an expensive light of glass, and they both dash to safety.

3. Love and Belonging Needs

These wants prime mankind in no small measure: in developing close ties with others, in joining social and professional groups, and in choosing occupations. In fact, psychologists have observed that infants who lacked mother love or mother-substitute love, became depressed and retarded, both physically and emotionally. A person who feels friendless and unwanted will exert great efforts to gratify love needs. All normal humans need to belong, to affiliate, to be accepted by others. No man is an island, and this is a reason why group pressures are so influential.

4. Self-Esteem Needs

With the achievement of biological, safety, and belonging needs, man works to gain his own respect and that of others as well. He wishes to prove his competence, worth, and importance, not only internally, but externally to his friends and colleagues. A powerful motivating force, it applies to everyone from the plumber's helper to the world-renowned designer. When a person lacks self-esteem, he may drain his energies solely in trying to convince himself and others of his worth, instead of effectively applying his talents and abilities.

5. Cognitive Needs

This urge for information and understanding helps to explain the enormous differences between man and animals. Animals seek only deficit needs, whereas man goes further. Anthropologists find this urge reflected even in the behavior of primitive man. How else could civilization progress and evolve without the efforts of some gifted geniuses? Such creative people invented the wheel, the wedge, the screw, and the lever—the basic principles on which all machinery runs.

6. Esthetic Needs

In daily experience, one recognizes the need for beauty. Observe the order and symmetry around us—buildings, paintings, books, theories, laws, etc. Some rare individuals possess this unique quality so strongly, they withstand fads and fashion, and create beauty and order.

7. Self-Actualizing Needs

Psychologists, on the basis of therapy cases, assume that human beings possess a motivation to self-actualize—to develop their capacity. Happiness lies in being what a man can be in terms of his unique capacity. Humans not only express this need creatively in their life styles, but in their whole beings. True self-actualization emerges freely only after one has successfully satisfied the lower levels of the hierarchy.

In addition to this conception of the hierarchy, Maslow further proposed that when man gratifies the lower or deficiency (D) needs such as safety, love, and self-esteem, he will then feel able to satisfy the higher, or being (B) needs, such as to know and understand, to seek beauty, and to self-actualize. A key element in this theoretical approach involves the distinction between deficiency and growth needs. A person directs his behavior to gratify D needs because of a deficit, whereas he seeks, because of natural *desire*, to satisfy B needs. The successful manager who fights forced retirement, the millionaire businessman who ventures into a new field, the esteemed architect who continues to work incessantly on a more beautiful monument are all cases that substantiate Maslow's proposal.

To summarize the distinctions between deficit and growth needs:

1. Man acts to get *rid* of *deficiency needs* (e.g., hunger and pain); man seeks the *enjoyment* of *growth needs* (to create, to appreciate beauty).

2. Deficiency motivation tends to reduce disagreeable tension; growth motivation maintains an enjoyable form of tension.

3. Man satisfies deficits to avoid illness and pain. Man satisfies growth needs to produce health.

4. All men share deficit needs; only particular individuals self-actualize.

5. Deficit-motivated people tend to be other-directed, more dependent on others for satisfaction and assistance, whereas the growth oriented individual tends to be more self-centered, more independent, and more able to help himself. (See Box 3.3).

Box 3.3 SELF-ACTUALIZERS

Do you maximize your potential?

On the basis of in-depth study, Maslow developed a list of characteristics most descriptive of those individuals who extract the most from their potential. In general a self-actualizing person:

1. *seeks reality, but can tolerate uncertainty,*
2. *accepts himself and others for what they are,*
3. *acts in a spontaneous fashion, seldom worrying about what other people think,*
4. *enjoys his own privacy,*
5. *remains faithful to his own values and independent of others,*
6. *appreciates the basic experiences of life around him, finding stimulation and pleasure in repeating experiences that absorb him,*
7. *establishes deep, satisfying, interpersonal relationships with few, rather than many, people,*
8. *believes every individual is worthy of respect, dignity, and esteem,*
9. *creates more because he breaks away from convention, and seeks new relationships,*
10. *has a good sense of humor because he tends to see relationships that strike him as funny,*
11. *makes decisions and accepts responsibility for these decisions,*
12. *focuses on particular goals with little wasted effort,*
13. *stays flexible; able to change his attitudes when he thinks it is appropriate,*

14. *takes a stand on important issues,*
15. *recognizes the effect he has on people, and*
16. *possesses ability to give and take.*

BEHAVIORS THAT LEAD TO SELF-ACTUALIZATION

1. *Experience life with full absorption and concentration.*
2. *Attempt new approaches rather than sticking to secure and safe ways. Be creative.*
3. *Give more weight to your own feelings in evaluating experiences, rather than to tradition or authority or the majority.*
4. *Be honest with yourself and others.*
5. *Assume responsibility for your decisions and actions.*
6. *Try your best at whatever you decide to do.*
7. *Try to recognize your problems and prejudices. Have the courage to change them.*

Maslow's scheme requires further scientific study and verification. This is especially true because the hierarchy is not a rigid process, and must be considered in the light of the particular backgrounds and values of each individual. Yet, the scheme does offer some interesting implications:

- Each individual possesses potential capacities, abilities, and talents.
- Unfortunately, often he fails to develop these potentials, and, consequently, wastes part of himself.
- Before effective development, the individual must satisfy deficit needs.
- By satisfying his growth needs, the individual maximizes his capacity to the fullest, and finds the process to be both enjoyable and natural.

The fact that people work for more than money and status supports these implications.

When asked how a person could recognize the self-actualization process within himself, Maslow stated that an individual must:

- Demand more of himself, raise his standards, and expect greater returns for his efforts.
- Continuously improve himself as a natural way of life.
- Increase his understanding of himself and the world around him.
- Maximize his abilities and develop his capacity to the fullest degree and diversity.

C. Motivation, Needs, and Occupation

For years organizational leaders incorrectly assumed that man hated work in principle and practice; that man performed effectively only under the threat of punishment; that man craved security, and worked only to make a living. Obviously, one can find fault with these assumptions. Otherwise, once a man earned sufficient wages for food and shelter, he would stop working. Man has built his civilization on nobler motives. Anne Roe, in her vocational studies, offered some notable insights gleaned from the theory developed by Maslow. On the basis of considerable research, she emphasized that an occupation involves much more than a paycheck. It is undeniably valid that, by means of his job, a person achieves the means to allay hunger and thirst, to provide shelter, and, to some extent, to gratify the sex needs. Additionally, the job provides safety and security via pensions and insurances. Slices from the paycheck pay taxes, which insure police and health protection. Occupations also offer the means to satisfy the higher needs. To work with a congenial group and to be accepted and respected by such a group may prove to be an outstanding factor in job satisfaction. A project run in a friendly, professional atmosphere certainly proves more satisfying than the opposite. A project manager may refuse a lucrative job offer because he "likes" his present employer.

Closely related to belonging, the importance of being recognized for competence and ability and being given the opportunity to establish a "name" may well be the dominant reasons why an individual chooses, and remains in, a particular career. A tradesman may surrender high hourly wages for the prestige of an office position. Prestige and respect are crucial components of any career. In fact, in our society, simply having a job carries esteem. Note the devastating effect on some individuals in times of layoffs and prolonged unemployment. Furthermore, people tend to suspect any adult male who lacks a definite job. Occupations distinctly reflect a measure of an individual's training, abilities, and overall competence. From the conferred status and respect may be derived the greatest source of satisfaction. The degrees of freedom, the opportunity to do research, or to fulfill a growth need may override the financial remunerations. Money, certainly of utmost importance, fails to tell the whole story. The perquisites and intangibles must certainly be considered.

In construction, designing is an obvious mode of expression, but, on a more personal basis, a proud craftsman may see beauty in a task well done. If a job fails to provide these "perks," the person may seek fulfillment in outside activities: photography, art, model building, and a hundred other outlets. Unfortunately, drugs and alcohol are considered too readily as relief mechanisms. Psychologists find a positive correlation between the increase of worker dissatisfaction and neuroses, and the increase of drab, mechanized jobs.

In summary, it appears that a career, especially professional, in addition to being a key element in satisfying basic needs, also holds the key to self-actualization.

PERSONALITY

*The whole of a quantity is equal
to the sum of all its parts*

Alegbraic axiom

Any normal individual resents being labeled or stereotyped as "average"—
a run-of-the-mill architect, a typical manager or *just* another plumber. Instead, he insists that such a label fails to do justice to his complex and highly
distinctive "being." All too often, however, he pins such generalized labels
on others—an engineer is practical; a contractor is aggressive; a manager
is a tyrant. Using his mental catalog, he classifies and typecasts other individuals into quick personality descriptions to help him maintain a ready
character reference on those he deals with. A specification writer will select
a piece of equipment from catalog descriptions of quality and standards;
some people use the same approach in describing humans. By labels and
stereotypes, they simplify the problem of identifying others, and predicting
their future behavior. One serious flaw exists in treating human beings as
catalog items, however. The shifting nature of personality and human behavior defies accurate classifications. People are often not what they seem
at first meeting, or the second or the third. Usually, it takes many interactions under varying conditions to obtain a reasonably correct view of what
a person is really like—the sum total of his personality. Even then, this view
is fraught with pitfalls.

"Personality" is a somewhat elusive concept that refers to the distinctive-
ness of the person. This concept tries to differentiate one person from another psychologically. Just as occupations tend to result in classification
of people, human scientists (and nonscientist for that matter) classify
people into certain categories. Even the crudist observation demonstrates
that human beings are alike, yet different, and it is these differences that lead
scientists to attempt to distinguish the manner, shape, and form of the variations. For example, when we merely look at a person, instantly we begin
to judge him. We form impressions by virtue of his physical looks alone,
sometimes consciously, other times subtly. We "read" the messages sent by
his physique, clothes, and mannerisms, some of which reflect his character
and competence. Accurate or not, everybody ties interpretations into these
messages. Consider the project manager who dressed like a cement finisher,
and spoke in gutter slang. What can be said about his technical competence? Actually nothing. Yet, the world is stuffed with irrationalities; people
judge by strange criteria, especially "personality."

In trying to describe a person, we observe and interpret those behavioral
traits that he exhibits (or fails to exhibit). We would like to know some-

thing about his motives, attitudes, skills and intelligence. How does he perceive the world? What drives him? What frustrates him? In short, what is his personality like? Knowing this may assist us in predicting his behavior under various conditions. Very intricate is this concept of personality, and highly susceptible to error. This section presents a broad overview of this complex subject.

A. Definitions and Difficulties

Essentially the concept of personality consists of various characteristics and patterns of behavior. Both account somewhat for how an individual responds to his environment. Specifically, personality consists of diverse combinations and permutations of an individual's major traits, values, and attitudes, his motivations and needs, his intelligence, abilities, self-image, and other behavior patterns that he has learned through experience. Most psychologists agree that a person's personality is dependent upon both heredity and environmental factors, and, in developing, he achieves a unique "identity." A person can be recognized from day to day by something other than his physical appearance alone.

Disagreement among scientists arises over the emphasis one places on genetics versus learning and the processes of development. When an infant is born, he looks different from others. He has distinct facial features, height, weight, size, and bone structure, and possesses specific traits, such as temperament and mood, which seem to be genetically dependent. As the individual grows and matures, however, the environment, in no small measure, influences the final outcome, the totality of the person—his personality. For example, one may be endowed at birth with a potential capacity for genius, but poor environmental conditions may stifle motivation, or offer no opportunity to implement it. Obviously, one's physical and psychological well-being heavily depend on both emotional and nutritional surroundings. A deficient diet may cause retardation; a harsh punitive upbringing may stunt mental growth. Research concludes that both heredity and environment interact dynamically, and both interact in different proportions. Heredity does indeed influence certain characteristics, but it also has a limited effect on other aspects of personality. For instance, as one deals with his surroundings, learning causes certain changes. The behaviorists feel that humans tend to repeat behavior that is positively reinforced. Certainly, we would reasonably concur that learning experiences and our roles in life (social and vocational) contribute in some degree and manner in molding our behavior. Although at birth one may have a particular temperament (or innate ability or handicap), society plays a major role in how this temperament is expressed. Therefore, it appears that learning and reinforcement serve to stabilize personality traits to the extent that we "identify" a particular person as an exclusive entity. Nevertheless, experiences impress on us that human beings sometimes act in totally inconsistent ways. Nothing really demonstrates this inconsistency more than observing the apparent contradictions in human behavior. At one time a person, perhaps considered well-known and stable, conducts himself in a precise, logical manner; yet at another time, in a similar situation, he darts about in a haphazard fashion. So many factors seem to be involved that one can do little but guess in predicting behavior. Too often we find it difficult to predict or understand our own behavior, let alone someone else's. Accepting the random unpredictability of behavior, one must still admit that most normal humans generally act in reasonably stable ways. Otherwise, civilization would degenerate into a virtual jungle of erratic strangers.

As proposed by Maslow, all humans have a hierarchy of needs. Although diversified and different, every healthy person strives to satisfy the majority of deficit needs, certainly the physiological ones at minimum. All humans experience emotions to some measure; love, anger, frustration, happiness, fear. Therefore, these common needs and emotions bring some uniformity and a cubit of confidence in predicting behavior. By way of this commonality (social customs, mores, laws, etc.) one feels, to some extent, confident in attributing a certain motive or reason to another's actions. When a contractor bids a job, one assumes his motive is to make a profit. Interpersonally, when one interacts with another person, he expects (predicts) certain socially acceptable responses. For example, suppose you say "Good morning" to a colleague. Instead of the expected response, he scowls at you and walks away without a word, or, worse, he explodes into curses. His unusual response certainly leads you to assume reasons for his strange behavior. Ill? Aggressive? Nervous? Personal problem? An array of questions flash through your mind as you compare and evaluate against the socially expected behavior. This example illustrates some factors that complicate the puzzle of behavior. Many people act in phase with their moods. Often a physical condition, such as fatigue or even a diet, may cause the personality to be directly affected. An overactive thyroid condition may cause hyperactivity and irritability, whereas an underactive thyroid may make an individual appear sluggish and unemotional. All are contributing factors—unforseen, capricious, random, unknown—but certainly factors that must be considered by psychologists in developing their assorted theories of personality.

B. Theories of Personality

In order to be strictly rational and scientific, early psychologists went beyond merely listing traits to describe a person. They attempted to uncover a single theme that would either disclose the nature of personality or encompass its structure under one broad umbrella. To their dismay, the complexity of human nature (inclusive of the researchers themselves) prevented the discovery of a single unifying theory. Instead, over the years several have emerged.

Fundamentally, all theorists want to describe a person accurately so they can predict his behavior, say, for screening job applicants or detecting character defects. As mentioned above, most scientists agree that all people possess an identity other than that based on physical features. This identity depends on both heredity and environment. Over the years several influential theories have been developed, and we now consider them.

1. Type

Type theorists simplistically put people into categories much as one classifies animals and plants. This theory originates from the age-old observation that some people seem to have personalities dominated by one trait. Frequently, we describe a person with a simple statement: "he is intelligent," or "he is aggressive," or some other oversimplification. In fact, there is a propensity (learned) to associate traits with facial features.

The square chin denotes strength, red hair signals a ready temper, and elephant ears signify stupidity. All too often, a person's personality is assessed solely on the basis of his body shape: fat people are jolly; solid people are courageous and athletically endowed; and thin people are meek and intellectual. Oddly enough at times these assessments prove accurate, probably because expectations are often self-fulfilling. A fat person "learns" to be jolly. Society, parents, and peers subtly push the solidly built person into sports and the frail one to the library. (See Box 3.4 for common types.)

Box 3.4. COMMON PERSONALITY/PHYSICAL FEATURE
STEREOTYPES

Since antiquity men have attributed certain personality traits to body shapes and features.

1. Body Types. In an extensive study, William Sheldon, a contemporary psychologist, found a close correspondence between physique and temperament. A major criticism is that environmental factors may well determine how a person "learns" to adapt to his physique. A strong, well-built person (mesomorph) may learn, via parent, peer, or societal expectations, to be tough, aggressive, and athletic. For the same reasons, a thin, weak individual (ectomorph) may be steered toward books and intellectual pursuits. Sheldon's body types and associated characteristics are shown on page 109:

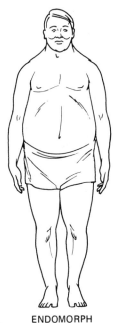

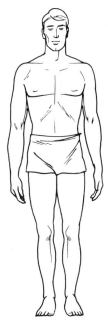

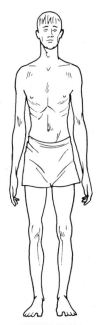

ENDOMORPH	MESOMORPH	ECTOMORPH
(Soft and Chubby)	(Hard and Rectangular)	(Thin and Fragile)
Jolly	Athletic	Shy
Indolent	Strong and tough	Morose
Loves comfort	Aggressive	Inhibited
Sociable	Adventurous	Secretive
Relaxed in posture	Prefers vigorous physical	Prefers mental activites
Gluttonous for food,	activity.	Possesses the largest
affection and people	Callous to the feelings of	brain in proportion to
	others	his size.

Can you identify the architect, the tradesman, and the civil service administrator? If you can, then that is all the more reason you must be wary of typecasting, especially when describing a particular individual. Although you may be correct one time, for certain you will be incorrect at another. The complexity and mystery of "personality" defy precision. Of course, many tradesmen are strong and aggressive, but others are: fat and jolly, thin and shy, fat and shy, athletic and intellectual, morose and adventurous—a million permutations are possible. Therefore, everyone should be judged on the merits of his totality and in context with the specific nature of the interaction.

2. Facial Features.   As with body types, facial features are common objects for stereotyping personality traits. Again, caution is essential.

From the works of Johann Lavater, 18th century Swiss clergyman, we have the following observations.*

FACE OF A HERO

FACE OF A SCOUNDREL

"The countenance of the hero: active, removed both from hasty rashness and cold delay. Born to govern. May be cruel, but scarcely; can remain unnoticed."

"Who does not here read reason debased; stupidity almost sunken to brutality? This eye, these wrinkles of a lowering forehead, this projecting mouth, the whole position of the head, do they not all denote dullness and debility?"

*Reference: "Human Behavior—The Individual" P. Good

In a more everyday vein, we all learn common (and often erroneous) associations as seen below.*

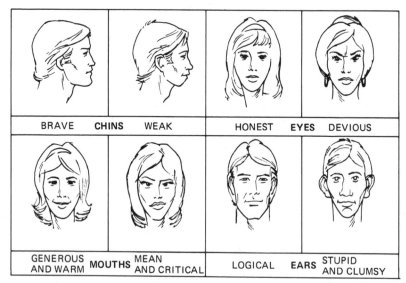

BRAVE	**CHINS**	WEAK
HONEST	**EYES**	DEVIOUS
GENEROUS AND WARM	**MOUTHS**	MEAN AND CRITICAL
LOGICAL	**EARS**	STUPID AND CLUMSY

*Reference: "Understanding Human Behavior"

> *Chapter 5 will show how physical attractiveness, undemocratic and veneered, governs how a person is evaluated—pro and con. (Of course if you happen to look like Michelangelo's* David, *so much the better for you.)*

Although simple, this theory fails in a number of aspects. For one, it allows no leeway for the inconsistencies of human behavior. Not all fat people are jolly. Furthermore, in a certain situation, a person may respond in atypical fashion.

2. Trait

Trait theorists argue that a more scientific approach is to define and establish, via test construction, a series of traits to best describe a person. Variations in personality are determined by testing and locating an individual's traits on a number of scales, each scale representing a different characteristic. For example, the values (theoretical, social, aesthetic, etc.) mentioned previously are such scales used to identify a person's dominant theme. In one such personality test, the Allport-Vernon-Lindzey Study of Values, engineers scored highest on the theoretical and low on the aesthetic. Businessmen rated positive on the economic and political, and negative on the aesthetic and social scales. A number of these tests will be utilized in Chapter 4 in drawing composite profiles of people on the construction team.

In lay terms, we all use traits to describe people. For example, when one describes another person as intelligent, anxious, or aggressive, he is essentially using the trait theory viewpoint. He labels the person by emphasizing a prominent (and *usually* stable and consistent) characteristic. One drawback to this approach concerns the danger that one will assume that the trait is the *cause* of the behavior. For instance, in a difficult problem situation, if an intelligent individual solves the problem, often it is assumed that he solved the problem *because* of his intelligence. Again, we assume a person exploded *because* he is aggressive. In actuality, the trait is simply a convenient psychological label, not a *cause* of behavior. Furthermore, there exists the inclination to assume that the trait is an inborn or unlearned characteristic within the individual, rather than arbitrary device for describing behavior. Traits, being economical, one- or two-word labels, say nothing definite about the characteristic, its development, or its consistency.

3. Developmental

Developmental theories stress that human development is a continuous process. Here, scientists assert that the key to understanding is to identify those past experiences that have shaped the personality. The Freudian approach views the earlier stages of psychosexual development as most critical with the result of a "fixed" personality, extremely difficult to change. Other psychologists, however, believe that one's personal identity results from a long process of resolving critical problems at various stages of life. Still others, from the behavioristic viewpoint, believe much of one's identity is learned (conditioned) by reward, punishment, and reinforcement in the formation of basic attitudes, habits, and emotional responses.

4. Dynamic

Dynamic theorists hold that the individual may be best understood by exploring the dynamic interplay between the conscious and unconscious: the conflicts that arise between one's traits and the demands imposed by his roles in society. The dynamic theorists attempt to define the concept of personality by observing how these conflicts are handled.

The reader may ask which theory proves to be the most accurate? This is a very difficult question to answer. Apparently all of these theories emanate from various viewpoints of mankind, and each approach presents certain advantages and disadvantages. Nevertheless, a few facts remain prominent:

1. Personality is a unique product of heredity and environment.

2. This summation, or totality, consists of genetically related factors (i.e., intelligence and abilities, activity and temperament) and environmental influences (values, attitudes, prejudices, interests, needs, goals, and motivational and emotional responses).

3. Although strongly influenced by early years, the personality can develop throughout life to achieve an exclusive "identity."

Whatever theory strikes one's fancy, it is important to realize that certain personalities seem to match certain careers. Since construction involves a potpourri of different occupations, it stands to follow that like politics, construction makes for strange bedfellows.

OCCUPATIONS AND PERSONALITY

*Nothing is really work unless you
would rather be doing something else*

Sir James M. Barrie

Since this book concerns primarily those occupations associated with construction, it is entirely appropriate to mention some psychological factors involved in careers. So far, the discussion has concentrated on the basics of construction management (especially the technical and legal aspects), then the basics of psychology, culminating with personality. The remainder of the text integrates these basics, with emphasis on the fact that people problems and misunderstandings cause undue hardship and waste in terms of time, money, and even health.

Whether an owner, architect, or construction manager (or any member of a construction team), one takes a positive step toward understanding his coworkers if he realizes some relationships between personality and occupation. Such knowledge leads to greater appreciation of others' viewpoints and values. With an understanding, one may consequently encounter fewer emotional blockages in friction situations.

Simply stated, a person's occupation mirrors his personality. This simple proposition has undergone considerable scientific research. Psychologists emphasize that to perceive correctly the role of occupation in an individual's life calls for a deep knowledge about his motives, needs, interests, and attitudes—his personality. It is widely recognized that a choice of occupation implies a person's general adjustment to life itself. The reader need only browse through the volumes of vocational books. The job descriptions invariably list values, interests, abilities—all personality factors—associated with a particular career. When an individual decides on a career, to some extent he selects those life patterns and roles most congenial to himself. His career gratifies needs and goals: at minimum, the physiological ones. Of course, one can eagerly argue that jobs and personalities often mismatch; every occupation abounds with round pegs in square holes. Even in those cases of job dissatisfaction (as one finds most common), it must be assumed that the worker has adjusted to some extent. Regardless of his woes and complaints about pitifully poor wages, insurmountable work loads, stupid, tyrannical bosses, and treacherous office politics, there must be at least a few redeeming factors that keep him on the job. Actions speak louder than words. After all, continuation in an occupation provides fairly good proof that the individual has achieved a minimum level of success, and that he has found the work somewhat agreeable. For example, it can be reasonably accepted that given ability, intelligence, etc., architects consciously choose the architectural profession because such careers offer gratification of certain needs, such as personal expression. In fact, studying thousands of architects, psychologists ascertained a number of traits attributable to this profession: artistic inclination; liking for work in unstructured, artistic setting calling for self-expression; dislike for problems that are severely structured or require gross physical strength. Chapter 4 explores this vein more thoroughly; suffice it to say here, that considerable study and observation demonstrate the factual relationship between personality and career.

Most adults work for financial returns that inevitably affect one's standard of living. Money directly buys food, drink, shelter, safety (taxes for police, army, etc.), and indirectly influences the other deficit needs (love,

sex, status, belonging, self-esteem, etc.). Basically every occupation provides a measure of status (see Box 3.5), partly related to income and partly
to self-esteem and recognition by others. All other factors being equal, a
highly paid union laborer seems to value his higher wages more than the
status of a more prestigious job.

In summary, a job not only expresses financial and status facts, but mirrors the individual's intelligence, abilities, aspirations, interests, self-image,
needs—the sum total of his identity. And, very important, a career invites
the means by which one can grow intellectually and esthetically—to maximize one's talents.

Box 3.5. JOB STATUS

*Roe notes "that social status is more dependent upon occupation
than upon any other single factor." It should be no surprise to anyone
that society values certain careers more than others. Generally, professions stand highest in the hierarchy and unskilled labor on the lowest levels.*

*From a number of studies on prestige, the following table has been
developed for 15 jobs. Because these rankings have been taken from
disparate lists, they should be interpreted only in relative terms. The
point to be appreciated is that a chosen career conveys a relatively
stable degree of status, regardless of culture and passage of time.*

Prestige Ranking

Occupation	U.S.[a]	U.S., 1925[b]	England[c]	Japan[c]
1. U.S. Supreme Court Judge	1			
2. Physician	2	2	1	2
3. College Professor	7			1
4. Architect	15			
5. Lawyer	15	3	3	
6. Civil Engineer	23	5		5
7. Author	31			
8. Building Contractor	33		12	
9. Electrician	44	13		
10. Carpenter	58	16	19	13
11. Plumber	59	18	20	
12. Local Labor Union Official	61			
13. Truck Driver	70			15
14. Bartender	85			
15. Janitor	85	23		

[a] *National Opinion Research Center, 1947; Anne Roe,* The Psychology of Occupations, *New York:
John Wiley & Sons, 1958.*
[b] *Counts, 1925; Roe,* The Psychology of Occupations.
[c] *Richard Murphy,* Human Behavior—Status and Conformity, *New York: Time, Inc., 1976*

Less scientific, but appropriate, is this observation from a 57-year-old stonemason who was interviewed by Studs Terkel*

> *I think a laborer feels that he's the low man. Not so much that he works with his hands, it's that he's at the bottom of the scale. He always wants to get up to a skilled trade. Of course he'd make more money. The main thing is the common laborer—even the word <u>common</u> laborer—just sounds so common, he's at the bottom. Many that works with his hands takes pride in his work.*

*From Working: People Talk About What They Do All Day and How They Feel About What They Do, *p. xlvi, by Studs Terkel. Copyright © 1972, 1974 by Studs Terkel. Reprinted by permission of Pantheon Books, a Division of Random House, Inc.*

A. Maslow's Hierarchy and Occupations

As previously mentioned, Maslow's theory of motivation bears directly on a discussion of occupations. That men work just to earn a living contradicts the reasons why civilization flourishes. Otherwise, with a paycheck, a full stomach, and a warm home, men would cease to work until the money ran out. Man, through the ages, has built; he has created on the basis of needs other than the physiological—the growth aspects.

Herzberg* researched those factors that led to worker satisfaction and dissatisfaction for engineers and accountants. The results showed that contentment originates from what a person does in his job:

- achievement,
- recognition of achievement,
- specific nature of the work,
- opportunity for responsibility, and
- potential for advancement.

On the negative side, those situations that lead to job discontent related primarily to job environment:

- company policies and procedures,
- supervision,
- financial remuneration,
- interpersonal relations, and
- working environment.

In a careful review of previous research into job satisfaction, Zander and Quinn (1962)* found job contentment related directly to the following factors:

*In Richard Kalish, *The Psychology of Human Behavior*, 2 ed., Belmont, California: Brooks/Cole Publishing Co., 1970.

- opportunity for self-actualization,
- opportunity to make decisions,
- congenial relations with colleagues and supervisors,
- perception of self-adequacy (via recognition and reward such as pay and status).

B. Determinants of Occupation

Understanding why a person chooses a particular career will better prepare any member of the construction team to deal with others. Therefore, this section examines some characteristics that seem instrumental, not only in choosing a career, but in being satisfied with that choice.

1. Personal Characteristics

Psychologists have conclusively identified the factors below, which influence a person's choice of vocation and his level of performance and contentment.

a. Interests, Attitudes, Needs, Goals—Personality. Investigations find that a person's choice depends on the degree of importance he places on certain internal values:

- Having a favorable self-concept (the desire to be popular or influential).
- Being personally comfortable.
- Enjoying artistic, creative tasks.
- Desiring prestige.
- Enjoying technical tasks.
- Having the opportunity to help others.

An engineer and a tradesman would be expected to enjoy technical tasks, whereas a manager would consider being influential more important. These expectations have been borne out in a number of studies, as will be discussed in the following chapter.

With respect to performance and contentment, the following points seem noteworthy: if a particular job interests an individual, if the tasks and duties gratify his prominent needs, if the purpose and policy of the organization coincide with his values, and if the work complements his personality, then, in all probability, that individual will succeed. Furthermore, he will probably enjoy himself and seek to maximize his potential. Still, not everyone finds accomplishment, or interest in his work. Unfortunately and all too frequently, people end up in careers they dislike. By lack of opportunity, training, ability, or misunderstanding the nature of the work, some people make poor initial choices. In time, as family and financial commitments grow and forks in the road disappear, these people find themselves firmly fixed in their jobs. Given initiative, however, anyone can find a number of careers that go begging for his talents and tastes. An extrovert may find sales or teaching equally compatible and rewarding. A project manager may find equal success and satisfaction in managing a drafting department.

b. Abilities.   Because different careers require certain abilities, as a prime consideration, an individual must accurately assess the congruity of his potential and the job requirements. For example, a construction manager must possess (or acquire) not only technical skills, but communications and supervisory expertise as well. For anyone to set his mark far above his talent leads to frustration and failure.

c. Education and Training.   Traditionally colleges prepare the professionals, whereas trade schools and on-the-job training provide the skills and knowledge for tradesmen. Some people feel that four years of college is a waste of time: four years of income lost and the tuition costs. The present high wages for union tradesmen seem to support that viewpoint.

d. Environmental Pressures.   Another determinant of occupation concerns the frequently overlooked influence of family and friends. Often unconscious, these pressures exert strong forces in the choice of a vocation. A contractor's son may be overtly (or subtly) persuaded to follow his father's career. Based on surveys in several countries, many sons do in fact follow their father's footsteps (see Box 4.1).

e. Miscellaneous Factors.   Additional characteristics that enter the choice include physical health, stamina, appearance, size, sensory acuity, etc.

2. Job Characteristics

So far the discussion has highlighted the qualifications and potential of the individual, but one must certainly look at the nature of the job itself.

a. Job Requirements.   Each vocation demands a unique pattern of functions. One field stresses human relations skills (sales); another emphasizes technical applicability (engineering); and a third may opt for profit (business). Each job requires a distinct matrix of abilities, interests, and personality traits with tolerances large enough to allow for an overlapping between people and jobs. Various jobs match one specific personality, and various personalities match one specific job. As seen, abilities associated with the management of construction are transferable to other careers and vice versa (i.e., managing a business or working in labor relations).

b. Job Tasks.   All vocations call for not only broad job scopes but the day-to-day elements as well. Often the most seemingly glamorous of jobs are, in actuality, very boring on the day-to-day level. For example, architecture involves creativity, but also a large dose of sheer drudgery, as any designer who has ever chased bureaucratic permits and approvals will heartily testify.

c. Working Conditions. Health, safety, physical labor, comfort, and hours worked are all practical matters that one must inevitably weigh. Apparently, wages must be high enough to motivate a construction tradesman to offset the punishment of the elements and the insecurity (physical and emotional) of the industry.

d. Income. As stated, most adults work for a financial return that dictates their standard of living. Few can deny the attraction of a liberal salary or the promise of future monetary rewards. And few can overlook the envy over paychecks that crops up in construction. There probably has been more than one designer or civil servant who has gritted his teeth as the apprentice steamfitter showed off his new Cadillac.

e. Social Status. Each occupation carries with it a status of some sort, as seen in Box 3.5. Often low paying, white-collar jobs are selected over a higher paying, blue-collar job; obviously status plays a part. Evidence from psychological studies indicates that high-status occupations lead to increased self-esteem. Like a self-fulfilling prophecy, it seems that the winners keep winning.

f. Opportunity For Growth. Another important job characteristic is the growth potential, not only in terms of salary, but for personal growth as well. Many jobs pay decently, but if a job offers little opportunity for an individual to improve, to learn, and to maximize his talents, he tends to feel frustrated. No one likes a dead-end job. Consequently, a person will search outside his job to satisfy his higher needs. Hobbies, leisure time activities, and even drugs are common outlets.

Bibliography

Anastasi, Anne. *Psychological Testing*, 3 ed. New York: Macmillan Publishing Co., 1968.

Biehler, Robert F. *Psychology Applied to Teaching*, 2 ed. Boston: Houghton Mifflin Co., 1974.

Editors of Columbia House. *Understanding Human Behavior*, vol. 1. New York: BPC Publishing, 1974.

Goldenson, Robert M. *The Encyclopedia of Human Behavior*, Vol. I and II. New York: Doubleday and Co., 1970.

Good, Paul, and editors of Time-Life Books. *Human Behavior—The Individual*. New York: Time, Inc., 1974.

Hall, Calvin S., and Gardner Lindzey. *Theories of Personality*, 2 ed. New York: John Wiley & Sons, 1970.

Hildick, Wallace. *Only the Best*. New York: Clarkson N. Potter, Inc., 1973.

Hilgard, Ernest R., Richard C. Atkinson, and Rita L. Atkinson. *Introduction to Psychology.* New York: Harcourt Brace Jovanovich, Inc., 1971.

Kalish, Richard A. *The Psychology of Human Behavior*, 2 ed. Belmont, California: Brooks/ Cole Publishing Co., 1970.

Murphy, Richard W., and editors of Time-Life Books. *Human Behavior—Status and Conformity.* New York: Time, Inc., 1976.

Roe, Anne. *The Psychology of Occupations.* New York: John Wiley & Sons, 1958.

Terkel, Studs. *Working.* New York: Random House, Inc., 1972, 1974.

Chapter 4

The Individual

Napoleon at St. Helena.

Abstract

As the title implies, we now look at the individual and those attributes that combine to form his identity. Seven self-assessment tables are presented to cover: abilities, needs, temperaments, personal values, job values, basic interests, and job preferences. Each table has been derived from a number of standard psychometric tests commonly used in vocational counselling and personality assessment.

With respect to the construction team, and based on considerable psychological investigation, the composite profiles are drawn for each member: the architect, engineer, administrator, contractor, project manager, superintendent, and tradesman. The objectives are twofold: (1) to establish the reader's profile in scientific terms frequently utilized and measured by psychologists; and (2) to compare the similarities and dissimilarities between "typical" members of the team. Then the reader may be able to recognize why individuals "see" and react to things, events, and people in unique and sometimes conflicting ways.

Finally, proven assertive techniques from the learning theory school are explained and illustrated via practical cases applicable to construction. Without being aggressive or timid, the individual, regardless of his job, can learn to better serve his self-interests by properly asserting himself. This he can accomplish with minimum negative consequences.

CONTENTS OF CHAPTER 4

SELF-ASSESSMENT
A. Basic Traits

WORKER TRAIT COMPONENTS
A. Dictionary of Occupational Titles
  1. Training Period
  2. Aptitudes
  3. Interests
  4. Temperaments
  5. Physical Demands
B. Guilford-Zimmerman Temperament Survey
C. Vernon-Allport-Lindzey Study of Values
D. Strong-Campbell Interest Inventory
  1. Realistic
  2. Conventional
  3. Enterprising
  4. Intellectual/Investigative
  5. Artistic
  6. Social
E. The Harrington/O'Shea System for Decision-Making

THE PROFILES
A. The Architect/Engineer Group
B. The Owner Group
C. The Contractor/Subcontractor Group
  1. The Proprietor
  2. The Project Manager
  3. The Superintendent
  4. Construction Workers

SELF-ASSERTION
A. Basic Definitions
  1. Nonassertive Behavior

THE INDIVIDUAL, CONCLUDED

QUESTIONS AND PREVIEW

1. Identify five worker trait components essential to adequate job performance.
2. How would you rank the dominant components of your personality? How do these characteristics relate, positively and negatively, to your job?
3. Name some traits considered necessary for success in the following careers: architecture, engineering, administration, contracting, project management, superintending, and crafts.
4. In light of the above, what possible misunderstanding and difficulties could emerge when these varied personalities interact in terms of communication, goals, and perspectives (say, between an architect and a roofing foreman)?
5. Describe the nature and consequences of inadequate social behavior, say, shyness or aggressiveness. Based on actual experiences from the project site, list some common examples.
6. In interpersonal relationships within the team, what approaches and personality traits usually contribute to a genuinely respectful atmosphere?
7. It has been found that many individuals hold a number of irrational assumptions to be true. For example:

  a. "One has to be loved and respected by virtually everyone," or
  b. "One has to be perfectly adequate in everything in order to be worthwhile."

What might be some damaging consequences of such irrational beliefs?

SELF-ASSESSMENT

*The most difficult thing in
life is to know yourself*

Thales

Now that the basics of psychology have been presented, the reader may well ponder its practical relationship with construction management. Therefore, in the remaining chapters, we propose to analyze some specific correlations, beginning with the individual. Because of the emphasis on human relations in construction management, and the positive correlation between traits and job types, it should prove worthwhile for the individual to examine his own makeup. After all, these traits play a crucial part, indeed, in the success of the project. As seen, there are a number of reasons why an individual, given innumerable options, chooses one particular vocation. Obviously, a combination of personality traits and values influences the choice, and, of course, the job itself enters the picture. Depending on an individual's value system, certain aspects of the job may be given more weight than others. For example, a design engineer, because of a desire to lead (and to receive more pay) may accept a managerial position, even though it may force him to relinquish the enjoyment he previously felt at the drafting board.

Recognizing the vast importance of compatible worker traits and occupations, psychologists, prompted considerably by industry and government funding, have devised ingenious methods to define and measure these elements. The *Dictionary of Occupational Titles*, which summarizes many of these research findings and defines job factors, refers to worker traits as those abilities, personal qualities, and individual characteristics required to achieve successful performance in a specified job.

For our purposes, an understanding of these factors should provide not only more insight into ourselves, but an appreciation of the values and interests of some personalities commonly met on the construction site. This combination, in turn, should lead to more efficient communication, and better overall relationships. As an approach to the subject of traits associated with members of the team, the reader is requested to first evaluate himself earnestly on a number of attributes that are measured in psychological testing.

First, however, we will give a few general comments about personality testing. Ordinarily, people use the word "personality" in a much broader and questionably accurate sense than that used in the conventional psychometric terminology. Often a charismatic person is said to have "personality," or a caustic boss may be said to have "an abrasive personality." Psychologists, aided by concepts of applied statistics, are much more restrictive and precise in their terminology and measurements. They apply personality tests to measure emotional, motivational, interpersonal, and attitudinal characteristics—as distinguished from those tests used to assess ability and intelligence. Several hundred of these instruments are currently available, especially the inventory and projective types. This text will explore only a few of the better known ones in four broad categories.

1. Personality Inventories

These inventories yield profiles of normal traits, such as sociability, emotional stability, the need to achieve, and a number of others. For example, on any site, one may encounter all sorts of individuals: the extrovert, the recluse, the aggressor, the achiever, etc. Two well-known tests to gauge some of these traits are the Guilford-Zimmerman Temperament Survey and the Edwards Personal Preference Schedule.

2. Interests, Values, Attitudes

This type assesses an individual's interests, values, and attitudes, all of which prove important in job performance. As mentioned, success is usually equated with interest and aptitude. Naturally, other factors enter the picture too, but, overall, if an individual inherits the necessary genetic ingredients, acquires the appropriate schooling and skills, and possesses the interest, chances are that he will enjoy success in his career.

Three tests to measure these traits are: the Strong-Campbell Interest Inventory, the Kuder Preference Record—Vocational, and the Harrington/O'Shea System for Career Decision-Making. Another device is the Allport-Vernon-Lindzey Study of Values, which appraises the strength of a person's basic approach to life. Keep in mind that how a person views a situation or event is colored by his values and interests, a vital consideration in communication. For example, a businessman-contractor who cherishes wealth "sees" a project in different light than, say, a plumbing engineer.

3. Projective

The projective test is utilized to survey a person's emotional response to an ambiguous stimulus. (See Box 3.1 for an example of a Rorschach Inkblot Test.) The information gleaned through projective techniques must be interpreted by a clinical psychologist.

4. Situational

The situational method is the fourth type of test, used to assess personality "under fire." The testee is required to face a realistic situation that calls for attitudes and abilities needed for the job itself. This approach could be considered somewhat akin to on-the-job training, except that it occurs before the fact. No attempt will be made to analyze this method here.

Before proceeding in self-assessment, we stress again that psychology works in the realm of probability, definitely not certainty. No one career or one job calls for only one type of person. Many engineers are successful businessmen, even though, occupationally, the vocational themes associated with engineers (intellectual theme) implies opposition to those of the businessman (enterprising theme). In the realm of vocational psychology, however, and with a valid sampling of the population, there is a positive correlation between specific jobs and certain worker traits.

It is to be noted that no test has been devised, nor is it likely that one ever will be, to measure irrefutably any one trait, let alone a totality as complex as "personality." These tools prove surprisingly accurate, however, and, in the strictest sense, both valid and reliable enough to be worth serious consideration, especially in this study of human behavior and construction.

A. Basic Traits

In order to compare your personality with those of other individuals, it seems constructive to first inspect your own house—to compile a personal punch list of sorts.

Tables 1 through 7 present a number of important characteristics excerpted from various psychological tests. These data should assist you in assessing your profile—your needs, values, interests, temperament, and abilities. Be honest, first and foremost, and be perceptive. Many people have difficulty in truly seeing the face in the mirror. Valid self-evaluation is very difficult, indeed, and fraught with pitfalls, because your self-concept reflects the qualities you see, not those seen by others. Not everyone can be a Napoleon, nor would everyone wish to be. Nevertheless, most people presumably possess a reasonable degree of insight into understanding and honestly evaluating themselves. Rate yourself on an arbitrary scale of 0–5, 5 being the highest value. It may be helpful and constructive also to review Box 3.3.

Table 1. Self-Assessment

ABILITIES* WHAT ARE YOUR STRONGEST (AND WEAKEST) ABILITIES?	SCALE					
	0	1	2	3	4	5
Artistic ability—drawing, designing; creating						
Numerical ability—speed and accuracy in working with numbers						
Math ability—solving math problems						
Scientific ability—doing experiments and understanding scientific principles; reasoning effectively						
Language ability—writing, speaking						
Principles of mechanics—working with machines or tools, repairing things, and understanding the principles						
Motor ability—working with your hands						
Spatial ability—seeing differences in size, form, and shape, and visualizing their relationships						
Social ability—ability to work with people; considered congenial by others						
Teaching ability—helping others learn; instructing people to perform tasks and activities						
Persuasive ability—able to talk easily with people; to influence others; to sell						
Leadership ability—leading group activities; able to get things started and to act quickly when necessary						
Clerical ability—providing or collecting information, accurate record-keeping						

*Adapted from the Harrington/O'Shea System for Career Decision-Making with permission. Moravia, New York: Chronicle Guidance Publications, 1976.

Table 2. Self-Assessment

NEEDS* HOW STRONG ARE YOUR PERSONAL NEEDS?	SCALE					
	0	1	2	3	4	5
Achievement—the need to accomplish things well, to be successful in overcoming obstacles						
Deference—the need to follow; to have a leader						
Order—the need to be neat and orderly, to have plans						
Exhibition—the need to attract attention, to be noticed						
Autonomy—the need to be independent, to defy authority, to come and go freely						
Affiliation—the need to form friendships, to join groups, to participate with others						
Intraspection—the need to be imaginative, subjective, analytical						
Succorance—the need to get help, to be dependent						
Dominance—the need to dominate or control others; to lead, to organize						
Abasement—the need to apologize, to accept punishment and guilt						
Nurturance—the need to help others, to empathize						
Change—the need to avoid routine, to be involved with innovation						
Endurance—the need to work hard, to persevere						
Heterosexuality—the need for relationships with the opposite sex						
Aggression—the need to express aggressive feelings, to punish						

*Adapted from the Edwards Personal Preference Schedule by permission. Copyright 1953 by The Psychological Corporation, New York, New York. All rights reserved.

Table 3.   Self-Assessment

TEMPERAMENT* WHAT ARE THOSE TEMPERAMENTAL FACTORS THAT MOST (AND LEAST) DESCRIBE YOU?	SCALE					
	0	1	2	3	4	5
General activity: hurrying, vitality, production, efficiency versus: slow, deliberate, easily fatigued, inefficient						
Restraint: serious-minded, persistent versus: carefree, impulsive, excitement-loving						
Ascendance: leadership, speaking in public, bluffing versus: submissiveness, hesitation						
Sociability: having many friends, seeking social contacts, attracting attention versus: few friends and shyness						
Emotional stability: evenness of moods, optimistic, even-keeled, composure versus: fluctuation of moods, pessimism, daydreaming, excitability, feelings of guilt, worry						
Objectively: thick-skinned, analytical versus: hypersensitive, self-centered, suspicious						
Friendliness: toleration of hostility, acceptance of domination, respect for others versus: hostility, resentment, desire to dominate, aggressiveness and contempt for others						
Thoughtfulness: reflective, analytic of self and others, mental poise versus: interest in overt activity and mental disconcertedness						
Personal relations: tolerance of others, faith in social institutions and authority versus: critical of institutions, suspicious, self-pitying						
Masculinity: interest in masculine activities, hard-boiled, inhibits emotional expression versus: interest in feminine activities and vocations, easily disgusted, fearful, emotionally expressive						

*Based on the Guilford-Zimmerman Temperament Survey (Profile Chart) with permission of Sheridan Psychological Services, Inc. Orange, CA 92667.

Table 4. Self-Assessment

PERSONAL VALUES* WHAT VALUES ARE MOST (AND LEAST) IMPORTANT TO YOU?	SCALE					
	0	1	2	3	4	5
Theoretical—values truth in the philosophical scientific sense; intellect; and the rational, empirical approach						
Economic—values the pragmatic and useful; money and material wealth						
Esthetic—values the artistic, both in form and grace						
Social—values social considerations and interactions						
Political—values power, prestige, the opportunity to influence						
Religious—values the religious aspects of the world						

*Adapted from Allport-Vernon-Lindzey Study of Values. Copyright © 1960 by Houghton Mifflin Company. Reprinted by permission of Houghton Mifflin Company. All rights reserved.

Table 5. Self-Assessment

JOB VALUES* WHICH WORK VALUES DO YOU PREFER (OR REJECT)?	SCALE					
	0	1	2	3	4	5
Good salary—being paid well						
Prestige—having a job that offers a great deal of status and respect						
Job security—having a steady job						
High achievement—being able to do things of importance or to succeed on a challenging job						
Routine activity—work that is uncomplicated, organized, and repetitive						
Variety—diversion—having the chance to do many and different things						
Creativity—having the opportunity to use your imagination and to be inventive						
Working with your mind—work that offers intellectual stimulation and allows use of your mental capabilities						
Independence—work that allows freedom to follow your own convictions with minimum supervision						
Working with people—working in close contact with people, being able to assist others						
Leadership—being responsible for directing the work of subordinates, making decisions affecting others						
Physical activity—work that calls for physical strength						
Work under supervision—working under the direction of others						
Work with your hands—a job where you can use your hands, machines, or tools to make or repair things						

*Adapted from the Harrington/O'Shea System for Career Decision-Making with permission. Moravia, New York: Chronicle Guidance Publications, 1976.

Table 6. Self-Assessment

BASIC INTERESTS* WHAT ARE YOUR BASIC INTERESTS?	SCALE					
	0	1	2	3	4	5
Realistic theme—prefer to work with machines, tools, things instead of people; rugged outdoors work						
Conventional theme—interested in highly structured activities; being a follower						
Enterprising theme—prefer to dominate, to lead, especially in the business sense						
Investigative theme—enjoy scientific activities, the abstract, intellectual						
Artistic theme—likes to work in artistic settings; self-expression						
Social theme—prefer work conducive to helping people, socially responsive						

*Adapted from the Strong-Campbell Interest Inventory of the Strong Vocational Interest Blank, Form T 325. With permission of Stanford University Press.

Table 7. Self-Assessment

JOB PREFERENCES* IN WHAT JOB SITUATIONS WOULD YOU RATHER WORK?	SCALE					
	0	1	2	3	4	5
Outdoor						
Mechanical						
Computational						
Scientific						
Persuasive						
Artistic						
Literary						
Musical						
Social service						
Clerical						

*Based on the *Kuder Preference Record—Vocational*, Profile Section, Men and Women © 1976, 1951, G. Frederic Kuder. By permission of the publisher, Science Research Associates, Inc.

WORKER TRAIT COMPONENTS

A right judgment draws us a profit
from all things we see

Shakespeare

Now that the reader has somewhat developed a self-profile using concepts common among psychologists, we now turn our attention to various traits associated with specific careers.

A major premise of this book centers on the hypothesis that groups within the construction team ascribe to different values, pursue certain goals, and use varied means of accomplishing those goals, which may be somewhat incompatible with the others. By virtue of contract and policies, each group member assumes defined roles and duties which certainly accentuate the "group personality." But more basic, each member claims a highly individualistic identity, which is reflected in his choice and tenure of career, and which, in turn, is modified by that choice in a dynamic fashion. A career reflects his needs, his self-image, his success in adjusting to life in general. That is not to imply that everyone who works in a particular occupation is a joyous bundle of success, satisfaction, and happiness. In fact, one needs only to survey his colleagues to uproot a tale of woes, mistakes and misfortune.

As stated by a 49-year-old crane operator in Studs Terkel's *Working**:

There's no job in construction which you could call an easy job. I mean, if you're out there eating dust and dirt for eight, ten hours a day, even if you're not doing anything, it's work. Just *being* there is . . .

I have one son doin' this work. But his youngest one, he's pretty intelligent, I'd like to see him be a professional man if he will. Of course, I wanted the other one too. But . . . there's so many changes now.

Many of the people from all walks of life interviewed by Terkel expressed this discontent in similar vein—dissatisfaction with their jobs for one reason or another.

Look at these complaints from a different vantage, however. Actions speak louder than words. If an individual remains in a particular career, given the generally available alternative opportunities to seek other jobs

---

*From *Working: People Talk About What They Do All Day and How They Feel About What They Do*, by Studs Terkel. Copyright © 1972, 1974 by Studs Terkel. Reprinted by permission of Pantheon Books, a Division of Random House, Inc.

(via similar fields, schools, new industries), at least *some* redeeming qualities in his present employment (money, prestige, congeniality, easy working conditions, etc.) tie him to that career. Although dissatisfaction exists, the fact that he remains indicates his adjustment—along with a message about his self-image, his abilities, values, etc.

Because of the economic and social impact of worker satisfaction and dissatisfaction, there have been many attempts to formulate a comprehensive way to investigate vocational choices. Carter, a psychologist using interest measurements, developed a theory that accounted for personality dynamics as well as the realities of the society, the job market, and the environment in which we live. He contends that one's vocational attitude develops in an attempt to make a reasonable adjustment to one's environmental condition. Each occupation offers various opportunities and rewards, and calls for certain mental and physical traits. Therefore, one's own capacity, motives, and, most important, one's family and social situation, all combine to limit (or expand) the avenues that are open to an individual. It should be no surprise that young people are steered by parents, peers, or a particular group into a particular occupation. (See Box 4.1.)

According to Carter, if the opportunity presents itself, and matches the individual's aptitudes and interests, chances are that the individual will enter and continue along this career line. If, however, serious obstacles arise, the individual may be reoriented into another vocation. For example, if an individual lacks the aptitude, opportunity, or motivation, he must seek other careers. For instance, an engineering aspirant who is mathematically illiterate or an effeminate roofer apprentice may do well to explore new jobs. When a serious obstacle occurs, the individual reassesses the total picture and eventually travels more promising avenues. This tends to form the basis for decisions and guidance in terms of long-time career planning.

Box 4.1. FOLLOWING THE FATHER'S FOOTSTEPS

Obviously parental upbringing exerts a strong influence on a child's sense of values, attitudes—i.e., his personality. Therefore, it could be assumed that this influence would be instrumental in an individual's choice of career. A number of surveys conducted over the last 30 years, have shown this to be true. In the major, industrial countries, a majority of sons choose careers in their father's job categories.*

**After R. Murphy*, Human Behavior—Status and Conformity.

United States

Office Workers and Professionals	71%		29%
Skilled and Semiskilled Workers	61%		39%

Germany

Office Workers and Professionals	80%		20%
Skilled and Semiskilled Workers	60%		40%

Japan

Office Workers and Professionals	74%		26%
Skilled and Semiskilled Workers	59%		41%

▓ Sons who followed Father's footsteps

☐ Sons who chose other careers

Nick Lindsay, a 44-year-old carpenter, in Working* *exemplifies the trend:*

> This is one of the few times in my life I had made a living at anything but carpentry. Lindsays have been carpenters from right on back to 1755. Every once in a while, one of 'em'll shoot off and be a doctor or a preacher or something. Generally they've been carpenter-preachers, carpenter-farmers, carpenter-storekeepers, carpenters right on.

*From Working: People Talk About What They Do All Day and How They Feel About What They Do, by Studs Terkel. Copyright © 1972, 1974 by Studs Terkel. Reprinted by permission of Pantheon Books, a Division of Random House, Inc.

Unfortunately all too often, an individual continues down the wrong career road, until life's commitments (wife, children, unending bills) form barriers before the few remaining forks in the road. There is no turning back. Redeeming alternatives and options for change, in this society, are always available, however, if one is actively motivated.

Another psychologist, Super (1953), lists the following factors that should be considered as determinants of occupational behavior:

People are unique, different in their needs, abilities—their profiles.

They are qualified, because of their wide range of traits, for a wide range of careers.

Each specific occupation calls for a special pattern of abilities and other personality factors with tolerances that overlap. Consequently, there are many careers that require certain traits, and a number of traits that match certain careers.

Because job situations change (i.e., new industries) and because people's self-images change with time and experience, their vocational preferences may also change. The continuing process shifts along with life's developmental stages.

The nature of a career pattern is determined by: parents; socioeconomic level; personality characteristics, such as intelligence and motivation; and, undeniably, opportunities.

Work satisfaction (and life satisfaction) depends upon the degree to which an individual finds adequate outlet for his personality and his value system.

Even in the absence of a flourishing job market, it appears that vocational choice depends in no small measure upon the emotional strength of the person. Given strong drive, aptitude, and interest, he can often wedge open any door and create his own breaks.

From the layman's point of view, we all often associate traits, even physical stereotypes, with certain jobs (see Box 3.4). For example, many people believe that an architect is highly creative, that a construction worker is rugged and aggressive, that an engineer is more interested in investigative aspects than in people, that businessmen are enterprising, or that salesmen are extroverts. Like most cliches, these are sometimes true, sometimes false. Psychologists, however, utilize statistical concepts to assist them in correlating the relationship between jobs and traits. Consider, on a national scale, the importance of identifying the compatibilities of occupations and the individual—no round pegs in square holes. Primarily, much of the testing has begun with studies of individuals who are already occupying particular jobs. Their interests, personalities, and necessary abilities and traits have been researched and established as significant criteria. Due to the vast amount of research data and the limitations of this book, our exposition will concern only a few members of the construction team.

From available research, a composite personality profile of each individual can be drawn, certainly not absolute but undeniably useful. Every businessman/salesman (or politician) strives to recognize his customer's (voters) needs and values—his makeup, and then behaves accordingly. Similarly, by understanding the key profiles of construction individuals, one can open doors to better relations on the job site. To develop such profiles, we will first examine a number of reference data compiled by vocational scientists.

A. Dictionary of Occupational Titles*

The handbook provides a wealth of information reflecting significant worker trait requirements necessary for a specific job. The following six distinct components are selected because they yield the broadest and deepest framework for the effective coverage of these requirements:

1. Training period
2. Aptitudes
3. Interests
4. Temperaments
5. Physical demands
6. Conditions of work

Obviously, each of these requirements is woven intricately with an individual's totality—his mental and physical potential, as well as his personality profile. With considerable ease, one should be able to relate these components to construction.

Each of these components will be briefly explained with special emphasis on aptitudes, interests, and temperaments that have been the focus of many personality type tests and research studies.

1. Training Period

This considers the amount of general educational development and the specific vocational training for a worker to acquire the knowledge and the ability necessary for average performance in a particular job. General educational development covers the broad aspects of education, both formal and informal. This includes the ability to reason and to follow instructions—i.e., "common sense," as well as specific knowledge such as language and math skills. Such education is obtained not only through schools but through experience, individual effort, and the college of "hard knocks." Vocational preparation relates to the amount of time required to learn the special techniques, to acquire the information, and to develop the ability needed for satisfactory accomplishments. This training may be acquired in school, apprenticeship (military or on-the-job training), and by the essential ex-

*See Appendix IV for complete job descriptions.

perience, exclusive of ordinary adjustment required in any new job. It is assumed that every competent individual in construction, in order to function reasonably well, has general knowledge. Each career or trade calls for different levels and types of education and training, however. For example, a professional engineer usually needs college and experience, whereas a plumber must serve an apprenticeship.

2. Aptitudes

These requirements refer to those distinct skills that an individual must possess to handle a job adequately. Such skills include the following:

- Intelligence: the broad learning ability to understand instructions and principles to reason and judge
- Verbal: the ability to understand words and ideas; to communicate clearly and effectively
- Numerical: the ability to perform arithmetical operations accurately
- Spatial: the ability to comprehend forms in space and to understand relationships of plane and solid objects.
- Form perception: the ability to perceive pertinent detail in objects or graphic material; to make visual comparisons and discriminations
- Clerical perception: the ability to perceive pertinent details in word or tabular form
- Motor coordination: the ability to coordinate eyes and hands rapidly and accurately
- Finger dexterity: the ability to move fingers and manipulate small objects
- Manual dexterity: the ability to move hands easily and skillfully
- Eye-hand-foot coordination: the ability to move all these in coordination.
- Color discrimination: the ability to perceive and recognize similar or different colors and shades

In this category we can cite as examples that a construction manager must have verbal facility (along with obviously other critical aptitudes), and a heavy equipment operator must have good eye-hand-foot coordination.

3. Interests

The third component embraces an individual's likes and dislikes. "Interests," in this context, refers to the preference for certain types of work as opposed to other types. As we all know: "one man's pie is another man's poison."

A like of one particular type of situation or activity implies lack of interest, if not actually dislike, in the opposing activity. The *Occupational Dictionary* lists five dual preferences:

- Working with things or objects *as opposed to* working in activities that involve people and communication of ideas
- Activities involving business contact *versus* situations that involve a scientific and technical nature
- Preferring routine, concrete, organized tasks *as opposed to* enjoying abstract, creative work
- Interrelating with people in social welfare situations *versus* preferring activities relative to processes, machines, and techniques.
- Job situations that result in prestige or esteem of others *as opposed to* job activities that provide tangible, productive satisfaction.

As shown by research testing, most businessmen would prefer business activities (profits and wealth) as opposed to abstract intellectual tasks. This conjecture has been neatly presented by Dr. John Holland (see Box 4.2).

4. Temperaments

This job component relates the different types of occupational environs to which an individual must adequately adjust, temperamentally.

- A variety of duties often characterized by frequent change
- Situations involving repetitive (or short cycle) tasks carried out in accord with set procedures
- Performing tasks only under specific instruction, allowing little room for independent action or judgment
- Duties involving the direction, control, and planning of a total activity or activities of others
- Dealing with people under actual job conditions beyond merely giving and receiving instruction
- Working alone in physical isolation from others, although the project may be integrated with others
- Influencing people's attitudes, opinions, and judgments about ideas and things
- Performing adequately under pressure when confronted with the unexpected or risky
- Evaluating (inclusive of generalizing, judging, and deciding) information contrary to sensory or judgmental criteria.
- Evaluating (inclusive of generalizing, judging, and deciding) information based on measurable or verifiable criteria
- Interpreting feelings, ideas, and data in terms of subjective viewpoints

Box 4.2. OCCUPATIONAL THEMES

Psychological research has demonstrated that human beings can be broadly described (and contrasted) by relating to their chosen vocations. Dr. John Holland developed a unique theory of career development in which the job field is broken into six broad occupational/interest themes: 1. Realistic (R); 2. Conventional (C); 3. Enterprising (E); 4. Social (S); 5. Artistic (A); and 6. Intellectual/Investigative (I).

Each theme tends to revolve around clusters of activities and interests; consequently, psychologists surveyed numerous individuals currently employed within each category. The results were utilized in developing interest inventories to aid in career selection.

These themes are arranged in hexagonal form in such a way as to show that occupational themes adjacent to each other are similar whereas those opposite are dissimilar.

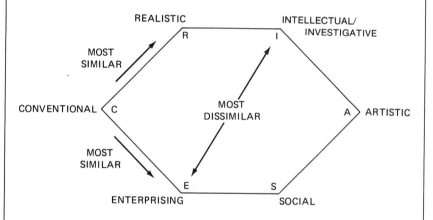

For example, using the Strong-Campbell Interest Inventory of the Strong Vocational Interest Blank, those occupational activities and interests which fall into the realistic category (i.e., skilled crafts) are more similar to those in the intellectual (i.e., engineer) and conventional (i.e., accountant) category than those in the social (i.e., administrator). Of course, it is to be understood that rarely does any individual have likes and dislikes so that he falls only into one pure theme. Like many strong traits, however, the strongest interests dominate, and, therefore, will direct him to those clusters of occupations that best satisfy his needs.

- Duties involving the precise attainment of established limits, tolerances, and standards.

By the nature of the beast, most construction people must adjust to a variety of duties in situations that change from job site to job site. As another example of temperamental factors, some people would rather be leaders; others do not care about the prestige (and responsibilities). For example, a bricklayer may feel the extra cents per hour are not worth the aggravation; therefore, he declines a foreman's position.

5. Physical Demands

This demand includes both the physical requirements of the work, and the specific capacities an individual must possess to satisfy the demands. Obviously a worker must possess these physical strengths in an amount at least equal to the job duties. Such factors refer to lifting, carrying, acute vision, etc. Because this book focuses on the psychological issues, little more will be mentioned other than to comment that there is a direct tie between values and physical requirements. A laborer may accept the rough rigors of the trade, in all probability because of high pay. He values the high pay over physical comfort.

B. Guilford-Zimmerman Temperament Survey

Temperament is a broad term used to describe a person's emotional makeup: his normal energy level, mood swings, and the tempo and intensity of his responses to people and situations.

Obviously, temperament bears profoundly on success (or failure) in dealing with others, as well as competence on the job. Witness the Chicken Littles: in times of a serious crisis, they scream and run nervously all around the job site. At the other extreme, observe the stoic steamfitter in a frozen trench at −12° F humming as he welds a condensate line. How often we all ponder, "What makes people tick?" Most psychologists generally believe that temperament is primarily determined by constitutional factors, but can be modified by life's experiences. In any case, as stated in the *Dictionary of Occupational Titles*, a worker must possess necessary traits to reasonably adjust to a number of situations or activities, or else job dissatisfaction or failure (mental, physical, and career) may result.

The GZTS survey is a self-report inventory that yields information about those traits (as presented in Table 3, Self-Assessment) that combine to describe a person's overall temperament.

Sample items from the test are expressed in the form of affirmative statements, rather than questions, such as:

1. You are often bursting with energy　　　　　　　Yes　?　No
2. Most people use politeness to cover up for ulterior motives　　　　　　　　　　　　　　　　　Yes　?　No

This survey has been given to various occupational groups.

C. Allport-Vernon-Lindzey Study of Values

Each of us has various predispositions, preferences, and prejudices as a part of our makeup.

As defined in Chapter 3, an attitude is a tendency to respond to a person, situation, or event in a certain way, favorable or unfavorable. Like a stereotype, it eases the judgmental process.

We all cherish numerous attitudes which basically originate from only a handful of basic values. Consequently, when a person cherishes something dearly, it certainly influences his perception, his goals, and his modus operandi. What one individual values as gold, however, another may perceive as dust. Therefore, it should prove useful to uncover those "things" that are cherished by the members of the construction team.

The AVL study is an inventory, designed to measure the relative strength of an individual's dominant, pervasive values. This instrument has much in common with interest tests and attitude scales, but it fails to fall clearly into either category. As discussed in Chapter 3, and seen in Table 4, Self-Assessment, six basic values are considered critical: theoretical, economic, aesthetic, social, political, and religious. A typical item used in this test is:

In your opinion, can a businessman best spend Sunday in—

- trying to educate himself by reading textbooks.
- trying to win at golf.
- going to a concert.
- hearing a good sermon.

The answers are rated in order of personal preference, in terms of most attractive and least attractive.

These tests have been given to a number of occupational groups and the results indicated significant differences between the strengths of the values. Although most individuals have various strengths in overlapping fashion, usually one or two themes are dominant.

The authors feel that the best way to understand an individual is to understand his value system, because studies indicate that he tends to construe and interpret his experiences and situations in terms of his unique system. Therefore, in spite of the inherent limitations, knowing an individual's strengths can help one to predict his response to various stimuli.

For example, test results summarized in Roe's *Psychology of Occupations* and other studies show:

1. By and large, engineering students rate highest on the Theoretical and Economic scale, and lowest on the Aesthetic.
2. Businessmen rate positive on the Economic and negative on the Aesthetic scales.
3. Skilled mechanics value the Aesthetic less, and the Economic and Theoretical more.
4. Artists score negative on the Economic, Political, and Social scales.
5. Selling specialties, as expected, value the Economic on the high side, and the Aesthetic on the negative.

Such findings, where applicable, will be incorporated into the construction profiles.

D. Strong-Campbell Interest Inventory

The intensity and the direction of a person's interests represent an important aspect of his personality. These traits generally affect the way he adjusts to his education, vocation, and interpersonal relations. Psychologists use various tests to try to measure and classify interests, because the consideration of this factor is of practical significance. If someone has a strong interest in a certain type of activity, all other factors being held constant (assuming he has the required aptitudes), he can usually do well in his job. It is noted that one may have the aptitudes to succeed on a job without necessarily having the interest, and vice versa, he may have an interest for a particular job and not have the capabilities. But for good adjustment and achievement, the two usually go hand in glove. People, under most circumstances, seek to satisfy themselves in a particular vocation that agrees with their personalities. Through the years, a number of interest inventories have been devised. One of the better known is the Strong-Campbell Interest Inventory. It was developed by questioning a large sample population concerning their likes and dislikes, over a wide variety of specific activities. For instance, a sample question, which implies a certain preference, is: "Would you rather repair a watch or solve a math problem?" On the basis of many similar questions, the population responses were then keyed to different occupational groups. It was found that persons engaged in various occupations were often characterized by common interests that differentiated them from other vocations, which extended beyond job activities. They also related commonly to the school; to hobbies; and to the types of books, leisure, and social activities the individual enjoyed. It, thus, proved to be a feasible screening device to see whether an applicant has the same interests as those successfully engaged in a specific career.

As seen in Box 4.2, there are six broad occupational themes; within each of these themes fall a number of job clusters, each having its distinctive array of interests, attitudes, and values.

Below are descriptions of the pure type of individual for each of the general themes.

1. Realistic

Jobs that fall under the realistic theme are mechanics, construction work, skilled trades, and some engineering specialties. In the extreme form, these individuals are rugged, practical, strong, and usually aggressive in their outlook. Usually, they have physical skills. Sometimes they find it somewhat difficult to express themselves in words, or to express their feelings. Preferring to work outdoors with tools, particularly large powerful machines, they would rather deal with things as opposed to ideas and people. They like to create things with their hands. Their political and economic opinions are essentially conventional; therefore, they are not overly receptive to radical new ideas. Again, we emphasize there are few extreme individuals who fall only in one occupational theme. For example, the carpenter quoted in Box 4.1 is also a poet who makes the rounds of colleges and coffee houses.

2. Conventional

This theme includes jobs such as financial analysts, computer operators, and bank tellers. Extremes of this type prefer highly ordered activities, especially verbal and numerical tasks that characterize office work. They seldom seek leadership; they respond to power and feel comfortable working in a well-established chain of command. Consequently, they fit well into large organizations. They tend to dislike ambiguous situations, opting for highly structured situations instead. The conventional individual has few interests in problems requiring physical skills or intense relationships. They describe themselves as stable, well-controlled, and dependable.

3. Enterprising

Under this heading are found, as expected, the businessman, the purchasing agent, and the lawyer. In the extreme case, this type of individual enjoys great facility with words, which he uses in social tasks—selling, dominating, and assuming leadership. Impatient, he dislikes tasks involving long periods of intellectual concentration. Rather, he likes power, material wealth, status, and expensive settings. Such people consider themselves energetic, enthusiastic, confident, and dominant.

4. Intellectual/Investigative

The intellectual theme includes design engineers, technical writers, and physicists working in scientific and technical situations. Extremes of this type are oriented toward a task. They are rarely interested in working around other people. Abstract problems, they enjoy, especially attempting to understand the physical world around them, and ambiguous challenges. They tend to think problems through, rather than to act them out, and they care little for highly structured situations with their rules and restrictions. Frequently, they hold unconventional values and attitudes; they tend to be original and creative, particularly in the scientific medium.

5. Artistic

This category embraces the author, the artist, and the architect to a lesser degree. Having few interests in highly structured or gross, physical strength situations, they try to express their feeling through the arts. Less assertive about opinions, they describe themselves as independent, unconventional, emotionally tense and sensitive.

6. Social

The pure type would rather work with people in sociable and humanistic situations. Concerned with the welfare of others, they choose occupations such as clinical psychologists or vocational counselors. They like attention in key situations that put them on center stage. They would rather solve problems by discussion or by arranging and rearranging relations between others. They have little interest in situations that require physical exertion or technical machinery. Such people describe themselves as good leaders, cheerful, popular, achieving, and concerned about the welfare of others.

As a final comment, again we emphasize that a person rarely falls under the heading of a pure type; no person is a pure anything. Normally, he has interests that overlap in various job settings. For instance the engineer has interests that fall in both Intellectual and Realistic categories. And the architect has been found to have Artistic, Realistic, and Intellectual interests.

The public administrator falls under the Social, Conventional, and Enterprising themes.

E. The Harrington/O'Shea System for Career Decision-Making

The final reference to be discussed is the Harrington/O'Shea system. Also based upon the research done by Dr. Holland, it contains a number of career clusters matched with compatible job values, abilities, and interests applicable to that cluster. The rated scales are similar to those discussed in the Strong-Campbell test: (1) Crafts; (2) Scientific; (3) Creative; (4) Social; (5) Business; and (6) Clerical.

1. Individuals who score high in the *crafts* are more interested in mechanical activities that call for physical strength. These individuals prefer to work with tools and objects, rather than with people and words. They want to build things, and they desire practical results. The associated occupations are: construction tradesman (carpenters, plumbers, electricians), cabinet makers, and machinists.

2. A second scale description is *scientific*. In this scale fall those people who value mathematics and scientific work. The individuals tend to be creative, theoretical, curious, and studious. They often prefer to work by themselves, and are commonly engaged in such careers as engineering, architecture, and mathematics.

3. The third scale relates to those interested in the *creative* activities, such as music, art, and entertainment. They are primarily nonconforming in life style, independent, and like to express themselves through the media. Common vocations are writers and artists.

4. The fourth scale is the *social*. These people are involved in teaching and social work. Typically, they are interested in the well-being of others, and they tend to get along with others. They have strong verbal skills, and look for the opportunity to express social concerns.

5. Under the *business* scale description are found those people who view themselves as leaders. Skilled with words they seek to persuade others. Business occupations include: sales people, administrators, business executives, and bankers.

6. In the *clerical* scale are people who prefer to work with well-defined duties. They enjoy routine tasks, and find office work to their liking. They often place a value on financial success and status. Examples are: office workers, accountants, and bank tellers.

THE PROFILES

*After a spirit of discernment, the next rarest things in the
world are diamonds and pearls*

Bruyère

With this lengthy foundation set in place, both in terms of the six worker
trait components and several personality tests, we turn now to members of
the construction team and their associated trait profiles:

A. The Architect/Engineer Group

Charged essentially with the design of the project, architects and engineers
should have many similarities. According to various tests, however, subtle
differences appear to exist, especially with respect to the artistic and creative factors.

Both the "typical" architect and engineer rate in the top 10 percent of the
population in terms of such aptitudes as intelligence, verbal-numerical-
spatial abilities, and form perception. Both these typical individuals enjoy
good visual activity and the spatial acumen necessary for graphic representation, imagination, and logical, organized minds.

They prefer scientific activities (as opposed to business or people tasks),
and are interested in abstract, creative endeavors (as opposed to the everyday routines). Their qualification profile implies that they have reasonably
adjusted to situations involving directing and planning activities, evaluating information against verifiable criteria, and meeting attainment of tasks
relative to established tolerances and standards. So alike are these two that
Drs. Harrington and O'Shea incorporate these two careers within the same
job cluster. In rank order they value:

1. Employment security
2. Being paid well
3. High achievement
4. Creativity; nonroutine tasks
5. Intellectual pursuits
6. Independence
7. Leadership

This would seem to jibe with observation and with commonly held stereotypes. The Strong-Campbell Inventory indicates that the architect is more

interested in, and committed to, artistic expression, whereas the engineer likes to work with things on a more practical level.

In fact, on the basis of the AVL Value Inventory, 508 engineering students rated Aesthetic lowest in esteem strength, well below the norm for 8300 college students. In another study, architects rated aesthetics highest whereas engineers rated it low. Of utmost importance, it should be borne in mind that contractual obligations and differing roles on the project somewhat alter this theoretical profile. The architect is legally responsible to the owner, not only for his own actions but for those of his consultants as well, and this unequivocally affects his behavior. In addition, personality is a product of both heredity and environment, which includes roles played within a group. As will be discussed in the next chapter, group pressures often override, and even coerce, an individual's preferences and convictions. Consequently, his overt actions may conform to the standards established in his group. Furthermore, many architects and engineers are themselves entrepreneurs, thereby adding a complex business dimension to their profiles as well as to their roles and duties. With caution as a keynote, however, these descriptive profiles seem to be fairly accurate in the collective genre.

A well-known investigation of architects was done by D. W. MacKinnon in 1962. The study was based on the hypothesis that architecture involves two types of creativity—artistic and scientific. Essentially a research on creativity, MacKinnon focused on the many diverse skills shown by successfully practicing architects: businessman, artist, engineer, lawyer, and advertising man all rolled into one neat package. MacKinnon concentrated on 40 of the most creative architects in the United States, who were carefully screened and selected. Implicit with the selection was the valid premise that if 40 most creative architects were not actually chosen, those who were chosen indeed represented a highly creative group. The results painted a composite personality structure that seems to bear out the above profile. Although by no means do all architects possess all of these personality traits, it is assumed that many, in fact, share similar attributes. These characteristics are ranked in order:

1. Favors aesthetic impression
2. Possesses a high level of aspiration
3. Holds his own independence in high esteem
4. Produces results
5. Enjoys above-average intelligence
6. Values intelligence and intellectual ability
7. Recognizes his own adequacy as a person
8. Performs dependably and responsibly
9. Is interested in a spectrum of subjects
10. Acts ethically consistent with his own standards

11. Projects social grace, poise, and presence
12. Likes sensualistic experiences involving touch, taste, and contact
13. Evaluates in critical, sometimes skeptical, fashion; seldom is easily impressed
14. Deals in a straightforward, candid manner
15. Typifies business qualities

B. The Owner Group

To conjure up a realistic image of an average owner is virtually an impossibility. Butcher, baker, candlestick maker—owners come in all types and temperaments. A frugal banker finances a shopping center; an aggressive realtor redevelops a slum; a board of directors expands a manufacturing facility. Possibly on the job front, a technical manager or a special architect could represent the owner's interest in day-to-day activities. Hence, the "typical" construction team employs the artificial, but reasonable, construct of a government agency headed by a public administrator—certainly a common situation, because of the vast expenditures committed to government construction. Even with the apparent limitation, the profile of the administrator should prove instructive. Should a nontypical project arise, the reader can cautiously modify the profile to suit the situation at hand.

The *Dictionary of Occupational Titles* rates the administrator in the top 10 percent of the population with respect to intelligence and verbal ability, and somewhat lower for the other aptitudes. His job requirements, assumed to be satisfactorily met, call for organizational capacity to plan, formulate, and execute policies, as well as the verbal facility to establish effective rapport with people at all levels. He favors working and communicating with people in social/welfare and business-oriented activities (as opposed to nonsocial, scientific-technical tasks). His temperament is such that the successful administrator has adjusted to situations that involve managing (controlling and planning) people and their duties beyond mere giving and receiving instructions. The Strong Vocational Interest Blank includes the public administrator primarily in the social theme category and, to a peripheral degree, in the conventional and enterprising themes. This would imply preferences for working (via words and ideas) with people on a social-business-leadership plane.

The Harrington/O'Shea system seems to bear out this implication; it associates the following abilities with the government administrator:

1. Social
2. Leadership
3. Persuasive
4. Language
5. Computation

His job values appear somewhat similar to those of architects and engineers:

1. Prestige, good salary
2. High achievement
3. Variety, creativity
4. Intellectual pursuits
5. Deal with people
6. Leadership

Again, it is cautioned that actual on-site conditions, as well as the group to which the administrator owes allegiance, definitely influence his actions. For example, the administrator may well be held responsible for expenditures of the project, but in a controversy, the money does not come from his own pocket, as is the case with a smaller contractor under a lump sum contract. Certainly, such a controversy would be viewed with different perspectives and grades of intensity, depending on which side of the wallet one stood.

C. The Contractor/Subcontractor Group

As with the "typical" owner, contractors come in all sizes and structures that defy precise description. In line with the "construction team" fabrication, however, the contractor and, moreso, the subcontractor specialties are assumed to be the entrepreneur type. Typically, he is a small businessman with a construction manager, project superintendent (or foreman), and tradesmen in his employ. This is a very realistic assumption, because over 80 percent of the 800,000 business firms classified as construction contractors are individual proprietorships. The remaining 20 percent are divided equally between partnerships and corporations.* In actuality, most owners wear many hats, and consequently perform several, if not all, functions. Being the doctor, lawyer, and indian chief precludes any stereotype of personality. For the purposes of developing personality profiles, however, it is assumed that the contractor group consists of: (1) the proprietor (small business contractors and subcontractors); (2) the project manager; (3) the superintendent (and trade foreman); and (4) the construction tradesmen. On every project such individuals are frequently encountered.

1. The Proprietor

Harrington-O'Shea includes the contractor in the "Management" cluster of jobs, with the same general abilities and job values as the government

*See Richard H. Clough, *Construction Contracting*, 3rd ed., New York: Wiley & Sons, 1975.

administrator. Yet, it would be prudent to shift the contractor more toward the businessmen characterization—dominating, leading, self-confident, and energetic, as described in Holland's Enterprising occupational theme.

As rated in an AVL value study, businessmen score strongest in the Economic and Political areas, and weakest in the Social and Aesthetic. They place high esteem on the practical, money, material wealth, power, and prestige and much less emphasis on the intellectual pursuits, artistic expression, and social interactions for humanistic ends.

A number of clinical interviews, as well as tests, have concentrated on the business executives who can be assumed to be similar somewhat to entrepreneurs in many respects. As presented in Roe's *Psychology of Occupations*, Flory and Janney believe that important factors for appraising executive functioning are:

- Intelligence
- Emotional control
- Skill in human relations
- Insight into human behavior
- Ability to organize and direct others' activities

Also presented were the results from a Guilford study, which concluded that there existed a definite relation between "success" and the following temperaments: sociability, self-confidence, cooperativeness, and masculinity. It appears that a successful executive, in order to be happy, drives hard in pursuit of achievement. All show a high degree of ability to organize and demonstrate decisiveness, activity, and aggressiveness. A report prepared for the Small Business Administration, asserts that the typical entrepreneur differs from the big business executive in that he finds it difficult to readily adjust to the framework of big business policies and procedures. Instead of trading his independence for the security offered by large corporations, he would rather be his own man, combining his skills, finances, equipment, and methods as he thinks necessary to make a profit. On the basis of a projective test (Thematic Apperception Test), a few certain dominant themes found in the small businessman were:

- A social value system steeped in middle class mores
- Punishing pursuit of tasks
- Unwillingness to submit to authority

In yet another management research study from the Small Business Administration, the following traits were associated with successful small businessmen (assumed typical of contractors):

- He works long, hard hours.
- He has the resiliency to recover quickly and persevere in the face of a setback.
- He is aggressive in both attitudes and actions.
- He is willing to defray immediate profit until he achieves an adequate financial position.
- He masters the technical and social skills that his operation requires.

Finally, on a less scientific level, but certainly an enlightening one, we conclude the proprietor profile with excerpts from an interview with a young entrepreneur, who rose from tractor mechanic to president of four corporations that he founded. In uncanny fashion, he exemplifies many of those traits measured to be consistent with the business stereotype.*

I'm enjoying what I'm doing. I'll make a good chunk of money in one thing, stick it back in the other thing, and just watch it grow. I'd get more out of it than hoarding it away somewhere. I'd say I'm better off than most twenty-six-year-old guys. (Laughs.)

I started working pretty young. When I was six, I had my first paper route. At nine I worked in a bicycle repair shop. At the same time I was delivering chop suey for a Chinese restaurant.

I worked as a stock boy in a grocery store for a year. This had no interest to me whatsoever . . . I always liked the feeling of being independent. Anything I wanted to buy, I always had the money.

I usually get out of here at one o'clock in the morning. I go home and eat dinner at two. I do my best thinking at night. I can't fall asleep until seven in the morning. I turn TV on. I don't even pay attention to it. They got the all-night movies. I just sit there in the living room, making notes, trying to put down things for the next day to remember. I plan ahead for a month. Maybe I'll lay down in bed about four in the morning. If something comes to my head, I'll get up and start writing it. If I get three, four hours sleep, I'm okay.

The world is full of people who don't have the guts or the balls to go out on their own. People want to be in business for themselves, but they don't want to take the chance. That's what separates me from the majority . . .

You want to be liked and you want to help people. I've found out you can't. It's not appreciated. They never thank you. If you're successful in business, you're around phonies all the time. There's always some guy slappin' you on the back trying to get you to buy something from him or lend him money.

*From *Working: People Talk About What They Do All Day and How They Feel About What They Do*, by Studs Terkel. Copyright © 1972, 1974 by Studs Terkel. Reprinted by permission of Pantheon Books, a Division of Random House, Inc.

You remember old friends and good times. This relationship is gone. The fun you used to have. They're envious of what you have.

There's no loyalty when it comes to money. I'm younger than most of the guys who work for me, but I feel older. It's like a big family. I have the feeling they're not here for the money. They want to help me out. They respect me.

When I first started to get successful, people in the business tried to hurt me. One of my biggest kicks is getting beyond them.

When you're young and in business, it's not an asset. The first time I walked into a bank they didn't want to deal with me. I used to be nervous. I'd look at the guy across the desk with a tie and a suit and everything. You could see what he was thinking. You oughta see that guy now when I come in. (Laughs.) When I go into banks now, I feel I'm better than them. And they know it.

It bothers them that somebody new should come in and be so successful. It wasn't easy. When other people were going out and just having fun and riding motorcycles and getting drunk and partying, I was working. I gave up a lot. I gave up my whole youth, really. That's something you never get back.
People say to me, "Gee! You work so damn hard, how can you ever enjoy it?" I'm enjoying it every day. I don't have to get away for a weekend to enjoy it.

. . . But I'll never retire. I'll take it a little bit easier. I'll have to. I had an ulcer since I was eighteen. I chew up a lot of Mylantas. It's for your stomach, to coat it. Like Maalox. I probably go through twenty tablets a day.

I guess people get different thrills out of business in different ways. There's a lot of satisfaction in showing up people who thought you'd never amount to anything. If I died tomorrow, I'd really feel I enjoyed myself. How would I like to be remembered? I don't know if I really care about being remembered. I just want to be known while I'm here. That's enough. I didn't like history, anyway.

2. The Project Manager

As discussed in Chapter 2, the project manager is charged with completing the project profitably within the contract time. He acts as a buffer between higher management and the numerous outside organizations that run the gamut from architect, engineer, owner, subcontractors, vendors, union officials, and last, but certainly not least, the public and the media.

The *Dictionary of Occupational Titles* describes managerial activities as organizing and coordinating the function of a unit originated for a specific purpose (say, a successfully completed project).

Such activities require the ability to: (1) manage programs (i.e., means and methods of construction); (2) understand, interpret, and apply procedures and directives (i.e., plans and specs); (3) control inventory (i.e., materials and equipment); and (4) maintain records (i.e., reports, minutes of meetings, financial data). Additionally, a manager must demonstrate leadership, verbal facility, and those social qualities necessary, not only to motivate employees, but to maintain good relations with other groups.

The *Occupational Dictionary* ranks the manager in the highest third of the population (exclusive of the highest 10 percent) in intelligence and verbal and clerical ability, but lower in numerical and spatial aptitudes. The key interests appear to involve a preference for activities that generate prestige (as opposed to tangible satisfaction) and for business and people contacts (as opposed to scientific and technical endeavors). A successful manager would have the temperament to adjust to a variety of duties subject to constant change—certainly a truism on any field site. Managerial contact with people, above and beyond exchanging instructions and evaluating information against verifiable criteria, is another situational adjustment required. For example, the project manager must assure that the work conforms to the contract documents. Because project management is a high-echelon position, it is included within the Management cluster of the Harrington-O'Shea system. Therefore, a project manager identifies with those worker traits of the administrator and the contractor: social, leadership, and persuasive abilities, and job values highlighting prestige, salary, achievement, and variety.

In broad terms, Clough (*Construction Contracting*) describes the project manager as directing his efforts to organizing, planning, scheduling, and controlling the field work. In this capacity, he must often act quickly and independently, and relate effectively with all types of individuals and groups. As stated in a lighter vein by V. Bush (*Construction Management*): "I have been trying to formulate a simple answer to the question, 'What does a project manager do throughout the project?' About the same thing as a housewife with a husband and five children does for the first twenty years of married life. They both do everything except furnish the money."

3. The Superintendent

In this profile are found the project super and the trade foreman. (Possibly one could justify including the Clerk of the Works here, even though he belongs to another camp, which undoubtedly influences his perspective and allegiances.) The *Occupational Dictionary* depicts the construction supervisor as coordinating the activities of tradesmen. Additionally, he skillfully uses appropriate tools and machines because, in difficult phases he may be required to work alongside the subordinates. He displays an in-depth knowledge of his trade, the facility to communicate this knowledge, and the proficiency to maintain harmony among workers and groups.

Significant aptitudes are motor coordination, finger and manual dexterity, as well as higher-than-average intelligence and verbal fluency.

His interests, as expected, involve choosing nonsocial tasks in relation to machines and techniques (versus communicating with others in a social/welfare environment). Another strong interest is for prestige-producing tasks, which bring esteem from others (and rejection of tangible satisfaction). He adjusts to frequent change and managing the work of others.

Because of the close relationship between the superintendent and the construction tradesmen, similarities between skills and job values seem evident. From the data of Harrington-O'Shea, these abilities are:

- Mechanical
- Manual
- Spatial
- Clerical
- Mathematical

The job values are:

- Work with hands
- Physical activity
- Work under supervision
- Routine tasks

In general, the project super is responsible for the daily routine of field supervision, coordinating the subs, supervising the means and methods, keeping activities on schedule, and, invariably, being at the vanguard of the problems and conflicts. In a nutshell, the project superintendent can make or break a job.

4. Construction Workers

By virtue of the transient and fluctuating nature of the industry, the average construction worker is usually bound to his particular trade and union more than to any one company. In the course of a year, he may work for several employers.

According to the Strong Vocational Interest Blank, the construction worker is solidly in the realistic occupational theme, being: rugged, robust, aggressive in character, and skilled physically. Construction workers prefer the outdoors and working with tools and powerful machines versus dealing with abstractions and people. Often they have difficulty in expressing feelings or communicating ideas. Typically conventional with respect to political and economic views, they are usually nonreceptive to the radical and innovative.

According to the AVL Study of Values, they choose the Economic and Theoretical, and minimize the Aesthetic theme.

The Harrington-O'Shea system lists their abilities as:

- Mechanical
- Manual
- Spatial
- Clerical
- Mathematical and Computational

They hold job values that provide:

- Work with hands
- Physical labor
- Performance under supervision
- Routine work

In line with these observations, the *Dictionary of Occupational Titles* states that this group is characterized by emphasis on applying manual skills: properly sequencing operations, using appropriate tools, reading blueprints, computing dimensions, and inspecting finished work. Critical aptitudes are motor coordination and dexterity, their intelligence and verbal and numerical facility ranging in the middle third of the population. As a group, they would rather do things for productive satisfaction rather than for humanistic ends. Their personalities must be so to function adequately in jobs requiring judgment and attainment within set tolerances and standards.

The following interviews bear out these observations:*

The 44-year-old carpenter:

. . . It's a real pleasure to work on it, don't get me wrong. Using your hand is just a delight in the paneling, in the good woods. It smells good and they shape well with the plane. Those woods are filled with the whole creative mystery of things. Each wood has its own spirit. Driving nails, yeah, your spirit will break against that.

A craftsman's life is nothin' but compromise. Look at your tile here. That's craftsman's work, not art work. Craftsmanship demands that you work repeating a pattern to very close tolerances. You're laying this tile here within a sixteenth. It ought to be within a sixty-fourth of a true ninety degree angle. Theoretically it should be perfect. It shouldn't be any sixty-fourth, it should be 00 tolerance. Just altogether straight on, see? Do we ever do it? No. Look at that parquet stuff you got around here. It's pretty, but those corners. The man has compromised. He said that'll have to do.

If you see a carpenter that's alive to his work, you'll notice that about the way he hits a nail. He's not going (imitates machine gun rat-tat-tat)—trying to get the nail down and out of the way so he can hurry up and get another one. Although he may be working fast, each lick is like a separate person that he's hitting with his hammer. It's like as though there's a separate friend of his that one moment. Unique, all by itself. Pow! But you gotta stop before you get that nail in, you know? That's fine work. Hold the hammer back, and just that last lick, don't hit it with your hammer, hit it with a punch so you won't leave the hammer mark. Rhythm.

A 57-year-old stonemason:
As far as I know, masonry is older than carpentry, which goes clear back to Bible times. Stonemason goes back way before Bible times: the pyramids of Egypt, things of that sort.

. . . But me being in the profession, when I hear something in that line, I remember it. Stone's my business. I, oh, sometimes talk to architects and engineers that have made a study and I pick up the stuff here and there.

Every piece of stone you pick up is different, the grain's a little different and this and that. It'll split one way and break the other. You pick up your stone and look at it and make an educated guess. It's a pretty good day layin' stone or brick. Not tiring. Anything you like to do isn't tiresome. It's hard work; stone is heavy. At the same time, you get interested in what you're doing and you usually fight the clock the other way. You're not lookin' for quittin'. You're wondering you haven't got enough done and it's almost quittin' time. (Laughs.) I ask the hod carrier what time it is and he says "Two thirty." I say, "Oh, my Lord, I was gonna get a whole lot more than this."

. . . So I take a lot of pride in it and I do get, oh, I'd say, a lot of praise or whatever you want to call it. I don't suppose anybody, however much he's recognized, wouldn't like to be recognized a little more. I think I'm pretty well recognized.

Stone's my life. I daydream all the time, most times it's on stone. Oh, I'm gonna build me a stone cabin down on the Green River. I'm gonna build stone cabinets in the kitchen. That stone door's gonna be awful heavy and I don't know how to attach the hinges. I've got to figure out how to make stone roof. That's the kind of thing. All my dreams, it seems like it's got to have a piece of rock mixed in it.

. . . The architect draws the picture and the plans, and the draftsman and the engineer, they help him. They figure the strength and so on. But when it comes to actually makin' the curves and doin' the work, you've got to do it with your hands.

There's not a house in this country that I haven't built that I don't look at every time I go by. (Laughs.) I can set here now and actually in my mind see so many that you wouldn't believe. If there's one stone in there crooked, I know where it's at and I'll never forget it. Maybe thirty years, I'll know a place where I should have took that stone out and redone it but I didn't. I still notice it. The people who live there might not notice it, but I notice it. I never pass that house that I don't think of it. I've got one house in mind right now. (Laughs.) That's the work of my hands.

SELF-ASSERTION

The world is governed only by self-interest

Schiller

At this point the reader may be able to identify the origins of many communication gaps, honest differences of opinion, and personality discords so frequently encountered in construction. There is much truth embraced in Goethe's comment: "As our inclination, so our opinions."

Experience on the site gives a fair idea of the assortment of personalities that will be met on most projects. Because most people possess insight into their own characteristics and roles, the reader can more or less predict those areas of potential harmony or hostility that he may have to deal with. For example, on a broad scale, if one assumes a positive correlation between personality traits and chosen occupation, an architect could be predicted to be aesthetically motivated and interested in the intellectual and creative aspects of the project more than, say, a construction boss, who would be, in all probability, practical, straightforward in actions, and oriented to things, machines, and profits. Furthermore, they both play differing roles. The architect is charged by contract to provide a functional design, as well as to serve as a general administrator for the owner. A contractor, if only for survival, commits his energies to building the structure within the bid price. Overall, both desire a "successful" job, "success" meaning different things to different people. Therefore, one should have a "feel" for how and when these profiles will mesh and, possibly, mismatch.

Of course, in the real world, there is considerable overlapping of personalities and roles. Many architects are in fact motivated by money, whereas many contractors are intellectually inclined. In terms of the population, however, tests, surveys and studies lend weight to the validity of the above composite personality profiles. Therefore, as the job progresses, sooner or later we should expect that a certain crisis or event will serve as catalyst to bring these individual traits, roles, and commitments together in heated dispute.

Regardless of what group one belongs to, he must deal proficiently with people, especially in emotionally charged predicaments. His job demands that he pursue the goals of his employer (or group). In this pursuit, he may win a few and lose a few—no one scores a thousand in any competitive game. Simultaneously, however, certain personal needs beg, as seen in Maslow's hierarchy, to be satisfied: esteem, belonging, money, self-actualization, and the like. In our society not every job goal or personal need can be had simply for the asking. Individuals, like companies and even nations, must compete for the prize in a general sense. In order to compete successfully and to protect one's self-interest, the individual must learn to assert himself appropriately without denying anyone his basic rights.

The importance of proper assertion cannot be overemphasized. Our society, with its multitude of organizations, values highly those socially talented individuals who can settle controversial issues without backing down automatically to the opponent's whims and wishes, or trampling the adversary in submission, thus inseminating a hatred that someday may return to haunt the aggressor. In construction particularly, a person must be neither a patsy nor a bully. Instead he must choose that social conduct that promises the best result. As a case in point, consider a hard-driving owner pressing for a questionable "no-cost" extra. The contractor's representative faces a number of options: (1) grumbling under his breath, he can buckle under the owner's demands; (2) he can curse the owner, "You pushy S.O.B.!" and stalk off the site; or (3) without undue emotion (flight or fight), he can point out the questionable aspects of the extra and explain that a change order is justified. Obviously, the latter choice, assertion, proves to be the wisest approach. Of course, the best choice may often fail to achieve the desired results. No system or technique can promise victory every time. The major purpose of assertive behavior is for the individual to look after his own best interests without feeling guilty, or "putting down" the opponent. Unfortunately, in many instances, aggression is construed as assertion—the aggressive boss, the tough business agent, the hawks and the hard-liners. But, aggression involves a "put down" of the recipient, whereas assertion contends that a person has no justification to trample or psychologically intimidate another in a human relationship. An owner has no right to be discourteous to a subordinate. An architect has no right to "talk down" to a laborer. Every human being has the prerogative to express his opinions and feelings. All people are created equal, and, although they occupy particular positions in an organization's hierarchy or project role, they still have their rights as human beings.

In trying to remedy any crisis (whether things or people) in or out of construction, the assertive person strives to walk the line between capitulation and total warfare, between being neither Mr. McGoo nor Attila the Hun, between being 100 percent winner and 100 percent loser. Neither extreme reaps satisfactory results. For an example, say a meeting is called. The opponent marches into the conference with an entourage consisting of two attorneys, a large Doberman Pinscher, and seven "experts," who loudly attempt to forge a solution to maximize their gains. One attorney opens the meeting with the claim, "The governor's my brother-in-law." One forceful expert shouts, "Everybody does it that way!" The dog growls. Naturally the element of intimidation pervades the discussion. An individual who is unsure of himself may drift along in acquiescence: a what-can-I-do attitude. Even though he may strongly resent the intimidation, he swallows his pride, and agrees to their proposed course of action. Why? One plausible explanation is that for centuries social structures were built upon certain premises: authority knows best, follow the leader, don't rock the boat, deny or suppress the self for the good of the organization. In this age, however, such premises are being scrutinized and held to be of questionable validity. Today, a number of astute individuals apply Franklin's suggestion, "God helps those that help themselves." Therefore, in accord with a me-first philosophy, it should prove instructive and profitable to examine some elements of assertive responses. This philosophy rests upon the basic belief that every person has the same fundamental rights as another person in terms of interpersonal relationships. Regardless of what slot one occupies in the hierarchy, he should demand his rights and not feel guilty about asserting himself to achieve his objective. The specific techniques are based on learning theory principles such that an individual can develop a healthy, durable behavior pattern with his self-interest first and foremost. He should avoid being overly concerned with a "good guy" image, so that he can honestly express his emotions, without violating the rights of others, or without manipulating others to gain his own ends. These assertive techniques are presented with the express purpose that the reader identify those situations in which assertion is necessary to facilitate a more respectful, give-and-take relationship with others. As with any psychological tool or suggestion presented in this book, the reader must measure the applicability and the risks involved, and consequently choose for himself. Refer to Box 4.3 for a self-inventory.

Box 4.3. SELF-INVENTORY TO TEST ASSERTIVENESS

The following are typical of many project/work/life encounters, the first eight general, the last twelve more personal. These questions should prove helpful in roughly assessing the reader's inclination toward reservation or aggression.

1. *When you stand before an authority figure (boss, official, etc.) do you become self-conscious or unable to express yourself?*
2. *The owner's representative is being uncooperative, or breaks his word. How do you approach him?*
3. *The designer submits the minutes of the meeting with certain statements to which you disagree. What is your reaction?*

4. *A subcontractor fails to correct a noncompliance, or he fails to comply with a directive. What is your next move?*

5. *There is a touchy borderline interpretation. Do you find it difficult to make decisions? Or rely on others? Do you trust your own judgment? Do you state your opinion in a heated debate?*

6. *The team makes a decision with which you disagree. Are you reluctant to present your case when there is a problem, or do you ride along with the group decisions?*

7. *A particular subcontractor is consistently late for meetings. Do you confront him? How?*

8. *A loud-mouth inspector is arguing with you. How do you handle the situation?*

9. *Are you prone to "blow your top?"*

10. *Do you express your anger, hostility, warmth, and compliments in a socially acceptable fashion?*

11. *When angry, do you resort to verbal abuse and obscenities? Do you bully or intimidate to get results?*

12. *When treated unfairly, do you speak out?*

13. *When criticized do you wither? Or become overapologetic? Or verbally hostile?*

14. *When you differ with someone, do you assert your own viewpoint, even though it may be unpopular?*

15. *Do you put words into people's mouths or finish their sentences for them?*

16. *Can you admit mistakes without being overly casual or overly apologetic?*

17. *Do you refuse unreasonable requests? How?*

18. *Do you prolong an argument even when the other person has relented? Do you have to speak the last word?*

19. *Are you openly critical of the actions, ideas, and opinions of others?*

20. *Do you maintain eye contact when speaking with someone? Use appropriate gestures or facial expressions? Do you roll your arms like windmills, and screw your face into a raisin?*

Every construction man, at frequent intervals, finds himself in disagreeable situations that often lead to tension. The purpose of assertiveness techniques is to provide him with a repertoire of responses such that he feels little anxiety or distress in these dilemmas when he pushes to pursue his objectives.

A. Basic Definitions

From the psychological stance, it is assumed that the person and his behavior under discussion are relatively normal and healthy. Extreme anxiety and hostility are well beyond the scope and the intent of this book. Still, all normal human beings at times find themselves in certain uncomfortable situations that cause a good deal of anxiety. These elicited emotions prevent them from responding adequately and constructively.

Assertive behavior is defined as the proper expression of any emotion, other than anxiety, toward another person. It is essentially that type of behavior in which an individual acts in his own behalf without a stomach full of butterflies. He expresses his honest feelings comfortably yet emphatically, without denying or trampling on the rights of other individuals. Although much of the research concentrates on singular interrelationships on a personal and social level, the results are easily extrapolated to construction management and to those individuals (and groups) that make up the team.

We will describe three types of behavior: nonassertive; aggressive; and assertive behavior.

1. Nonassertive Behavior

Generally a weak response indicates that the individual is inhibited from expressing his true emotions. Possibly he sacrifices his objectives because of an unreasonable fear of stepping on a few toes. He allows himself to have others choose for him, instead of relying on his own judgment. He may be reluctant to express his opinions especially when they differ from those of his friends or colleagues. Justified or not he finds himself unable to criticize a peer or a subordinate because his "nice guy" image may be injured, or because he believes the irrational assumption that he must be loved by everyone to be considered worthwhile. All too often he feels so frustrated that he cannot find the correct behavior to stand up and be counted without anxiety. Sometimes, this timid person thinks of an appropriate response, but at a later time, when the appropriate opportunity has passed. These individuals display passive behavior patterns; they are what one might call the patsies, the chronic victims. People shove them aside, not literally, but figuratively. Others seldom accept their opinions, or respect or appreciate their assets. Why is it some individuals seem to be such perpetual losers, so that people tend to take advantage of them, or act as though they didn't exist? Is it that these individuals wear a neon sign that flashes: "I am a loser!"? No, but they might as well, because their expression, gestures, tone of voice, absence of eye contact, and posture, all elements of nonverbal communication—send an unfavorable message that identifies them as "easy marks." Consequently, opportunists snatch up the advantage like a shark at a hunk of meat.

Here are some descriptive components associated with a nonassertive person:

- He seldom speaks up. If he does, he does so feebly. Therefore, rarely will an adversary take this person seriously.
- Usually he acts hesitant. He pauses, unsure of himself, which in effect flashes a nonverbal cue: "I am unimportant; therefore, you do not have to listen to me or respond favorably."
- He avoids eye contact. Generally, eye-to-eye contact indicates forcefulness and attentiveness. Consequently, if one avoids eye contact, he sets himself apart, so that the recipient can easily ignore him.
- He edges away. At construction meetings, some individuals drift into the background, to the rear of the room. Like blending into the woodwork, they occupy places of isolation. If they fail to make contact, the reason is they are *actually* unnoticed. The nonverbal message may read low self-esteem, indifference, or laziness.
- He assumes poor posture. The humped shoulders and the hunched walk indicate low self-esteem. Sagging muscles do the same. When an individual walks humbly, head bowed in deference, as though on the way to chapel bells, the world associates this mild expression with his character, and acts accordingly.

2. Aggressive Behavior

At the other extreme is the aggressor, the bully, the intimidator. To gain his objective, he explodes. He responds too vigorously, causing a rift in communication. Later, after a cooling-off period, he may feel embarrassed and regret his outburst. He wins countless battles, but precious few wars.

Often these offensive tactics achieve the objective, but at the expense of injuring someone else—denying their rights and causing hurt and humiliation. Consequently, he sows potential seeds of hatred and vengeance. Unfortunately, this type of behavior pattern reinforces itself, because, in many cases, the recipient backs down, thereby rewarding the aggressor's mode of operation. Habits, good and bad, originate and mature on the learning theory principles: people repeat those responses that reward and attenuate those that result in punishment.

Here are some possible descriptive elements associated with an aggressive person:

- He seldom speaks; he shouts. He comes on straight-out—very vigorous in his speech. In fact, he may very likely curse or threaten—any mea-

Box 4.4. "So *this* is where you design those innovative bridges."

Gerry Fox

sure to gain his ends. He specializes in name-calling and other propaganda techniques.

- He moves doggedly, aggressively. If he fails to get his way, he romps and stomps and breaks into a tirade—slamming his fists on the table, and other hard-line gestures.
- He seldom looks. Instead he stares through people, and often wears a scowl.
- As though he is ready to attack, he leans close, inappropriate for the recipient's comfort space. This is a subtle maneuver to intimidate his opponent.

A serious disadvantage of being nonassertive or aggressive is the emotional consequences of such behavior. Often people overlook the assets and abilities of both shy and aggressive individuals, and, consequently, incorrectly evaluate them. For instance, a shy person may strike others as bored or snobbish, or an aggressive person may seem a tyrant or sadist. Therefore, the resultant feedback is negative, which, in turn, leads to lowered self-esteem.

3. Assertive Behavior

In general, the assertive person is open and ordinarily concerned with the rights of others. At the same time, he looks out for himself first and foremost. He may or may not achieve his desired goals; however, he chooses for himself; he does not calmly accept the decision of another. In most circumstances, he is in control of his emotions, and can enter into interpersonal relationships with successful results. He is confident without being cocky, generally spontaneous, and aware of his own feelings as well as those of others. If he takes exception to anything, he expresses legitimate opposition, and makes his demands in socially acceptable ways.

As an illustration, consider a boss, a tyrant type, who demands from a worker unfair performance standards (quality as well as quantity) under grueling tension. Other than flood the market with resumés, the subordinate faces several courses of action: (1) say nothing but seethe inside, while he lays awake nights with a headache; (2) snarl, grip the culprit by the throat, and shake him vigorously like a rag doll; or (3) confront the boss with the complaint—"I feel as though you're taking advantage of me." By using the assertive approach, the anger or displeasure is expressed in a way that is socially acceptable.

No one's rights have been denied—no insults and threats have been voiced. Whether or not the unfair workload is reduced depends on the personalities in question, but at least the air is clear. And typically, the silent bystanders—those who lacked the courage to speak—look up to and respect the assertive person. Peculiar to, and pervasive in, our society, a fair segment of the population holds the irrational belief that one should respect the whims and wishes of others to the detriment of one's own good. Parents, teachers, and authority figures preach that one should be tactful, polite, respectful, a child-should-be-seen-and-not-heard philosophy. One learns not to climb over people to get ahead. Yet frequently, observation demonstrates the opposite. In order to win or to reach objectives, a person usually must compete in tough fashion. As coach Woody Hayes quipped, "Show me a good loser and I'll show you a loser." This ambivalence carries over in the occupational scene. In keeping with status quo, authority-knows-best philosophy, employees are typically told not "to rock a boat."

Even if a decision of management borders the bizarre, one is expected to go along with it. If a rebel or deviant falls out of step, he often suffers punishing consequences—the 0 percent raise, the transfer to Siberia, or his walking papers. It certainly is true that conformity and uniformity are essential to the survival of any organization, company, country, or civilization, but conformity breeds some negative results, as will be examined in Chapter 5. For the present, suffice it to say that by inference or blunt publication, the organization-to-subordinate relationship is such that one is pressured to conform to group standards and goals. In essence, what all this boils down to is that jobs, rules, policies, and procedures, all praise and reward nonassertive behavior. Yet people must recognize that the following assumptions are untrue:

- Bosses are better than employees.
- Executives are better than laborers.
- Architects are better than inspectors.
- Owners are better than contractors.
- Contractors are better than subs.
- Managers are better than plumbers.
- Generals are better than privates.
- Engineers are better than foremen.

Our social structure perpetrates these and similar myths. Such fallacies cause human beings in the lower strata to be treated as though they were actually of lesser value as human beings, rather than in the context of the roles that they occupy. People must rid themselves of the assumption that the lives and goals of others (executives, professionals, politicians, etc.) are more precious or worthwhile than their own lives and wishes. Assertive techniques equip an individual with a philosophy and a mode of dispensing with such myths.

B. Elements of Assertive Behavior

Behavioral scientists have done considerable research into what constitutes assertive behavior. They have identified several elements, which we discuss below under three categories.

1. Strategy

The best strategy involves two elements: contradiction and timing.

a. Contradiction.   If you disagree with someone, or take exception to his behavior, avoid pretending agreement or acceptance. State your objections and viewpoints with as much vigor and emotion as is reasonable.

b. Timing.   For maximum effect the assertive act should be initiated at the appropriate time: right there and then. Occasionally, however, it may be more appropriate to confront the person in private. As a general rule, though, you should try to respond immediately and avoid delay.

2. Nonverbal Signals

This includes the following:

a. Eye Contact.   When asserting, you should look at the person with whom you are speaking. Not in the sense of staring at him, but in normal non-intimidating eye-to-eye contact. As mentioned previously, if you refuse to meet another's eyes, it is a nonverbal communique that you are setting yourself apart—that he is not to recognize you.

b. Facial Expression.   A proper display of emotion on your face should be compatible with the occasion. For instance, if you are angry, then your face should indicate this anger (without undue contortions).

c. Gesture.   Your gestures should be forceful, but not too emphatic. They should reinforce your words. Holding yourself erect, firm, muscles tightened, complete your sentences in gestures. This indicates that you are sure of yourself, and that you fully intend to achieve your objective, whatever it may be.

d. Posture.   To edge away or to sag humbly communicates a lack of self-esteem. Stand tall; stand authoritarian as a soldier does. Posture definitely affects your personality. Therefore, the weight of your messages carries more impact if you stand close to the person and hold yourself erect.

3. Message

Both the content and the delivery are vital.

a. Voice. Your voice should be well modulated, the tone being strong and clear. It should accurately reflect the emotions that you feel. Obviously a monotone will fail to impress anyone that you mean business. To speak in a whisper, defensively, or indecisively defeats your purpose. Without a doubt, shouting or swearing brings defensive reactions on the part of the recipient, so be decisive in your words and fully complement them with the supporting gestures to demonstrate that you are sure of yourself.

b. Content. With respect to the contents, although what one says is important, sometimes it is less important than you think. Often just making a statement forcibly with a spontaneous expression is enough to achieve what you want. In fact, just saying something—anything—at times can be very fruitful. So instead of pondering about the right word or the best word, it is more important that you express yourself adequately and promptly. Of course, it is essential that the discussion be kept on a smooth, intellectual basis.

c. Style. Keep in mind that you should always state your feelings in such a way that you accept the responsibility for your own emotions. You should use the word "I" as much as possible, because it involves you in the statement. For example, it is one thing to say "I am angry," but quite another to shout, "You S.O.B.!" The latter expression is a definite "put down," whereas "I am angry" is an assertive expression. Everybody gets angry at times, but it is important to recognize that you are the one who feels the anger, not the one who provoked it. The best way to handle this (and any) emotion is to express it spontaneously in a healthy style without escalating the provocation. Finally, avoid the build-up of hostility over a long period of time. Prolonged stress contributes nothing to the solution, but it does wear the worrier down with ills from headaches to hypertension. Here are some assertive statements that have been found to be useful:

1. "I am angry" (it is assumed the reader could easily conjure up a raft of descriptive phrases).
2. "I strongly disagree with you."
3. "I am angry when you say or do that."
4. "It bothers me that you are using this approach" or "I don't really like that technique (approach, method . . . etc.)."
5. "Will you please call back, I'm busy now."
6. "Would you kindly stop talking during the meeting."
7. "You have kept me waiting for a half an hour."
8. "I hate your attitude (goofing-off, complaining, nonsense)."
9. "I'm sorry, but it won't be possible."
10. "I would rather not say."

Obviously such expressions are more acceptable than browbeating someone with threats and curses, or tying psychological motives to his behavior. Overall, the best strategy seems to be a gut-level response that is tactful, honest, and spontaneous. Although such expressions may fail to accomplish your ends, at least it helps you blow the fuse and clear the air.

It is important to realize that assertion also involves complimentary statements to convey feelings of warmth and appreciation. Some commendable assertions would be:

1. "That was a clever remark."
2. "I think you did a fine job."
3. "I admire your tenacity (talent, skill, etc.)."
4. "That was really well done."
5. "I understand what you mean (feel, say)."
6. "I'm glad we're working on this project together."
7. "I'm glad to see you again."

On the nonverbal side, a firm, warm handshake, a pat on the back, a smile, extended eye contact—all convey good vibrations.

Probably none of these statements present a new thought to you. In fact some of them you may find difficult to say, primarily because of embarrassment. This is especially true of those that concern more interpersonal expressions because they usurp the tough macho figure of society's design (another *learned* attitude). Many people are unaware, or fail to consider, that all humans like to be admired and like to receive favorable attention or even a cubit of recognition. Everyone likes to receive positive feedback for a task well done or a talent well appreciated.

C. Adverse Reactions

Here we stress that assertion involves a risk—make no mistake about it. There will be definite negative reactions from many people. One major reason is that the recipient may be unwilling, or unable, to cope with the definition or the rationale behind an assertive act. Therefore, you should never engage in an assertive action that is likely to punish and cause unpleasant consequences. For instance, it may be unwise to give an unreasonable boss a piece of your mind—unless you are prepared to pay the price. Remember that some people drive to win all the time while others, because of their aggressive nature, may be unwilling to change. Also, timid people may be so shy that their reactions to your assertion may be painfully negative.

In the final analysis, however, a person should do for himself what he feels is in his best interests. Instead of letting other people choose for him, or manipulate him, he should express himself vigorously and in his own interest. In response, the recipient may be disgruntled, and react on a strictly emotional level, indulging in name calling and underhanded techniques. Unfortunately, if the asserter retreats, then it tends to reinforce the nasty behavior of the recipient. The asserter must be steadfast. Remember, if one stands up for his rights, takes a positive stand, in the future the aggressor will be less inclined to be obnoxious. Stated differently, if one backs down in a situation, the aggressive person will be reinforced to repeat his behavior, whereas if one holds his ground, the aggressor may be less likely to initiate hostile actions.

Obviously, one need not be assertive under every circumstance. An individual should decide whether or not to pursue a particular issue. For instance, there are times when it would be best to let an issue die. Suppose someone momentarily loses control and snaps at you. Later he apologizes. Even though your rights were violated, it would be more appropriate to acknowledge the apology and say nothing else.

We now discuss a few adverse reactions you may encounter.

1. Aggression

At times the aggressive recipient of your assertion may become outwardly hostile. He may scream and swear. The wisest strategy is to avoid worsening the condition. You may choose to express regret that he is upset because of your disagreement, but that you feel your position is in your best interests. Remain cool and steadfast. This is vital because if you back off once, then, in future contacts, he will be encouraged to repeat the response. Ignore his reactions. In the long run he will begin to take note of your sincerity, and will adjust to your style.

2. Revenge

Another adverse reaction you may experience is revenge. Possibly a spiteful individual may try to settle the score. As time goes on he may try to make life miserable for you by indulging in unscrupulous activities. The best recommendation under those conditions is to speak with the individual discreetly. Confront him directly with the evidence or with your interpretation of the situation. Tactfully demand that he cease the vengeful tactics.

3. Backbiting

After you assert yourself, a typical retort is a disgruntled complaint: "Big man, big deal!" or "Who does he think he is?" Pay no heed to these childish tactics because to do otherwise would only reinforce the behavior.

4. Overapologizing

Occasionally, the other party may be overly apologetic or humble toward you. Point out that his behavior is unnecessary. In later encounters if he seems overly deferential, you could possibly assist him by suggesting the above methods for more assertive behavior.

We end this section with the comment that *choice* is the key word in assertion. An individual should understand that he can choose to assert himself or not as he pleases, in accord with the setting and the risks. These techniques promise few absolute answers or easy outs for everyone. Many people are happy with their present style; others are reluctant to test any new approach. Each man listens to a different drummer. The choice lies with the reader.

D. Case Studies

As any job progresses, everyone experiences some degree of frustration due to schedules and delays, claims and counterclaims, errors and non-compliances, and accidents and plain bad luck. If all members of the construction team interacted in appropriate fashion, assertively tending his own garden without trampling on another's crop, these frustrations could be weeded out more easily to everyone's benefit.

In order to demonstrate typical conflicts, the available alternative responses, and some probable consequences, we analyze ten case studies below. Although none of these studies, per se, involve a technical difficulty, certainly all entail the people-problem dilemma, which affects the ebb and flow of the progress.

The reader should try to empathize with each situation. Imagine yourself in the same predicament, and examine how you would act with your present behavior repertoire.

Case Study #1

At noontime, your supervisor says he wants you to work late that evening on a special assignment. On this particular night, however, you have a previous social engagement, which has been planned for a number of weeks. Here are some alternative responses:

1. You can say nothing about the engagement and simply stay at work, grumbling to the world at large about such short notice, or "he could have chosen someone else."

2. You can blow your top, shouting: "Who does he think he is? Ruining a good time that I've planned for weeks." "Get someone else," you mumble over your shoulder as you return to your desk.

3. With the appropriate eye contact and gesture, you inform him in a clear, firm voice of your important plans, that you will be unable to stay this night, but that, with sufficient notice, you will be available at other times.

Case Study #2

Periodically a meeting is cursed with a loudmouthed buffoon who seems bent on dominating the discussion. Inside everyone is seething, but no one speaks up. Here are some alternative reactions.

1. You remain silent even though you boil over "with this brain of feathers and a heart of lead." Meanwhile, his avalanche of words buries every constructive idea. Everyone loses. After adjournment, little cliques form, voicing their specific beefs, but none confront the loudmouth.

2. You slam the table, and shout "For God's sake, shut up!" You follow with a tirade of obscenities. Unfortunately, three weeks later, the loudmouth purchases the company that employs you.

3. You explain to the verbose individual that the purpose of the meeting is to discuss everyone's point of view, and that you feel he is getting an inordinate share of the time. Directly but tactfully ask him to limit his discourse so everyone can enjoy equal time. Appeal to his sense of fair play. Be aware that, invariably, you will be supported fully by the group.

Case Study #3

Your superior receives a memo from a colleague unfairly criticizing the method in which you handled a small crisis. After hearing your explanation, your boss dismisses the matter. Nevertheless, it bothers you that anyone would resort to such underhanded tactics. Your choices are:

1. Say nothing, or with a squeaky voice, slumped posture, and averted eyes, protest weakly to the colleague.

2. If he's not too big, you can wait outside in the parking lot. Or you simmer until the office Christmas party; then you confront him head on with a barrage of alcoholic obscenities.

3. Using the proper assertive elements, you can meet the colleague in private. Tell him "I resent that memo. Why did you write it?" Another tack would be to arrange a meeting between the superior, the colleague, and yourself to straighten out any misunderstandings.

Case Study #4

Since each person follows a different biological, or temperamental, time clock, some individuals make a habit out of tardiness. They arrive late for work and engagements and, unfortunately, for conferences. Consequently, each member wastes time that could have been more profitably spent. What alternatives do you face?

1. Live with the problem—and continue to waste everybody's time.
2. Reduce the issue to an emotional level, calling him "a lazy slob, etc."
3. As with the case of the loudmouth, appeal to his sense of fair play. Explain that his consistent tardiness is, in effect, causing considerable hardship and aggravation. Tell him that each member is expected to arrive on time unless delayed by some unavoidable circumstance.

Case Study #5

Another situation involves indecision on a contractor's part. The same problem continues week after week (say uncorrected punch list items). As the owner, you have three general courses of action:

1. Learn to live with the items.
2. Get very upset, and make nasty threats.
3. Explain that the punch list has yet to be corrected. Ask why it has not been resolved. Then state that if no action takes place, you fully intend to bring the issue to higher authority (i.e., upper management, bonding company, etc.).

Case Study #6

In the design phase, the owner queries the engineer about the operating costs of the proposed heating system. In an abrupt manner the architect claims the chosen system is the most suitable. He implies that the owner is meddling. The possible responses are:

1. The owner lets the engineer choose as he wishes.
2. The owner berates the architect, and threatens to terminate the contract.
3. The owner asserts that he fully expects to have the architect/engineer provide sound answers to all his questions.

Case Study #7

The owner, in the working design stage, arbitrarily and sporadically, changes some design parameters, not dramatically, but in small increments that require many revisions in the drawings and specifications. The job captain gets instructions from his accounting section: finish the design before it loses money.

1. The job captain leans on his designers and spec writers to make the many minor revisions. He complains to everyone but the owner, toward whom he feels very hostile.

2. Up to his eyeballs in anger, the job captain tells the owner he is sick and tired of making all these changes. He also tells the owner that he doesn't "know his toe from his elbow."

3. Using the proper behavioral patterns, the job captain informs the owner of the consequences of the many minor revisions. He explains that he will comply with the owner's wishes, but that there will be a charge for extra services (in accordance with the specific contract provisions).

Case Study #8

A sheetmetal foreman (as mentioned in Chapter 1) misses a detail on the plans. The HVAC engineer picks up the oversight. Angrily, the foreman criticizes the design: "Stupid design!" He causes quite an embarrassing scene. The engineer faces three options.

1. Say nothing. Try to ignore the abuse, even though it is scathing.

2. He shouts back, "Can't you read!" He sharply calls him down for failure to see what's in front of his face.

3. He states that he takes exception to the nasty comments. Calmly, he indicates where the detail appears on the plans and specs. Then he requests that the contractor perform the task per contract documents.

Case Study #9

The architect and owner flood the contractor with small, insignificant extras. In the interest of good public relations, the contractor has performed these items at no cost, but the situation is getting out of hand.

1. The contractor mildly complains, but continues to take care of the "freebies."

2. He tells them all bluntly to go to blazes, and watches them sharpen their punch list pencils.

3. He lists all the extras that he has completed to date, explaining his reasons for performing them at no cost. Then he informs them that if their requests continue, he will start filing claims.

Case Study #10

The contractor is involved in a minor noncompliance, say, the quality of paint finish in a small mechanical room. The general shrugs off the issue: "It's nothing." Then he berates the others for nickel and diming him.

1. The architect accepts the item, with the rationale that it is only minor. Yet it bothers him.

2. The architect blasts the contractor. He writes a nasty letter stating that this is a definite noncompliance. Finally, the contractor consents, but he, too, is now very hostile, and he begins to inundate the project with claims. Meanwhile, the owner and architect draw battle plans.

3. The architect shows the contractor the plans and specs, and informs him that the noncompliance must be completed. He tells the contractor that he expects all noncompliances to be corrected promptly in the future.

Of course, the reader can think of other alternatives to these case studies. As a supervisor, you could fire subordinates; as an ex-wrestler, you could throttle people; as a worker, you could find another job. You could blacklist, undermine, call bonding companies, etc.—but at what price, and what consequences? You be the judge.

E. Foundations For Assertive Behavior

If an individual wants to change his style, and weighs the risk/benefit ratio, he may decide to try assertive techniques. He should expect no immediate payoffs. First, he must practice and modify these new patterns. As he begins to be rewarded with good results from his efforts, he will become more comfortable and facile. Therefore, one of the first things he notices is that his new behavior can be self-rewarding, not only in achieving his goals, but in having others pay more attention. People show more respect and recognition. The asserter gets positive feedback, which leads to higher self-esteem. We present the step-by-step process, which the reader can adopt or modify.

Step 1. Identify behavior.   You should be cognizant of those specific situations in which you tend to be aggressive, assertive, or nonassertive. Try vividly to imagine yourself in a particular meeting; try to review your typical responses. Be aware of those components of assertion that lead to maximum effect: eye-to-eye contact, posture, appropriate gestures and expressions, and the content of the message.

Step 2. Observe an effective model.   Watch other members of the construction team and others with whom you have contact. Analyze how they handle situations. Be critical. Note their strengths and weaknesses. In order to gain insight, watch their eye-contact and posture. Listen to their expressions and tones of voice; identify those components that really come across as acutely potent. If possible, discuss "style" with these people.

Step 3. Develop a comfortable style.   With the information gained either by observation or by communication, consider modifications and improvements to suit your style. Try to pinpoint what methods, statements, postures you could implement more effectively. In addition to observing effective models, you should be keenly observant of nonassertive and aggressive behavior. Identify those negative components, so you can avoid them. Again, consider alternative techniques that "fit" your personality.

Step 4. Actual participation.   Once you have identified certain behavior, and have chosen your general approach, watch for an opportunity that almost assures you of positive results. For example, take a minor issue at a conference, and assert yourself. Analzye the responses. Look for other opportunities. Repeat this step as often as possible. Try different approaches and role-playing to gain experience.

Step 5. Feedback.   Monitor the results, especially the positive aspects of your behavior. Review all assertive elements. Was the eye contact steady? Was your gesture emphatic? Was your voice firm? What phrases and language did you use? Observe carefully the consequences of your actions, not only from those whom you directly acted upon, but from other members of the construction team. Sometimes vibrations can be easily read. If possible, get verbal feedback from friends and close colleagues.

Step 6. Reinforcement of behavior.   Once you begin adopting certain methods, reinforce or shape your behavior so that it becomes your normal behavior pattern. It is very important that you reinforce (reward) your style by remembering the purpose of assertion—to gain one's goal, to place self-interest above others if one so chooses to do so. As long as no human rights are denied, this style often results in profits, both physical and psychological: positive feedback, raised self-esteem, confidence, and, of course, the specific goal in question.

THE INDIVIDUAL, CONCLUDED

> *Of all knowledge the wise and good seek*
> *most to know themselves*
>
> Shakespeare

In this chapter, we have discussed considerable psychological research and test data, with construction personnel in mind. We now end the chapter by merely mentioning a few related topics.

A. Irrational Assumptions

Albert Ellis, a psychotherapist, has listed a number of irrational assumptions that he feels many individuals hold to be true. Many of these erroneous hypotheses originate in our environment and our ties to society, which teaches us to value competence and expertise. For example, one notion widely held in our society is that a person must be competent in everything he does. Another irrational assumption, according to Ellis, is the belief that when a person commits an error, it is tantamount to catastrophe—a critical flaw in an otherwise perfect record. To attempt to meet these impossible criteria can only lead to distress and failure. Essentially, Ellis is stating that a great deal of emotional doubt and worry are engendered by these unrealistic criteria. By recognizing the negative consequences of trying to attain such unrealistic standards, however, the individual can change his behavior patterns to be more in tune with reality.

Eight such irrational ideas, which the reader should be able to relate to construction, are examined below.

Irrational Idea No. 1

"It is absolutely necessary for you to be loved or approved by virtually everyone." Obviously if one strives to achieve such an unrealistic goal, the attempt becomes frustrating and self-defeating. A rational person does not sacrifice his own self-interest and desire to this end. On every project, both friendships and adversaries will be established. To expect otherwise is ridiculous.

Irrational Idea No. 2

"One must be perfectly adequate in everything in order to consider oneself worthwhile." This impossibility leads to a sense of inferiority—the inability to lead one's life because of a constant fear of failure. The rational individual strives to do well for his own sake, rather than for others. He resorts to activity; he would rather learn from mistakes than foolishly strive for absolute perfection. In construction, no one person knows it all: design, building, financing, etc.

Irrational Idea No. 3

"When things are not the way one would like them to be, it is a disaster." Obviously, in construction everyone faces conflicts, not all of which can be resolved to everyone's satisfaction. There is no reason why things should be different than they are in reality. Getting upset rarely improves the problem. Often an irrational person avoids getting involved in unpleasant situations. He tries to escape. He fails to admit the problem's existence. A more rational approach is to work at removing or improving the difficulty. Remember: conditions can be disturbing, but they are never catastrophic unless one defines them so. It is never the event—it is how one views the event.

Irrational Idea No. 4

This idea states that "unhappiness is caused by unfavorable circumstances over which one has very little control." An individual should realize that he is not necessarily at the mercy of environmental factors whenever he makes an evaluation. Circumstances can be changed. The intelligent person will realize that, although he may be irritated by, or angry at, external events, he can change his reactions by the way he perceives these events.

Irrational Idea No. 5

This idea concerns the belief that "if something is potentially dangerous, then one should do nothing but continuously dwell upon it." Construction and risk are synonymous. Obviously, everyone risks life and limb, money, or reputation in one fashion or another. If one continuously worries about the possibility of a dangerous event, his energy may be consumed in unnecessary tension. Because he exaggerates the dreaded consequences, he may cause the situation to be worse than it actually is. A rational person recognizes that the potential dangers are seldom as catastrophic as they may appear. Therefore, he can more readily direct his effort to improve the situation.

Irrational Idea No. 6

"It is easier to avoid certain difficulties and responsibilities than to face them squarely." This irrational assumption causes one to assume that avoiding difficulty is easier and less painful than actually remedying the situation. The rational individual does what he has to do. He intelligently avoids unnecessary tasks, but, when he confronts an obstacle, he analyzes the situation and then tries to overcome the obstacle. He recognizes that certain risks have to be taken and, even if an attempt results in failure, the failure should not be construed as catastrophic.

Irrational Idea No. 7

As discussed under assertion, many timid people allow themselves to depend completely on others. "Let someone *stronger* make the decisions."

To some extent we are all dependent on other people. Nevertheless, we should minimize this reliance, for it leads to a loss of independence, equality, and self-expression.

Irrational Idea No. 8

Some individuals believe that "there is always a perfect solution to every problem." There is no such gem as the perfect solution. To attempt to find one can lead only to delay and indecision. The rational person accepts the imperfections of reality. When confronted with a difficulty, he explores various definitions of the problem, develops a number of reasonable solutions, and finally selects the most promising for evaluation.

All these fallacious ideas are embedded in our society. For many people, they are accepted and reinforced by continuous self-indoctrination, and, because they cannot be lived up to, they cause considerable and unnecessary heartache and confusion.

As far as construction is concerned, there has probably never been, or never will be, a large project without difficulty or disagreement. Therefore, one should free himself of these illogical precepts. Unquestionably, he will face unpleasant, controversial situations, but, if he holds a tight rein on his emotions, and perceives the situation in a realistic manner, in all probability he can work out a good solution.

Bibliography

Alberti, Robert E., and Michael L. Emmons. *Your Perfect Right*, 2 ed. San Luis Obispo, California: Impact, 1970, 1974.

Allport, G. W., P. E. Vernon, and G. Lindzey. *Study of Values*. Boston: Houghton Mifflin Co., 1960.

Anastasi, Anne. *Psychological Testing*, 3 ed. New York: Macmillan Publishing Co., 1968.

Bush, Vincent G. *Construction Management*. Reston, Virginia: Reston Publishing Co., Inc., 1973.

Chambers, Edward J., and Raymond L. Gold. *Factors in Small Business Success or Failure*. Washington: Small Business Administration, 1963.

Clough, Richard H. *Construction Contracting*, 3 ed. New York: John Wiley & Sons, Inc., 1975.

Collins, Orvis F., David G. Moore, and Darab B. Unwalla. *The Enterprising Man*. Washington: Small Business Administration, 1964.

Edwards, Allen L. *Edwards Personal Preference Schedule*. New York: The Psychological Corp., 1953.

Goldenson, Robert M. *The Encyclopedia of Human Behavior*, vols. 1 and 2. New York: Doubleday and Co., Inc., 1970.

Guilford, J. P., and W. S. Zimmerman. *Guilford-Zimmerman Temperament Survey Profile Chart*, Orange, California: Sheridan Psychological Services, Inc., 1955.

Hall, Calvin S., and Gardner Lindzey. *Theories of Personality*, 2 ed. New York: John Wiley & Sons, Inc., 1970.

Harrington, Thomas F., and Arthur J. O'Shea. *The Harrington-O'Shea System for Career Decision-Making*. Moravia, New York: Chronicle Guidance Publications, 1976.

Kuder, G. F. *Kuder Preference Record—Vocational*. Chicago: Science Research Associates, 1976, 1951.

Murphy, Richard W., and the editors of Time-Life Books. *Human Behavior—Status and Conformity*. New York: Time, Inc., 1976.

Dictionary of Occupational Titles. U.S. Department of Labor, Bureau of Labor Statistics, 1965.

Roe, Anne. *The Psychology of Occupations*. New York: John Wiley & Sons, Inc., 1958.

Strong, Edward K., and David P. Campbell. *Strong-Campbell Interest Inventory*. Stanford, California: Stanford University Press, 1974.

Terkel, Studs. *Working*. New York: Random House, Inc., 1972, 1974.

Wolpe, Joseph. *The Practice of Behavior Therapy*. 2 ed. New York: Pergamon Press, Inc., 1973.

CHAPTER 5

Group Dynamics

Abstract

As stated by the noted historian, Will Durant, "Almost all groups agree in holding other groups to be inferior to themselves." Although historical in context, the statement applies somewhat to construction, in that all groups, as well as individuals, have self-interests at heart. Each group within the team harbors unmistakable attitudes, needs, interests, and motives. In doing so, it acquires a unique personality, and, to no small degree, it exerts pressure on the individual members to conform with its norms, overt and subtle.

In this chapter, we discuss group processes: leadership, norms, attraction, communications, and cohesiveness—elements found in any group. From social psychology studies, we analyze intergroup conflicts: nature of conflicts, development, escalation, and methods of resolution.

CONTENTS OF CHAPTER 5

GROUP PROCESSES

A. Definition
B. Construction Management and Groups

LEADERSHIP

A. Nature of Leadership
B. Functions of a Leader
   1. Mobilize, Define, Coordinate, and Direct
   2. Maintain Cohesiveness
   3. Maintain Group Norms
   4. Provide a Symbol for Identification and Commitment
   5. Represent the Group to Others
C. Traits of Leadership
D. Types of Leadership
   1. Task-Oriented Leader
   2. Social-Oriented Leader

GROUP NORMS

A. Conformity

ATTRACTION

A. Components of Attraction
   1. Physical Attributes
   2. Intelligence and Competence
   3. Social Behavior
   4. Mental Health
   5. Similarity
   6. Reciprocal Liking

COMMUNICATIONS

GROUP COHESIVENESS

A. Stages of Development
B. Group-Think
   1. Illusion of Strength, Expertise, and Invincibility
   2. Illusion of Solidarity
   3. Pressure Toward Conformity
C. Preventing Group-Think

GROUPS IN CONFLICT

A. Interactions Between Groups
B. How Intergroup Conflicts Develop and Escalate
   1. The Nature of the Conflict

    2. The Past and Present Relations Between Parties
    3. Defining the Problem
    4. Strategies Employed and Contingent Results
  C. Resolving the Conflict
    1. Establish Common Goals
    2. Improve Communications
    3. Utilize Spokesmen
    4. Utilize Third Parties
    5. Fractionate the Problem

QUESTIONS AND PREVIEW

1. Describe some similarities and differences between the O, A/E, and GC/S groups in terms of attitudes, interests, perspectives, and goals.
2. What is the nature of leadership? Functions? Traits? Types?
3. Identify the qualities of a "good" leader.
4. Indicate ways, formal and informal, by which a group influences a member's behavior. Discuss the strength and drawbacks of conformity.
5. List those factors that determine like or dislike for another person.
6. What conditions affect the quantity and quality of communication within a group or between groups?
7. Why is morale so important? Explain how esprit de corps would strengthen a groups's performance. Identify some negative consequences of cohesiveness and high morale.
8. Name common areas of disagreements within the construction team. How do they develop and escalate? What steps can be taken to resolve these differences?

GROUP PROCESSES

It is far easier to know men than to know man

Rochefoucauld

Having investigated the individual, we now focus attention on unit groups and the processes that affect their collective behavior. Every normal human being belongs to a number of organizations, but very few give conscious thought to the psychological aspects of group actions. Usually a person affiliates with others because of a mutual goal (i.e., a labor union, a political party, or a project) or because of fellowship (i.e., a social club or a professional or trade association). Some organizations serve both purposes, goals and good fellowship. In any case, such affiliations, because of rules, objectives, and information disseminated, influence the individual's aims, interests, values, and attitudes (and prejudices). For example, it is reasonable to assume that each group of the construction team (the architectural group, the owner group, and the contractor group) affects each of its members with regard to established objectives, expectations, and policies on a formal level and, more personally, with respect to accepted behavior, attitudes, and, of course, job performance. Each member generally marches in step with the lead drummer, or else he gets fired or ostracized. Every group in construction, in fact any association, calls into play a number of extremely relevant processes: levels of trust, friendship, and esprit de corps; leadership and followership; and effectiveness of communication. Psychologists include these topics under the broad heading of "group dynamics." This, in turn, encompasses two areas of study: (1) training and (2) experimental.

One area refers to training groups (T-groups) and sensitivity training, in which participants interact with one another under the guidance of a trainer. The purposes are viewed as educational—to learn about one's self and one's relationship with others. Specifically the aims are fourfold:

1. To examine one's behavior and to experiment with new modes of relating to others
2. To learn more about human nature
3. To improve (emotionally and effectively) working relations with people in a respectful but assertive atmosphere.
4. To develop skills to resolve disagreements without resorting to coercion, manipulation, or aggression.

To these ends, the previous discussions in the text have attempted to inform the reader of some of the basic definitions and concepts: learning, needs, personality, composite profiles, and assertive techniques.

The other area of group dynamics (experimental) concentrates on the underlying components of group behavior, such as:

1. Leadership types, functions, traits
2. Pressures exerted by the group
3. Attractiveness
4. Communication
5. Development and cohesiveness

This chapter deals primarily with this latter area, and begins with a definition.

A. Definition

Group dynamics is the study of group behavior with special emphasis on the interactions that occur, not only among the members, but also with the surrounding social environment. Kurt Lewin, an authority on this subject, stresses that dynamic studies should not accent the dissimilarity of members but, instead, their interdependence. Admittedly man is a social animal. Through the years he has developed complex networks from small units consisting of a few individuals to large political parties. Our very society relies upon thousands of such networks of one sort or another: legal, institutional, religious, educational, and, closer to home, construction. All these groups combine to strongly influence how a person perceives himself. So strong is this perception that an individual tends to associate or identify personally with the success or the shortcomings of his group. In construction when a project succeeds, everyone inclines to bask in the sun. When the project slides, however, the mud wipes off on all parties.

Referring again to Maslow's hierarchy, many of man's needs can be satisfied only because of certain groups: farmers, truckers, and merchandisers serve to feed the population; police and armed forces provide the needed safety; and the family unit and friends gratify most of an individual's love wants. Higher on the hierarchy, on the self-esteem level, a person's perception of himself is in proportion to the type of reaction he receives from others.

The quality and quantity of feedback help to formulate his opinion of himself. If he receives commendation, his self-image rises. If, however, he catches disapproval and abuse, his evaluation sinks; he sees himself as inadequate, or worthless. At the apex of Maslow's pyramid, self-actualization for many people often hinges on group settings: an architectural award is a complimentary recognition by a board of judges; a promotion or a raise in pay is an expression of approvement from management.

B. Construction Management And Groups

The study of psychology attempts to understand and to predict behavior. If a person can reasonably predict another's behavior, then the chances are favorable that he can coordinate his efforts to accomplish goals more easily in a cordial atmosphere—as opposed to locked-horn clashes in an aura of hostility. What holds true for individuals also holds true for organizations, even more so. Therefore, a basic knowledge of group elements and processes should prove to be an asset. This is especially true in the construction industry where several distinct groups invariably interrelate with each other. Forwarned is forearmed.

The architect, owner, and contractor, each individually, contributes a vital component to the project, whether the simplest possible building or a contemporary wonder of the world. Coordination, cooperation, and communication are absolutely essential. Suppose there were a total lack of communication or little trust among the groups, or, worse, out and out aggression. Without question the project would suffer technically, as well as emotionally. The same result, in proportion, would occur if leadership lacked direction or forcefulness or if members failed to define the roles and duties of each individual or one group unfairly manipulated the others. These processes affect each and every individual, whether or not he is aware of the ongoing persuasive, manipulative, or coercive techniques. From a pessimistic viewpoint, it is emphasized that many people (i.e., politicians and advertisers) do, in fact, understand group behavior. Consequently, they apply that understanding to their advantage, with moderate success, often to the detriment of others. For example, in a construction meeting, one often hears this form of propaganda (bandwagon tactic). "Everybody does it that way! What's wrong with you!" Or two groups may team up to present a formidable "might-makes-right" front against a third group: say the architect joins with the owner in a concerted drive against the contractor—a common situation. Or the most verbal member, Babbitt with a construction helmet regardless of technical ability, may subtly usurp the authority of the formal leader, and, consequently, run the show to his own profit. Such practices occur repeatedly in project after project. Therefore, a basic knowledge of groups prepares construction personnel to recognize when someone is using such tactics. In addition, one may become cognizant of those charismatic but incompetent pied pipers who use glib tongues and persuasive tactics to lead others down the garden path—a basic knowledge of leadership types and tasks certainly adds to one's defensive arsenal.

On the more positive side, construction, with its cost and complexity, drives home the need to work in harmony within the group and with other groups. In fact, our modern society places a premium on one's ability to get along well with others, and rewards such talent. As a mature adult, one must learn to overcome interpersonal obstacles and manage his affairs, especially in business, with facility and discretion. The aggressive individual, whose problem-solving technique consists of ranting and stamping and telling everyone off, in all probability will, one day, perish by a clever sword. It is extremely important that the reader accept the fact that he will face problems, delicate and difficult, and that he must resolve these problems by dealing fair and square with others, on both an individual and a group basis. He must learn the techniques of give and take; he must cope with people of all ages, all types of education and background, and particularly, people with different values, abilities, goals, and roles. We stress again that, although individuals differ, they are also identical—in that everyone has needs they wish satisfied. On the social level, all normal people wish to feel important, to have the opportunity to express opinions, and, at least, to have this opinion treated with respect. Each member likes to think his contribution to the project is relevant and respected. Therefore, whether acting on a group basis or on a personal basis one should recognize that this human commonality (so well expressed in "do unto others . . . ,")" forms the groundwork for communication, cooperation, and coordination. Courtesy may well dictate that one refrain from an explosive, profane attack on another. Yet an inconsiderate remark, a tactless gesture, a crude letter, or a cool indifference to duty may do twice the damage. It is important, therefore, that we mention some critical components that determine a group's behavior.

Realistically, companies and corporations are rarely democracies, in that few members share equally in duties and rewards. One or a handful of officials at the top issue orders to the many workers who form the lower stratum. Most organizations designate a leader and a line of command (often emphasized in the form of a published chart), for, without defined authority and responsibilities, few businesses could survive. Members would act in haphazard fashion. Therefore, the founder (or higher management) appoints specific people to assume the ultimate responsibility for what, when, where, who, and why. The company's long-range objectives are usually decided by the upper echelon; the middle management, foremen, and line workers handle many of the routine matters.

Most companies follow this pattern. As discussed previously, each group in the construction team will usually be organized along these lines. Leaders are designated; they carry certain authority and play traditional scripts, all of which influence their behavior and the collective actions of the group. The subordinates, in turn, also assume certain duties and responsibilities; they conform to major policies and procedures, and compromise with minor ones. Leaders and followers recognize each other's roles in implementing company objectives. Members communicate with each other, grow, and develop to form (possibly) trust and cohesiveness. All the above are somewhat informal in nature, but are critical components in the dynamics of any group. These informalities bear directly on how well the group succeeds in reaching its objective, not only in terms of the final pot of profits, but also in the emotional prices paid along the route. How well members get along with each other in no small way affects the project. For example, in construction, by direct experience alone, one can see that it is much easier to work in a congenial setting with trust, respect, and mutual appreciation of each other's "identity." Distrust, prejudice, and lack of communication or consideration, especially in small groups, lead to discord, too much precious energy being consumed on petty griping and defensive strategies. For better or worse, the quality of leadership holds the key to most of these informal components. Therefore, it is notably imperative that managers, job captains, and directors acquire a firm understanding of these processes.

LEADERSHIP

I carry off the chief share because
I am called the Lion

Phaedrus Fables

For centuries the question of what constitutes leadership has puzzled philosophers. Many schools of thought have attributed special traits to leaders. Others have argued that leaders are a product of their eras; fortunately, they happened to be born at a time that provided fruitful opportunities. With respect to dynamic processes, almost every group distinguishes between the role of a commander and the role of a follower. One could reasonably state that the function of the leader is to modify, direct, and control the actions of a particular group; this is a more or less traditional definition associated with executives, managers, supervisors, and foremen. Psychologists, however, transcend this definition and study leadership from several points of view: the nature of leadership; functions of a leader; traits of leadership; and types of leadership.

Whenever people come together in small groups, whether the membership be political, social, or construction-management, several things occur. With remarkable regularity people begin to exchange ideas, opinions, and interpretations. They interact and influence each other, in positive or negative ways. For example, at a monthly meeting, the architect's job captain may present his views to the contractor's superintendent; in reciprocal fashion the contractor presents his thoughts. Because of this exchange, both affect the behavior of the other in certain ways. Within a particular group, the content and the method by which one communicates influence each member and vice versa. Certain individuals, however, by choice, official or casual, seem to wield a greater dominance over the group, which causes scientists to ponder the question, "What is a leader?"

A. Nature of Leadership

Scientific findings show that different circumstances or situations call for different types of guidance or command. Obviously, many groups have different personalities and functions. Techniques and strategies that are required to direct and control one group may not necessarily work well with another. A boss roofer's approach would in all likelihood fail with an architect's staff. A leader must satisfy the needs of his group. If he cannot provide satisfaction, his influence will diminish, and, consequently, another leader will emerge.

As stated, when people gather together, even in a completely unstructured environment, certain actions take place. People start communicating, and, as they begin to affect each other, sooner or later leaders emerge. Within formal organizational settings, the leadership, in all probability, has been designated to a few individuals. Even in the most informal situations, however, scientists have observed one or two persons rise above the crowd. These individuals usually take over primarily because they participate more than others. Because of this active participation, other people tend to look upon them as the leaders. Apparently the ability to command successfully involves more than a set of personality traits relative to the commander alone. The followers must be considered. One perspective, the leader/follower paradigm, emphasizes the interpersonal transactions between both parties. This concept views the interrelationship as a fluid process among various members. It involves such variables as prestige, legitimate authority, role playing, and the emotional relationship between the group and the leader. Some studies indicate:

1. Leadership implies a social differentiation: to have a supervisor implies the existence of a subordinate. Therefore, consideration of the worker must be perceived in the scheme of things.

2. Leadership also entails a script, whether by random circumstances or by recognized authority. This role can dramatically dictate behavior (and self-esteem).

3. Certain types of behavior are expected of those in charge. A leader is expected to give suggestions and directions, and to exert influence on the actions of the subordinates. He is expected to communicate effectively, to speak with more authority and dominance, and to be more forceful in action. He is expected to be a loyal member of the group, defining and abiding by company policies and procedures—in short, to set a good example for others to emulate. If a manager were to adopt a lackadaisical manner, disobey company policies, perform his duties with inconsistency, subordinate performance would almost certainly follow suit—in any case, morale would suffer. If a boss roofer takes a two-hour lunch break in the local tavern, what productivity can be expected from the roofing crew? When a person occupies a command position, he usually has certain personality traits and needs that put him in that position in the first place. Yet the specific duties at hand often determine how well the traits and needs match the job. In some situations, he may be called upon primarily to complete a task without considering social or likeability factors. For example, a government official in charge of the safety systems of a nuclear plant, or a job captain punching out a project would be expected to uphold strict standards. In another situation, the goal may emphasize the social aspects, say a personnel manager building company morale.

4. Leadership calls for specific drives within the individual (i.e., reasons why one would desire a managerial or supervisory position.) The American way promulgates that a person strive to improve himself—to move up socially and economically. Often management offers both monetary and status rewards. Still, one must pay the piper. One must accept such responsibility that may require extra time and effort and often wears a person down physically and mentally. Many times the leader may be the object of much criticism and hostility, much of it unjustified and based on envy. On the positive side, supervisory positions provide gratification of the monetary needs (more pay); a higher salary improves one's standard of living and satisfies esteem and status needs. Although less profitable, being a subordinate also promises redeeming advantages, many of which depend upon a person's personality. For instance, if one is a follower, he has an easier time emotionally and physically, because he can avoid the extra time or burdens associated with command. Then again, on the negative side, the follower has less status, less money, less control over his environment, and less glory. There exists a balance between the rewards and the costs that each person must recognize and evaluate for himself.

B. Functions of a Leader

A leader's functions can vary widely, depending upon the particular group and the tasks at hand. Nevertheless, many social experts believe that the functions of leadership will entail most of the five duties discussed below.

1. Mobilize, Define, Coordinate, and Direct

The supervisor defines certain goals, establishes and coordinates necessary tasks for the particular members, and helps to prosecute those actions that result in attainment. For example, any construction meeting will find the leaders of each group executing these duties.

2. Maintain Cohesiveness

In maintaining an effective group, a leader will encounter conflicts and clashes between various members of the group. It is the leader's duty to reduce these tensions; to resolve these differences; to try to blend the group into a cohesive unit with maximum esprit de corps. In construction, if such a clash persists, instead of beating heads against the wall, iron out the discord—or transfer the disputants.

3. Maintain Group Norms

A supervisory position calls for disseminating formal policies and procedures, and establishing acceptable (and unacceptable) behavior patterns as well. Not only must the leader insure that all members understand and abide by these norms, he must himself unerringly present a proper model for the others to copy.

4. Provide a Symbol for Identification and Commitment

In times of success the members may attribute a fair share to the leader, and, consequently, may emulate his performance and personality. In good times, upper management may profusely reward the leader with money and titles. In times of defeat and conflict, however, the leader will serve as a scapegoat. Just or not, one bad project can irreparably damage a manager's career.

5. Represent the Group to Others

In this role the leader, whether in fact or by implication, represents the personality (values, goals, motives) of his group. All too frequently he finds himself compromising his values in favor of the objectives of the group: not every contractor or designer admits to errors and omissions. Because his group is committed to profit, he may be coerced to compromise his integrity.

C. Traits of Leadership

Psychologists have investigated what factors produce a leader. Their findings imply that leadership is similar to personality—a combination of factors deriving from heredity and environment. Personality theory warns that, even though a positive correlation may be found between certain traits and leadership in general, the results may prove inapplicable to a particular individual in any number of situations. To further complicate the issue, a leader in one situation may be a follower in another.

Scientists have traditionally examined prominent leaders and their characteristics. One investigator allocated the personality traits most closely associated with effective leadership into the following five categories:

Capacity—verbal facility, ability to judge, intelligence, originality
Achievement—education, knowledge, expertise
Responsibility—self-confidence, motivation, aggressiveness, initiative, dependability
Participation—activity, flexibility, and sociability
Status—social position, economic position, and popularity

Another investigator stated that, although the leadership scripts change as the environment changes, a person who commands under one set of circumstances usually stands a better than average chance of commanding in another situation. This implies that leadership roles do share common elements, found in greater frequency in executives than in followers. Executives often have the following qualities: (1) physical health, (2) intelligence, (3) ability to communicate, (4) social awareness, (5) good adjustment—self-confidence, dominance, sense of humor, responsibility, sociability, and tact.

Other studies confirm that leaders tend to display a cluster of traits: (1) adjustment, (2) extroversion, (3) intelligence, (4) dominance, (5) masculinity, (6) interpersonal sensitivity, and (7) conservatism. Although a person may actually possess all these personality traits, a major criticism concerning the trait perspective is that the environment contributes in no small measure, and must be considered in the analysis. For example, subordinates usually behave differently toward their bosses than they do to their peers. Such respect or deference would affect the manager's self-image, possibly reinforcing those traits such as dominance, achievement, etc. From the environmental vantage, if an individual manifested these traits, the appropriate opportunity must appear before he could apply leadership capabilities. These situational factors are extremely important not only in determining whether or not a person becomes a leader, but additionally how the roles modify the behavior of the manager and subordinates alike. For example, if an executive is high on the pyramid, subordinates may demonstrate their respect by changing their opinions to fall in line with his. Consequently, the executive, given this support from his group members, feels more positive about himself, a reinforcement to his esteem needs. Furthermore, a leader in the prosecution of his functions tends to direct more and to communicate more than others. He influences behavior because of this verbal and written communication. In fact, a person who is *more verbal*, or *verbally fluent*, will more likely be perceived as a leader.

Another situational factor is the size of the group. As the group increases in size, there will be a greater possibility that one or two members will rise to the top. As the group grows larger, the demands and duties of the top executive will grow in proportion, certainly having an impact on his ego.

Crises often illuminate specific traits, or their absence, commonly associated with leadership. In times of crises, certain people tend to be more forceful; they make more suggestions; they have more ideas. Therefore, the group may follow their guidance. In other cases, especially ones posing an internal threat, groups look to strong, forceful command, as opposed to socially oriented guidance. This finding bears out the folk saying "Everybody's a captain on a calm sea."

All in all it is doubtful that leadership can be explained either by traits or by situational factors alone; a combination of both is more likely. Some tasks require certain traits combined with certain situations. A boss laborer requires different traits than those a construction manager needs. Other tasks require special skills that only certain individuals seem to possess. A case in point: a job captain must be technically competent and socially adept, too.

D. Types of Leadership

There is evidence that each situation may call for more than one type of command. For example a study by Bales in 1955 distinguished between two types: (1) a task leader whose orientation was to get the job done as efficiently as possible; and (2) the socially oriented leader whose orientation was to create a verbal, harmonious climate within the group. In one experiment a small group of people were presented a problem. Each member was observed by trained investigators, and was rated according to: the quantity and quality of interactions; giving and taking information; offering and asking for suggestions; advising and receiving; showing agreement and disagreement; tension and antagonism. From this study, two general types of leaders were hypothesized: the task leader, and the social leader.

1. Task-Oriented Leader

In general, this type directs his energy to the problem at hand: he defines problems to his group; he insures that his role is understood; he requires the group to follow standard operating procedures or norms; he expects them to maintain the standards that have been established; he assigns various tasks to the group; and he expects the performance needed to accomplish the objectives. More specifically:

1. He initiates explanations to the membership concerning goals.
2. He defines the problems.
3. He gives facts and requests information. He offers his own suggestions and ideas.
4. He clarifies and presents the alternative solutions.
5. He evaluates and checks on the group progress.

Usually a task-oriented leader does well in a variety of group situations that require skill at organization and the ability to maintain emotional distance. Because his main objective is to accomplish a goal, he often antagonizes people because, in general, they do not like to be directed, especially in a socially oriented setting. He sacrifices likeability for results. In these cases, and more so if he lacks genuine leadership traits, disagreements and hostility become paramount. Trade foremen exemplify the tasks perspective. Their job is to produce the maximum output in the shortest time.

2. Social-Oriented Leader

This type concerns himself with the warmth of personal relationships, the establishment of trust, and the willingness to listen to other group members and to encourage participation. He expresses feelings; compromises; tries to understand the members and appreciate their positions. Specifically, the social leader:

1. Encourages the members of the group; he is warm, friendly, tactful, and respectful.
2. Expresses group emotions and moods; expresses his own feeling; shows regard for the welfare of the members.
3. Harmonizes; tries to reconcile discord and reduce tensions.
4. Offers compromise in his own position, admits wrongs; disciplines himself.
5. Assures that others have their say.
6. Expresses standards that will assist the group to achieve; tries unique approaches to improve group efficiency and morale.

In general, studies have shown or suggested that social leaders are likeable leaders. They perform well in many groups where effective functioning is dependent upon interpersonal relations.

Which of the two types proves more effective? One investigator (Fiedler 1964, 1967) found that task-oriented types were more effective where: (1) good leader/follower relationships existed and either a highly structured task or a strong position of power for the leader, or both combined. Task leaders were also effective when: (2) poor leader/follower relations existed with an unstructured task and low power-position of the leader.

The social leaders were more effective in situations where there were (1) good relations between the leader and the group, an unstructured task, and a weak power position for the leader, or (2) poor leader/follower relations, a highly structured task, and strong power for the leader. Both the task and social functions may be carried out by one person or by different persons. In a particular situation where there is a great deal of hostility toward the leader, or where there are unsettled questions concerning power, values, communications or status, usually the two functions will be allocated to different people. One leader may devote himself to the social aspects of the organization, and the other carries out the task; these are, respectively, a public relations/personal type and a project manager/superintendent type.

If the assigned authority is legitimate, however, and defined by company policy, these two functions may be carried out by the same person. He may carry out a particular task and simultaneously handle the interpersonal relationships of all members of the group. It has been found through study that, in productive companies (and construction management), supervisors work on both functions—the task and the social aspects. These men spend time planning and supervising work and also satisfying the needs of the particular group. In the first sense, when the supervisor is planning and directing the group toward the accomplishment of a particular task, simultaneously, he is involving himself in the social aspect of the group by addressing intergroup relationships, personal problems, and the overall morale of the individual members.

The reader should readily recognize that often the task-oriented supervisor may fare poorly in social circumstances, and vice versa. An aggressive, no-nonsense construction manager in a public relations meeting with a community may unwittingly sabotage a project. Therefore anyone in a supervisory position should differentiate between the nature of the task at hand, and the appropriate approach to gain the best results. (See Box 5.1.)

Box 5.1. EFFECTS OF LEADERSHIP STYLES

There have been a number of experiments to determine the affects of leadership styles on group morale, productivity, and general behavior, a subject of great international and corporate significance. Within any group, and specifically groups in the construction team, it can be observed that the climate set by the leader has a direct impact on performance. As mentioned in Chapter 1, the psychological problems aggravate the technical obstacles, especially in poor leadership areas. Lack of direction, dedication, and assertiveness, or worse, indecision are all factors attributable to leadership. The autocratic project manager suppresses a superintendent's warning; the job captain keeps putting off a decision on a sticky interpretation; the owner's rep gambles away the afternoon at the race track. How can anyone expect a group to constructively function in such a climate? In their classic studies, Lewin, Lippitt, and White (1939) and White and Lippitt (1960) conducted a series of experiments to establish the effects of three styles of leadership: autocratic, laissez-faire, and democratic. The subjects, all young boys engaged in hobby activities, were divided into small groups, equal in quantity and personal and social makeup. During the course of the test, each group was given tasks to accomplish and was directed by adult leaders specifically trained in each style of leadership, described as follows:

1. The authoritarian leader: determined all group policies; directed all techniques and activities one step at a time; frequently criticized the members; refused to listen to suggestions; and remained aloof from group participation except when giving orders.

2. *The laissez-faire leader: allowed complete freedom; remained on the sidelines; took no part in work discussion; offered no comments nor information unless requested; and made no attempt to appraise progress.*
3. *The democratic leader: encouraged and assisted the members in making decisions and assigning the division of tasks; suggested, but did not dictate, procedures; gave objective, helpful guidance when needed; and praised, criticized, and participated in the activities without doing much of the work.*

Each group experienced each type of leadership with these results:

1. *Autocratic. Under authoritarian leadership, the group produced more work, but showed little independence or creativity in their activities. When the leader left the room, the group stopped working. When criticized about the work, the members did not defend it, but responded "He told me to do it that way." The autocratic style produced apathy in some members, and hostility in others, including aggression against scapegoats.*
2. *Laissez-Faire. The effects of complete freedom were less work and inferior quality. With the leader absent, the members goofed off and, at times, became destructive.*
3. *Democratic. The democratic climate resulted in a substantial amount of work, high morale, considerable originality, and little hostility toward the leader or between members. When left leaderless, the group continued its activities. At the end of the experiments 95 percent of the members preferred the democratic leader over the autocrat, and 70 percent chose the laissez-faire over the autocrat. Admittedly, one may argue that the experiment was conducted with youngsters in hobby activities—a far cry from construction management. Still, the implications and generalization are applicable to the adult world: a democratic style of leadership yields the best overall results. This implication holds true for all types of leadership situations, whether one is a partner in an architectural firm or a roofing foreman. Both leaders must produce; if not they are replaced. Yet, the style they adopt to get results is an important factor. For example, consider the options open to roofing foreman. If he adopts the laissez-faire approach, one can be reasonably sure that if he leaves the site on a scorching afternoon, the crew will idle the time away under a shady tree with a case of beer. If he is autocratic, the work will indeed be produced (and appreciated by the roofing subcontractor), but at what cost? Constant vigilance*

and much hostility. A better overall style is the democratic: en-courage ideas and suggestions; give guidance when needed; praise and criticize as appropriate; and build esprit de corps. The work will be done with little interpersonal strife.

GROUP NORMS

We take our colors, chameleon-like from each other

Chamfort

On a moralistic scale, society builds upon the premise that people will adhere to certain laws and rules. To achieve objectives requires that a culture set certain regulations and laws, rooted in those mores, or institutions, that give the individual certain guidelines to follow. Such rules more or less define those aspects of behavior that society holds in esteem and also those that society considers to be maladaptive. If a nation or a culture is to function and flourish, then the majority of citizens or members must share certain kinds of behavior that have been deemed appropriate (i.e., most citizens pay taxes, abide by the laws, etc.). This pressure to abide by the rules begins at birth and continues throughout life, affecting one's value system and, consequently, his overt actions and cognitive processes.

In construction management, obviously, emphasis is on a much smaller group, but this idea of norms and accepted behavior and values applies equally well, if not quantitatively, then qualitatively. Whereas attitudes apply to individuals, norms apply to groups. Norms, or standards by which one's behavior is judged, pressure the individual to think, feel, and act in an expected way. To be effective, in fact relevant, these rules and regulations must be *shared* by the rank and file to a reasonable degree. These shared expectations influence an individual's relations with others by helping the member know what is expected of him and what he should expect from others. The reason group life is orderly and somewhat predictable is partly due to norms. They are like road maps that show members just what is expected of them (i.e., doing one's job competently and being loyal to one's group, which sometimes involves a personal compromise).

Analogous to organization charts, norms are signposts to appropriate behavior, for, without guidance and direction, group behavior could be confusing or, worse, chaotic. If one knows what he is supposed to do and has the compatible means and methods, the norms give him a sense of security and belonging. In fact they can reduce the tensions associated with potentially inappropriate behavior. Collectively, everyone's behavior is somewhat stabilized toward the shared, expected, and monitored criteria of the group. To a large extent, social norms determine how one feels about himself, and how he evaluates whether or not his actions, thoughts, opinions, and attitudes are sound and appropriate to the membership.

Because they establish criteria to guide us, norms influence an individual's perception, how he views both the physical and social aspects of his job; how he thinks; and how he evaluates himself and his behavior. Perceptually these norms determine how he sees a particular situation or event—as we quoted previously, "All looks yellow to the jaundiced eye." If the architect group stresses esthetics, a designer who conforms will probably feel accepted. From the cognizant point of view, norms also affect thought processes. They may influence how a person reasons or how he analyzes and remembers or even how he participates in achieving group goals. For example, if the owner group places a premium on economy, then quality or quantity must suffer. Obviously, this group process exerts considerable force on every member to conform to the collective with special emphasis on goals and methods of attaining these goals. Closer to home in construction, by acute observation, it can be recognized that the norms set by owners, architects, and contractors press and at times coerce members of those respective groups to keep in step. A construction manager may be expected to run a profitable project, even at a cost of absolute compliance with the contract; a job captain is ordered to overlook certain gray-area issues, possibly contrary to his personal esthetics; an owner's inspector may receive an order from his superior to be adamant on certain issues possibly because of a past grievance. Ethically questionable or not, these are all facts of life in the construction business. Each group wields a threatening club over the members; the price of nonconformity or disobedience may well be termination. It has been found that many people evaluate their level of performance by referring to the group with which they identify and the shared standards of acceptable action (inclusive of roles to be played, enthusiasm, abilities, interests, and viewpoints). Be aware that each group on the construction team judges by different standards, a vital point that should be recognized by everyone in construction. Of course, norms must be set within the range of reasonable behavior. Also, they must allow considerable latitude for individual differences. Otherwise, members, depending upon their particular preferences and pride, would disobey the rules to the detriment of the collective cohesiveness. We again emphasize that norms must be shared—members must agree that they are acceptable.

The strength of a norm's influence depends positively on several factors:

1. The group is a highly cohesive group—high morale, enthusiasm, dedication, etc.

2. The norm is highly relevant, reasonable, and steadfast.
3. Each and every member understands: the group criteria; accepted and rejected behavior; and the duties, responsibilities, and roles each member plays.
4. The group serves as a gratifying (or threatening) force in the individual's career or life style.

Under such conditions, the probability is high that people will conform to the collective.

A. Conformity

In a stable organization most people conform; in fact, some rigid individuals (or company men) obey so unflinchingly that they exceed the normal definition of loyalty. At the other extreme, there will invariably be those who refuse to march in step. If this nonconformity becomes too objectionable, pressures may mount until employment may be terminated. (Thoreau would find little welcome on a construction team.) Everyone who works for a living somewhat banks the fires of his independence and complies with convention. In essence, this bowing to convention strengthens the solidarity of the group, although such pressure can also cause adverse effects. So important are these effects that there has been considerable study in this area. It is believed that individuals often conform because of fear of group disapproval in the form of criticism, rejection, and banishment. This pressure to conform usually begins in childhood, and carries throughout our lives— from school, teachers, peers, classmates, and, finally, from society's institutions, and very much so from the construction groups. From a thousand angles and sources, these rules and regulations, all geared to check and modify his behavior, bombard everyone.

Therefore, for one's sanity and peace of mind, he should examine questionable norms and their roots with a keen eye. Are the collective goals and rules reasonable or tolerable? As explained earlier, Albert Ellis, psychotherapist, asserts that too often rules and pressures become irrational assumptions so ingrained that they hinder personal development. Is it an absolute necessity for a person to be loved and approved by virtually everyone? Must one be thoroughly competent in every possible task to be considered worthwhile? When things go wrong, is it always catastrophic? No, a resounding no to all these questions! Yet, for many people, those beliefs become almost gospel. In fact, so strong is the desire to be loved and accepted in our society, that one may sometimes seek approval from a complete stranger, or agree with a stranger's judgment even though the situation contradicts the individual's perception.

There have been a number of experiments that dramatized the influence of a group judgment. A classic experiment done by Asch in 1951 pitted an individual's unmistakable perception against the perceptions of other people. All subjects were asked to judge the length of a line. (Group members were secretly instructed to give an incorrect length.) The result was that, even though the individual knew the length was correct, he voted with the majority. In additional repeat experiments, even those individuals who opposed the group's judgment felt anxious. This demonstrated that merely asserting a contrary opinion is so unpopular that some people conform to the majority view, even though what they see is not in agreement with what they have stated. From a more constructive viewpoint, it is acknowledged that norms regulate a person and give him solid reference for appropriate behavior. In addition, they provide psychological comfort and security to each member and, consequently, solidify the group effort. When members abide by the shared conventions (i.e., loyalty, dedication, trust, etc.), the group in toto functions more effectively. A closed fist is more powerful than five open fingers. Conformity has its place, but sometimes the desire for convention goes beyond one's better judgment. To be sure, conformity is certainly an easy way to get along, and for many people it is a congenial way as well. As implied by Asch's experiments, however, it can operate in ways that adversely influence a person's judgment, especially when the condition is unclear or ambiguous, encouraging that person to opt for the majority opinion. With this said, the reader should recognize the fallacy inherent in the bandwagon tactic in propaganda: "But everyone does it that way!" So what! A majority choice is not necessarily the right choice.

ATTRACTION

A good face is the best letter of recommendation

Queen Elizabeth I

Another informal aspect of group dynamics concerns attraction between people. Why does a person like or dislike another? This is a very important question especially in light of the fact that individuals who admire and respect each other interact more efficiently than out-and-out enemies. It is certainly pertinent to understand how people perceive one another and how a person generates hostility or attraction. When we meet someone, we usually go beyond the information our senses receive. Simultaneously we engage in acts of judgment based on self-characteristics that we feel influential. For example, suppose an individual values intelligence very highly, then likely he would view an intelligent person as an attractive person, even to the degree of overlooking obvious negative qualities. At the other end of the scale, if a person has a trait that one holds in low esteem (even on a prejudicial level) that person would tend to be disliked. A robust, aggressive plumber may hold in contempt an effeminate, sensitive designer who wore shoulder-length golden hair. Why? Different value systems. All human beings require some close personal friends to feel secure, worthwhile, and mentally comfortable. Therefore, if one achieves positive feedback from his interpersonal relationships, he will have higher self-esteem. On the other hand, if one gets negative reaction, he tends to feel rejected and to have a lower self-esteem, which, in turn, hinders his performance. All in all, the more attractive and congenial the group is, the likelier each member will share the norms and perform acceptably within their limits.

A. Components of Attraction

Because of the distinct importance of group morale, attraction and liking have been targets of many industrial and social psychology studies. Experimental results suggest several reasons why people like or dislike others, and we will discuss six of them here.

1. Physical Attributes

It seems undemocratic and superficial, but research indicates that physical appearance plays an important part in how a person is evaluated. In fact, because of stereotypes, one tends to identify physique with "associated" traits. Often an architect is perceived as slight of build and more inclined to intellectual "looks," whereas a construction worker is perceived as stocky, square-chinned, aggressive, and athletic. Good looks seem to be very important in evaluating someone. Unfortunately, if one is handicapped or disabled, prejudice and nonacceptance may be his lot.

On a basic, practical level, one can do little to alter his inherent physical appearance. However, it would seem reasonable that a person who dressed well, kept a neat and clean demeanor, stood erect, and projected a confident, energetic manner, would be making himself more attractive. As stated before, it is important to realize that truth and expertise sometimes come in strange packages: the laborer stuttering in broken English may speak more truth than the grandest of architects, Biff Woodsley, polo star and graduate from Harvard School of Design.

2. Intelligence and Competence

Society traditionally and justifiably places high value on intelligence. (The surest way to gain an enemy is to call someone stupid in public.) Therefore, intelligence is considered an asset to social attraction, as long as the intelligence is neither too high or too low. Brilliant people, especially non-conformists, are sometimes viewed as oddballs, and are not readily accepted. Slow people, especially if they behave in socially inappropriate ways (showing clumsiness, poor coordination or extreme shyness) are often disliked. Related to intelligence is competence. Although some studies indicate that those with the best skills and ideas are not necessarily the best liked, competence does indeed seem to be a cause for liking. Because of mixed results, probably the optimum is to be facile but not so perfect as to cause envy and hostility. The practical lesson: be smart and competent, but not to the extreme.

3. Social Behavior

A person is rated as attractive who exhibits interpersonal behavior that is supportive and helpful to others. If a person is aggressive and quarrel-some—an Ivan the Terrible—naturally, the reaction he receives is that people dislike and will probably try to avoid him. This carries back to one's perfect right to be assertive but appropriately so. As we saw for someone very timid and shy, chances are that people may not react favorably, and may often overlook his positive qualities. The same appears to hold true for laziness and laxity to duty. Therefore, be energetic, dedicated, and as-sertive, leaning neither toward aggression nor timidity.

Note that in construction management, the job situation represents only one aspect of a person's totality. His social behavior may be completely different from the behavior he exhibits at work. If one knows that he is being judged by another person, he puts on a good front and tries to project a favorable impression. Therefore, true character may not always be evident. For instance, and this is especially true in political circles, many impressive maneuvers are deliberate attempts to create good public relations.

4. Mental Health

Hand in glove with social behavior is mental conduct. If a person is well-adjusted and has a high opinion of himself, there seems to be a strong probability that he will be accepted and liked by his peers. Adversely, if a person is maladjusted, defensive, hostile, and unstable, people usually dislike him. In essence, reasons for liking another are enhanced when he is physically attractive, coordinated, skilled, outgoing, socially effective, intelligent, and very stable. This is like a vicious circle, for it seems everyone loves a winner.

If people like a person it enhances his self-worth, which, in turn, reinforces him. Unfortunately, if one has a poor self-image, people do not readily accept him, thereby reinforcing inferiority feelings. A point to ponder: try to keep an even keel; avoid blow-ups and tirades of curses. Sure, anger is normal, and erupting volcanoes of sputtering curses and threats somewhat release the internal pressures, but in the coolness of afterthought, such behavior accomplishes little except to display one's immaturity and lack of leadership abilities.

5. Similarity

People are predisposed to like those with whom they can identify and associate. Generally ethnic and religious similarities play a major role in the racial and social development of many friendships. Studies show that a strong reason for attraction between two persons is the similarity of their beliefs, values, attitudes, and other characteristics. As aptly stated by the proverb, "Birds of a feather flock together." People are inclined to like those who agree with them. For instance, a group member who more or less conforms, who acts and behaves and maintains the proper attitude toward the norms, will in general be accepted and liked much more than the out-and-out rebels. Those who break the norms, have dissimilar values, and rock the boat stand a fair chance of being punished or avoided.

As with mental health, self-fulfilling prophecies exist. If one is liked, he receives favorable attention that, essentially, rewards and reinforces his behavior. Therefore, he continues to hold certain beliefs or attitudes until they become a habitual part of his personality.

A practical observation: most people like to be liked; therefore, if a group norm rewards a certain value or attitude, any normal individual may find it more profitable or expedient (consciously or otherwise) to adopt that attitude. This is one reason why members of each group (O, A, GC) of the construction team may be so inclined to adopt the values, goals, and means of the particular group to which they belong.

6. Reciprocal Liking

If a person likes someone, it usually shows, and studies indicate that liking leads to reciprocity. A case in point: if one likes himself first, emanates warmth and sensitivity, along with the collage of the attributes previously cited, in all probability he will be liked and respected.

COMMUNICATIONS

*What would the science of language be without
missions*

Max Müller

Much of the decision-making in our world depends upon small groups communicating in one form or another. It is the method by which a person shares his thoughts, verbalizes his feelings, expresses his opinions, conveys his ideas, and transmits knowledge—the process by which he tries to influence others. Without communication civilization would spin into a spiral of confusion and chaos. No wonder why this topic occupies a prominent position in social psychology research. Unfortunately, communication is one of the least understood features of the group processes. It can be said with confidence that in positive group settings (inclusive of cohesiveness and trust) there is usually a great amount of dialogue and feedback between members, primarily because there is trust, empathy, and understanding. People are essentially interacting with those they like, respect, and can work with. At worst, communicating in an atmosphere of trust eliminates many defense mechanisms, for if a person mistrusts another, his suspicion leads to inhibition of open, honest exchanges. The interaction becomes, then, a game of strategies and subterfuge. By direct observation of many meetings, it should be evident that cohesive groups more likely produce best results, other factors (abilities, motivations, values, etc.) kept constant. Usually, in these settings, people understand their roles; they have specific tasks and goals; they have a good working relationship with people; and they share the norms and objectives of the group. Even though disagreements and conflicts may surface, dialogue continues. Of course, we do not imply that the message is always understood. Frequently the opposite occurs, leading to not only misunderstanding, but perhaps dislike, even hatred.

With respect to formal information theory, communication always involves a transfer of energy, a transfer of information, which is defined as any message that reduces uncertainty. The systems involved are always made up of five basic parts:

1. the source of the message (say the sender's brain)
2. the transmitter that converts the information into the form of a coded message (i.e., the human voice)
3. the channel of transmission (i.e., the air that carries the sounds)
4. the receiver (i.e., the recipient's ears)
5. the destination (the receiver's brain)

Regardless of whether the mode is speech, gesture, writing, mechanical or electrical devices—these components are involved. Research has pinpointed a number of variables that influence the nature of communication: the physical and emotional climate of the exchange (trust versus hostility); the state of sender and receiver (ill, angry, etc.); nonverbal factors (tone, gestures, even seating arrangement), and, of course, the message itself.

Certainly the roles of the speaker and the listener lend weight and, at times, credibility to the message. If the speaker has expertise, authority, prestige, a pleasant appearance, a good voice, and attractive social traits and mannerisms, social research indicates that these factors have a direct bearing on the persuasiveness of the content. In addition, the personality and role of the receiver also affect the interpretation of the information. All these elements will be discussed in the next chapter. Here, we merely observe that if a person is unable to convey or receive information correctly, he is seriously handicapped. This is especially so in construction, where we have inherent communications problems. The architectural group (including designers, engineers, and spec writers) prepares the documents. The contractor and his subs then interpret these plans and specifications. If there is a misunderstanding or a misinterpretation, it will certainly lead to money lost on the job. Sometimes this condition is not readily accepted by many businessmen, with the inevitable result: noncompliances and corner-cutting.

As a job progresses, undoubtedly those shades-of-gray problems will arise, calling for clear communication in speech and listening—not quite as simple a proposition as one may assume. For thousands of years, in all corners of the earth, man has consistently misunderstood his fellows, triggering tragedy and war as a consequence. Therefore one should appreciate the active effort that is required in the process of transmitting information. Different words carry various connotations for different people.

GROUP COHESIVENESS

By uniting we stand; by dividing we fall

John Dickinson

By way of definition, cohesiveness is considered to be the result of all the forces and processes that act upon the members of the group. These underlying elements work simultaneously to influence how a member feels about the group, his sense of identity with other members, and his feelings of participation and belonging. All those processes previously discussed play a vital part in solidifying the members (i.e., leadership, norms, attraction, and communication).

There is general agreement among psychologists that groups differ in this sense of trust and belongingness. High morale members participate more, show more loyalty, uphold the standards with much more vigor, and value the group to the extent of defending it against internal and external threats. Under such favorable circumstances, individuals are prepared to tolerate upsets and disagreements, consuming most of their energy in achieving the shared objectives instead of useless bickering. When an individual feels a sense of belonging, he will often override his personal preference for the collective good (or because of internal pressure).

From a number of experiments, scientists generally have observed some specific consequences of this cohesiveness. Members will:

1. Try harder to influence other members.
2. Be more flexible to the input from the group.
3. Be more willing to listen; be more accepting of others.
4. Have a greater sense of security and relief from tension—consequently, have more trust.
5. Participate more readily at the meetings and functions.
6. Protect the shared norms and exert more pressure on those who deviate from these standards.
7. Be less susceptible to disruption if a member terminates or leaves the organization.

Research in industrial organization has shown the importance of cohesiveness concerning morale and productivity. Psychologists have positively correlated it with the productivity of a work unit; namely if the norm of the unit was to produce efficiently, and if cohesion existed production rose. (On the negative side, it was also found that some groups propagate negative norms, which consequently pressure people to perform less.)

It is common knowledge that construction workers not only work together, but also associate with their peers socially. Again quoting the crane operator in Terkel's *Working**

Oh yeah, every union has a clique. I don't care what union it is, their own people are going to work more. I mean their brothers and their son and such like that. And as the machinery gets more complicated, you have to learn how to read them. Somebody has to teach you. But if you're just another person and have no pull, why then you're not gonna have an opportunity to learn it.

You're tense and most everybody'd stop and have a beer or a shot. They'd have a few drinks and then they'd go home. They have a clique, like everybody has. Your iron-workers, they go to one tavern. Maybe the operators go to another one. The carpenters go to another place. They build buildings and tear 'em down in the tavern.

And the same could be conjectured with respect to architects, engineers, and other construction people, only probably to a lesser degree.

A. Stages of Development

We should recognize that groups, like individuals, proceed through developmental stages as they mature. As theorized in Erikson's personality theory, all humans pass through a period of emotional development. Through life one faces certain problems, and before one can reach another level of maturation, he must resolve these problems successfully. Thus, psychological growth can be viewed as both sequential and successive. Each stage follows another in time. The solution to problems in one stage depends upon the resolutions made in previous stages. Analogously, groups also must pass through successive stages as they develop. In fact, psychologists identify four distinct stages of development.

Stage One.   At the initial meeting, impressions are being formed; members tend to seek a secure place. Each member may be reticent, fearful of presenting a poor image, anxious about being rejected. Therefore, people tend to go slow and to put their best foot forward. For example, ordinarily this will be the case when an individual first joins a company or attends his first construction meeting.

Stage Two.   Once a member feels he is part of a group, then patterns of influence begin to develop. Members begin to form into cliques having common interests and values. Leadership begins to emerge, along with patterns of communication. The group begins to devote itself overtly to the specific tasks at hand, and covertly, it moves to maintain the social aspects of the membership.

Stage Three.   In this stage, there is considerable communication. There is planning, evaluating progress, and resolving problems and discord. Members learn to accomplish duties, to play certain roles, and to socialize with others.

Stage Four.   In the final stage, cohesiveness and trust develop to the point where members gradually feel that they have a common bond. There is an increase in mutual trust, a submergence of individual differences, esprit de corps, and, consequently, a strong commitment to achieving the collective objectives. Although each of the above processes have been studied with respect to a particular group, their applicability to the construction team appears promising. In construction management, if all groups work in an aura of trust and respect, then, even with their inherent differences and goals, in a spirit of cohesiveness, any project will run more smoothly.

All the processes operate not only on each group, but on the team as well—leadership, norms, attraction, communication, and cohesiveness. Psychologically, discord begins with the failing of any process: ill-defined or poor leadership; ineffective norms, whether because of ambiguity, irrelevance, or disregard; on a personal level, dislike for any reason; and misunderstanding or deceit.

It may be true that a project can be completed without a successfully developed team, but it is equally true that with team cohesion the project could be completed more profitably.

Understanding these processes can lead to a more beneficial exchange within the group, and the team as well. One should appreciate that in each faction of the construction team (O, A, GC) many common features are shared: a leader; some sort of structure; certain norms; attractiveness; and a sense of purpose. But a major feature is that it is to everyone's benefit to work on a project with a minimum of people problems. Finally, an understanding of dynamic processes prepares one with a knowledge of how to identify and avoid the pitfalls of group-think.

B. Group-Think

Even though a group may be fully mature and have an impressive degree of expertise, able leadership, realistic norms, and solidarity, often it fails to make wise decisions. Its own brilliance blinds its members to the obvious. This condition has been termed "group-think,"—the stifling of realistic judgment because of in-group pressures. Consequently, the membership makes faulty decisions because it considers itself infallible. As a result of high morale, intelligence, and dedication, the group may insulate itself from any opposing viewpoints or criticisms. Although the term was originally applied to foreign policy decision and fiascoes (i.e., the Bay of Pigs invasion), the concept applies equally well to construction management or to any organized group. In a study done in 1972, a social psychologist named Janis took exception to the social scientist's assumption that cohesiveness and dedication to purpose were the primary badges of a healthy and proficient group. He emphasized that this united and positive esteem held by the membership often caused them to stifle, if not ignore, criticism and disagreement. Consequently, only a collective "we-are-so-good, we-can't-be-wrong" atmosphere pervaded every decision.

As stated previously, conflict and disagreement on an eye-to-eye level often result in improvement. When the disagreement remains on the surface, i.e., no vital energy is wasted in a guerilla warfare of bickering and backbiting, a healthy group can, and should, tolerate differences in opinion. When cohesiveness, high morale, and norms reach such heights that members feel reluctant to voice dissenting opinion and consequently "go along" with the colleague's "expertise," however, they become victims of groupthink. Janis identified several symptoms, discussed below.

1. Illusion of Strength, Expertise, and Invincibility

This occurs when members are overcome by a pervasive sense of superiority and strength, so much that they actually believe themselves infallible. Construction history is full of accounts of the follies of world renowned experts. The Tower of Babel must have required considerable public relations, before and after the fact. As another example, suppose a group of eminent architects was assembled to design a certain structure. Obviously, a sense of superiority would influence their collective behavior. Who would be bold or impertinent enough to criticize such a panel of experts? Still, civilization and progress thrive on the boldness of the innovators and critics—as witnessed in the history of invention.

2. Illusion of Solidarity

Because of a sense of unity and the high respect members may have for each other, an individual may be reluctant to oppose such a formidable collection. Also, such an expression of disagreement may be ignored or glossed over by the majority. All too often in construction meetings, might (majority) means right, not, unfortunately, always yielding the best results. Despite that, this type of collective decision-making frequently occurs, probably because there is safety in numbers. Instead of "I decided" it is much more secure to cop a "we decided." "We signed off the plans" is preferable to "I signed off the plans."

3. Pressure Toward Conformity

In a high morale, solid setting, a dedicated individual may be reluctant to deviate from the majority or the shared expectation. He may so like or respect the others (or feel subtly intimidated) that he chooses to keep in line even though, internally, he may still hold reservations.

The risk of ridicule may also dictate conformity. For example, the vice president of a contracting firm, a powerful and persuasive figure, decides to bid a questionable job with the expressed intent of using a revolutionary method to build the structure. Everybody rants and raves about what a great idea it is and the profits that will be realized. Everyone, that is, except a new resident engineer. He holds a strong belief that the standard method is better. Yet, who is he, so he rationalizes, to challenge his colleagues, especially the vice president, an expert in construction. If he argues long and loud, he will be pegged as disloyal, an outcast, and possibly an unemployed outcast. So he bites his tongue and stands mute in Rome with the other Romans.

C. Preventing Group-Think

A number of preventive measures are suggested to alleviate, if not prevent, the influence of conformity and group-think. (In the chapter on creativity, this concept will be analyzed more thoroughly.)

1. A devil's advocate role should be assigned to various members. They should be instructed to air criticism, objections, and disagreement. The leader, as well as all other members, must support and reinforce this vital task. For example, when exploring a design or bid proposal, or solving any problem, the advocate should question, challenge, critique, and dissect these collective decisions. He must stress the necessity of an uninhibited forum. Often such an approach leads to a more rational decision, and more so instills confidence in the group process, especially when members can safely express their doubts and misgivings without fearing intimidation.

2. The leader, especially the aggressive taskmaster, should be cautious when initially defining a problem or objective. He should limit his preferences at the outset, for they often influence the members. Instead, he should strive to maintain an open, inquisitive atmosphere of active give-and-take among all individuals. Such participation encourages more alternatives on which to make the final decisions. In brainstorming sessions to develop new ideas, it may be more prudent for the leader to be absent, thus bypassing another opportunity to press for conformance and convention.

3. In the interest of diversity, the group can be subdivided into separate units (including different leaders and devil's advocates) to work on the same program. Later these units can converge to present their findings and recommendations and to forge the final solutions. For example, an owner's organization, in planning a new building, may find it fruitful to assign two or three committees to submit independent programs. Later each program can be modified and assimilated into the final plan.

4. At times, independent consultants, or other qualified members within the organization but outside the immediate group, should be invited to

offer their input for critique and consideration. The role of the "critic" may prove extremely effective in thus stimulating original discussion. Such a technique ensures new ideas and insights, especially if the individuals are beyond the normal sphere of conforming pressures. Under certain circumstances, it may prove worthwhile for a contractor to call in outside assistance to help him resolve a technical problem.

5. When dealing with an outgroup, especially in a conflict situation, one often does well to analyze the problem from their vantage. In this way, one can often anticipate the opponent's intentions and strategies, thus preventing surprises at the actual meeting.

GROUPS IN CONFLICT

> *In victory the hero seeks the glory,*
> *not the prey*
>
> Sir P. Sidney

Up to this point the chapter has emphasized the single group and the related proceses that affect its behavior. As presented, considerable research has indicated the important influences that organizations have on the personality and self-esteem of the members. Cohesiveness, trust, and high morale are all signs of a healthy and essentially effective group. At times, however, stringent norms and blind loyalties can exert such extreme pressures that certain individuals conform to authority even when the demands oppose one's values and beliefs.

In construction management, there are at least three groups on any one project—in a "typical" scheme of things the owner/reps, the architects/ engineers and the general contractor/subcontractors all contract to complete the job. As noted, each of these parties may have a unique leadership style, a potpourri of personalities, and different attitudes and values in reaching its goals. This special collective identity often causes friction within the construction team. Therefore, it would seem reasonable, if not prudent, to investigate how a knowledge of dynamic processes can be applied to the interrelationships between various groups. A few questions seem relevant. What factors stimulate cooperation (or hostility) between groups, say the owner (O) and general contractor (GC), or between the A/E and GC/S? What effects do these interrelationships have on the individuals in each organization? Most critically, what techniques can be utilized to spur harmony, respect, and the three Cs—cooperation, coordination, and communication? As stated in the major premise of the book, each project faces certain technical difficulties. These problems can be either minimized or distorted out of all proportion by the personalities involved, the methods used to attack the situation, and the overall rapport between the factions. If the people problems are held in check, the project runs smoothly, and, therefore, tends to reinforce the positive interactions. If personalities lock horns, however, or rival leaders toe the line, obviously unfortunate consequences will result. One side may attempt to inflict injury on the other side—monetary/reputation/psychological (i.e., the endless punch list, assassination of reputation, numerous criticisms and innuendos). Lines of communication may be closed, or misused to either "knock" the opponent or blow the problem all out of proportion in Chicken Little fashion. Additionally individuals may be subtly influenced, so as to stereotype and disparagingly highlight the differences between each party: "us" versus "them"; "we" are experts—"they" are know-it-alls; "we" are efficient—"they" are cheapskates; "we" believe in fair compromise—"they" are grabby.

Often one may generalize from a single experience to indict "all architects" or "those owners" or "every contractor." As discussed in personality theory the inherent danger in such generalizing is that prophecies tend to be self-fulfilling. If an individual is considered deceitful, he will be treated with suspicion, thereby causing him to respond with the very behavior that was expected in the first place. Even if the opponent made conciliatory efforts, trying to establish an atmosphere of trust and congeniality, an overly suspicious group would attribute these attempts to questionable ulterior motives and, therefore, would squelch the friendly gestures. Reasonable trust appears to be a necessary condition in any successful encounter. For years social psychologists have tried to uncover those causes that lead to the development and escalation of conflicts between groups. We will discuss the results of their findings next.

A. Interactions Between Groups

Dynamic processes, formal and informal, offer keen insights into how one can understand and reasonably resolve intergroup conflicts and disagreement. Various social scientists have extrapolated the knowledge gleaned from small group study to interrelationships between political parties, associations, and even nations. In this book the extrapolation is further modified to focus upon the construction team. Although this extension may appear questionable, it is apparent that most decisions and interactions in construction (and even on a national level) are made in small settings.

Typically most construction meetings are held with only a few select representatives seated around a conference table or huddled over a planning board. It would be highly unusual, if not impossible, to have *all* members of each faction in the construction team attend every meeting. Chaos would result. Normally a few key members, representing the interests and attitudes of their organizations, will suffice to handle most situations.

Realistically speaking, because the architect represents the owner, the two often join together to present a unified front against the general contractor and subs. For example, the owner may feel that a higher quality of concrete finish is required; therefore, he notifies the architect who, after interpreting the plans and specs, may side with him. Together they argue the case. The contractor will perceive the finish from a different vantage, however. Higher quality means higher costs, hence less profits (on a lump-sum bid basis). As a consequence, a disagreement exists, which must be remedied by a few select personnel. Obviously, the case presented is somewhat ambiguous. If a definite noncompliance has occurred, by law the contractor must correct the deficiency, or else the courts will be required to settle the dispute. Neither side wins in a court case, however. It was emphasized at the beginning of the book that primary focus will be on those garden variety types of problems—the shades of gray issues that call for a little give-and-take on everybody's part. Remember that if a contractor fails to install the roof or the engineer misses the total plumbing system or the structure collapses or some other catastrophe occurs at a cost of hundreds of thousands of dollars, the case will undoubtedly wind up in court. There is absolutely no possibility of negotiating in a trailer. It becomes a legal issue to be handled as seen fit by the lawyers and higher management.

Another important point to consider in any interaction is the moral or psychological climate. If either side is totally committed to steal or cheat or intimidate or come across like Attila and the Huns, then nothing stated in this discussion (or anywhere else) is going to change that deviant philosophy. Barring that type of behavior, we assume that all parties, although striving to reach their particular goals, act in relatively good faith. We further assume that the issues involved are reasonable in cost, as well as essentially nonlegal in nature, and that each party is willing to compromise and to trust the other—up to a prudent point. For example, suppose, from a disinterested point of view, the concrete finish was borderline. With marginal effort on the contractor's part, the finish could be touched up to be acceptable under normal standards. It would seem that a compromise could be reached: if the contractor cleaned up the finish, then architect and owner could subdue their esthetic drives and settle for less than a masterpiece. No one wins 100 percent, but then again no one loses 100 percent. Now suppose all three groups distrusted each other, even hated each other, to the extent that no one would budge an inch. What would be the probable outcome? Arbitration? The courts? In either case, all parties would lose: the owner might not get what he wanted; the contractor might lose money;

the architect might suffer a damaged reputation. Unquestionably, each would lose something in time, money, and emotional aggravation. This is a no-win situation that could be avoided if all parties understood the basics, which play a crucial role. If each were willing to cooperate and to settle for less than 100 percent, then probably everyone could gain, or at least minimize the losses.

Whenever two parties (or companies, races, nations, etc.) meet on a business or diplomatic basis, one point should stand paramount in everyone's mind: except for a few benevolent billionaires, no one is a philanthropist. Expect neither favors nor quarter. Each side is there for one purpose: to maximize profits or gains. These profits are usually monetary. A contractor may demand a change order for what he considers "extra work"; a subcontractor may argue for a less costly piece of equipment to be substituted for an "or equal." Gains can also be psychological. As inferred from Maslow's hierarchy, an architect may stress higher quality in order to create a gem and fulfill his need to self-actualize; a union negotiator may strive to increase his esteem by winning a "sweetheart" deal from management. In any case, the name of the game is to win. On the other side of the coin, if a group cannot win, at least it tries to minimize the losses, again usually money, but reputation as well. Rare is the human being or group who wants to lose face, to look stupid, or to be labeled "Mickey the Dunce."

When two sides confront each other, certain explicit or implicit considerations should remain supreme in everyone's mind. Each party should acknowledge that, as with the individual, their rights and interests come first, as long as no other person or group is denied its rights. Therefore, on a collective level, assertion is called for—along with a recognition and appreciation of what factors are interacting. Members see each other and the opposing members in a way dependent upon the nature of the problem and the rapport between the parties. If one faction perceives and evaluates the other side in a favorable manner, then individuals may be influenced to respond likewise (via norms and the effect of leadership). For example, suppose the owner's management has a strong friendship with a particular architectural association, or the contractor was the governor's brother-in-law, then it could be assumed that the attitudes of the owner's inspectors would be somewhat toned down. This is not to say that all personalities will mesh compatibly; that is highly unrealistic. Yet, under these circumstances, the tendency to do so is apparent. If one side acts hostile, however, and poses a threat (tangible or psychological), then loyalty and forceful leadership become salient as the membership coalesces in a united front.

Pressure to conform becomes so intense that any criticism may be construed as deviant behavior or, worse, treachery. Say a job superintendent sided with a consulting engineer in a hot dispute with the result that his company lost money; justified or not, he could find himself unemployed. A crucial factor in this interplay is the role of leadership. In tough situations it seems that strong direction may be called for, not, however, so strong as to prevent compromise and reconciliation. With these factors in mind, we now examine how and why intergroup conflicts get out of hand.

B. How Intergroup Conflicts Develop and Escalate

Although there is much truth in the proverb, "Princes fight for the same reasons as butchers," psychologists take a more scientific approach. In order to unravel the complexities involved, we next consider four pertinent elements.

1. The Nature of the Conflict

In a broad sense, friction between groups may occur not only because of a competitive goal, but also because of the means used to obtain that goal. Say two contractors bid on a particular job. On a lump-sum low bid, obviously, only one contractor can win. This is a conflict of goals. Relative to conflict of methods, say an owner and an architect agree on a mutually accepted solution, but disagree on the means or procedures to be used to achieve the desired end. For example, to clear up a punch list, a mutual goal, an architect may opt for verbal persuasion, whereas the owner may favor pulling the bond. In construction management, some conflicts develop because of other variations on this broad theme, and are, furthermore, complicated because three distinct groups are using parochial methods to achieve an overall mutual goal—the completed project. Underlying this mutuality, the contractor strives to maximize his profits (money and possibly reputation); the architect certainly considers monetary profit and, because his reputation determines future clientele, he strives to maximize his reputation; finally, the owner, like any consumer, wants the most for the least cost. Therefore, the specific nature of disagreement or conflict must be defined.

2. The Past and Present Relations Between Parties

Both the present and past history emerge as important in the development and continuation of hostility. A painful experience on a past project may cause lasting effects, which guide a person's present and future behavior. On the other hand, if past projects or encounters have been mutually successful and favorable, the potential of trust and cohesiveness on a team level is evident. This relationship between all factions will affect the membership (and leaders) in a generally constructive fashion. A positive atmo-

Box 5.2. INTERGROUP CONFLICT

"Just definitions either prevent or put an end to disputes"
Emons

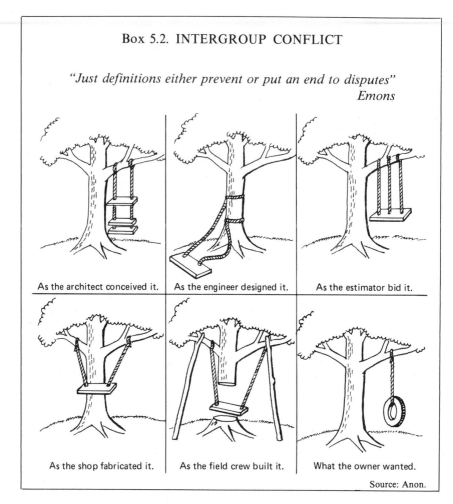

| As the architect conceived it. | As the engineer designed it. | As the estimator bid it. |

| As the shop fabricated it. | As the field crew built it. | What the owner wanted. |

Source: Anon.

sphere usually breeds positive results. Even with the ever-present elements of competition and self-interest, cooperation and communication will be more easily developed in a congenial respectful setting. When dislike and distrust predominate in the interactions, however, small-group experiments have demonstrated that the opposing sides are inclined to emphasize incompatabilities and differences. Issues then become clouded as prejudices take hold. All too often discord and distrust arise solely because a leader, or a membership, dislikes the outgroup for one reason or another. Such a dislike can lead to aggressive behavior in which injuring (monetary, reputation, psychological) becomes the primary goal. On a job site, say an inspector, hits it off badly with a subcontractor's foreman. Therefore, the inspector becomes unfairly harsh in his evaluation of the work— not so much to fulfill the job requirements but to cause injury.

Frequently, if a party has been offended actually (or imagined) retaliation may occur. Say a contractor feels he has been unfairly denied payment for a small extra; therefore, he may pad an unrelated change order request, or cut a corner elsewhere. If discovered, such a maneuver will instigate the owner to escalate the hostility (via the inspector).

3. Defining the Problem

Often a problem is complicated because all the subsurface factors are overlooked. It must be unequivocally determined whether the friction results from a technical difficulty or a personality clash.

The anomalies of any building project call for everyone's cooperation, coordination, and communication. A misfire with any one of these elements will cause hardship for everyone. Problems must be defined, but, in addition to defining the technical issue, the underlying personalities and prejudices must also be considered, for they directly influence both the goals and the means. Say a contractor misinterprets the plans, the architect misses a detail, or the owner discovers that what he got was not what he wanted— how does the team maximize the gains and minimize the losses physically and psychologically? Besides defining the factual, physical problem at hand, one would do well to define each groups's goals and methods, too. Are they mutually exclusive? What limits of compromise could be entertained? Are the psychological factors a help or a hindrance? As mentioned previously, as emotions intensify and the group draws up battle lines, stereotypes are commonly perceived by the members—usually negative stereotypes that distort and aggravate the original cause of conflict.

4. Strategies Employed and Contingent Results

When two or more factions clash, various strategies provoke various consequences. Strong threats and gestapo tactics may well effect counterstrategies from the recipient and, consequently, intensify the hostility. Though oversimplified, it is true that hostile acts usually result in hostile responses. Communication becomes sporadic or degenerates to exchanging unfriendly messages and insults. Say a general fails to complete a questionable item (in actuality an omission on the designer's part): after lengthy, heated arguments, the owner unfairly notifies the bonding company, via a brutally frank letter, and slanders the contractor from one end of town to the other. How would the contractor respond? Not by turning the other cheek. It would seem plausible that many unflattering (and visually descriptive) remarks would fly back and forth in the construction trailer, few of which would contribute to the reconciliation and resolution of the questionable item.

C. Resolving the Conflict

As discussed, intergroup conflicts can develop and intensify for a number of reasons. We now turn to a few research applications that serve to reduce, if not completely resolve, certain disagreements and discords. In construction management, the overall goal is to complete the job successfully— theoretically to the mutual benefit of all concerned. Commonly, the actual dispute involves the methods and instruments used to reach that goal—say a contractor shortchanges on the quality of workmanship, or an owner inundates a sub with a wave of freebies. Consequently, patience wears thin; friction increases until a small spark begins to smoulder; suddenly a blaze erupts. In this situation, two psychologically strategic options are available: (1) lash out and prepare for the counterattack until the suspicion and hostilities destroy the integrity of the project; or (2) define the problem, external and internal; clear the air of sparking personalities and prejudices; and concentrate energies to iron out the differences. After a serious dispute has developed, how can workable relations be effectively established between groups? Social psychologists list a number of methods: (1) establish common goals; (2) improve communications; (3) utilize spokesmen; (4) utilize third parties; and (5) fractionate the problem.

Before discussing these specific techniques, we present some elements of bargaining that should be understood to gain some insight into these methods. Basically, friction between groups is caused by differences in either the objective to be achieved, the methods used to gain these ends, or both. (Sociologists have determined that it is easier to resolve a conflicts of methods.) In any case, there are numerous ways of handling any conflict, war being one extreme and surrender being the other. In construction, one side may steamroller or eliminate the opponent—say, in court or via the bonding company—or harass them into submission. Another approach would be to avoid, or withdraw from, the situation—say a contractor walks off the site or an owner claims bankruptcy or a union calls a strike. Neither of these approaches is very productive in the long run, especially for the construction team. By far, groups settle their differences by extending offers and counteroffers until they reach a settlement acceptable to both sides. Although it is certainly true that the owner, the architect, and the general contractor are bound by legal documents, it is equally true that not all questions are decided on a legal plane. Building is a very complex endeavor, and the plans and specifications involve an inherent communication gap.

Not every issue is cut and dried, black or white, or precisely definable. Consequently, one is often required to compromise judiciously, or, said in another fashion, to bargain. When a contractor submits a request for a progress payment, there is an element of bargaining, unless, of course, the work to date is precisely known. More than likely, however, the amount of work actually completed will be estimated to within certain limits, say between 30–35 percent. The contractor requests 40 percent payment; the architect claims 30 percent. They check off item by item, trade by trade, giving a little here, taking a little there, until an agreement is reached, say 34 percent. This process occurs without giving much thought to some of the underlying elements. Suppose little trust existed between them, that, in fact, the designer disliked the contractor (and vice versa). Both sides would be reluctant to compromise. Even if the actual work completed was 40 percent, and the general requisitioned for 35 percent, the architect might be suspicious of his motives. Such is the atmosphere on a negative project. Examples of bargaining or compromise occur in many shades-of-gray situations: change order versus contract work; pricing of claims; interpretations of plans and specs; punch lists; errors and omissions; "or equal" evaluations; guarantee issues; retainage to be held; and, of course, payment requisitions. Few decisions, especially those that involve relatively small costs, are made by lawyers in the courts. More likely the team has bargained to some extent.

Sociologically, bargaining refers to that method whereby people attempt to settle a situation in give-and-take fashion. Normally one side submits a proposal, typically more than what the other side will accept. The counterproposal will fall short of the acceptable. Back and forth goes the bargaining until a mutual agreement is reached. It must be recognized that bargaining is far from an all-or-nothing process. The aim is not to destroy the opponent, but to reach a solution acceptable to both sides. Suppose a union drives such a hard bargain that contractors close their shops. In that case both sides lose. More on the bargaining process will be discussed in the following chapter. Here we discuss some specific techniques to resolve intergroup conflicts.

1. Establish Common Goals

One method of reducing conflict in the construction team is to emphasize common goals (and mutual losses). In general it is to everyone's advantage to resolve differing attitudes, values, interests, etc.—and to proceed in a concerted effort, so that the project can be completely profitably. Even in those situations that involve serious technical difficulties (i.e., a serious delay), a positive atmosphere can help at least to minimize the losses for all concerned.

2. Improve Communications

As hostilities intensify, there is increased distortion and distrust and poor channels of communication between opposing sides. Therefore, one way of restoring a psychologically effective relationship is to close the communication gap. If the parties can be brought together, and can express their opinions and viewpoints openly, on an intellectual level, tensions can often be alleviated. It is cautioned, however, that, in situations of a extreme dislike or seriousness, open communication may prove ineffective in remedying the dispute. In such cases, the utilization of a third party, or a spokesman, may prove more prudent.

3. Utilize Spokesmen

Another method of abating intergroup disputes is to use a spokesman, especially one with authority and expertise. During construction, when trouble slows the job to a standstill, and the immediate parties (O, A/E, GC/S) cannot seem to break the deadlock, the problem can be appealed to higher management. In this case the agency director, the partner in the architectural firm, and the president of the construction company may meet to reach a detente. Usually a leader of an organization, by virtue of his prestige, his authority, and his expertise, may be able to settle disputes more readily than subordinates. In some instances he may possess a unique point of view or, because of experience, he may be more sensitive to the bargaining process. By his greater authority he can make more concessions or stronger demands. We should mention, too, that a spokesman or official is limited somewhat by the expectations, values, and goals of the membership he represents (i.e., a union negotiator is required to drive a tough bargain, irrespective of his personal feelings). Our culture calls for leaders to be competent, effective, and tough in dealing with others. Therefore, a leader may be under pressure to save face, stand firm, and yield few concessions. Still, as mentioned with respect to bargaining, without a willingness to give and take, negotiation is virtually impossible.

4. Utilize Third Parties

On a formal level, this method is used frequently in construction disputes, in the person of an arbitrator. A third party often proves to be a key instrument in reducing conflicts, especially if each side agrees to recognize his legitimacy and willingly to accept his recommendation up to a reasonable point.

From the sociological viewpoint, here are some important functions of a third party:

1. He reduces emotionalism and tension by encouraging the opponents to vent their feelings.
2. He presents alternatives by recasting the issues in more acceptable terms. Since he has no ulterior motive, when he proposes an alternative, it can be taken at face value.
3. He can provide an opportunity to establish meaningful intercourse.
4. He can arrange and conduct meetings, prepare the agenda for discussion, and offer technical or legal expertise, and sound judgment.

Obviously, a third party must possess the right qualifications: be a recognized authority; be impartial; be trustworthy; be knowledgeable; and be perceived as fair. Although, in the strict sense, third parties are seldom used in construction projects, their use certainly offers some outstanding advantages.

5. Fractionate the Problem

The final method of reducing tensions is to break the major problem into smaller, more manageable components. Many large technical problems can be broken down into smaller items. Sometimes the poor performance of a project can be attributed to two factors, one physical, and the other psychological. Each can then be dealt with separately. Usually, solving the easiest dispute first helps to rebuild the elements of trust, therefore leading to more productive relations. A minor compromise or concession from one side may create a good impression on the other side, thus ending the row.

Box 5.3. CONSTRUCTION GROUP PROFILES

Similar to individuals, groups also seem to take on certain characteristic identities. Although more complex, and therefore less accurate, a group "personality" results from a multifaceted web of individual traits, group processes, and contractual obligations. Admitted to be scientifically questionable, in the interest of comparison the reader could draw a reasonably accurate composite for each of the construction groups. From simple observations, it can be seen that the O, A/E, and GC/S groups behave in different styles and patterns. Some "collective traits," as listed below, should appear to be valid descriptions of the many influences that help to shape a group's behavior pattern. With a healthy caution, the reader should select and modify these group traits to coincide with the actual personnel and conditions as witnessed on an given project.

As a beginning the following generalized profile traits are assumed to be influential precursors to overt actions.

OWNER

1. *Contractural Obligations*
   a. *The owner pays for services rendered and all extra work.*
2. *Attitudes*
   a. *The owner holds the finances.*
   b. *The owner is not responsible for the design or the construction.*
   c. *In public funding, money may take on less of a personal significance, in that government employees share in neither the profits nor the losses.*
   d. *He is subject to pressures and control from politics, bureaucratic policies, and procedures, as well as the pitfalls and peculiarities of civil service.*
3. *Interests and Goals*
   a. *In all likelihood, the owner wants the structure to be simple, economical, and functional with the ultimate users in mind (i.e., doctors, students, office workers, etc.).*
   b. *Being essentially a consumer, the owner expects the best quality for the least cost. (This is the rationale behind lump-sum bids.) Therefore, the owner tends to construe the plans and specs from the "high" side of tolerances, "or equals," and shades-of-grey issues.*
   c. *Because the owner lives with the project long after the designers and contractors have departed, he will be keenly interested in maintenance and operating costs. Sometimes he considers the guarantee period to be a free ride from maintenance.*
4. *Skills*
   a. *The owner relies heavily on the technical expertise of others. Therefore, his leadership style may tend to be laissez-faire.*
   b. *The owner is administratively inclined, and limited to certain proscribed procedures and processes.*
   c. *He is prone to inspect thoroughly, and to compile reports and other documentation.*
5. *Miscellaneous*
   a. *Often the owner is required to pay for change orders that are caused by a designer's oversight.*
   b. *No cash-flow problems threaten the owner.*
   c. *He is unaffected moneywise by weather, strikes, late deliveries, etc.*

d. He suffers few personal consequences of errors, especially since he did not design or build the structure. It is very easy to pass the buck.

e. The end-users (students, patients, office workers) care nothing about design or construction problems. (For example, a politician/administrator/director may be more concerned with the grain of his new desk or the color of the rug than with the total sanitary, electrical, or air conditioning systems.)

ARCHITECT

1. Contractural Obligations

   a. The designer is responsible for the design and the work of his consultants.

   b. He provides general administration of the job.

   c. He renders decisions on interpretation of plans and specs (i.e., the quality of workmanship, materials, etc.).

2. Attitudes

   a. The architect values to the utmost his reputation for integrity and ability.

   b. Since he acts as the agent of the owner—a possible future client—he may be somewhat prejudicial in favor of the owner's interests.

3. Interest and Goals

   a. The project offers the opportunity to enhance (or damage) his professional reputation in terms of expressing (actually advertising to the public) forms, lines, materials, and original combinations. Excellent source of future work.

   b. Because the design fee is dependent on the project cost, and architecture is, after all, a business, greater quantity or quality means higher fees.

   c. Problem projects, regardless of who is to blame, threaten the designer's reputation.

4. Skills

   a. The project requires aesthetic, intellectual, and administrative abilities of the highest caliber.

   b. The architect is responsible for the overall quality of the leadership. If a problem is discovered, the designer must identify its nature and must designate a satisfactory solution.

   c. Architecture demands a great facility with words and abstractions in order to translate the owner's needs into a form from which a contractor can build. Any gap or mistake in this translation process blemishes the designer's reputation.

5. *Miscellaneous*
   a. *Designers may be politically influential.*
   b. *He is relatively unaffected moneywise by weather, strikes, late deliveries, etc.*
   c. *Other than gross errors or omissions, oversights and misjudgments can be corrected via contract change orders paid for by the owner.*
   d. *Unnoticed noncompliances by the contractor and misoperation by the owner often reflect on the designer's ability, justly or not.*
   e. *Contingent maintenance and operating headaches damage a designer's reputation.*
   f. *Costly "errors and omissions" because of designer negligence may be difficult to prove.*
   g. *A design error invariably involves three parties contractually: the owner versus the designer, and the general contractor versus the owner.*
   h. *If a pure theorist, the designer may sacrifice durability and practicality for appeal and sensitivity.*
   i. *In his relations with speciality consultants, the architect may be nonreceptive to their objective technical needs (i.e., Where do we locate the cooling tower, piping, ducts, or equipment? What about the energy consequences of all glass walls? "Hide it," or "Live with it," may well be the ground rules).*

GENERAL CONTRACTOR

1. *Contractural Obligations*
   a. *He is responsible for means, methods, sequences.*
   b. *He is responsible for the work of his subcontractors.*
   c. *Work must be completed for a specified sum.*
2. *Attitudes*
   a. *He risks money in hopes of a profit.*
   b. *Money, especially in a small propriertorship, takes on personal dimensions. Any error (i.e., a missed detail, poor judgment, or lack of coordination) means money lost, often out of personal finances.*
   c. *Regardless of performance, even if superior in quality, he must bid competively on future work.*
   d. *Because of itinerant nature of construction, tradesmen may feel "It's just another project."*
3. *Interest and Goals*
   a. *The contractor tries to maximize profit, primarily in terms of money, but possibly reputation as well.*

    b. *He is more concerned with practical matters than with beauty and intellectual concepts. Ordinarily he is conservative in nature because innovative ideas that backfire cost him money.*

    c. *He tends to interpret plans and specs on the "low" side of tolerances, "or equals," etc.*

4. *Skills*

    a. *He must be able to estimate and build a project competively and successfully.*

    b. *He is responsible to translate words, lines, and concepts into a physical structure within the restrictions of a lump sum and a defined schedule.*

5. *Miscellaneous*

    a. *The contractor is affected by weather, strikes, late deliveries, etc.*

    b. *He suffers most the results of poor general leadership and other psychological deficits.*

    c. *He is vulnerable to cash-flow difficulties.*

    d. *He pays directly for his errors.*

    e. *On a personal level, an error may result in the loss of the job or even his company (i.e., a project manager who misses a detail may be fired).*

    f. *He is more susceptible to harrassment by officials, inspectors, etc.*

    g. *His work is inspected by designers, owner's inspectors, maintenance user staff, local officials, etc.*

    h. *In the situation of questionable designs or owner operation, the contractor usually stands "guilty until proven innocent."*

    i. *He is liable for subs, vendors, equipment and material suppliers, etc.*

    j. *Tendency toward autocratic, aggressive leadership is the modus operandi for contractors.*

    k. *He is susceptible to union policies.*

    l. *Any "cut corners" (noncompliances, lower quality, etc.) mean higher profits.*

    m. *May be politically connected.*

    n. *When lowest bidder is considerably below the next proposal, the contractor may feel, it is "money left on the table," and he consequently begins the project with a have-to-catch-up outlook.*

    o. *Change orders, being noncompetitive, are often viewed as lucrative sources of revenue.*

Bibliography

Durant, Will. *Our Oriental Heritage*. New York: Simon and Schuster, 1963.

Fabun, Don. *Communications, The Transfer of Meaning*. Beverly Hills, California: Glencoe Press, 1968.

Goldenson, Robert M. *The Encyclopedia of Human Behavior*, vols 1 and 2. New York: Doubleday and Co., Inc., 1970.

Hilgard, Ernest R., Richard C. Atkinson, and Rita L. Atkinson. *Introduction to Psychology*. New York: Harcourt Brace Jovanovich, Inc., 1971.

Kalish, Richard A. *The Psychology of Human Behavior*, 2 ed. Belmont, California: Brooks/Cole Publishing Co., 1970.

Murphy, Richard W., and the editors of Time-Life Books. *Human Behavior—Status and Conformity*. New York: Time, Inc., 1976.

Raven, Bertram, H. and Jeffrey Z. Rubin. *Social Psychology: People in Groups*. New York: John Wiley & Sons, Inc., 1976.

Schmuck, Richard A., and Patricia A. Schmuck. *Group Processes in the Classroom*. Dubuque: Wm. C. Brown Publishers, 1971.

Steinberg, Rafael, and the editors of Time-Life Books. *Human Behavior—Man and His Organization*. New York: Time, Inc., 1975.

Terkel, Studs. *Working*. New York: Random House, Inc., 1972, 1974.

Thompson, William R., and Richard C. DeBold. *Psychology: A Systematic Introduction*. New York: McGraw-Hill Book Co., 1971.

Wheeler, Ladd, Robert A. Goodale, and James Deese. *General Psychology*. Boston: Allyn and Bacon, Inc., 1975.

Yalom, Irvin D. *The Theory and Practice of Group Psychotherapy*. New York: Basic Books, Inc., 1970.

Chapter 6

Communications and Meetings

The Tower of Babel. In the biblical account, Jehovah struck the builders with confused tongues and they were scattered, thus spreading different languages throughout the world. (After a painting by Peter Bruegel, Flemish artist.)

Abstract

Communications and meetings, both crucial components in construction management, are examined here in detail.

First the listening and speaking processes are analyzed, and a number of skills are presented to improve the quality of transmission. Such skills include: paraphrasing, perception checking, feedback, and awareness of nonverbal messages. This latter skill, although overlooked in many cases, is instrumental to understanding, because nonverbal cues flavor the context and delivery of the message.

The chapter then identifies the most troublesome personalities and strategies that sabotage so many meetings. On a more positive note, the elements of a productive conference are presented. These are proper preparation and judicious application of certain methods that mitigate the impact of common difficulties.

CONTENTS OF CHAPTER 6

GENERAL COMMUNICATIONS

VERBAL COMMUNICATIONS
A. Listening
  1. Actively Work at Listening
  2. Think About the Content of the Message
  3. Listen Patiently and Without Interruption
  4. Capitalize on Your Thought Speed
  5. Resist Distractions
  6. Disregard Symbols of Authority
  7. Avoid Blind Spots and Prejudices
  8. Strive for Clarification
B. Speaking
  1. Do's
  2. Don'ts

NONVERBAL COMMUNICATION
A. Common Signals
  1. Face
  2. Eyes
  3. Hands, Arms, Fingers
  4. Voice
  5. Space
B. Signals In Construction
  1. Personal
  2. Job Site
  3. Meetings

COMMUNICATION SKILLS
A. Specific Skills
  1. Paraphrasing
  2. Behavior Description

3. Description of Personal Feeling
4. Perception Checking
5. Attending
6. Acknowledgment
7. Open Question
8. Active Listening
9. Feedback

MEETINGS

A. Why Meetings Fail
1. Twenty-Five Reasons
2. Trouble People
3. Torpedo Strategies

THE EFFECTIVE MEETING

A. Negotiations
B. Preconference Preparation
1. Initial Planning
2. Preparing the Agenda
C. Execution
1. Mechanics of Meetings
2. Dynamics of Meetings

QUESTIONS AND PREVIEW

1. Name some factors to which a listener must attend in the speaking and listening exchange.
2. How do nonverbal cues affect the meaning of a spoken message?
3. List some ramifications conveyed by personal appearance, site cleanliness, meeting locations, and seating arrangements.
4. Identify some specific skills that augment the quality of conversation.
5. Name some reasons why meetings fail to achieve expected objectives. Identify behaviors and questionable strategies that are frequently observed in group discussions.
6. Explain how the following factors influence the character of a conference: initial planning and brainstorming; size and composition of the groups; location and suitability of the conference room.
7. Why are negotiations relevant to construction management?
8. What are the mechanics and interpersonal dynamics associated with the construction meeting?

GENERAL COMMUNICATIONS

What is not fully understood is not possessed

Goethe

As cited in earlier chapters, construction involves no end of planning and precision in all the sequential stages, whether these be the owner's conceptual financial study, the designer's plans and specifications, or the contractor's bid and build. Each organization utilizes some system of internal checks and balances to preclude errors and omissions, thereby reducing unnecessary costs and frustration. When these parties face each other to exchange ideas and information, however, especially in meetings, too frequently the scene resembles a contemporary Tower of Babel. Each person speaks or hears his own personal language, often foreign and having nuances and internal definitions that are misunderstood by the others. Sure, everyone converses in English, but even the most commonly used words (and ideas, events, and situations) convey different meanings to different people. For example, as mentioned in Chapter 2, the typical phrases "or equal" or "good workmanship," used to describe a piece of equipment or quality of finish, may be interpreted by the contractor to mean anything on the minimum side (and least expensive) to satisfy the requirement. The owner may read it to mean the best (and most expensive)—a Cadillac. And the potential for dispute increases when working in the less precise (and less documented) medium of the spoken word.

Basic to most gaps and bungles is the unfounded belief that most people consider themselves to be linguistic experts in transmitting and receiving ideas lucidly and cogently. This hazardous misconception probably originates in childhood, where we all learn our native tongue. We speak and hear so naturally we assume mistakenly that comprehension follows as a logical outgrowth. If that were true, if language were so simple, then why all the blunders and fumbles? Communication is, in actuality, a very deceptive, complex subject inherently imprecise and ill-defined. Accepting these limitations, however, it is a learned skill that demands, like any learned ability, honing to a sharp edge.

At this point a brief review is in order. So far this book has built a framework, presenting, first, the basics of construction management and then the basics of psychology. Next, individual and the "typical" profiles were interlaced. The text then defined groups, group processes, and the relationship of the three dominant groups within the team. Now all these elements are merged in that vital network called "communication." Facility in this area is one of the germane skills required in construction management. In one way or another, it touches everyone in diverse forms. At its root, it includes the legal documents, plans, and specs, carefully constructed yet imperfect, as errors and change orders bear witness. Less precise or definitive, communication may be: instructions from a leader to his group, dialogue between leaders of different groups, or a conversation between members of small groups attempting to arrive at a solution to a particular problem. Essentially, that is what construction management is all about: several groups communicating with each other in the joint venture of building a structure.

As seen in Chapter 5 much of the decision-making in construction depends upon small groups. It is the method by which an individual shares his thoughts, verbalizes his feelings, expresses his opinion, and transmits his knowledge. Much of this exchange is for persuasive purposes; at other times it is to clarify and to define. Little wonder then that the nature of communication is so important for everyone to understand. Without that understanding, they will be severely handicapped.

Construction management usually has three options available to remedy a dispute: (1) the courts; (2) arbitration; and (3) meetings. Time and money being precious commodities, the courts and arbitration are generally avoided. The meeting remains the most viable route to clear up differences. Granted that, if a bridge collapses or a building topples—both extremely costly mishaps—an army of lawyers will begin to mobilize their briefs. But by and large, and fortunately, few disputes reach these proportions, and, consequently, they are addressed in meetings. Furthermore, and again fortunately, most projects are seldom a series of awesome obstacles. Nor are meetings infused with the intensity or impact of the United Nations on the eve of war. Normally, a project involves ordinary meetings to periodically review and inspect; to evaluate progress and payments; to transmit information and clarify questions; and even to offer the opportunity to establish solid friendships and expand one's experience. In any case, whether the meeting is formal or informal, or has 2 or 22 people, clear discourse is the crucial vehicle to a smooth-running job. Clarity depends on everyone grasping that each group, as well as each individual, has a unique personality and a host of roles and goals, all of which affect one's "language." The A/E group is committed to the design—in fact their success determines future clients; the owner, gripping the bankroll like most consumers, wants the most for his money; the contractor, gambling on the lump sum, is striving to maximize profit. Within each group are the members, each with a distinct profile, and a highly individualistic perception of words, ideas, and concepts, i.e., the expressive architect, the practical engineer, the worldly businessman and contractor, the straightforward tradesman. Such factors must be considered in communication because they all crop up on the site and sometimes lead to misunderstanding and frustration. Each individual must assess his own profile and his group's roles and goals, and recognize that others do not "see" and "hear" as he does. Many times a particular attitude, or prejudice, held by a person determines how he perceives things and how he interprets or sends messages.

VERBAL COMMUNICATIONS

The tongue is but three inches long, yet it can kill a
man six feet high

Japanese proverb

Think back over the last week or so. Chances are that you can pinpoint wasted effort, a frustration, or an argument that originated with a faulty message. Review past construction meetings. The contractor missed a final inspection because he got his wires crossed. The work completed was condemned because the electrician misread the plans. The owner locked horns with the designer because of a misinterpreted project scope.

Historically it has been claimed that man alone has the dubious distinction of talking or gesturing himself consistently into problems. For millions of years, humans have been most proficient at misreading one another, causing tragedy, catastrophe, even war. Examples leap to mind: a crane operator kills a laborer because of a misconstrued hand signal; a roof collapses because of a missed decimal point; a boiler explodes because, "I thought he checked the safety valve!"—ad infinitum. Which of us has never sat in a meeting only to discover, after two hours of "sound and fury," that we had no idea of what had transpired. Have you ever read, in the minutes of a meeting, statements directly contrary to your understanding at the meeting?

If each of us consistently understood one another, construction would run like a frictionless top—precise and steady. But reality contradicts this "if." The top often falls and skitters about in a spiral of confusion. Why? Because most people believe communication to be as easy and as natural as breathing. The words flow from our mouths and will be accurately construed, so we erroneously believe. To cut to the core, if people kept a few of the following points in mind, the number of errant messages would diminish.

1. The ability to communicate correctly is not inherited. Instead it is learned, skillfully or maladroitly. Just because you speak plainly is no assurance that you will always be comprehended. Just because you listen attentively again does not guarantee that you will accurately receive the

speaker's true message. How many disputes have been sparked by "But you said . . . ," and exploded by "That's not what I meant!"

2. At best, our senses, perceptions, and interpretations of what we "see" or "hear" are inherently limited and fragmented; they are invariably textured by our personality and the roles dictated by our group. In addition, a person's immediate psychological state (i.e., anger) or physical state (i.e., flu) affects the total process. A profane "insult" from a smiling friend would draw a response markedly different than the same insult from a tight-lipped adversary.

3. Words, even the most commonly used words, do not transmit the same meaning, or pull the same weight from individual to individual. As mentioned in discussing propaganda, "loaded" words can carry peculiar connotations and ambiguities. To call a contractor "sharp" may mean that he is long on competence or short on integrity. No word sounds the same chord in all ears.

4. Whenever we describe a situation or event, we are describing our interpretation of what occurs within us, not necessarily outside of us. What happens inside one individual is not necessarily similar to the same process churning within someone else. Suppose an architect, an owner, and a contractor viewed the Taj Mahal. From the personality profiles, one could expect the architect to "see" the symmetry and beauty. The owner may "see" only hoards of maintenance men armed with mops in an around-the-clock effort to keep the place scrubbed. The contractor may reconstruct the building methods, possibly contemplating the use of cheaper, used red brick and secondhand wallboard. "Why not," he may rationalize," a building is just a building." Like the Rorschach inkblot, we have an identical stimulus, but three varying internal processes.

If a person is party to faulty communication, the defect probably stems from ignoring one or all the points above. The individual alone must identify the problem and take steps to remedy the deficit. One must carefully examine his own skill in sending and receiving messages, and not blandly assume he knows all about this complex subject. With this thought in mind, we now explore the most frequent form of exchange, the listening and speaking processes.

A. Listening

Listening and speaking usually go hand-in-glove, but in that self-interest and ego reign supreme, people in general like to speak more than to listen. Anyway, according to the misconception, listening is much easier. A person can sit, apparently mesmerized, uttering only a few token aha's and sometimes nodding. Meanwhile, his mind is a thousand miles away.

To be sure attention is a crucial element for a good listening strategy (and courtesy) as acknowledged by most of us—hence the nods and affable grunts. But the interest should be reasonably sincere without "suffering fools gladly."

Under normal circumstances, meetings use the listen-speak process (enraged silence being a ready exception) to unravel the macramé of issues. Information is transmitted. Ideas and opinions are exchanged. This interchange requires both the ebb and the flow of words on everybody's part. But, since we potentially learn more from receiving than sending, listening will be discussed first. Unfortunately, many people fail to appreciate that dexterity in listening depends solely on the hearer. If a message is sent, regardless of how limited or ill-spoken, the listener is obliged to seek clarification. Otherwise the speaker will assume, erroneously, that he has been received. Therefore, a few broad rules encompassing the art of listening are discussed below.

1. Actively Work at Listening

Admittedly, listening is hard work requiring concerted effort. Yet it can be one of the best investments you can make. A message, misread, regardless of all other factors, is virtually useless. Better it were never sent or heard. Concentrate on the message being transmitted. Appropriately look the speaker in the eye. Try to give the impression of interest because it tends to stimulate his best conversation.

2. Think About the Content of the Message

What is the speaker saying? What is he driving at? What are his main ideas? What data substantiates his statement? Most importantly, what information does he leave out? Many are the victims of the supersalesman who overwhelmed them with glowing attributes about his product or service, only to find themselves, after the guarantee period, saddled with some unforeseen white elephant: maintenance costs, fuel bills, or discontinued equipment. (This is another example of propaganda—the glittering generality.)

3. Listen Patiently and Without Interruption

Do not interrupt the speaker by interjecting your opinions or finishing his sentences. When you listen, do so without criticism or judgment. Take care that you do not communicate impatience or criticism nonverbally. For instance, a scowl on your face will indicate nonapproval and engender anxieties at his end. Let him tell his tale even if "it is a tale told by an idiot, full of sound and fury, signifying nothing." Hear the speaker out. Avoid a direct confrontation when he is speaking, irrespective of your approval or disapproval.

4. Capitalize on Your Thought Speed

On the basis of what has already been said, try to anticipate what the person is talking about. Ask yourself "What is the speaker trying to get at?" "What point is he trying to make?" Weigh the speaker's evidence by mentally questioning it. If he spouts facts or statistics, ask yourself, "Are they accurate?" "Are they from an unprejudiced source?" "Do they present a full picture?" Look for other signs. Few speakers put everything that is important into words. Notice the changing tones and the volume of his voice. Observe his facial expression, the movements of his body, and his gestures—forms of nonverbal messages. In an emotional situation, if the speaker shows no emotion whatsoever, speculate as to whether or not he is withholding something. As will be discussed later, however, in reading nonverbal cues, you must proceed cautiously and carefully recheck your initial perceptions.

5. Resist Distractions

Good listeners tend to adjust quickly to any kind of abnormal situation, and they instinctively fight distractions. If there is distraction, a good listener tries to concentrate on the message, not on the disturbance. That is why meeting places should be conducive to conversation: no jangling telephones or jack hammers six feet away. Also take only minimum notes if they tend to inhibit listening. They are essential at times, but too often they may become a hindrance, and frequently the results are ambiguous if not outright inaccurate.

6. Disregard Symbols of Authority

Judge the content of the message, not the delivery. In order to listen fully, you cannot be overawed or unduly impressed by the speaker's power, rank, attraction, social facility, or position. These things are not necessarily evidence that what he is saying is true and reliable. Remember that the quality of his voice, color of his skin, shape of his eyes, height, weight, and age guarantee nothing nor detract from the wisdom of what he says. Truth can be lisped, stuttered, mispronounced and ungrammatical. Whether it comes dressed in an attache case, a brown paper bag or a toolbox is actually of little importance.

Actually, this suggestion may be very difficult to put into practice for one major reason: society thrives on the pecking order. As discussed previously, if the speaker has expertise, prestige, authority, good looks, a stentorian voice, and an abundance of leadership qualities, the listener will listen more receptively than to a speaker of lesser stature. Social scientists, in experiments on persuasion, have found this to be the case, and, in one sense, justifiably so. After all, if one has the credentials, he should be accorded the respect and weighty consideration. Nevertheless, the critical point is to judge the content of the message on its face value, not on the speaker's status. After all was said and done, Columbus was proven right, not the experts.

7. Avoid Blind Spots and Prejudices

Keep your mind open. Avoid tunnel vision and oblique notions that impair your ability to be objective and logical. Everyone has certain likes, dislikes, values, etc. Everyone has a unique makeup and life style. Some people are highly resistant to change; others are highly influenced by argument. Persuasibility has been shown to be somewhat dependent upon personality traits. Therefore, know your hangups and prejudices. Identify those words and phrases that trigger unnecessary emotions and cause unjustifiable alarm.

8. Strive for Clarification

If you actively listen to a speaker and are still unsure of what he is saying, you should make every effort to clear up the troublesome points. Ask questions, preferably by rephrasing his words in terms of how you understand them, such as "Do I understand you to mean that . . . ." Remember plans and specs are objective documents in black and white. Even so, their interpretation frequently brings confusion and ambiguities. The spoken word, fleeting and subjective, is more prone to being misunderstood. Learn not to overreact one way or the other about the speaker's statements until you are certain you have correctly understood his message.

B. Speaking

When in the position of the speaker, reverse the techniques given for good listening. Clearly, you must place yourself in the position of the listener. Remember that he is not a student guru or a clairvoyant trying to unravel one of life's great mysteries. More likely he has a specific job to do, and is actively listening to what you are saying. At least that is the underlying assumption that a speaker must make. Therefore, the speaker must be as active in putting across his point as the listener is in trying to understand.

From language studies, a list of dos and don'ts have been compiled.

1. Do's

Do think about the recipient and the difficulty of his position. Make every effort to ensure that he "reads" you correctly.

Do provide objective, complete, and factual information, including necessary substantiating data. Therefore, weigh and measure your words with care before speaking.

Do speak neither too fast nor too slow. Use common language, preferably simple, concrete words in short sentences, as opposed to long-winded abstractions that muddle the mind. Crystallize this approach with the appropriate inflection, facial expressions, and gestures to lend emphasis and clarity to the verbal message. A Navy Department study found that speakers who spoke too fast were less apt to be understood than their slower paced colleagues. In no case should a speaker use words or terms that he suspects the listener may not comprehend. It serves little useful purpose for an HVAC designer to explain the intricacies of an enthalpy chart to an apprentice tin-knocker who has a sparse background in thermodynamics. The sheetmetal apprentice will fathom little of the discussion, and will probably be uninterested anyway. More likely he may take offense because the engineer "puts on the dog." Use your common sense—honk your horn elsewhere. Express—don't impress.

Do get to the main point immediately and fully. Brevity is a virtue, and it eases the task of the listener. But never sacrifice lucidity for brevity.

2. Don'ts

Don't use generalities when you can be specific. "Hammer" is more precise than "implement."

Never, especially from a position of authority or expertise, talk down to anyone. As emphasized in regard to assertion, every person, regardless of his place in the pecking order of work and abilities, deserves, and rightfully expects, his share of respect and courtesy.

Avoid the hard-line approach. Even if you feel strongly about an issue, always take the edge off your words. To insult someone causes anger or other responses (possibly physical) that inhibit if not destroy good interpersonal relations.

In a similar light, the reading and writing process may well find use for most of these pointers. The major differences concern the longevity of the message and the substantial absence of nonverbal communication. (Refer to Appendix III, "Written Communication and Documentation.")

NONVERBAL COMMUNICATION

There was speech in their dumbness; language in their very gesture

Shakespeare

In assertiveness we saw that nonverbal communication was an extremely relevant form of sending messages, many of which are read uncorrectly. This unspoken counterpart includes facial expressions, body movement, eye contact, and hand gestures. All signal emotions. Unfortunately, many senders are oblivious to their implications. For an illustration, a worker tries to explain a point; his boss drums his fingers on the table—in effect indicating his impatience or frustration. In a meeting, an ironworker offers an idea; the structural engineer frowns—sending the subtle response that he thinks the idea ludicrous. Possibly neither the boss nor the engineer intended any such transmission; yet, such a signal was sent and "read." Although verbal messages receive a fair share of incorrect interpretations, gestures or facial modulations, can foster equal damage. Such unspoken communiques are just two of the many signals that constitute the highly elusive, yet pervasive, silent language referred to as kinesics—the language of the body. Sometimes such gestures accurately describe the inner emotions to the nth degree. Other times they fall short of the mark. Consequently, we must attend to our own nonverbal actions, as well as the cues sent from others. Taken in context with the climate of the conversation, astute attention will result in more accurate "reading," sent or received. Simply proposed, the awareness of nonverbal communication is often a key to personal relations. It may well be the secret of success used by so many men in handling others. Such people are able to interpret body language. They manipulate people with their bodies as well as with their voices. For instance, a listener's warm smile will ordinarily encourage the speaker to engage in his best conversation. A boss who leans over the subordinate's desk intimidates the worker even before the first word is spoken. Beyond this awareness of body language and the ability to interpret it, one also cultivates an awareness of his own body language. He begins to receive and interpret messages that others are sending, and, in response, monitors his own signals to achieve a greater control over the exchange. Long after Shakespeare wrote the quotation above, Freud, the father of psychology, observed, "He that has eyes to see and ears to hear may convince himself that no mortal can keep a secret. If his lips are silent, he chatters with his fingertips." Although in itself a questionably accurate statement because of cultural orientation, scientific research has experimentally verified the significance of body language. The medical profession has long suspected that, through our organs, we unconsciously express feelings, impulses, and conflicts: tension causes headaches; anxiety reveals itself through a variety of psychosomatic ills such as hyperventilation, rashes, backaches, and mysterious pains; and the rigid face, slumped posture, and reduced gesticulation indicate depression. More far reaching are the serious dysfunctions attributed to long-term stress: ulcers, hypertension and heart attacks. These are all couriers of the body, which are well recognized in our society, and which most of us can sometimes experience in ourselves, especially in emotional situations. Some psychoanalysts believe that the everyday clichés "can't stomach something," "lump in my throat," "he gets under my skin," and "pain in the neck" originate from such relationships.

Dr. Allport, coauthor of the *Study of Values*, went so far as to hypothesize that a person's personality could be understood by observing his posture, his manner of walk, his handwriting, and other such mute considerations. Sheldon, another theorist, found a positive correlation between personality and body types. A fat person, by stereotype, wordlessly tells us that he is extroverted and jolly. Not necessarily valid, this is a nonverbal signal nonetheless.

Whereas the average adult acquires a vocabulary numbering thousands of words, Dr. R. Birdwhistell of the University of Pennsylvania believes that the face alone is capable of 32 basic expressions and 250,000 different combinations of gestures. Other scientists have determined that many interpretations change from culture to culture, although some gestures are universally accepted.

Little wonder then, that nonverbal elements add enormously to (and vastly complicate) the variability of communications. Each day, in the course of the simplest transaction, people supplement their words through eye contact, smiles, nods, arm and head gestures, and even personal spacing. Astonishingly pervasive, this often-ignored form of language reveals more than the face value of the spoken words. Many gestures are more quickly understood. Being transmitted more quickly, body movements are preferred in moments of danger when instant and unmistakable response is essential. Because such signals are transmitted visually, they travel much faster than the spoken word, and are unaffected by the noise that drowns out speech. For instance, during an initial high-pressure boiler test, if one were to observe several engineers madly dashing for the exits it would seem prudent to join the race and to ask questions later.

Because kinesics is a voluminous study in itself, only a few signals, of which several are especially pertinent to construction, will be examined here.

A. Common Signals

These nonverbal messages, many of which are unique to our society, blend variety and richness with everyday conversation. Although fragmented into separate entities here for analysis, all may be (and usually are) used simultaneously in normal circumstances, and should be interpreted in this light.

1. Face

Being the most obvious, the facial expression is one of the more predominant sender of signals—the arching of the eyebrows, the curve of the lip, the wrinkling around the eyes, and even the nod of the head. People normally change their expression while they are speaking, the smile being the most readily understood. Usually a grin indicates pleasure or approval, but some-times this turns out to be the most ambiguous. Some individuals tend to smile in times of stress, embarrassment, or when stoically accepting bad news. Therefore, the reader must read the expression (as with all other ges-tures) in the context of the situation and the spoken words. As is well under-stood, the frown, the snarl, and the "bared fangs" indicate negative at-titudes—anger, disagreement, or disapproval. Another point to consider concerns the poker face. A blank expression may well imply that the sig-naller is withholding or hiding something.

2. Eyes

After the mouth, the most expressive part of the face is the eyes. Albert Mehrabian, a psychologist, found that if a man dislikes another with whom he is conversing, he avoids eye contact as much as possible. To shuffle papers or gaze out the window while someone speaks to you reveals your lack of interest, contempt, or hostility. Avoidance of eye contact may indicate low self-esteem or possibly intimidation—as occurs when the sergeant or the boss calls for volunteers for a dirty detail. To meet his eyes may well be tantamount to accepting the assignment. (Hence all the troops begin to gaze at their shoelaces or off to the horizon.) Refusing eye contact can also mean that the listener finds the conversation boring or dubious in content. By observation, many of us learn to construe movements of the eyes, brows, or lids to carry certain meanings. Squinting of the brows may reveal anger or puzzlement. Wide Orphan Annie eyes imply high joy or shock. Holly-wood's questionable cliché tells us that shifty-eyed people are dishonest whereas "straight shooters" maintain a steady gaze. Which of us has never experienced the uneasiness of a prolonged stare (voluptuous young maidens being exempted)?

Whether speaker or listener, it is essential to realize that appropriate eye contact is imperative because it is an indicator of attention, respect, and interest.

3. Hands, Arms, Fingers

As is the case with the face and eyes, the hands can speak just as forcefully. Everyone tends to use his hands, consciously and often unconsciously. Therefore being aware of one's motions and the gestures of others, one must consider the impact of these signals. In most sports, we read the upraised arms to mean a score. In everyday work and street activities, we acknowledge a wide variety of accepted gestures. The simple chopping downward hand motion may well spell a "cut" project. The oscillating palm facing downward may mean "slow down." The circle of thumb and forefinger means ok. The upraised clenched fist signifies defiance, and, of course, the upraised phallus of the middle finger tells us that the sender is aggravated about something or someone.

These everyday signs are equally apparent: folded arms to imply rejection; drumming fingers to convey impatience; a finger pointed in accusation; clenched fists to indicate anger, possibly the onset of a fight; rapping or pounding the desk to mean emphasis (pro or con)—all of which must be put in the proper perspective of the ongoing events.

Box 6.1.

"Gracious! It's just delightful to see everyone in agreement with my decision."

Gerry Fox

4. Voice

Other invariable concomitants to speech are the vocal cues—the change in the pitch and tone of voice and the emphasis with which the speaker flavors the words he is uttering. Like the other expressions, tone and inflection can have a profound influence on the meaning of what is said. They frequently contradict the apparent meaning of the words. "Ya, that's great!" dripping with sarcasm plainly supplants the literal translation of the phrase.

George L. Trager, a researcher on vocal cues, identified a number of nuances that people project with their voices. At his option a speaker can yell or whisper, vary his pitch, or drone along in montone; speak forcefully or chatter in a happy fashion; or groan and whine. Each style carries its own unique message.

Most people resent a whine; it conjures up the image of a irritable, whimpering child. An audible sigh can mean boredom or despair, possibly in mockery. A whisper warns of potential skulduggery. A slow deliberate approach, commonly used by politicians and those in authority, implies that the speaker has given weighty thought to the subject, and is handing down, emphatically, his decision.

In our Western culture there is a widespread prejudice in favor of the man who speaks in a low, resonant voice, especially when he speaks slowly and manages to avoid pomposity. (Who would believe a news broadcaster who sounded like Donald Duck?) Included in this vein is silence, a definite form of rejection. If we ask a foreman, "How's the job progressing?" and he fails to respond, his silence sends a message. Of course, we must put the response in proper perspective—busy, rushed, ill, frustrated, or just failed to hear us? Nevertheless, when a speaker asks a question or makes a comment that normally calls for a response, and he receives no such response, a serious gap has developed. Silence builds walls. Holding one's tongue may often be wise, but generally this approach proves nonproductive in righting any wrong.

5. Space

Probably one of the most overlooked, but nevertheless significant, cues is the communication of space. Every individual has a certain territoriality, a comfort zone in which he likes to hold conversation. Usually, the better people know each other, and the closer their relationship, the shorter the distance between them is likely to be. This private space is as if we walked around with a plastic bubble hovering over us. Violating another's space may cause discomfort or hostility in him, because this may imply a feeling of intimacy that the individual is not prepared to accept, either emotionally or because of cultural upbringing.

Edward Hall, in his study of spatial communication, concluded that the normal conversational distance between white Americans is approximately two feet. Closer than that, Americans tend to become ill at ease, and may back off. The minimum distance is the bodily contact, and this gesture can hardly be missed and seldom misinterpreted. A firm prolonged handshake and a pat on the back are good strokes. A limp, sweaty handshake is a bad stroke.

In America, office locations and arrangements project status and importance. Large, well-furnished corner offices carry the most prestige, their occupants, as mentioned previously, often wielding considerable influence over the visitor. Individuals with less authority (and assumed lesser abilities) occupy offices around the windowed perimeter of the building. Finally, distributed in the middle spaces sit those people with even less prestige and import. Although this generalization is not necessarily true, it is a spatial suggestion nonetheless.

B. Signals In Construction

Although not actually singular to construction, these signals highlight much of the previous material. In Chapter 1, we saw that psychological problems frequently seen on a project included such defects as lack of dedication, direction, confidence, respect, and discipline. In the course of living in a society, and working in an occupation such as construction, we invariably observe one another, thereby forming individualistic assessments and opinions on the basis of these observations and interactions. Not only do we evaluate on the basis of what is said and heard, but certainly on overt behavior as well. This can be considered an offshoot of nonverbal communication. After all, psychology is defined as the study of behavior, regardless of the nature of the behavior: verbal, nonverbal, overt, or internal. Many of our personal assessments may be astute, others incredibly inaccurate.

1. Personal

We must realize that everything about us adds to our tale, both verbal and nonverbal. For example, the manner in which one dresses mirrors his personality and possibly his competency. Whether fact or fiction, the cliché "clothes make the man" carries some weight in our society. In any case, the style and color tell something about the wearer. If you parade into work dressed as the village beggar or as the fourth musketeer, panache and all, or wear a frayed shirt splattered with last week's menu, a very damaging signal is flashed to the observer. Furthermore, such a beacon radiates clues about your personality and technical expertise. (Would you visit a surgeon who operated out of an old garage?) In construction, everyone should be aware of the impact and side reactions (real or fancied) of similar nonverbal elements such as those discussed below.

a. Career.   The fact that an individual chooses a particular career sends a message about himself: his self-esteem, his values and interests, his intelligence and overall life style—his totality. This is certainly a questionable inference in any individual case, but humans learn many maladaptive habits—hence prejudices and labeling.

As soon as a construction manager states his occupation, he creates an impression, often stereotyped, but certainly a different impression than if he claimed to be a booster on the local midway. Therefore, be cognizant of career stereotypes and how they color your perceptions and responses.

b. Job Roles.   Somewhere in a company, a person occupies a certain organizational slot, which transmits a number of implications about his expertise, salary, duties, and responsibilities. Many of these implications may prove true via documented charts and job descriptions. Some, however, may prove false (i.e., political "hacks"). Caution should be the keynote when dealing with titles and organizational charts.

Another silent element under this category relates to work habits and attitudes. A group member, especially a leader, who operates in a professional manner—competent, dedicated, fair, and assertive—sets a good example, not only for his group, but for the construction team as well. On the negative side, a malcontent who "knocks" the project, bickers and moans constantly, goofs off, and acts obnoxiously, infects, via a contagious signal, not only his colleagues but the image of his organization as well. The same can be said for sloppy reports, rife with inaccuracies and misspellings; marginal workmanship; and, of course, incompetent work.

On a lesser scale even a sloppy work area—whether pyramid of catalogs and letters on a spec writer's desk or a trailer strewn with tools from here to Tibet—mutely testifies to a disorganized mind, singular or plural. Similarly, neatness, logic, and attention to detail convey a favorable image.

c. Personal Appearance.   Research data substantiate that a pleasant physical appearance, good physique and low, resonant voice all contribute to attractiveness—favorable nonverbal cues. Few are the lucky individuals genetically endowed with such complimentary qualities. For the majority of the population, the most rational approach is to make the most from materials on hand. Even if you have the misfortune to look like Quasimodo, hunchback and all, you can still be clean, well-groomed, and dressed appropriately.

2. Job Site

As stated in the beginning sections, an unsafe, dirty site is a subtle but insidious nonverbal message that pertains to everyone on the construction team, including upper management. Somewhat akin to the captain of a ship, the leaders stand responsible for their subordinates, not necessarily legally nor psychologically, but prejudically, as far as an observer is concerned. Fair or not, reputations, both personal and corporate, are built upon this premise. A scaffolding collapses, killing two bricklayers; a truck crushes a child—whatever the mitigating circumstances, unavoidable or not, the message still sears everyone, above and beyond the actual human tragedy. Check any newspaper or TV report for a telling illustration.

Traditionally construction has always entertained risk. Anyone in the trade realizes this. Be that as it may, however, most accidents can be avoided by stringent precautions. Psychologically, a forceful safety program builds worker morale. After all, think of the implications (nonverbal) to the workers, the public, and the future clients of such a program: management cares. Sure, the ulterior motive may be to reduce insurance costs, improve productivity, etc., but the implication goes beyond monetary concerns.

A clean, well-maintained project is another form of silent communication that extends beneficially to possibly unrelated factors, such as competence, organizational ability, public concern—the project "personality." Be conscious of the resultant pubic relations consequences. A site need not compete with a lawn party, but it need not resemble the Normandy beachhead either.

3. Meetings

With regard to a conference location, a busy, cluttered trailer, workers tramping in calling up the local bookie or otherwise interrupting the train of thought, is hardly the location to conduct a fruitful conference. Granted, many judicious decisions are made in such environments, but a more conducive climate could engender more and better results. As mentioned relative to assertion, if an owner consigns a meeting to a dungeon in the cellar, in effect, he sends an uncomplimentary message, not just about his own personality, but about his respect for the other parties.

a. Room Arrangements. Another nonverbal aspect of the conference, often overlooked, is the seating arrangements that affect the flow and quality of conversation. For instance, a "classroom" type of seating arrangement is normally less favorable to active dialogue than would be the roundtable, at which all participants interact face to face.

Experiments have shown that, as in family settings, the prominent member, questionably assumed to exercise more authority and expertise, usually sits at the head of the table—the "godfather" seat. Consequently, people tend to listen more attentively and to give more substance to his words.

The distance a person allows between himself and another is another nonverbal signal. If he is inches away from another's ear, chances are that he will speak lower, possibly whisper, which may be read by an observer as secretive. At a distance of several feet, however, the exchange may be private, but its nature has changed. It appears less furtive.

Two other seating signals worth mentioning are: (1) the individual who constantly sits on the "outside" of the meeting may be implying rejection or indifference; (2) because groups normally sit together, possibly to present a united front, members may feel threatened if they are arranged in random seats.

b. Language of Time.   We all have a tendency to feel that time is experienced pretty much the same by everybody. Yet consider the variation of time as felt by a designer, excitedly sketching a pet project, and a roofer ripping up a roof under a blistering sun. The designer loses track of time in his excitement, and the roofer is suffering. "When the hell will this day end?"

Every human has his own special time scale depending on his temperament, his role, and the immediate situation at hand. Failure to appreciate that one's clock may not coincide with another's can lead to difficulties. To be one hour late for a critical meeting with a busy corporation officer will probably result in a different reaction than to miss a coffee break with a peer.

With that said, consider some of the implications of time. Suppose a successfully built structure is completed far ahead of schedule. Everyone is pleased. Such exemplary effort nonverbally attests to the individual's (and company's) ability, dedication, perseverance, and the like. It may very well be that an abnormal run of good weather is the actual hero, but observers who overlook factual causes and read instead the silent extensions are legion. Conversely, a perverse winter may cause a project to run long over. Although this is a legally justifiable delay, its nonverbal message may still slight all parties.

At periodic conferences, a certain person may be relentlessly tardy. In effect, he is silently rejecting all the others, the hint being that his time or expertise or ego is more valuable. Frequently members may resent such an insult, and respond with hostility or revenge. Then again, suppose a person shows up early for a meeting. This may be an ambiguous cue that he is overly concerned, conscientious, or enthusiastic.

In summary, whether hidden or overt, nonverbal language is a vital component in everyday dealings with people. Unfortunately, all too frequently, these signals are misinterpreted. Therefore, one has to be extremely cautious that he zeroes in on target. To do this, he must constantly check his perception—one of the skills to be discussed in the next section.

COMMUNICATION SKILLS

Intercourse is the soul of progress

Buxton

With the thought in mind that poor communication may be worse than none at all, we now present a number of skills. Essentially, these skills appear to be relatively simple; often, however, they are difficult to put in practice consistently. Still, as with sharpening any dexterity, practice makes perfect.

A. Specific Skills

1. Paraphrasing

When you paraphrase, you are restating what another person has said, using your own words. Doing so means that you have listened, that you have cared about what the other person has said, and that you are showing respect in responding effectively. Some useful lead-ins when you paraphrase are: "Am I correct in understanding that you say . . ." or "Is this what you are saying?" This type of lead-in will assist you in mirroring the person's thoughts. The vital function of paraphrasing is a check to see that all parties have understood correctly.

2. Behavior Description

In using this skill, you describe the actions of another person, without judging them or attaching a particular motive to his behavior. For instance, if a person is late for a meeting, it is best to state, "This is the third time that you have been late." You have stated a fact, without going beyond that fact. To say something to the effect, "Why are you late? Are you trying to aggravate us! Or are you just plain lazy!" ties in a psychological interpretation. This, in turn, sets up defenses and possible retaliation, seldom improving the situation.

3. Description of Personal Feeling

This skill involves expressing your emotions straight out. In this approach, the other person need not rely upon his interpretation of your words and signals. You have told him how you feel about his actions or words. For example, with an individual who is always late, you can be direct or indirect. A direct statement would be, "Yes, I feel angry that you're late," whereas the indirect approach would be, "I'm angry," and say nothing. Both express your feelings but attribute no psychological motives to his actions.

4. Perception Checking

Always check that you understand what the other person is feeling. Crystallize both verbal and nonverbal signals to avoid any erroneous interpretations on your part. Suppose someone appears angry at a decision that you just made. He says nothing but his face shows a deep, fuming scowl. Sure, you could ignore, or misread, the signal, but this blocks the avenues of communication. A better tack is to find out for certain. Therefore, say, without judging the underlying feelings behind his scowl, "I get the impression that you are angry at this decision." This is very important because many times it is difficult to "read" a person's expression, let alone correctly comprehend his spoken statement. For instance, "Today is a great day" could be interpreted as a statement of joy or a sarcastic condemnation. Perception checking attempts to have the other person express his feeling, his internal processes, so that you understand exactly what he is trying to get across.

5. Attending

Attending is an essentially nonverbal ability. It is the behavior that shows that you are attentive to the speaker, that you respect him as an individual, and that you are interested in what he has to say. By paying attention, you will enhance his self-respect, establish rapport, and help him express himself as well as possible on the issue.

Sometimes silence can be the most effective form of communication. It encourages the other person to keep talking, and it can prompt a reticent individual to speak up. If a person is uncooperative, say nothing, and look at him expectantly. Your attitude should clearly convey that you are waiting for information, and that you expect to receive it. Remember that the other person may be less comfortable with the pause than you are because, as mentioned, silence can be menacing.

6. Acknowledgment

Acknowledgment is a skill somewhat similar to silence. Acknowledgment tends to keep another talking. Instead of engaging in conversation, you simply bounce the ball back to the other party. This strategy shows that you have heard the previous statement, understood it, and are waiting for more information. For instance, one may echo or repeat a key phrase that has been used by the speaker. If he says "And this occurred. . . ," you might respond with "And yes?" One-word questions are also extremely useful, such as "Then?", "And?", and "So?" Objective attending and acknowledgment require a good tone of voice and appropriate facial expressions and gestures. This is crucial because you have to combine your verbal and nonverbal cues.

7. Open Question

The open question is a skill that invites more elaboration. For example, queries, such as "Would you tell me how this occurred?" or "How do you feel about the situation?", are difficult to answer in a single word. Therefore, such questions provide excellent tools for gathering information because they emphasize the other person's input rather than your own. Other useful statements are "Tell me more," and "Give me an example."

Ask questions not to offend nor to put a person on the spot, but to get answers. This entails knowing what to ask, how to phrase it, and when to ask it. Be aware that, by judicious use of inquiry, you can secure attention, maintain interest in the item under discussion, and direct the course of the conversation. Be aware also of some important functions of asking questions:

1. To cause attention—what is your problem?
2. To obtain information—what, how, when?
3. To give information—are you aware that you could do this?
4. To promote thinking—what would you suggest?
5. To bring to a conclusion—isn't now the best time to accomplish this task?

8. Active Listening

Without belaboring the point, we agree that active listening is a very difficult skill to master. In the most advanced form, it requires that you not only understand what has been said and "read" the signals, but that you have assessed the hidden meaning behind the words and cues. It involves two distinct steps: (1) listen to the words, observe the nonverbal behavior, and make an educated guess as to the emotional content of the complete message; (2) check your perception—using short statements, paraphrase your interpretation in such a way that the action returns to the speaker. Such a technique demonstrates your interest to continue the dialogue. "And 'this' is how you feel?" often does the trick. It assesses what you believe to be the situation. You may be wrong, but the obligation to correct the misunderstanding now rests with the other person.

9. Feedback

The final skill is establishing what effect you have on others—how you are "coming across." As seen in Maslow's hierarchy of needs, all normal human beings use reactions from others in forming their self-concept. Likewise feedback is critical in communication. All the abovementioned skills can be used to test the responses of others to your words and actions. For example, paraphrasing and feedback are combined in the question, "What do you think of what I just said?" Perception checking and feedback can be joined in "Am I wrong in assuming that you feel. . . ?" Regardless of the combinations of skills, such questions or statements should be as specific and concrete as necessary to help you, as the communicator, to understand the quality of your messages.

MEETINGS

The joy of meeting, not unmixed with pain

Longfellow

Universally, human beings join together for a wealth of reasons: to share information, to make laws and decisions, to solve problems, or simply to socialize. Business studies report that managers spend an impressive percentage of their work week in conferences, estimated to be on the order of 15 percent. The higher one climbs the organizational ladder, the greater the percentage of time devoted to conferring with others (say 30–50 percent). Construction, being a business, requires no less conferring. Ask any designer, contractor, or project manager how much of his time is consumed in meetings with bankers, accountants, lawyers, bonding companies, licensing agencies, and tens of other red-tape bureaucracies, let alone with members of the construction team. Some dog days seem to call for 30 hours just to keep abreast of the basic necessities.

During the span of any project, a number of conferences will be scheduled sequentially to:

1. weigh the owner's needs within the confines of the funds available
2. review preliminary or working plans and specs
3. discuss conformance with plans and specs
4. evaluate progress, coordination, and direction
5. identify and resolve problems
6. document progress and difficulties

Through such conferences pulse the life of any project, for it is here where the project succeeds or fails. Perhaps, at this point, the reader recognizes the rationale behind this text's strategy in examining first the CM/psychology basics, personality profiles, individual and group dynamics, and methods of communication—the skeleton that supports the meat of the construction process, the meeting.

As seen in group dynamics, most decisions throughout the world are made by small groups. In construction management it is handily discerned that, although a conference may involve only three people, the ripple effect of their decision often touches the jobs of several hundred others, as well as great sums of money. Furthermore, construction meetings carry other serious consequences—time for one. First and foremost, you should realize that to assemble members from various groups in one location for a period of hours is an expensive proposition. A progress conference may include: the architect and his engineering consultants; the owner's representatives (project engineer, inspectors, clerk of works, etc.); the general contractor and his subs; the superintendent; trade foremen; and, finally, the project manager. In salaries alone, this amounts to several hundred dollars per meeting. Multiplying this amount by the frequency leads to thousands of dollars per project. Consider the money lost when time is wasted because of poor communications, lack of preparation or effort, and personality and group discord.

Prized is that individual who can master those social techniques that smooth the relationships between people working with people. Everyone knows that it is much easier to function in a respectful and congenial setting than in one that emanates distrust and hostility. Yet knowledge does not necessarily lead to implementation. Some people have a totally adverse reaction to meetings. They consider them a waste of time and energy—a lot of hot air. Such attitudes lend little to a solution. Nevertheless, if we learn bad habits and attitudes we can try to unlearn them. If everyone pulls the rope instead of pushing, the combined force adds vectorially. When all members, especially the leaders, energetically endeavor to improve the substance of a meeting and the process by which they conduct it, then certainly all groups will benefit in time and money. For example, if an architect or contractor arrives late or ill-prepared for a conference, his laxity translates into money lost from everyone's pocket, a monetary fact not always expressed or realized.

Therefore, accept the dictate that construction meetings are neither social events nor places to kill a few hours away from the office. They are expensive investments whose primary purpose is to bring together those people necessary to build a structure. Its two major expectations are: (1) to exchange information and ideas (progress, coordination, scheduling, etc.); and (2) to solve problems. Although individual effort can produce tangible results, often the group effort is the only practical means to reach an end. Such is the case in construction. No one individual could excel in all the intricacies of architecture, engineering, and the contracting specialties.

This is not to suggest that each task requires a conference. Justification should be the first consideration. For example, group ventures may produce inadequate or unsuitable results when the objective is to draw detailed analyses or to translate concepts into ideas. These objectives require intense concentration, which an individual can more aptly handle (i.e., designing a detail, writing a spec, reading a blueprint). On the other hand, groups of individuals, more so than one person, produce more ideas and enjoy larger resevoirs of information, qualitatively and quantitatively. This is due to multiplicity of backgrounds, perspectives, and talents.

Box 6.2. EFFECTIVE GROUP DISCUSSION

Frequently in-house meetings are called to provide advice and data in support of a management course of action. Often the responsibility for the ultimate ruling rests solely with one person, say the president of the architectural firm or the subcontractor's proprietor. Periodically, however, major decisions are provided by the membership in total. For example, in a brainstorming session, the function is to generate new ideas and original solutions.

It is true that group decisions may be slow and frustrating, but in many cases, they have been found to be successful for a number of reasons:

1. *Often the group is better able than a single person to develop fresh alternatives. A free exchange of opinions and information allows each member to draw upon the contribution of his colleagues. This increases the probability of a good decision, because from the quantity of available options springs quality.*
2. *A group decision implies that the entire membership has participated, and, by acquiescence, compromise, or acceptance, has agreed to the final judgment.*
3. *Individual members are more inclined to conform to a collective decision, especially if all the issues and evidence have been openly aired and fully critiqued.*

Social psychologists propose a number of broad guidelines that lead to effective group discussion:
1. *Define the issues. Explain goals.*

2. *Present ideas and information without imposing preconceived solutions. Explore all avenues.*
3. *Give careful weight to the ideas of others. Often a marginal idea may trigger a profound solution.*
4. *Avoid arguments or playing politics. The outcome is not to win a point, but to find solutions. Establish a tolerant climate.*
5. *Be brief and direct. Limit the discussion to one topic at a time before moving on to others.*
6. *Periodically, summarize the progress of the meeting. This not only illuminates the progress, but helps to spotlight misunderstandings.*
7. *Ensure that everyone participates.*
8. *In concluding the meeting, review the important decisions.*
9. *Document and distribute the outcome.*

As with any tool, a conference can be applied correctly or misapplied. It is frequently fruitful to hold a conference when:

1. An individual or leader seeks input or advice from the membership.
2. A leader wants to involve the group in a particular decision or an assignment.
3. There exists an issue that needs clarification.
4. There are certain problems or data that the leader wants to share with his group as a whole.
5. The group members have requested the meeting.
6. There is a conflict that involves people from other groups.
7. There is confusion concerning job responsibilities; who is to do what and when.

One should avoid scheduling a meeting when:

1. The issues at stake are personal: negotiating salary, evaluating job performance, etc. Such matters are best handled by the supervisor and the subordinate in question.
2. There is insufficient time for adequate preparation.
3. The objective could be better communicated by phone or memo (or on a one-to-one level if only two people are involved).
4. There is confidential material that cannot be shared with others.
5. The decision has already been made.
6. The subject material is trivial.
7. There is too much emotion, especially anger and hostility. People need time to calm down before resuming contact.

These introductory comments having been made, the remainder of the chapter proposes to answer such fundamental questions as:

1. Why do so many meetings fail?
2. What constitutes an effective meeting?
3. How should a meeting be prepared and conducted?
4. What are the mechanics of meetings; what are appropriate leadership strategies?

Regardless of what group one belongs to, he anticipates technical difficulties in all phases of the contract life—an omission here, a late delivery there, a granite wall hiding behind an innocuous wallboard here, a large boulder buried there. Whether these obstacles can be remedied easily or painfully is directly proportional to the quality of leadership, motivation, respect, dedication, and the other psychological and people factors brought into focus in the introductory chapters. More often than not difficulties are brought to light in meetings, especially progress meetings. Unfortunately, too often the team is assembled with a specific objective or function in mind, and yet nothing materializes. The road to hell is indeed paved with good intentions. For one or a number of reasons, the meeting fails.

A. Why Meetings Fail

"Happy families are all alike; every unhappy family is unhappy in its own way." So wrote the great Russian novelist Tolstoy in the perceptive opening sentence of *Anna Karenina*. The same could be said for meetings (and projects for that matter.)

All good conferences seem to be alike: well-planned, well-executed affairs in which a majority of members actively and constructively participate. And all bad ones are "bummers" in their own distinct way.

1. Twenty-Five Reasons

For a starter, here are 25 causes that in general terms encompass the more readily recognized malpractices and misfits. The reader should be able to identify most, if not all, of them.

a. Lack of Preparation or Motivation.   Half the participants show up with only a vague concept of "what it's all about." Plans and specs are missing. Critical documentation is locked in the office file and the key is missing. Lacking an agenda, the meeting is played by ear. After a late start and a casual affair with the coffee wagon, the meeting breaks early for lunch. Several members fail to return.

b. Unclear Responsibility About Who, What, When, and How. Someone always misses the message. "I thought you were supposed to do that," is his trademark. Or, "But you said next week, didn't you?" and "Oh him? He's out of town."

c. Negative Attitudes. Even before the discussion commences, individuals have already decided the outcome. Negotiation or compromise is absolutely out of the question. It is win or nothing.

d. Vague Problem Definitions. Everyone has an opinion, but no one has the facts. Evidence is all hearsay, incomplete, or distorted to suit one's interest. Even the expected outcome is muddled.

e. Misguided Energy. With the rationale of lemmings bound for the sea, everybody scurries off in different directions, all jabbering simultaneously. Everyone talks; nobody listens.

f. Feast or Famine. Communication is either too much or too little. Pauses of silence are punctuated with outbursts of activity.

g. Too Much Ground. Too much content is stuffed into one meeting. Consequently, when a good idea is presented, it gets smothered in the avalanche.

h. Unbalanced Dialogue. A few people become orators hawking their own interests without allowing equal time for other viewpoints.

i. Unresolved Issues. The meeting begins on the same sour note, the unresolved complaint or issue that resurfaces again and again.

j. Poor Meeting Location. Inside a crowded trailer, the cramped participants seat themselves on top of desks, tables, and upturned wastebaskets. Telephones and workers constantly interrupt the dialogue. Cigarette smoke fogs the interior like a poolhall.

k. Faulty Record-Keeping. The minutes are either too late, too slanted, or out-and-out inaccurate. Three single-spaced pages elaborate on the successes of the job; four abstract words imply something about a precariously leaning wall.

l. Misuse of Authority. Via steamroller tactics, the leader coerces: "It's my way or else!"

m. Manipulation. Self-appointed leaders or "experts" dominate the meeting by filibuster or intimidation.

n. Wavering Decisions. Trading off anything in the name of harmony or "good guy" images, decisions are constantly changed to appease the most vocal faction at that particular moment.

o. Tardiness. Consistently a member shows up late, and demands to be informed of the previous discussion.

p. Repetition. To the detriment of all other matters, a dogmatic member keeps harping on his pet peeve.

q. Avoidance of Problems. Blinded to the obvious, a member refuses to recognize a difficulty. "Everything is just A-O-K." Meanwhile the wall tilts more.

r. Stonewalling. A member adamantly refuses to cooperate with another. Even if he can easily lend assistance, he figures, "Let him stew. I don't like him anyway."

s. Attack. A volatile member, quick to take offense, attacks anyone whose idea runs counter to his perspective. Anyone who disagrees with him is either stupid or an enemy.

t. Nonentities. These silent individuals vegetate and contribute nothing.

Each of the previous twenty causes erodes the underpinning of any conference, whether in-house or with other groups. To these are added the following shortcomings, which are descriptive of a poor construction team atmosphere.

u. Group Think. One group or faction may have the illusion that it is so strong or so talented as to be invincible—it cannot make an error or make a concession. Such a group may feel that its position is such that bargaining or even listening to others is unworthy. For example, the overzealous leader of an owner group may demand that each and every contract provision, regardless of practicality or applicability, be stringently enforced to the high side of the gray areas. Otherwise, he will notify the bonding company or terminate the contract. Group think could well apply to an eminent architectural team also; its definition of beauty is the only acceptable definition—period.

v. Group Solidarity. Meetings may fail because of group pressures. Each group educates its membership as to the acceptable means and objectives, some of which are incompatible with the philosophy and values of the other groups. Therefore, a loyal, dedicated person may feel reluctant to oppose the members of his particular group. He subdues his individual preference, and adopts the group approach and methodology. He may circumvent the facts and turn a deaf ear to the others, as he tries to protect the interests of his own group. In settings of mistrust and misapprehension, he may receive instructions to the effect that "a good offence is the best defence"—anyway it is "them" against "us." Make no mistake about it: groups standards certainly impress upon the membership the need to conform and to suppress individuality for the achievement of the group objectives. These group norms tend to influence the individual dramatically, pressuring him to think, feel, and act in an expected way. After all, they are the standards by which one's behavior is judged and rewarded.

w. Opposing Personalities. Vocational studies assert that statistically positive correlations exist between careers and personality traits. The architect is verbally expressive and somewhat sensitive and unconventional; the tradesman is aggressive, oriented toward things and machines, and less verbally inclined; the engineer is practical and logical; the contractor/businessman is wealth-directed and dynamic. One man's pie is another man's poison, and sometimes this diversity fuels a controversy.

Contractual consequences can widen these differences, especially in times of difficulty. It is one thing for a civil service inspector/architect to push for condemnation of a marginal piping installation—it is no money out of his pocket. It is quite another matter for the plumbing sub. He sees a shrinking profit margin and possibly business failure.

x. Ineffective Communication. At the root of any meeting miscarriage is lack of proper communication, whether or not the problem is technical or psychological. The wisdom of much of our decision-making depends directly on the quality of the communication (verbal and nonverbal) especially in small groups.

As discussed, unfortunately for constructioneers, communications remains one of the least understood of the group processes. Especially when money or pride is at stake, often the most innocent and unintended non-verbal cue, whether it takes the form of a squeezed fist, or a flicker of the eyelid, sets off a chain reaction of animosity and ill will. The antagonized person or group then sets a battlement of defense mechanisms, leading to games of strategies and subterfuges.

y. Poor Leadership/Supervision. As discussed in Chapter 1, this includes the following areas: (1) direction; (2) decisions; (3) confidence; (4) dedication; (5) planning and execution; and (6) assertiveness.

Recognize any defects? Of course! From job to job, these ills appear and reappear as faithfully and irritably as the hayfever season. Whether allied with designer, owner, or contractor, who has never suffered the misfortune of attending a long, boring session that accomplished little but to cause a splitting headache? Unstructured, or torpedoed by maladroits, it was virtually a waste of time. Individuals saunter in a half hour late; others stare out the window. Several clusters simultaneously carry on different conversations—one clique loudly threatens a $1 million lawsuit; meanwhile, at the other end of the trailer, another cluster calmly rehashes the World Series. Gripes, empty promises, unasked questions—gaps and mismatches in understanding and motivation, no rhyme or reason—ad nauseam. Fortunately, not every meeting degenerates to this level, but too many conferences do, in fact, suffer some of these defects, causing wasted time, lost money, and unnecessary aggravation.

In order to outline a plan of attack for corrective measures, these 25 reasons are subdivided into two groups: trouble people and torpedo strategies. Later in the chapter, after identifying those qualities of a good meeting, we will comment on how to prevent or alleviate these defects, but first, we explore the problem people.

2. Trouble People

Whether leader or follower, introvert or extrovert, saint or sinner, there are essentially 15 types of individuals whose behavior causes many a conference to fail to achieve a successful outcome. Whom do you recognize—yourself?

a. The Bully. The bully is an aggressive individual who always unfairly pushes his point of view, regardless of the merits of the opposition. There is no compromise—he must have his way.

b. The Loudmouth. Cousin to the bully, the loudmouth allows no one to have a turn at speaking. Offensively he interrupts, interjects his views, concludes statements, and finishes sentences for other people.

c. The Attacker. He launches personal attacks on all members of the group. He sometimes resorts to name-calling, profanity, character assassination, and dubious innuendoes.

d. The Latecomer. When he finally arrives, typically half an hour late, the meeting must stop at his request to rehash and review previous discussion.

e. The Early Exist. Always pressed by other commitments, he leaves early, often conveniently, at a crucial point when his head is on the block. Besides interrupting the interchange of dialogue, this misfit sends demoralizing nonverbal messages.

f. The Busy Body. Throughout the meeting, he darts in and out, taking phone messages, going for coffee, cigarettes, etc. Upon returning, he wants to know what he missed.

g. The Dropout. He contributes not one iota of effort. Typically nested in the back of the room, he takes no notes, and seldom offers a comment other than an occasional, "Ah, who cares—who's buying lunch?" In quiet moments, his snoring distracts everyone's concentration.

h. The Broken Record. A living contradiction to the dropout, he keeps repeating the same point over and over again (i.e., a pet peeve, an injustice, or a complaint).

i. The Know-It-All. This self-styled expert on every phase of construction prefaces his every statement with "I've been in this field for twenty-two years . . ." or "I've got a Master's degree from . . ." It matters little to him that he worked the 20 years as an apprentice laborer, or that his Master's degree is in anthropology. In any case, he epitomizes the Monday morning supercritic, emphasizing what should have been done.

j. The Doubting Thomas. Each time an issue is discussed, he shakes his head, rolls his eyes in despair, and emits a low keening of doomed failure. "It'll never work—never in a hundred years" is his battle cry. Verbally and nonverbally, he negates everything, and discourages everyone.

k. The Whisperer. Always in a furtive whisper, he constantly talks about irrelevant topics. Sometimes he makes a good point vocally to the other members, but most times not.

l. The Rumor Monger. His forte is to pass along rumors. Fact or fiction, he expresses them as though they were as immutable as Newton's second law.

m. The Interrupter. He speaks for other people. Jumping into the sentence of another, he finishes the thought because he "knows" what the other person "means." Three quarters of the time, his interpretation is wrong.

n. The Cave Man. Whether because of shyness, insecurity, or natural reticence, he dwells in a cave. Even if he possesses knowledge and expertise, he is reluctant to share it.

o. The Hesitator. Besieged with self-doubt, he finds the most obvious decision a traumatic experience. Hemming and hawing, he ponders ever so carefully every decision, critically conjuring up all consequences. By the time he is ready to make a decision, the meeting has been adjourned or the project has been completed.

3. Torpedo Strategies

It is indeed difficult, if not impossible, to separate people and their methodology. After all, it is the people who implement the methods. For the sake of analysis, a few propaganda techniques and dubious strategies, commonly employed, will be examined. By no means do we suggest that you are to use these techniques; one should recognize, however, that these strategies are used and should be prepared to act accordingly.

a. Sandbag the Project. Pretend to go along with plans, specs, and decisions, but in fact do as you wish. "Sure I'll correct it—right away." But you never do. By doing nothing, and making empty promises, you hope that the problem (say a guarantee item or a minor noncompliance) will disappear or will, in time, become accepted because the owner wearies of all the hassling.

b. Stall the Project. "Let's study the problem." "Let's call in another consultant." "Let's set up a committee." This approach gives an impression of concern and noble motives, but, again, the ulterior reason is the same as in the preceeding illustration.

c. Wait and See. Test everybody's reactions. Try anything that you think you can get away with, such as knowingly substituting cheaper quality goods or workmanship or submitting for a 50 percent progress payment when only 20 percent of the work has been completed. Act surprised (or insulted) when confronted with the situation.

d. Be Absent. At decision time, be absent (out of town, incapacitated, or sick). Send a representative who has no authority to make a commitment.

e. Browbeat the Other Groups. Be completely unreasonable. Shoot for the moon. Demand your rights. Inundate everybody with paperwork protesting anything and everything. Lay the ground work for future claims. Pound at the opponent's weaknesses or harass him with incidentals. Keep calling meetings. If someone is doing something incorrectly, let him continue to do so until the end of the project. Then lower the boom. Notify your attorney.

f. Divide and Conquer. Especially when you are the guilty party, try to create dissension within specific groups, say between a GC/sub or between designer/owner. Then blame them for the shabby cooperation.

g. Mobilize Your Forces. Bring in a large team of experts to intimidate the opponents. There is safety in numbers, and the element of social pressure can become menacing. Cast your own experts into specialist roles (i.e., a lawyer to assist in "defining" and "resolving" problems). Also use good guy/bad guy team techniques—the bad guy, obnoxious and unyielding, sets up the opponent for the empathetic good guy. Bring a stenographer, a tape recorder, or both for the ultimate in intimidation.

h. Dodge the Questions. There are numerous ways to not answer a question:

1. Sidestep the question. Avoid answering completely or directly. Instead answer with a longwinded statement that defuses the actual question and muddles the issue.
2. Ask that the query be put in writing (so as to stall for time).
3. Answer incompletely by using such phrases as "As I understand you . . ." or "Let me rephrase the question . . ."
4. Leave the questioner with the impression that he has been answered.
5. Before answering, cause a distraction—go to the men's room.
6. Display indignation; claim that the question is insulting to your intelligence, or that it is impossible to answer. Claim that the inquiry is tantamount to an inquisition.

i. Use Propaganda. Appeal to prejudice and emotion—not to intellect and enlightenment. At times everybody is susceptible to propaganda. These devices work best when people are too lazy to think for themselves. They let others do their thinking. Of the devices available (loaded word; transfer of testimony; bandwagon; card-stacking; arousal of needs; and appeal to prejudice), three illustrations are given below:

1. Using the loaded word, assassinate the character of your opponent, or question his integrity or expertise. Even more effective, add the bandwagon device. "Everybody knows you're unfair (indecisive, incompetent, cheap, etc.)." Use common negative stereotypes.

2. Stack the cards with glittering generalities and "facts," preferably those that cannot be checked. "It's in the trade journals—all the statistics!" Avoid identifying any specific reference.

3. Arouse needs with statements such as: "All right, you want me to return the equipment! It's a two-year delivery! Are you going to accept the responsibility for a two-year delay?"

j. Flee the Scene. Finally, in moments of desperation, leave the meeting. Feign illness or insult, or claim that another, more important engagement forces you to leave. Even better, you can claim ill-preparedness because you were ignorant of the specific intent of the meeting. Then throw the guilt onto your opponent by asking indignantly "Why didn't you give me proper notification beforehand? Why wasn't I sent an agenda?"

We hope no actual project is burdened with a high percentage of misfits or unethical strategies, somewhat overstated here for emphasis. On a lesser scale, however, many meetings flounder because certain individuals fail to recognize or to correct their offensive behavior. Furthermore, such behavior is often left unchecked or unacknowledged. Consequently, the team bears the brunt. As to what remedies are available, each individual must decide for himself the best approach to handle the case in point. In normal circumstances, assertion and communication skills should yield good results. Yet, if the offenses are too severe, then the only recourse is to refer the issue to the proper authority: management or legal counsel. The text assumes that only generally minor infractions are involved. Even so, these contribute to less productive meetings.

THE EFFECTIVE MEETING

> *If a better system is thine, impart it; if not,*
> *make use of mine*
>
> Horace

In contrast to the negative sides of meetings, inclusive of the misfits and shortcomings, the text now identifies some positive elements affiliated with a productive conference. To this end, we hope the reader can find practical application of those methods and concepts covered in the previous sections: assertiveness; individual and group personalities; and communication skills.

A. Negotiations

Within the readily acknowledged restrictions imposed by contract, negotiating and bargaining techniques are examined because they offer some interesting and useful concepts that may improve the yield of any meeting.

By virtue of the contract documents, construction obligations are defined in no uncertain terms. Legal responsibility for every reasonable situation is laid at someone's doorstep. As a matter of practicality, however, as witnessed on every project, not every issue is settled in the courts. There is always a margin in every interpretation—another side to every story. There is always a doubt in every decision—the best one can do is to choose the best alternative at his disposal. We emphatically do not suggest that anyone trade off what is due him. As seen in the discussion of assertion, we are all governed somewhat by self-interest, and should appropriately assert ourselves. The owner buys a product and, rightfully so, he expects the product signed, sealed, and delivered. The architect is held to furnish a working design, and the contractor to build in conformance. If there is a definite breach, serious and costly, then so be it. Call a spade a spade, and muster the attorneys. But, in less serious matters consider the psychology involved, as well as the common sense angle: many disputes and decisions are best handled via compromise. In the life of every project, one encounters those "gives and takes," a favorable interpretation in one case—a hard line in another, a helpful gesture here (i.e., a small extra)—a dogmatic objection there (i.e., change order claim). Above and beyond contractual obligations, an owner can lean over backward to provide sufficient storage areas, allow easy access routes for traffic, willingly suffer some inconveniences in shutdowns, and muzzle an overzealous inspection crew. In reciprocity the contractor can extend an extra effort without undue expenditures, can expeditiously correct nuisances, and provide incidentals to improve public relations. Whatever the situation, the human factor is ever present. For example, when a designer evaluates the percentage of job completed, necessary to establish the progress payment, or interprets a hazy point in the specs, obviously there is some tolerance, plus or minus. Very possibly on those happy, sunny days when he receives an unexpected bonus, and especially if he likes the contractor, he judges favorably. But on those dark, bleak days when he is depressed, or in the throes of a mini male menopause, he may well decide "thumbs down." (Such mental states and such factors cannot be divorced from many decisions). Ideally by final completion, the score evens for all parties with the result that the satisfied owner receives what he bought; the designer enhances his reputation (and potential for future clients); the contractor makes a fair profit and adds another star to his catalog of successes.

The following discussion is limited to issues that are within the letter of the contract, and are certainly not sufficiently serious to require litigation or arbitration. Basically, in intergroup conflicts, there are three approaches to any settlement: (1) trample the opponent; (2) flee the scene—quit the job and let someone else worry about it; (3) iron out an agreement. Fortunately, most agreements are reached by the bargaining process, which sociologically refers to that process whereby groups attempt to settle in a give-and-take fashion. Formal negotiations can occur only if the following conditions are met:

1. There has to be two or more people or groups.
2. A conflict must exist.
3. The groups must be in attendance voluntarily. Although they compete, they must also cooperate.
4. The activity is centered on resolving one or more issues that can be compromised. Success depends on the free discussion of ideas, positions, and interpretations. This defines areas of agreement and contention—obviously a definite, expensive noncompliance is completely out of the question, but a border line interpretation is within the scope.

5. Each party must be willing to yield to a reasonable extent. Parties interact through a number of offers and counteroffers—give and take, trading value for value appropriate to their self-interests. Negotiation is not a game, nor a war. The goal should be to achieve agreement, not total victory, because, generally, a mutual compromise will result in lasting accord.

6. The parties must trust each other to some extent, or else they will be immobilized with "safety clauses" and a them-against-us philosophy.

As explained in the bargaining example of Chapter 5, a similar procedure, although more informal, is often followed in construction. For example, a designer specifies a piece of equipment along with the phrase "or equal"; the contractor submits a shop drawing for a piece of equipment that is inferior (and less costly). The designer rejects the shop drawing for not conforming to the specs. The two bicker back and forth, one emphasizing the merits, the other highlighting the deficiencies. As is often the case, the piece of equipment finally accepted may be somewhat inferior to the one originally specified (but within the intent of "or equal") and of better quality than the initial submission—hence, a compromise. Every spec has limits of precision—inherently a flaw in any language process. Of course, one can take a strong position, truly believing himself to be absolutely right. He can be stubborn and unwilling to concede an inch. In this case, bargaining will be impossible. If the other side feels just as strongly, a standoff results. Then the dispute must be referred to the upper echelon, where bargaining may or may not be successful, and so on to the docket. It is true that hard lines win many battles, but it is equally true that hard lines lose many wars. If, for the sake of illustration, the contractor is forced to relent, in spite of his true belief that he was justified in his first submission, he may well slack off in other matters, say marginal materials or workmanship—within the contract but just barely. Or worse, he may resort to the torpedo strategy of attempting anything that he thinks he can pull off.

The *Handbook of Construction Management and Organization* mentions a case whereby a "tough" agency unfairly knuckled reputable contractors to the point where they refused to submit future proposals. In a similar light is the union that hammers out a sweetheart package with the result of bankrupt contractors and curtailed building programs. Who really wins? No one.

Call it by any name—a reasonable compromise, bargaining, or negotiation—it is an essential process in the world in which we live. Every construction project will encounter problems that must be solved, often requiring tradeoffs as the best practical alternatives. In a respectful, assertive climate, no one need feel he has to relinquish his just due, only to discriminate between the various shades of gray and other perspectives. Few contracts, especially those as complex as construction documents, regardless of how well-written or how well-executed, are carried out to the exact letter with all parties satisfied to the nth degree. There are always a few t's left uncrossed, a few periods omitted, and maybe a misspelling here and there. To expect, or demand, otherwise is unrealistic.

B. Preconference Preparation

As with any task, the key to a successful conference is adequate preparation. The more refined a group plans initially, the greater the probability it will benefit at the conference table. In general terms, as far as methodology is concerned, there are three basic ingredients for an effective meeting—necessary but not sufficient conditions.

1. There must be a common focus on the content—for what purpose was the meeting called: progress? problems? to register a claim or protest? Brainstorm?

2. Each group must assign a specified individual not only to act as an authorized representative, but to ensure that his subordinates actively prepare and participate.

3. Everyone, particularly the group leaders (job captain, owner's rep, and project manager), must be instrumental in maintaining a tolerant, yet disciplined flow of dialogue. Each must bear the responsibility of airing his views without attacking or intimidating others.

Although commitment to these points will not guarantee success, it is a good beginning. On more specific terms, each group should attend to (1) initial planning, and (2) preparing the agenda.

1. Initial Planning

First and foremost several questions need to be answered by each group leader.

a. What? What are the objectives, implications, and expectations of the meetings? To discuss the progress on a smooth-running project calls for preparation markedly different from that needed for addressing a serious protest. One must determine the nature of the beast; otherwise, he will be unable to assemble the necessary personnel and relevant data. In parallel, he must define not only his obligations, assumptions, and positions but anticipate those of the other groups. It may well be required that he brainstorm with the in-house staff to formulate ideas and alternatives.

b. Who? Predicated on the nature of the conference, the leader must decide who should attend to best serve the intentions of the group. Experts? Top management? Furthermore, tasks must be assigned in advance—who is to do what and on what schedule? From a psychological view, the leader should consider the effects of group size. A one-man group has the following advantages:

1. It prevents the other groups from directing questions at the weakest member, or creating intergroup discord.
2. It places complete responsibility on one individual.
3. It lends itself to quick decisions.

However, a large group offers some favorable points:

1. Each member has a specialty, and can correct misstated facts.
2. Two heads are better than one. It enables a pooling of judgment and planning in advance.
3. It presents the other groups with large opposition, which in the name of oneupmanship, can be somewhat disconcerting.

c. Where? Regardless of the actual general location, the room itself should be conducive to an orderly, comfortable environment (i.e., normal temperature, adequate smoke exhaust, sufficient lighting, etc.). The importance of the meeting should be evidenced by the physical arrangements. To hold a preconstruction meeting in a hissing steam tunnel starts the project off on the wrong foot, physically as well as nonverbally. Noise and other distractions must be curtailed, if not completely avoided.

As with the psychology associated with group size, a group leader must also weigh the pros and cons of the conference site. Some advantages of choosing your offices are:

1. It enables you to get approval that may be necessary for difficulties that you failed to anticipate.
2. It discourages your opponent from adjoining the meeting prematurely and leaving.
3. It gives you a psychological advantage over your opponent—you are in home territory.

But, if you meet at another group's site:

1. You can devote full time to meeting without in-house distractions and interruptions.
2. You have the option of going over your opponent's head to higher management.
3. The burden of arrangement lies with the others.

d. When? Choose a convenient time and one that promises the best return. To schedule a late-afternoon conference on Friday is virtually a waste of time; to begin at 11:00 o'clock leaves just one productive hour until the lunch break, less if members are tardy. Each situation must be judged on its own merit, but, in all cases, allow ample time to cover all important topics.

2. Preparing the Agenda

Every group leader can help stimulate construction-management meetings, by developing an agenda for himself. Whether a designer, an owner, a general contractor, or a sub, you will do well to list your questions and concerns. By doing so, you put on record—a concise record—issues that you consider important, at least to you. Furthermore, from a psychological point of view, you demonstrate to the other participants that you have spent the time and the effort to prepare adequately, and you tactfully indicate, therefore, that others should prepare likewise. Your agenda need not be an iron-clad sequence to be forced upon the others. Instead, it should be flexible and as detailed as necessary to serve your best interests. Besides being a good device to jog your memory, it eases note-taking. Appendix III shows a sample agenda used at a preconstruction meeting.

C. Execution

To define all the components necessary to execute a good meeting is like attempting to encapsulate the best methods of motherhood—virtually an impossibility because of the complex factors involved. As with preparation, however, certain methods are listed with the understanding that the reader implement in tune with his style and his situation.

1. Mechanics of Meetings

The following format is suggested for consideration.

a. Schedule the Meeting in Writing.   If possible, personally confirm the time and place with all parties. Too often, for a number of reasons (i.e., misplaced mail, etc.), someone misses the boat.

At the first meeting, emphasize that all groups should be punctual and prepared. Do this without sounding like a dictator or a Yale cheerleader. Instead, impress upon everyone that punctuality is mutually beneficial, as is one conversation and one topic at a time. Initially, all groups should be appraised as to authority and limitations of individual leaders. It should come as no surprise, but point out that unforeseen obstacles and disagreements will be encountered and will have to be resolved. Therefore, set the tone and request that each party cooperate in a spirit of professionalism and courtesy. Again point out that it is to everyone's advantage. As quoted,

"Well begun is half done" seems applicable to construction meetings, especially the first.

b. Opening.   Always try to open a meeting on a cordial note.

c. Attendance.   Have all attendees sign in.

d. Pass Out the Agenda.   Flexible but comprehensive, it should be the framework for the content of the conference.

e. Review Past Problems.   Determine what has been accomplished regarding past difficulties. Identify unresolved issues and the reasons for delay. Ask questions instead of barking orders and ultimatums or attributing psychological motives to the delinquent.

f. Discuss Progress and Schedules.   Throughout the project, establish reasonable, specific objectives and milestones. These must be clear to all parties and must not be changed lightly. Each group must understand what results are expected and when they are due.

g. Routine Matters.   Resolve routine matters and clean up immediately nuisance items that aggravate one group or another, whether they take the form of debris, irregular reports, or minor punch list items. In minor matters, make immediate decisions. There should be no valid reason why a leader must ponder and weigh an issue that involves only inconsequential depth. Remember that minor grievances, left unattended, have perverse ways of turning into ugly conflicts.

h. Serious Problems.   Depending on the case at hand, discuss less serious problems first. Leave the most serious issues until last. If appropriate, dismiss those parties not involved. When defining a conflict or interpretation, be precise. First and foremost, carefully check the plans and specs to set the case on solid ground. As a leader you must take three important steps: (1) get all the facts concerning the disagreement; (2) get all sides of the argument; (3) settle the matter as promptly as feasible. Whenever a definite decision is called for, act quickly (assuming that you have the authority to make it). You should realize that you can never get all the facts. Judgments are based on the best of available options. Therefore, collect all the data, cut the fat from the meat, and then decide. Normally people will excuse a mistake, but they will seldom excuse a man who consistently walks the fence. Calm, thoughtful deliberation of the problem, followed by logical reasoning, is the surest way to establish confidence and rapport. Of course, not everyone will welcome your final choice. Under such a circumstance keep in mind that if a man disagrees with you, it does not mean that he is conducting a personal attack on your integrity, or that he is either stupid or foolish. He is certainly entitled to his opinion. Avoid talking down or becoming angry—neither enhances understanding or rapport. Remember, your job is to solve problems, not to create them.

As mentioned in the discussion of communication, it is imperative that the specific nature of any disagreement be clearly identified. If it appears that there is any confusion, request that each party paraphrase the disagreement so that it becomes clear what is contested and what is agreed upon.

As a leader, you must regulate the flow of dialogue. Slow down or speed the meeting up depending on the impact or severity of the topic (i.e., a cracked window versus a cracked foundation). When the participants get hung up or fixed on a sticky point, try something else or move on to another topic and return later. If the energy of the group gets low, if it shows loss of interest or signs of frustration, take a short pause or serve refreshments. Sometimes this breaks the deadlock. Then, review what has been previously accomplished. If a lull develops, be prepared to handle silences. Silence often produces the most tension, but different kinds of silence convey many meanings. Is the group just pondering a point? Is it a natural pause? Is the silence the result of confusion? Hostility? Find out what is happening. Ask a question, and, if there is no response, wait a while. Finally, if a definite impasse is apparent, you may decide to take the bull by the horns and adjourn the meeting. Beforehand, schedule a conference date, allowing sufficient time for each group to research and prepare accordingly.

i. Minutes. Usually the architect keeps the minutes, since he is charged with the overall administration. In any case, the pertinent transactions of every meeting should be astutely recorded and expeditiously distributed. This report must be detailed, comprehensive, timely, and, of course, accurate. There is much truth in the Chinese proverb, "The weakest ink is better than the strongest memory." If at times there is a question concerning the accuracy or scope of the conference notes (or any other correspondence). the issue must be quickly addressed in writing. See Appendix III for particular suggestions.

2. Dynamics of Meetings

Although the preceding format is somewhat mechanistic for strict adherence, it does offer an overall antidote for the many causes of inept meetings. This concluding subsection examines the meeting on a more dynamic, interpersonal level, and provides a few counter strategies and approaches to offset problem people and their torpedo methods.

First, we acknowledge that there are unethical or neurotic individuals or groups who, in extreme cases, commit themselves to achieving a certain goal by any means. Whether this goal is money, glory, or fear of failure is inconsequential. What is consequential is their willingness to jeopardize the legitimate interests of other members of the construction team for their personal ends. For example, if a person or group were inclined by makeup to cheat, lie, bully, or withdraw, to the detriment of everyone else, you must acknowledge such behavior, but you do not have to live with it! In such radical cases you must appeal to the proper authority. As stated previously, nothing contained in this text can remove such woes.

Barring such fanaticism, all of us have personal habits, oddities, and approaches that others may find offensive. And since we are social, rational beings, if such characteristics are identified in a tactful way, we usually take steps to modify these characteristics to avoid displeasing others. Of course, this is not to imply that we should dart around in a vicious circle trying to satisfy everyone's standards and wishes. Our self-interests come first and foremost, as long as we deny no one's rights. But, as we saw in the section on learning, society (parents, peers, school, etc.) teaches us to be courteous, sociable, and respectful of others.

For example, if you unwittingly took advantage of someone or offended him, and he forcefully asserted himself, chances are that you would avoid a repeat occurrence. If you hurriedly scribbled a report, and a supervisor pointed out a number of misspellings or inaccuracies, in the future you would be more careful. By analogy, these examples could be extended to problem people and their methods. Whispering is certainly not annoying to the whisperer, but it distracts everyone else. It may very well be that he is unaware of the distracting consequences. The same could be said for the others: the bully, the know-it-all, the doubting Thomas. You can choose to identify their behavior to them, tactfully and assertively, or live with the annoyance. But parallel to living with the situation is the wasted time, lost money, and aggravation of less efficient meetings.

The following potpourri of illustrations incorporates the necessary measures of assertiveness, common sense, and communications to handle most normal situations.

a. The Aggressor. At times an aggressive person might verbally assault your decision. One technique is to thank him for his consideration, be silent for a moment, and then toss the conversation back to him: "How would you suggest that I . . . ?" If the aggressor emotionally attacks another: "That's a stupid idea!" you, as the leader, should emphasize that "In the interest of open communication, everyone is entitled to hold an opinion without abuse. The purpose of the meeting is to work with problems, not an individual's emotions."

b. Lack of Participation. Essentially there are two major obstacles that limit effective participation: (1) difficulty in getting a chance to speak, and (2) fear of ridicule. Therefore, you must ensure that each group member has an equal opportunity to be heard, protected from personal attack as described above. There are a variety of ways to handle the first situation. If people are talking at the same time, you can say something appropriate: "Hold on, only one at a time." Then signal to the individuals pointing to them in sequence. "Why don't you go first, then you, and you. Everybody will be given his chance to speak." The best approach to bring a silent member out of his cocoon is to simply ask, "What do you think about this?" or a similar question.

As for the dropout, nested on the periphery of the conversation, possibly doodling, reading a magazine, or yawning, you can ask, "What do you think about that?" After a few seconds of awkward silence, he may well pay attention. If this fails to turn the trick, you can always use the assertive methods after the meeting—likewise, for the busybody, early exit, or latecomer.

c. Overparticipation.   With respect to the painfully talkative know-it-all, especially one with actual expertise—"I've been in construction (engineering) for 30 years . . .", you can recognize his expertise, but with qualification. "We appreciate your opinion, but other people have other views." The same techniques could be applied to the broken record, the rumor monger, the interrupter, etc.

The doubting Thomas overparticipates in a negative way. He tends to put a damper on any constructive idea. Not only verbally: "It'll never work," but nonverbally as well. By dramatic gestures, such as grimaces, head shaking, crossing and uncrossing his legs, he can disrupt a meeting just as forcibly as if he shouted. Confront him straight on with a perception check, such as, "I see you're shaking your head. Does that mean you disagree?" Then boomerang, "Well, what would you suggest?" If the skepticism persists, then assert yourself.

d. Torpedo Strategies.   First and foremost, these discussions are limited to minor infractions. Even so, they disrupt meetings. You must correctly identify and assess each situation individually. Is someone stalling, or legitimately in need of sufficient time to study the situation? Is the strategy a case of business oneupmanship, or one bordering the unethical? Judge for yourself, and act assertively, especially at the outset. If you give an ounce, there is always the predator who drools for a pound. If a strategy (or any act) brings a reward, psychological behaviorists tell us that the act will most likely be repeated. Habits are formed in this fashion. So, if you allow a strategy to become the status quo, then all the more effort will be required to change it.

Concerning propaganda and dodging questions, once they are recognized, they should be easy to handle. Approaches such as, "Who cares if MIT uses this equipment (design)? Explain how that is relevant in this case?" should defuse the transfer of testimony.

Because the remainder of the book concentrates on solutions to technical problems via creativity methods, this chapter closes with one final comment relative to the interpersonal side of construction. If you know yourself (strong points and hangups); if you recognize the potential for disparity that exists because of varying individual and group perspectives and personalities; if you understand the pitfalls of communications and develop a few skills; and, finally, if you have the courage to properly assert yourself, then you have circumvented many unnecessary obstacles, whatever your career may be.

Box 6.3. MEETINGS—EVALUATION

	YES	NO

This checklist can be used to jog the reader's memory in evaluating the success of any particular meeting or in planning and conducting the conference.

I. PRECONFERENCE PREPARATION

1. *The issues and questions were carefully studied so that the purpose of the meeting was underscored with why, what, who, when, and where in order to accomplish tentative expectations and goals.*
2. *An adequate meeting room was reserved.*
3. *The agenda was prepared; the items to be discussed were compatible with the time allotted.*
4. *Explicit notification and schedules were forwarded to the proper parties in time to allow for sufficient preparation.*

II. CONFERENCE

1. *The structure of the meeting was appropriate to the task and the occasion. (For instance, in-house brainstorming would call for a leaderless type of structure.)*
2. *All the participants recognized and accepted the topics being addressed.*
3. *Everybody knew where the final authority lay to make the final decision.*
4. *The right people were involved: those with the rele-*

YES | NO

vant expertise, knowledge, or experience; those who were affected by the problem; and those who had the authority to represent their groups.

5. The conference began promptly on schedule with all in attendance.

6. The atmosphere for the meeting was conducive to the occasion, neither too formal nor too informal.

7. The levels of light and heat and the room size were suitable. Distractions were negligible.

8. The objectives of the meeting were clearly stated in the agenda, so that the participants knew what to expect.

9. All issues were clearly defined and understood by everyone.

10. Each group had enough information or expertise to analyze the problems at hand.

11. The groups examined the various alternatives before stating their respective positions.

12. Everyone participated in a courteous, respectful manner.

13. The leader tried not to dominate the meeting; everyone was given his say in a free exchange.

14. The agenda was flexible enough to allow the participants to revise the format.

15. Each leader was effective in getting his group to concentrate on the common tasks.

16. At the end of the conference, the results were reviewed, so that each person was apprised of who was to do what and when. Decisions were reviewed and acknowledged.

17. A future meeting was tentatively established, along with the probable agenda.

18. The conference notes were taken and expeditiously distributed to each participant.

19. This memo was accurate, detailed, and understandable even to those who were not present.

Bibliography

Bonny, J., and J. Frien, eds. *Handbook of Construction Management and Organization*. New York: Van Nostrand Reinhold Co., 1973.

Brown, James I. *Efficient Reading*, rev. ed. Lexington, Massachusetts: D. C. Heath and Co., 1962.

Doyle, Michael, and David Straus, *How to Make Meetings Work*. New York: Wyden Books, 1976.

Fabun, Don. *Communications, The Transfer of Meaning*. Beverly Hills, California: Glencoe Press, 1968.

Fast, Juluis. *Body Language*. New York: M. Evans and Co., Inc., 1970.

Goldenson, Robert M. *The Encyclopedia of Human Behavior*, vols. 1 and 2. New York: Doubleday and Co., 1970.

Raven, Bertram, H., and Jeffrey Z. Rubin. *Social Psychology: People In Groups*. New York: John Wiley & Sons, Inc., 1976.

Schmuck, Richard A., and Patricia A. Schmuck. *Group Processes in the Classroom*. Dubuque: Wm. C. Brown Publishers, 1971.

Thomson, David S. and the editors of Time-Life Books. *Human Behavior—Language*. New York: Time, Inc., 1975.

Van Dersal, William R. *The Successful Supervisor*, 3 ed. New York: Harper and Row, Publishers, 1974.

Chapter 7

Problem-Solving and Creativity

Fire-Escape.

No. 221,855.   **Patented Nov. 18, 1879.**

UNITED STATES PATENT OFFICE

IMPROVEMENT IN FIRE-ESCAPES

Specification forming part of Letters Patent No. 221,855, dated November 18, 1879
Application filed March 26, 1879

" . . . This invention relates to an improved fire-escape
or safety device, by which a person may safely jump out
of the window of a burning building from any height, and
land, without injury and without the least damage, on the
ground; and it consists of a parachute attached, in suitable
manner, to the upper part of the body, in combination with
overshoes having elastic bottom pads of suitable thickness
to take up the concussion with the ground. . . . "

After A. E. Brown, H. A. Jeffcott, Jr., *Absolutely Mad Inventions*, New York: Dover, 1970.
Reprinted with permission of Dover Publications, Inc.

Abstract

Throughout life, in and out of construction, an individual will be confronted with a continuing array of problems and conflicts that he must learn to overcome. Therefore, the remainder of this text discusses a number of methods that lead not only to solutions but to better solutions.

After we identify those factors that inhibit effective problem-solving, the Dewey system is examined. A generalized procedure applicable to any problem, Dewey's system asserts that the most effective approach is to adopt the "experimentalistic," or pragmatic, point of view: define the problem, develop hypotheses, and test them empirically.

Creativity is analyzed: definitions, associated traits, and the processes involved, such as preparation, incubation, and illumination. In the development of hypotheses, a number of well-recognized techniques are presented, notably Osborn's "Applied Imagination," Gordon's "Synectics," and Parnes' "Idea-Stimulation Techniques." All these techniques have to be altered to suit the construction field.

CONTENTS OF CHAPTER 7

    3. Motivation and Persistence
    4. Sensitivity to the Environment
    5. Fluency
    6. Flexibility
    7. Originality
    8. Humor
  B. A Small Business Administration Study
    1. Alertness
    2. Curiosity
    3. Adaptive Skill
    4. Constructive Dissatisfaction

CREATIVE APPROACHES

  A. Composite Approach
    1. Steps to Originality
  B. Osborn Method
    1. Problem Definition, Preparation, and Analysis
    2. Production and Development of Ideas
    3. Verification and Decision
  C. The Synectics Process
    1. Personal Analogy
    2. Direct Analogy
  D. Miscellaneous Techniques
    1. Functional Visualization
    2. Idea-Stimulation Techniques
  E. Final Comment

QUESTIONS AND PREVIEW

1. Explain how one's personality traits affect problem-solving, pro and con.
2. What steps should be followed whenever confronted with a difficulty or making a decision? What, invariably, is the final step?
3. With respect to construction and construction management, identify some areas that could stand improvement: predesign, design, bid, and construction phases.
4. List some traits that seem conducive to originality.
5. Name important inventions commonly seen on the project site. Identify some examples of ingenuity: design, means, procedures, materials, machines, interpersonal relations.
6. What considerations are essential in decision-making? Why should the quantity of alternatives improve the quality of the solution?
7. What are the benefits and drawbacks of group decisions? How are group cohesiveness and communication related to brainstorming?

PROBLEM-SOLVING

Troubles are often the tools by which God fashions us
for better things

H. W. Beecher

In *The Encyclopedia of Human Behavior*, Dr. Goldenson states,*

"Problem Solving. There is no need to justify the study of problem solving, since life is a continual series of obstacles, difficulties, and frustrations from beginning to end. In fact, this type of behavior is probably the most characteristic activity of the human being, especially at a time when every phase of our existence is rapidly changing and ideas which worked in the past can rarely be used in unchanged form today.

This statement applies to all types of problems, both psychological, in the construction management context of this book, and technical, to which the remainder of the text devotes itself. Furthermore, Dr. Goldenson asserts that the basic methods of attacking these problems have changed far less than the situations themselves. Therefore, our efforts will converge on, first, general steps commonly employed to correct an undesirable physical situation or difficulty. Next, the nature of originality will be examined. Then systems to generate creative solutions will be analyzed, inclusive of specific approaches that an individual or a group can implement to solve the actual situation at hand.

Like medicine and banking, construction is a somewhat conservative industry. Essentially a one-shot (and risky) proposition, construction encourages most designers and contractors to opt for the tried and true. Simplicity, economy, and functionality are usually the keynotes dictated by owners. For example, many spec writers *assemble* specifications rather than *write* them—a Frankensteinian operation of cutting, chopping, and joining previously used paragraphs and sections to fit the design under contract. (In some staid offices the master specs, through the years, begin to yellow and curl like ancient parchments.) For the most part, it is a rational, justifiable approach because of the pressures of time and money. "Let someone else pioneer a new product (or design or construction means and methods), I've got to clean this up in two months. And it's got to be right the first time around!"

Yet competition, even survival, in the face of spiraling costs and explod-

*From *The Encyclopedia of Human Behavior* by Robert M. Goldenson. Copyright © 1970 by Robert M. Goldenson. Used by permission of Doubleday & Company, Inc.

ing techniques forces everyone to improve on old methods. As reported by Dun and Bradstreet, in recent years construction contractors have failed in disproportionate numbers, with respect to total business failures. Why? For a number of reasons: financial, managerial, and technological. Regardless of the specific cause, however, the failure rate underscores one crucial point: improvement, innovation, new methods, creativity—call it what you will—is imperative to any viable organization. With win/no-win, lump-sum competition, the high costs of labor and materials, and sometimes a shrinking economy, all accepted constituents of the construction industry, each group needs to improve its modus operandi. For an explicit comparison of ever-surging building costs (albeit mitigated by inflation) refer to Box 7.1. Similarly, the labor/productivity dilemma is no mystery to the contractor, estimator, or owner.

New ways are urgently needed to solve persistent problems—if they result in improvement and, hence, cost savings and higher payback. Note that the road to hell is paved with good intentions. Enthusiasm and innovations are certainly virtuous attributes, but only when blessed with wisdom and discipline. No one need create a white elephant by chancing risks or using the project site as a personal research and development center. With a good grasp of the problem, however, and with judicial, careful planning, and selective utilization, everyone can fare extremely well.

As stated before, the tools and techniques exist, many based on solid psychological and industrial research. The correct application rests solely with the user faced with a unique dilemma.

As a first consideration this chapter considers some personal, mental obstacles that block productive problem-solving.

A. Factors that Hinder Problem-Solving

From the behavioristic (learning theory) school, whenever an individual (or organism) confronts a barrier to a certain goal (or reward), he faces a few basic choices. He can give up and avoid the situation—psychologically a very nonproductive behavior because he will unlikely ever learn to overcome the barrier. If a baby, after a few tumbles, gave up—he would never learn how to walk. Unfortunately, some individuals adopt this general avoidance reaction, often with damaging consequences. Since time immemorial, nobody nowhere has ever advanced under such a negative philosophy. The self-actualizer, the expert, the genius—all capitalize on their mistakes. Errors are pretty much a part of growth.

A more rational method to achieve a blocked goal is either to change the goal or to circumvent the barrier. Rephrased less scientifically, there are many ways to skin a cat. Such is the case with solving problems. Box 7.2

Box 7.1. COMPARISON OF BUILDING COSTS (1889–PRESENT), DOLLARS PER CUBIC FOOT.

		Actual costs[a]	1977 Median costs[b]
1. BANK Eight-story Bank and Office Building, Atlanta, Georgia	1904. Fireproof; quite elaborate	.41	$3.90 Banks
2. HOTEL Brown Palace Hotel, Denver Colorado	1892. Nine stories; flat roof; all rooms face st; 350 guest rooms, 160 private baths, 17 public toilet rooms, all tiled; steel construction; fireproof; provided with electric light, ice refrigerator plant; laundry; four elevators	.30	$2.35 Apartments
3. LIBRARY Public Library, New London, Connecticut	1889–90. One-story stone bldg; ordinary construction	.36½	$2.80 Libraries
4. HOSPITAL Hospital Bldg., New York City, New York	1890–95. Seven stories; pressed-brick front; stone trimmings; fireproof; thorough heating and ventilating plant; plumbing; much marble and tiling	.40	$4.25 Hospitals
5. SCHOOL Newark High School, Newark, New Jersey	1897–98. A large three-story building, mostly fireproof construction. Cubical contents from basement floor to mean point in roof 1,803,000 cu. ft.	.10¾	$2.05 Schools Sr. High
6. OFFICE BUILDING Manhattan Building, Chicago, Illinois	1892. Sixteen stories; five elevators; two fronts; pressed brick, terra cotta and granite.	.17¹/₃	$2.90 Offices

[a] Actual costs per cubic foot from Frank E. Kidder, *The Architect's and Builder's Pocket-Book*, 15 ed. New York: Wiley, 1908. Reprinted by permission of John Wiley & Sons, Inc.
[b] Approximate costs from *Building Construction Cost Data 1977*, R. Means Co. This information is copyrighted by Robert Snow Means Company, Inc. and is reproduced from *1977 Building Construction Cost Data* with permission.

presents five step-by-step systems that one may follow to reach his objective, whatever its fundamental nature.

For our purposes at present, we study such factors as motivation, definition, hypothesis, and testing. To miss, or stumble on, any of these steps usually leads to detours and failure—easier said than done. By virtue of the chart, it may appear that the road to success is well posted, utterly logical, and quite clearcut, but the world does not work that way. Even if one were to use his talent and logic with such skill as to delight Aristotle, success might still elude him. One major reason is that problem-solving expertise is more than just a function of our logic, knowledge, and experience. It is dependent on some factors that may seem almost unrelated to the difficulty in question, whether it is personal or physical.

1. Lack of Recognition and/or Acknowledgment

Every human being has needs, as classified by Maslow in rank order of strength. A problem is a difficulty, a challenge, an unsatisfied need. Whatever the actual motive, before a person can churn the wheels, he must recognize and acknowledge that a problem indeed exists. Outwardly this statement may seem alien to the observer, but most normal individuals experience anxiety and depression without being able to accurately pinpoint any particular cause. Other individuals persistently ignore even the most serious difficulties. How often we hear: "I don't want to hear about it!" On a more interpersonal level, an aggressive person may see no need to change his offensive behavior because he fails to recognize the consequences of his tactics. For centuries, ignorance, poverty, and slavery were accepted as facts of life, and, therefore, never recognized to be genuine ills. It may be true that ignorance is bliss, but not in construction. Untold lives and finances have been wasted because of the failure to "see" and acknowledge, or even contemplate, the potential of trouble. "No sweat—everything's just fine!" has prefaced many a disaster. That is not to say one need be a mystic or run around the site like a robed "Prophet of Doom," but sometimes small irregularities and wisps of smoke seem to find a way of erupting with volcanic force. Admittedly, many disasters and, on a lesser scale, difficulties are completely unpredictable; but some are in fact the result of failure to acknowledge existence of a problem—in many cases a psychological refusal to see the apparent. As a few cases in point: unenforced safety programs, deteriorating, uninspected equipment, and unexplained abnormalities (cracks, hisses, rumbles, distortions, etc.).

2. Erroneous Definition

Obviously dependent on recognition and acknowledgment, is the definition of the difficulty. Although it is axiomatic that a problem well-defined is half-solved, too often people approach issues blindly—darting here and there

Box 7.2. STEPS IN PROBLEM-SOLVING

Through the years philosophers and, more recently, psychologists have formulated a number of sequential processes for solving problems. Here are five such formulations:[a]

(System) →	**Dewey**	**Osborn**
(Steps to be followed) ↓		
1.	Motivation to recognize and solve difficulty	Orientation: identifying the problem
2.	Delimitation—define and restrict the problem	Preparation: collecting relevant material
3.	Hypothesis—develop tentative solutions	Analysis: breaking down the material into cause/effect relationships
4.	Test the hypothesis	Hypothesis: developing a wide range of alternatives
5.		Incubation: letting ideas simmer in order to invite illumination
6.		Synthesis: assembling and digesting all information
7.		Verification: critical judgment of ideas
8.		

[a]More formal, in terms of broad philosophical traditions, the Dewey system is used to solve general problems of all natures often without an individual giving the process much thought. The more recent Osborn and Synectics systems (actually refinements of the all-encompassing Dewey system) are well-known techniques to develop creative solutions.

Synectics	Work Simplification	Military Method
State the actual problem in concrete terms	Select an area or job that needs improvement	Identify problem
Analyze and discuss to render the strange familiar (and vice versa)	Collect the facts	Research; assemble and analyze facts and data
Purge the immediate solutions	Challenge the details and implications	Define the actual problem
Restate the problem	Improve old methods	Brainstorm for innovations and new ideas
Use analogies, evocative questions, reversals, improbabilities, and other methods to compile many ideas	Implement the improvements	Screen and clarify ideas. Judge the applicability and consequences
Follow ideas to conclusions and implications		Test against external criteria
Apply original and new problem statements to force new perspectives		Execute
Explore new perspectives; repeat steps if necessary		

with little thought to rhymes and reasons—wishfully waiting for "Eureka" to pop into their heads. After repeated failures, they may accept defeat, primarily because they failed to understand the true ilk of the obstacle in the first place. Although, in many concrete situations met on the project, it may prove very difficult to actually discover the exact nature of the problem, the more adequate the definition, the better the odds of a solution. In fact, as we shall see later, the more alternatives that are developed, the more favorable the odds for success. Whatever methods or system one chooses to adopt, he must invariably define precisely those factors that produced the problem initially. For example, during the withdrawal of the First Marine Division from the frozen Changjin Reservoir in Korea. First Lt. R. Glendinning was faced with an almost insurmountable obstacle. At one point the narrow road was cratered entirely across by shelling, causing the column to be halted in the heavy snow and susceptible to enemy attack. In his own words,*

> The dozer tried to fill it with dirt, but the ground was frozen so hard that is was impossible to dig up. The supply of explosives on hand was insufficient to blast loose earth. Bridging the crater was out of the question; there was neither the material nor the time.
>
> All along the line of march, the weary column halted in the heavy snow despite the risk of being hemmed in by attacking Chinese. Something had to be done, and done quickly. What would you have done?

What actually was the trouble? To span the crater? But in the light of the frozen conditions, how? The actual definition was that the hole needed to be filled. Therefore, Glendinning's solution:

> The engineers used the bulldozer to push the snow into the crater. Then they packed it down until the hole was filled. It supported even heavy vehicles and the division marched on.

3. Lack of Motivation

Without motivation it is unlikely that any difficulty will be remedied. Thomas Edison defined genius as "99% perspiration and 1% inspiration." When he was conducting his light investigations, he tried dozens of substances to find that one that would glow without being consumed by electricity. As a matter of record, he was so motivated that he tried 6000 different bamboo specimens before selecting three that worked moderately well. Even so, he

---

*S. J. Parnes, R. B. Noller, and A. M. Biondi, *Guide to Creative Action*, New York: Scribner's, 1977. Reprinted with permission of Charles Scribner's Sons.

continued until the best and final answer was found to be filaments of tungsten. We can safely state that one must be adequately motivated to overcome an obstacle. Too much can be as fruitless as too little, however. It does not logically follow that the stronger one is urged (internally or externally) the more rapidly and easier the goal is reached. If one is too enthusiastic, he may be blinded. With poor organization and plan of attack, he may rush along one road, probably the most obvious route, but one leading to a dead end.

4. Prejudice and Preferences

Without question, training and experience lay the foundation on which one learns to correct troubles. It is certainly gratifying, and somewhat mysterious, to hear of the young designer who brilliantly overcomes a serious obstacle, or to see a crusty old timer glance at a tough question, and, in an offhanded manner, instantly offer the answer. In both instances, the success was a product of, respectively, schooling and experience (if not a combination of both).

Sometimes, however, training and experience, in addition to personality, can hinder a recognition of other routes. Few individuals live their lives by logic and objectivity in the purest form. When beset with difficulties, as discussed in previous chapters, our biases, and preferences—both learned—influence how we perceive the situation, and consequently the approach we take. Through the years, all individuals form habits and develop "comfortable" ways to tackle issues. Sometimes these habits become so rigid that the individual falls victim to what psychologists refer to as "mental set"—the negative effect of clinging to old ideas. The individual walks the same barren path over and over again.

As a simple illustration of this concept try these two puzzles.

1. Pronounce these four words:

    Mactavish   Macdonald   Macbeth   Machinery

2. Think of four-letter words that end in "any."
   Now think of a four-letter word that ends in "eny."

Like many puzzles, these require no genius to solve, only "common sense." Experiments find that many people: (1) pronounce the word as "MacHinery," whereas the correct pronunciation is "machinery"; and (2) fail to think of the word "deny" because as originally phrased, the "y" sounds as "ee" (many, zany, and wany), whereas in "deny" the "y" sounds as the long "i." These two illustrations demonstrate on a small scale how "mental set" determines how one thinks or attacks problems. Had "Machinery" or "eny" been given first, the chances of obtaining the correct solution would have increased.

In construction, men pride themselves on their practical ability. Yet sometimes they stumble and bumble because their "common sense" and past experiences hinder them from attempting new techniques. We emphasize that common sense remains a necessary ingredient of construction. Without it, nothing safe and sound would be built. But these side effects of preferences and bias sometimes hurt, especially in those areas of solving problems creatively.

5. Poor Attitudes and Atmosphere

Since the beginning of time, statements like: "It'll never work" (bias); "But it's always been done this way" (propaganda); and "That's a stupid suggestion!" (aggression) have sabotaged numerous good ideas. Fortunately, the world is full of disbelievers and deaf people. If a person just quits and throws up his hands in futility, believing the trouble to be insurmountable, then, as far as he is concerned, the trouble will, in fact, be insurmountable. Therefore, regardless of the circumstances, think positive. Few problems are completely solved in the absolute sense, but a partial solution is better than none at all. All humans have esteem needs—no one likes to be ridiculed or torn apart by caustic remarks; consequently, in poor group settings, a potential hero may remain silent instead of making suggestions. This may be personally prudent, but it lends nothing to solving the issue. This point will be reexamined when discussing brainstorming.

With these pitfalls behind us, we will give some virile techniques, beginning with the most general system of Dewey.

B. The Dewey System

Preeminent in three fields (philosophy, psychology, and education), Dr. John Dewey wrote in his book *How We Think* (1910) that the most effective procedure to solve any kind of problem was to go through the same steps that are applied in the purist scientific circles. His pragmatic, four-step sequence included: (1) motivation—a difficulty is felt; (2) definition and delimitation—the difficulty is located and defined; (3) hypothesis—possible solutions are suggested and consequences considered; (4) testing—after verification, a best solution is selected. Concise yet extremely comprehensive, this procedure applies to practically every type of reasoning, creating, and problem-solving encountered in human activities. (The other patterns are elaborations of the Dewey system.)

1. Motivation

As mentioned, an individual must face a challenge, feel a need, or confront a barrier, as a prerequisite to seeking a solution. He must recognize and acknowledge that a difficulty causes his discomfort or unrest and therefore warrants correction. His motive may be extremely diverse: ambition, curiosity, or fear—but the driving force must exist. This is a required, but not necessarily a sufficient, condition. For example, in any construction meeting, difficulties are brought to light whether they take the form of late delivery or an uncovered noncompliance. The contract (particularly the payment provisions) usually motivates the parties to act accordingly.

2. Definition and Delimitation

Before the actual attack, a person must define and delimit issues, so that the relevant factors are involved. As an illustration, if the workmanship fails to meet acceptable qualities called for in the specs, it must be determined specifically where and in what degree. Is the total heating system in non-compliance or just two feet of dented duct? This step is often the crucial point in the process because defining the actual difficulty helps to: plan the effort; look for information in the right places; and make observations and tests that suggest best returns. Otherwise, one may bark up the wrong tree. In the long run, time invested in separating fiction from "fact," and asking directive questions will provide a good return. Is the lengthy punch list indicative of poor construction or a personal beef between an inspector and a subcontractor's foreman?

3. Hypothesis

Every decision should be based on the most promising alternative. When faced with trouble, one must develop a number of tentative answers, which often depend on the nub of the problem as defined. If one incorrectly describes a situation rife with incidental features, irrelevant details, and out-and-out inaccuracies, then how can he possibly hypothesize effectively? In the case cited above, if the punch list is indeed accurate, then the contractor is bound to correct the deficiencies. If the conflict originates from a personality clash, however, the most apparent alternatives are either to settle the personal grievances or to remove one of the disputants from the job site.

With regard to quality of guesses or hunches, it is usually the old dog for a hard road. A person with considerable previous experience in similar situations usually outshines the novice. He is less likely to stomp over unfertile ground. Yet, as will be emphasized later, especially in creativity discussions, a chief danger is that he may resist novel, potentially good approaches, electing to stick to the old ways (mental set). It must be borne in mind that a good hypothesis must also be clearly defined, so as to lead the baptism of fire where it is either verified or disproved. A hunch that is nebulous and ill-formulated is like a snake eating his own tail—you go nowhere except around and around in an ever-consuming circle.

4. Testing

The only way to check the validity of any idea is to test it. As demonstrated in Edison's case, testing a hypothesis is frequently a long, arduous process— a series of trials and errors until the needle is plucked from the haystack.

In construction, this process is somewhat shortened. The contract calls for one design and one only. And the actual construction, if in compliance, checks the validity of the design, a potent reason why, in matters of large consequence and finance, radical departures from the standards should be viewed with caution. A job site is far from a testing ground—instead it is a here-and-now affair, undeniably risky at best, with marginal tolerance for error. Nevertheless, in less costly matters, innovations and improvements, executed in proper perspective and with tempered enthusiasm, can prove profitable, if not competitively crucial.

CREATIVE PROBLEM-SOLVING

Where we cannot invent,
we may at least improve

Colton

Creativity is not restricted to eminent artists, writers, scientists, or geniuses. It is a universal attribute utilized since the beginning of time by mankind in his relentless search to improve his lot. From Neanderthal man shaping a new club to an engineer developing a new safety device for a nuclear plant, the creative process seems essentially the same: a problem is recognized; facts are collected and manipulated somehow, so that a unique idea is formed; the idea is tested and verified. As T. W. Higginson quipped, "Originality is simply a pair of fresh eyes." Any ordinary person, on any given day, can create to some degree, depending upon his relevant background and personality. In concept, creativity involves a fresh way of seeing things— a somewhat heightened perception and a sensitivity to recognize associations or combinations. Additionally, it involves the courage to persevere so that these unique hypotheses meet the test of applicability. The patented fire escape in the opening of this chapter is certainly original in concept; however, one would be reluctant to verify its usefulness voluntarily from the pinnacle of the World Trade Center.

In construction, a laborer with a fourth-grade education can be inherently more creative than an architectural professor. Of course, architecture offers more of an opportunity to create than, say, laboring, but, with respect to one's life style, the laborer, through a hobby or avocation, can be very original—more than the architect from a psychological point of view. It is

also reasonable to assume that because all men can be creative to some extent, then men who fail in this respect are failing to maximize their true potential. Everyone can be original. In fact, Maslow told of a woman who was "uneducated, poor, a full-time housewife and mother"—noncreative in the conventional sense. And yet she was a marvelous cook, mother, wife and homemaker. With little money, her home was beautiful. Her meals were banquets. Her taste was impeccable. "She was in all these areas original, novel, ingenious, unexpected, inventive. I just *had* to call her creative."*
According to Maslow's definition, "original, novel, ingenious, unexpected, inventive" seem to be the qualities necessary to creativity—qualities that may be found in anyone.

In construction, within certain individuals, these qualities are apparent. The richness and novelty of how they produce ideas sets them apart from their peers. This text proposes to explain the essence of this originality and to list steps that everyone can follow to produce potentially useful results.

That is not to imply that every problem can be permanently solved with only *one* right solution possible. By experience, one can easily identify many difficulties that are open-ended—many options are available. "What is the best way to do . . .?" welcomes many answers, some of which will be contradictory, depending on one's personality and roles. Since every decision is based on the best of alternatives, however, it follows that, from a statistical viewpoint alone, the more viable options a person generated, the better his chances of making a better decision. In fact, how would a construction manager know what *should* be done until he explored every conceivable option that *might* be done. Both the Osborn and Synectics systems provide the means that help to expand quantity of the alternatives.

As a beginning, we must appreciate that humans think in different ways, depending on the nature of the problem that confronts them. Psychologists, in this area of originality, have invested considerable research, which has returned some interesting and practical findings. Obviously "thinking" is a very complex subject. Therefore, this text limits discussion to only a few cursory comments about some of the different kinds of thought processes. By definition, thinking is defined to be: cognitive behavior in which we remember or manipulate symbols and concepts that represent objects and events. On a less refined basis, we think on three wide levels—analytical, judicial, and creative—as shown in tabular form below:

ANALYTICAL	JUDICIAL	CREATIVE
Aristotelian logic	Law	Inspirational
Mathematics	Testing	Serendipity
Systems analysis	Quality control	Hunches
	Human relations	

*Paul Good, *Human Behavior—The Individual*, New York: Time, Inc., 1974.

Many problems, including those of construction and management, will probably require all three levels, with emphasis on one of them as predicated on the situation at hand. Suffice it to say that the nature of the problem plus the personality of the solver are essentially the two most important factors in determining the methodology to be used along the route.

Osborn (*Applied Imagination*) views mental capacities from a functional standpoint, oversimplified as follows:

1. Absorptive—the ability to perceive, and to concentrate
2. Retentive—the ability to memorize and recall
3. Reasoning—the ability to analyze and judge
4. Creative—the ability to generate ideas, to "see" unusual associations, combinations, and relationships

He asserts that, although computers can perform the first three functions (i.e., via storage, input-output, "Do" and "If" commands) no machine will ever "create" ideas. For example, mathematics demands that one think analytically—objectively, unemotionally, and logically. This is suitable for the computer. An equation, such as: $\$11.70/\text{hr} \times 460 \text{ hr} = ?$, has only one correct answer, but open-ended questions beg for many responses, such as: "What piece of equipment could improve the safety and output of underwater construction?" To be sure, a computer could be fed data bits, so that it calculated millions of times and spewed forth a ream of numbers, but it is extremely doubtful if the computer could have created a solution as did Sir March Brunel. He overcame serious barriers by observing a shipworm tunneling into timber. As the worm moves forward it constructs a tube for itself. By direct analogy, Brunel made this ingenious association with underwater construction. Hence, the classical notion of caissons was created.

The Encyclopedia of Human Behavior defines creative thinking as "a form of directive thinking applied to the discovery of new solutions to problems, new techniques and devices. . . ." It also distinguishes between two types of thinking: divergent and convergent. Convergent thinking (closed system) is the conventional method devoted to solving those problems that have only one answer (i.e., $2 + 2 = 4$). By assembling available facts and adhering to proscribed rules, the answers usually fit into place.

Many difficulties, however, are such that defy the conventional approach. Like Brunel, we must resort to "open system" divergent thinking—referred to as creative and adventurous. On this tack, a number of options must be generated and submitted to the test of consequence and judgment; the best is chosen, the rest discarded. In all probability, Brunel discarded many less suitable ideas, but the one he invented was spectacular.

Whether an engineer, designer, or contractor facing daily routine problems, an individual can solve them by assembling available information and applying established rules. If confronted with a question, "How many yards of concrete are required for . . . ?" he looks in his handbook or charts for the one answer—a cookbook solution. There are no improvements here, no evidence of originality is here, and actually none is required.

Occasionally, however, he is confronted with a unique situation that has no cook-book answer. For example, what is the best method to . . . ? Conventional thinking leads to unoriginal results. Like Brunel, he must brainstorm: he must invent. He must assemble data from his cookbooks in an unusual way, so as to obtain a novel result. This is called divergent thinking. Explore new roads. Take intellectual risks. Traditionally, we associate this open type of thinking with the artist, the inventor, the genius—the so-called creative endeavors. It is this type of cognitive ability that leads to advances, whether in the arts, in politics, in philosophy, in technology, and, in our case, construction management. A hundred years ago, who could have envisioned the machines, the materials, and the methods so commonplace in contemporary construction? Even the past ten years have brought about dramatic changes.

A. The Nature of Creativity

Einstein stated that: "Imagination is more important than knowledge." Although, in some circles, this statement could be challenged, it remains unquestionable that the two combined can render vast, far-reaching results as exemplified by Einstein himself and greats like da Vinci—a virtual volcano of masterpieces ranging from the Mona Lisa to sketches of tanks and flying machines.

It would appear that creativity is somewhat of a blessing, prized universally. But just what is it? Obviously, it is a function of imagination (as seen in the novelty of the fire escape patent). To this must be added knowledge, for, without an adequate background, it appears dubious whether a creation can be produced. It could be said that creativity, in essence, is a function of knowledge, imagination, and evaluation—any one of which is closely intermeshed with an individual's personality. Originality is commonly described as the ability to associate or combine facts into a unique and relevant configuration. The apparent conclusion is that, if one were to possess certain catalytic traits, relevant training and experience, and an awareness of methods to stimulate the possibilities of creativity, then he, too, could create. To these ends, psychologists have pioneered many avenues.

1. Definitions

There are many definitions of creativity:

1. The process of inventing something new and novel and useful.
2. Thinking of new ideas that are useful.

3. Heightened perception of our surroundings, resulting in a unique outlook.

4. The ability to make connections from various pieces of information in a novel way, and to bring these ideas to a fruitful result.

5. New ideas, improvements, inventions, innovations are all forms of creativity. A country or a company, in order to survive, is dependent on the quantity and quality of new ideas, new methods, advanced technology—Yankee ingenuity. So important is creativity to a country that, as a consequence, the United States (and most others) has the present patent system, by which patents are granted by Congress for the public benefit. The inventor is rewarded for disclosing for public knowledge a complete description of his invention. With respect to patent law, an invention involves two factors: (1) conception of the idea, and (2) reduction of this concept to practice (building a model).

6. Finally, our preferred definition: Creativity is the invention or expression of that which is both original to the creator and is useful. This is not unlike the Patent Office definition of an invention.

Even with these definitions stated, the exact nature of the creativity process continues to be somewhat mysterious, and to defy analysis. What "makes" a da Vinci, a Newton, and an Edison? What prompted Faraday, one of the great founders of electromagnetic theory, to envision himself as an atom under great pressure? By doing so, he gained insight into the behavior of an electron. What caused Einstein to fantasize about what would happen to a man who traveled in space at the velocity of light?

What is the creative urge—the need for some individuals to create? What personality traits contribute to originality? What occurs before and during the creative act? And, most importantly, how can creativity be cultivated?

For a number of years, psychologists have attempted to answer such questions. Their methods include studying the process itself; the personality characteristics of acknowledged original people (from both a biographical angle as well as an introspective view); testing and measuring imagination and originality; and, finally, examining the process by asking artists, novelists, and scientists to describe the internal processes that went on within them when creating.

These investigations have determined that creativity can be cultivated. Although originality is commonly associated with eminent people, everyone can be creative—to some degree—dependent on training, motivation, flexibility, and other traits to be discussed.

B. The Creative Processes

Among psychologists, there is general agreement that three major processes are involved in the birth of original ideas: (1) preparation, (2) incubation and illumination, and (3) appraisal.

1. Preparation

Without proper training no one is going to achieve a major breakthrough in science, technology, or the arts. A solid foundation is necessary to solve most difficult problems. In construction, in order to perform their jobs satisfactorily and creatively, the original engineer, the designer, and the contractor study the work of their predecessors, whether in school or on the job. They learn the facts, the relationships, the errors, and the hypotheses; nothing can replace a proper background. As seen in self-assessment, each job requires certain levels of skill and intelligence. The same holds true in creativity. It is indeed the "old crab whose claws are hardest." Inspiration may be crucial, but Edison felt that perspiration far exceeded inspiration. It is a fact that many inventors underwent years of vigorous, meticulous study and experimentation before they found their mark. Following the Dewey steps, the creator usually aids himself by laying a solid foundation, in the sense that he assembles facts, airs his thinking, phrases questions, and starts to form hypotheses. Finally, he investigates promising leads. If need be, he refines and repeats the process. Many times people overlook the importance of preparation in the creative process. It seems more dramatic when someone achieves a discovery supposedly by the Eureka method—the instant solution! But typically discoveries are far from accidental. It is highly unlikely that a person untrained in a particular field will discover anything significant, probably because he would fail to recognize important details and associations. A solid foundation is critical. The next task concerns insight into the conception of an idea. The inventor may vaguely have the notion that something has to be done, and he prepares thoroughly for his investigation. He reads, takes notes, discusses, questions, defines, and begins to weigh his premises and postulates. He starts to play with different ideas. For example, during the schematic stages, a designer may sketch a wide range of structures for possible consideration. A contractor, when estimating, is collecting facts, via plans and specs, obtaining quotes, and entertaining various ways to cut costs so as to be competitive. Of course, one must also know what has gone on with his predecessors. What approach worked well, and what one failed. (How many bids have proved too low because of the ignorance of previous failures?) These successes and failures may be the springboard from which to leap, thus launching new ideas. Of course, the individual must discipline himself to his particular craft, knowing what and what not he can accomplish—a little bit of knowledge can be dangerous. But again, this is the result of training and experience.

2. Incubation and Illumination

Often this process of incubation and illumination is overlooked. It may be true that many ideas are flashes. The likelier route, however, is that one successfully defines the problem and energetically pursues a solution. During this pursuit, his mind continues to mull over the puzzle, possibly on a subconscious level. There is something of an air of mystery about what actually happens in this period, because incubation defies description, and the moment of illumination is unpredictable. It may be that when the individual is asleep a solution may be germinating, and may slowly rise weedlike to the surface, or burst through like a volcano. Many psychologists disagree as to what actually occurs during illumination and the incubation period. It has been conjectured that after a period of relaxation, one may approach the problem from a different vantage point, and this ability to change viewpoints has been found to be an important impetus to originality.

One psychologist explains that, during the incubation period, after the conscious mind has laid the foundation, the unconscious begins to activate itself. In this free-ranging unconscious world, many associations are taking place—analogous to a computer on an If-Do loop. From the vast storehouse of the brain, data are being compared, mixed, questioned, etc., in an unknown fashion until an unexpected connection is made—flash!—an inventive answer! Whatever the internal process, further insights into the nature of illumination have been provided by a few creative individuals in the arts and sciences who have written about the processes that occurred within them at the moment of the flash of light. One of the best known descriptions comes from Henri Poincaré, who worked incessantly on a very difficult mathematical problem. His mind was blocked and, although he worked day after day for weeks, a solution was not forthcoming. Then after fifteen days of futile work, in his own words, "One evening, contrary to my custom, I drank black coffee and could not sleep. Ideas rose in crowds; I felt them collide until pairs interlocked, so to speak, making stable combinations. By the next morning I had established the existence of a class of Fuchsian functions." A geology trip interrupted Poincaré's mathematical studies for a period. However, without consciously thinking about mathematics, one day as he stepped on a bus, another solution popped into his head. "At the moment I put my foot on the step the idea came to me, without anything in my former thoughts seeming to have paved the way."

The classic example of spontaneous insight is attributed to the great Greek scientist, Archimedes, who was presented a formidable assignment. The king, so goes the legend, had purchased an intricately designed crown. He wished to know if the crown was all gold—had he been shortchanged by the maker? (Even in those days the plans and specs were not always followed.) The critical aspect of the dilemma was how could Archimedes measure the volume of a very complex structure? After considerable thought and no results, one day, when Archimedes was taking a bath, he noticed that the amount of water displaced by his leg equalled the volume of water displaced. Immediately he associated the idea that if he submerged a crown into the water he would displace an equal volume. Therefore, he could accurately determine the volume of the crown, and, knowing the density of gold and silver, he could weigh the crown, and from this he could determine if the crown was pure gold. (As it was, sources disagree whether or not the metal-smith had complied with the specifications.) Archimedes solved his problem in that flash of brilliance; "Eureka!" (I have found it!). One must appreciate that Archimedes, being a scientist by training, was well-prepared to recognize the association between density and fluid displaced—an association not recognized by thousands of his predecessors and peers.

3. Appraisal

Verification is the final component in the process of creativity. Ideas are a dime a dozen. Which one of us has not "invented" until we try to build or test the "invention." No idea is generally creative until put to the test—whether in the laboratory or on the construction site and verified through observation and experimentation. (From the artist's point of view, the verification may be highly subjective. Geniuses like Shakespeare and Michelangelo have survived the test of time, however, and are acknowledged as true creators in the finest tradition of the word). Without question, the finished product or idea must be evaluated on the basis of intelligence and judgment. This sometimes calls for refinement and revision in cyclical fashion, until the final solution is chosen. And often the cycle of trial and error to verify may lead to further insights—sometimes of an altogether different kind.

In summary, the creative cycle seems to have several phases, which, although logically distinct and descriptive, are rarely so separated in experience. An individual, well-prepared, faces a challenge and, if motivated to accept it, he gathers all the facts and develops hypotheses. During the incubation process, the solution may be churning on a subconscious level, and, if forthcoming, illuminates the conscious. Finally, after a period of evaluation, alteration, and revision, the final choice is made.

As stated in *Guide to Creative Action**

> The effectiveness of creative productivity also depends, of course, on the evaluation and development of embryonic ideas into usable ideas. Without knowledge, imagination cannot be productive. Without imaginative manipulation, abundant knowledge cannot help us live in a world of change. And without the ability to synthesize, evaluate, and develop our ideas, we achieve no effective creativity.

With the nature of creativity explained, it may prove useful to examine the traits of these people who produce original ideas and things.

---

*S. J. Parnes, R. B. Noller, and A. M. Biondi, *Guide to Creative Action*, New York: Scribner's, 1977. Reprinted with permission of Charles Scribner's Sons.

CREATIVE TRAITS

They who have light in themselves, will not
revolve as satellites

Anonymous

We are all aware that certain individuals are geysers of creativity: Einstein, Newton, da Vinci, Edison. What common traits did these geniuses possess? How can we identify these traits?

Certainly construction people, especially leaders and managers, should be most interested in knowing which individuals within their organization possess such traits. In fact, it may do us all good to investigate our own personalities. Creativity can often be rewarding—salarywise.

There has been considerable psychological investigation in this area. Unfortunately, few consistent findings have resulted. A few general findings do, however, indicate that social nonconformity is highly correlated with creative problem-solving ability. Fluency, flexibility, and the ability to elaborate also seem important. It was also found that creative intelligence is not identical with academic intelligence, and that creativity involves nonintellectual factors, such as: openness to novel experiences, and a relaxed attention to problems.

As discussed in Chapter 4 one interesting study (D. W. MacKinnon, 1962) focused on American architects, who were chosen as a category because architects are involved in two avenues of creativity: artistic and scientific. In addition it was felt that a successful architect must have diverse skills in: business, law, art, engineering, and advertising. The results of the study indicated the most general characteristics of the creative architect are:

1. high level of effective intelligence
2. openness to experience
3. freedom from petty restraints and inhibitions
4. mental flexibility
5. esthetic sensitivity
6. independence in thought and action
7. high level of energy
8. commitment to the creative endeavor

A. Specific Traits

Other studies have proposed similar traits to be associated with creativity. The reader should also compare these traits with Maslow's self-actualizer.

1. Intelligence

Above-average intelligence seems to be required, but not a top I.Q. Many highly intelligent people are far from creative, whereas many highly creative people are not overly bright. In a classical, long-range study of highly intelligent individuals, conducted by Lewis Terman (Stanford University), the results showed that, although these gifted people fared well in life, not one produced any outstanding creative work. Of course, some fields of endeavor require various levels of intelligence. As implied in the *Dictionary of Occupational Titles*, for an architect or engineer, a high I.Q. is usually more important than it is for, say, a tradesman.

2. Nonconformity

The creative person is open to new experiences and ideas, unprejudiced, skeptical of accepted ideas and conventions. As explained, construction, being a complex, costly, and risky venture, tends to breed conservative methods and to mistrust the radically innovative. Therefore, the creative individual, especially on the construction site, is something of a maverick— a rebel of sorts, skeptical of conventional means and methods and receptive to the novel. Nevertheless, sometimes a virtue and, by the nature of the business, sometimes a vice, this trait is correlated with creativity.

3. Motivation and Persistence

The creative person is interested in the creative endeavor; he follows a novel idea to achievement; he persists in the face of time and obstacles; and he has the tenacity to return again and again to the problem. The annals of history have been written of people driven by an insatiable urge to create. Without motivation or commitment to solve a task, an individual will produce little of importance. Because few difficult problems are easily solved, persistence may have to be sustained over periods of time in the face of overwhelming barriers. Although it took Einstein five weeks to write his revolutionary treatise on relativity, he spent the previous seven years in extensive study and fact-gathering. Edison persevered through thousands of experimental failures. Goodyear (vulcanized rubber) all but starved to death before he hit his mark.

4. Sensitivity to the Environment

The creative person is alert to experience and aware of colors, textures, relationships, similarities, concepts, differences, personal reactions, etc. Psychologists have found that, in the natural course of development, humans learn to perceive both similarities and differences in stimuli. Otherwise, we could not adequately deal with things or people, nor could we develop concepts needed for thinking and communication. The original person perceives more acutely. He notices things and experiences that other people fail to "see" or "feel." Because originality involves both novel associations and "redefinition" of the conventional, the innovator is especially aware of his surroundings (within the confines of his interest).

5. Fluency

The creative person is capable of producing more ideas (verbal and nonverbal) than an ordinary person. The creative artist, designer, and engineer may produce more nonverbally, via painting or sketches. In our society, however, since most activities call for verbal communication, the creative person is usually the more articulate.

6. Flexibility

The creative person attempts a variety of approaches, transforming, translating, and thinking up unusual uses for things. Generally the inventor is more flexible than other people; thus, he generates more ideas, associations, etc. He is able to change his viewpoints readily, emotionally involving himself in the problem, as did Faraday when he imagined himself to be an atom under high pressure.

7. Originality

Capable of producing unusual ideas and unique solutions, the creative person toys with ideas. He is curious. Somewhat closely allied with flexibility, originality is a broad trait that can be seen in the uniqueness of response or the ability to produce ideas or remote associations that are statistically infrequent for the population.

8. Humor

The creative person has the ability to perceive the unusual or subtle meanings, and the ability to react spontaneously to incongruent meanings and implications. It is this humor, a release of emotional intensity, that allows the creator to express what ordinary people repress.

B. A Small Business Administration Study

A Small Business Administration study identified four traits consistent with creative people: (1) alertness; (2) curiosity; (3) adaptive skill; and (4) constructive dissatisfaction.*

*Bruce Goodpasture, *Creative Thinking: A Commonsense Approach*, Washington, DC.: Small Business Administration, 1963.

1. Alertness

Creative thinkers are alert to their environment and the consequences of what they observe. For example, the discoverer of lithography (a playwright) stumbled on this unique principle while writing a shopping list with a crayon on a piece of sandstone. His alertness to the consequences, when he accidentally printed a duplicate list from the stone, led to this principle used in offset printing.

2. Curiosity

This trait, common to creative people, is essentially that mental approach of digging below the surface to find the whys and wherefores.

3. Adaptive Skill

Creative people are skilled at making adaptations—manipulating, tailoring, even distorting what they see, read, and hear to suit their own situations.

4. Constructive Dissatisfaction

The original person is committed to the creative endeavor. Somehow he is dissatisfied with the status quo, the conventional; therefore, he tries to improve, often in a novel way.

With creativity defined, its processes examined, and its practitioners characterized, it remains now to be seen what steps can be applied to produce originality.

CREATIVE APPROACHES

Second thoughts they say are best

Shakespeare

First and foremost, no single definitive approach can be developed to solve problems creatively, such that the promised outcome shakes the very pillars of technology. Actually too little is understood about creativity (or any other mental process) to talk in terms of absolutes. Nevertheless, through the years, a number of excellent techniques have been devised that serve as well-documented tools to improve the chances of success in creative problem-solving. These are certainly applicable to all phases of construction.

As stated initially, Dewey's system is very comprehensive, and uses the same steps as traditionally utilized in the formal scientific method: defining and delineating the difficulty, constructing and generating hypotheses, and testing them empirically. Like many generalities and far-reaching principles, practical applications sometimes prove extremely elusive when reduced to everyday obstacles. Not every problem is easy to define or is superficially obvious. How do you think up hunches or brainstorm ideas? How can one learn to be flexible and receptive to unusual associations? How can one force unique transformations, translations, and combinations of existing facts? We hope the following discussion will aid the reader who commonly faces construction (and interpersonal) obstacles, regardless of what roles he plays on the construction team—designer, owner, project manager or tradesman.

For example, it would be reasonable to assume that any contractor or subcontractor could, and should, improve in several, if not all, of these areas.

1. Organization, administration, records
2. Personnel selection and training
3. Bid strategies and estimating
4. Finances, borrowing, accounting
5. Bonding and insurances
6. Equipment maintenance and repair
7. Coordination of trades and scheduling
8. Expediting and purchasing
9. Safety programs
10. Public relations

It would also be reasonable to assume that everyone on the construction team could reexamine the construction, contractual, and psychological phases, as shown in Box 2.4, and pinpoint 5, 10, or 20 recurring ills that should be remedied. In the construction phase alone, one can identify 20 technical problems, independent of encountered personalities who unfailingly tangle the knots. Since the bottom line is of utmost interest to everyone, to improve is any of these should save time and money: (1) change orders; (2) differing site conditions; (3) noncompliances; (4) errors and omissions; (5) weather (in terms of mitigating the impact); (6) interpretation of plans and specs; (7) delays; (8) claims; (9) "or equals"; (10) payment requisitions; (11) punch lists; (12) strikes; (13) guarantee items; (14) retainage; (15) safety, accidents; (16) payment for stored material; (17) theft, vandalism; (18) suspension of work; (19) acceleration of work; (20) legal problems. How? There are a number of ways.

The forthcoming discussion and techniques offer no guarantee of transforming anyone into an overnight genius, but they do uncover within the would-be problem-solver a wealth of ideas and knowledge that lay dormant in the passage of his brains. To this end, four general methods will be examined: (1) the composite approach; (2) the Osborn method; (3) the Synectics process; and (4) miscellaneous techniques.

A. Composite Approach

Based on various studies, including the Osborn and Synectics methods, the following steps should prove useful as an overall guide. Some of these steps will strike one as strange, even ludicrous, yet their rationale will be explained in the discussion of the Osborn and Synectics approaches. For now, we say only that the main objective is to solve a problem, to innovate and improve, to render wiser decisions—in this case the end justifies the means. Therefore, in the spirit of being open-minded, when a situation exists such that an improvement can be made (as is always the case), make it a habit to try to be creative. Try to improve on existing means and methods, even if for years "it's always been done that way." Attempt to give a little extra thought to obvious solutions. Strive for better answers. Before making a decision, assemble as many alternatives as feasible and practical. Defer judgment until all the options have been listed, and then discard the less promising. Remember, as Osborn points out, the greater the quantity of ideas—regardless of the unfamiliarity of the steps taken—the likelier the chance of a quality decision.

The creativity checklist shown below attempts to break the normal habit of response. Too many times a person finds himself in a rut, and, consequently, repeats some response over and over, with usually sterile results. Frequently, a potentially great idea is nipped in the bud because of an instant judgment, "Forget it. It'll never work!" All creativity methods require that the person delay his criticism and forego his verification until a substantial quantity of ideas and options have been gathered. At this point, but not before, evaluate, verify, test and retest. Normally, during this last step of testing and verification, a number of options will readily appear to be worthless. Buried within the remaining group of relevant, more promising alternatives, however, may be the *one*—how many thousands of materials did Edison test until finally proving tungsten filaments to be superior? Consider your brain analogous to a kaleidoscope, containing a million flakes of facts, data, memories, observations, etc. Creativity methods simply ask that you twist and shake the kaleidoscope a number of times, and examine the various patterns that crystallize. Unique viewpoints yield unique solutions.

1. Steps to Originality

The following eleven steps prove useful in creative problem-solving.

1. Be open to experience—not only in your job, but in everyday living. Develop a free-spirited attitude; keep your senses alert and receptive. Enjoy

the exhilaration of a new idea. Above all, avoid blind spots, prejudices, preconceived beliefs, and the fear of ridicule.

2. Accurately define the problem. List all the parameters and the goals. List similar problems. Break the problem down into more manageable details. List the attributes of the problem. Delete irrelevant material. Rephrase the definitions, and ask open-ended questions in different ways (i.e., In what ways. . . ? How many techniques. . . ?), and from various viewpoints. Ask "Why?" to extend the level of abstraction. Phrase the problem in terms of two words: an action verb, and a noun; then change the verb.

3. Compile all available facts and ideas on the subject. Plow through books, reports, magazines, trade journals, etc. Constantly look for previously unknown or unrecognized relationships. Fill page after page—list everything that comes to mind, no matter how seemingly irrelevant or trivial.

4. Play spontaneously with ideas, colors, shapes, relationships, similarities, differences, etc. Juggle elements into impossible combinations. Make mental images to represent the elements of every problem. Sketch. Make lists.

5. Make wild assumptions. Express the ridiculous. Repeal the laws of nature. Fantasize. Exaggerate. Make the impossible possible and vice versa. Consciously deceive yourself. Invert, reverse, distort, translate. Change the environment. Sketch. Write.

6. Identify yourself personally with the problem. Think of yourself as the "thing." Pushed. Pulled. Fabricated. Place your self inside, outside, on top of the obstacle. Make it a part of your body.

7. Transform the problem into improbable equivalents. Change it into an animal. Use analogies from nature, animal life, art, music, etc. Think in concrete terms. Change the everyday ways of looking at people, ideas, and feelings.

8. Notice the qualities of things and how they are alike and dissimilar. Sort things into types and families, according to their similarities and differences. Make a list of these characteristics.

9. Break the whole into parts. Analyze each part. Remove components. Identify essentials. Reverse assemblies. Shift functions. List merits and liabilities.

10. Recognize how things happen in successive stages. Reverse the sequence. Identify how time changes the concept.

11. Let the ideas simmer. Relax. Let the lists lay idle. Read a book; take a break. Return to problem at a later time. Then choose the best of the lot, the simplest, the most practical. Test and retest.

Essentially, the most important feature is to let your imagination flow unrestricted. Record your thoughts; think in terms of concrete images. Ideas breed more ideas; an illogical thought or fantasy may trigger a stroke of genius. Be open to the creative process.

B. Osborn Method

The previous steps are somewhat broad in nature, whereas Alex Osborn, in his classic text, *Applied Imagination*, presents a neat cluster of specific suggestions. Box 7.2 lists Osborn's seven steps to be used in problem-solving: (1) orientation; (2) preparation; (3) analysis; (4) hypothesis; (5) incubation; (6) synthesis; (7) verification. For the purpose of this discussion these steps are incorporated into three procedures: (1) problem definition, preparation, and analysis; (2) production and development of hypotheses; and (3) verification and decision. Each of these procedures will be explained in detail.

1. Problem Definition, Preparation, and Analysis

This first procedure calls for recognizing the problem for what it is, and, consequently, gathering and analyzing all the pertinent facts. Accurate definition cannot be overstressed, for this determines in part the avenues to be explored. Is the "problem" (whether a punch list, an interpretation of quality of workmanship, low productivity, delays, lack of coordination, mounting paperwork) based and defined on objective facts instead of on personal whims and wishes? In personal, as well as technical matters, wrong definitions often lead down dead-end streets. Be aware that not all "problems" are assigned or presented as such—one must be sensitive to any situations or methods that can stand improvement.

In construction, for instance, the contractor's management may be satisfied with (or oblivious to) the status quo way of storing material on the site. Yet, an astute project manager may hit upon an innovative plan for efficient material distribution, thus saving unnecessary labor and moving costs. Actually no "problem" was assigned or thrust upon the manager, but he improved the situation because he wondered how to cut costs, and, consequently, he narrowed the possibilities to the placement of materials. Many difficulties and tasks are forced upon an individual by the nature of construction—the bulldozer breaks down. What do we do? Repair? Lease? Purchase? At other times, an individual must explore new problems and question the traditional processes. He must constantly strive for better ways to solve recurring difficulties especially ("How can we expedite equipment deliveries at least cost?"). Generally, it proves useful to begin with problems of wide focus (i.e., "How can I cut costs?") and then narrow the field down to specifics (i.e., "How can I cut material storage costs?"). A simple question may lead to another of greater impact, particularly if the question is phrased in divergent fashion such as: In what ways. . . ? What are the possibilities of. . . ?

A designer may well ask, "By what method can I design a more balanced cost/esthetics structure?" The HVAC engineer may ponder, "In what ways can I conserve energy?" The owner may try to initiate methods to ease the red tape: "How can I improve the documentation systems?"

Of course, if the trouble is apparent, so much the better. With a good handle, one can begin to gather all the pertinent data. Here previous knowledge and experience become the most readily accessible sources. Reading, research, and investigation provide other sources of information that may be analogous to a miner prospecting for gold. One must dig, even at the risk of finding "fool's gold." The dead ends can be somewhat minimized by properly analyzing the overall situation, especially the cause/effect relationship. By clarifying the objectives so as to make the goals more specific, one can save time and effort by condensing the fact-finding to those that best suggest pay dirt.

2. Production and Development of Ideas

With the problem defined and the facts assembled, the second procedure involves thinking up tentative ideas as possible leads. It is Osborn's belief that the output of these ideas, in terms of quantity customarily left to chance, can be deliberately increased by following two basic principles:

Defer Judgment. Instead of evaluating the merits of an idea one at a time in sequence, as is normally the case, defer judgment until an adequate list of options has been established. Then transfer your mode of thought to the analytical and judicial level.

Quantity Nurtures Quality. The more options one has to choose from, the better his probability of finding a better solution. Because questions spur ideas and give conscious direction to thinking, Osborn outlined approximately 75 questions to prod the imagination. This text discusses only a select few. With a little effort, however, the reader should be able to fill in the gaps, and modify to his particular situation.

Basically the question technique works as follows: first the problem or subject is defined; then the imagination is bombarded with loose questions of the divergent kind, such as: "What if. . . ?", "What else?", and "How else." With these open-ended questions, one can amass a quantity of ideas—some found to be good and some useless. From the good ideas come the alternatives; therefore, a more effective decision can be made.

Below is a list of questions (adapted from those suggested by Osborn) to assist one in maximizing his imaginative potential.

a. Other Uses? What are new uses as is (i.e., construction equipment, materials, methods, design systems, etc.)? If modified, what other uses? Note the following examples.

1. In 1935, at the onset of the synthetic material explosion, the question "How can threads of spun glass be used?" was posed. Today, most

construction projects have innumerable uses for fiberglass products: in-sulation, pipe, machinery housings, plumbing fixtures, electrical equip-ment, etc.

2. A plumber accidentally dropped a piece of pipe into a batch of molten glass. Upon retrieval, the glass adhered to the pipe. He had dis-covered a new way of making glass tubing.

3. *Guide to Creative Action** cites the following problem, demonstrat-ing other uses for even commonplace objects.

CAPTAIN HAYDEN'S PROBLEM

In the midst of the drought last summer, an Army post not far from New York City faced an emergency. It got its water through an underground pipe from a lake six miles away. Gradually the flow decreased to the point where it was plain that the pipe was getting stopped up. To clear the pipe and insure adequate water, a "go-devil"—a small machine propelled by water pressure in such a way that it rotates a set of blades as it goes—was dropped into the pipe at the lake intake. Three hours later the flow through the pipe fell off to a slow trickle and it became obvious that the "go-devil" was stuck somewhere. The problem of locating it was urgent. But how could it be found? Would it be necessary to tear up the six miles of pipe? Under the circumstances, what would you have done?

CAPTAIN HAYDEN'S SOLUTION

The post signal officer did some atomic-age thinking. He suggested that about two grams of mildly radioactive metal be dropped into a volley ball, and floated down the pipe. A group walked above the pipe and followed the ball's course by means of a Geiger counter. The blocked area was located when the ball halted four miles from the lake. By taking up one length, the pipe was cleared and the water supply replenished.

b. Adapt? What else is similar or parallel? What other ideas does this suggest? How can they be adapted to this situation (i.e., an owner in the predesign stage could inspect an existing similar structure for ideas)? In like fashion, designers and contractors could study designs and techniques used by predecessors and peers to incorporate into their operations.

1. Over 2000 years ago, Hero of Alexandria built the first "steam en-gine." It was virtually useless from a practical viewpoint until (approxi-mately 1705) Thomas Savery and Thomas Newcombe began their ex-periments. Savery, a British sea captain, while dining, noticed a bottle partly filled with boiling water. As the steam condensed, the resulting partial vacuum sucked the stopper into the bottle. This gave him the idea

---

*S. J. Parnes, R. B. Noller, and A. M. Biondi, *Guide to Creative Action*, New York: Scribner's, 1977. Reprinted with permission of Charles Scribner's Sons.

for a pumping engine, which functioned as follows: (1) the steam acted directly on the surface of the water, with the steam under pressure forcing water from the chamber to the pipeline (and crude check valve to prevent reversed flow); (2) after the chamber was clear of water, the steam was cut off (by hand); (3) cold water flowed over the chamber, condensing the steam, and causing a partial vacuum, which sucked in another chamber full of water, and so on, repeating the cycle.

2. In 1849, an ingenious American inventor, Walter Hunt, repaid a $15 debt in a few hours by twisting a piece of wire into the first safety pin.

3. Elmer Sperry revolutionized navigation by inventing the gyrocompass, an idea attributed to a simple question asked by his son, "Why does a top stand up as it spins?"

4. George Westinghouse faced the difficult problem of how to brake a long line of trains to a simultaneous stop. Upon reading that compressed air was piped over long distances to drillers in tunnel work, he adapted this principle to fashion the air brake and connected it to his long line of trains.

c. Modify? How can the present situation (operation, means, methods, etc.) be modified? A new approach? Change meaning, color, layout, systems, shape, form, material? Essentially, this is what occurs as the design progresses through the schematics, preliminary, and final design stages. Another modification is the change order.

1. For over four centuries after da Vinci's era, the roller bearing was a straight-sided cylinder. In 1898, Henry Timkin modified the cylinder by tapering the sides. This slight modification resulted in great improvements—a bearing that could withstand both radial and thrust loads.

2. Although da Vinci is credited as the inventor of the elevator, in 1852, Elmer Otis patented the first no-fail safety device—a modification that is essential to every elevator today.

3. In 1775, Alexander Cummings, a watchmaker, invented the water closet with an important modification—the trap—which is essential to any effective sanitary system.

d. Magnify? What can be made bigger? Taller? Stronger? Faster? More Frequent? Larger? What can be added? Duplicated? Multiplied? Lengthened? Stretched? For example, a construction team could well ask how the project could be completed faster. A contractor could question how a machine output could be duplicated. An owner could plan a dual function for his usable space.

1. During one lunchtime, William Mason, researching a new form of porous insulation composed of wood fibers, forgot to turn off the heat

and pressure on an experimental press. Upon his return, he discovered that the prolonged heat and pressure had not ruined the batch, but had resulted in a dense, hard smooth board. Hence, Masonite was invented.

2. A chemist unintentionally broke a bottle full of collodion on the floor. As he picked up the pieces, he noticed that the fragments stuck together—leading to shatterproof glass (layer of plastic sandwiched between layers of glass).

3. In the last century, as cities grew and land became precious from scarcity, someone (designer? owner?) hit upon the idea of buying minimal land and building *higher*—the high rise of today. In fact, as land became even more precious (and probably cities more congested) someone(?) found it more favorable to expand into contemporary suburban developments.

e. Minify? What can be deleted? Streamlined? Split up? Reduced? Condensed? Lightened? Understated? (Each group could think about how the organization can be streamlined or ways to reduce paperwork. In times of budget restrictions, an owner will be required to delete some of his predesign expectations and fringes.)

1. Prior to 1856, the two most common metals were cast iron and wrought iron. Cast iron takes compression adequately, but is susceptible to failure under shock and high tensile loads. On the other hand, wrought iron, because of the absence of carbon, can function under shock and tension, but is too soft for practical applications. By forcing hot air through the molten mass, Henry Bessemer, by decarbonizing the cast iron, removed carbon, silicon and other impurities. To the molten, decarbonized mass at a certain temperature, he added a mixture of manganese, iron, and some carbon, and lowered the temperature. The result was a metal, hard but not brittle—steel.

2. Glenn Martin, the airplane designer, studied stationary bridges to learn the stress and strain relationships, which he ultimately used for smaller aircraft structures.

3. Walter Irving, the creator of the mats used for ready landing fields in World War II, began the idea by developing sidewalk grates for subways. Noting that women's high heels sometimes got caught in the openings, he solved the problem by making the grate openings smaller—leading to the idea for landing fields.

f. Substitute? Other material? Equipment? Machines? Power? Places? Procedures? Facial expression? The contractor may substitute another piece of equipment provided it meets the "or equal" clause. The designer may elect to substitute one material for another.

Box 7.3.   DISTORTION

Below are a few examples to illustrate the results of magnifying, mini-fying, and modifying. Often a sketch underscores the effects of im-plementing these manipulative verbs.

Building   *(1)*   *(2)*

$a = b = c$ $a = c$ $a = b$

                           increase b   *increase c*

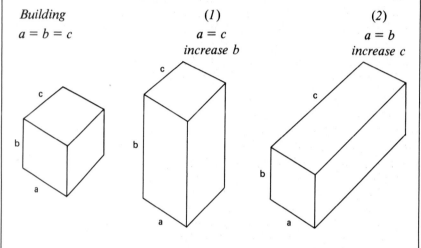

Two completely different buildings emerge: (1) a high rise would im-ply an office building, whereas (2) would tend to conjure up a vision of a factory building.

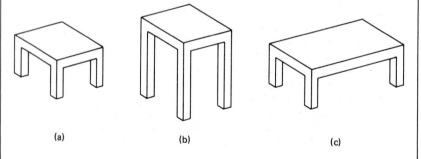

(a)   (b)   (c)

A piece of furniture implies different usage as the dimensions change.

1. In his electric light bulb experiments, Edison substituted a number of substances, such as carbon, platinum, straw, paper, tar, cellulose, cork, and 6000 bamboo specimens. He is credited with saying "I'll try anything—I'll even try Limburger cheese!"

2. Transmissions in trucks were greatly improved by substituting metal worms for coventional cogs.

3. In the building industry alone, witness the material substitutions, as technology provides new options (and as raw material supplies diminish): the families of plastic substituted for metals and woods; prestressed concrete beams in place of steel I beams; steel cables for rope.

g. Rearrange? Interchange parts? Sequences? Switch cause and effect? Schedules? Machines? Systems? A designer may use blocks of wood and models to "play" with the components of the structure before the actual design. A contractor could do likewise in determining the best transportation routes or site layouts.

1. Eli Whitney, well-known inventor of the cotton gin, was also instrumental in developing the vital ingredients of mass production: tooling and interchangeability of parts. Prior to the 1790s "manufacture" meant "to make by hand." In France (1780s) Jefferson met an inventive mechanic named Honoré Blanc who had developed a system of interchangeable parts for making guns. But it was essentially Whitney, in 1798, signing a contract to manufacture 10,000 guns, ramrods, and bayonets, who put the idea into practice.

2. Helicopters have the propellers on top, a rearrangement from traditional aircraft.

3. Every construction project contains countless rearrangements of the four basic principles on which all machines run: the wheel, the lever, the wedge, and the screw.

h. Reverse? Turn it backwards? Upside down? Reverse roles? How about opposites? Consider the other opinion? Turn sequences around? A designer or contractor may schedule design tasks or operations by working backward from the completion date. An individual may gain insight from "wearing another's shoes."

1. During World War II, Henry Kaiser increased ship construction dramatically by building whole sections upside down—welders found it quicker and easier to work downward than overhead.

2. Michael Faraday, in 1831, discovered that by moving a magnet in and out of a coil of wire, he caused an electric current to flow—the first generator. The electric motor is primarily the reverse of a generator. Whereas a generator requires a force to turn the armature (via diesel en-

gine, steam, or water power) to produce electricity, an electric motor requies an electrical input to provide mechanical power.

3. Sometime around 1844, Elias Howe, the inventor of the sewing machine, instead of putting the eye of the needle at the opposite end of the point, located the eye at the point.

i. Combine? Combine components, uses, units, and assortments. Combine ideas? Combine purpose and operations? When an architect (and general contractor) retain consultants (and specialty contractors) they are effectively combining forces. A laborer sometimes uses a shovel to bang a stake into the ground—a simplistic example of combining two functions.

1. Joseph Aspdin, a stonemason in England, was seeking a better mortar for his masonry in 1824. First he pulverized and burned limestone and combined it with clay and water to make a plastic mass. He then dried the combination, burned it again in a kiln, and purified the results. He was the first to combine these ingredients in correct proportions. Because the mixture resembled building stones quarried in Portland, England, he called his product Portland cement.

2. When inventing the reaper (1834) to harvest wheat, Cyrus McCormick was the first man to combine *all* the essential elements: the knife, the iron fingers to hold the grain against the block, a large reel to push the stalks against the blade, and a platform to catch the severed stalks.

3. Thermal windows wed both characteristics of transparency and insulation.

3. Verification and Decision

Osborn's final procedure (as well as all the others) calls for appraising and verifying the tentative ideas via test, execution, etc.—sometimes a long arduous process. Granted that many discoveries are made quite by accident, flashes of light, and pieces of luck, the history of inventions is written in the "blood, sweat, and tears" of work and dedication. For years Charles Goodyear struggled in deprivation, his family living in an abandoned rubber factory on Staten Island, reputedly so poor that one day on a ferry trip to a pawnbroker, he had to leave his umbrella as collateral for the ride. At another time Goodyear surrendered himself to debtor's prison. Finally, he hit upon that invention of vulcanizing rubber. He gained fame, but doubtless he paid his dues.

Great inventions demand great efforts. Although few individuals are inclined to sacrifice life and limb in the pursuit of creativity, all can contribute their intellect and effort to improve on existing ideas, methods, things, tasks, and all those facets necessary to functioning in a technological society. Regardless of the means taken to arrive at the hypothesis, it is imperative that the validity be tested thoroughly. As observed by Shakespeare, "Thoughts are but dreams till their effects be tried." In this vein a few comments are offered concerning the process of decision-making. Because of the multi-dimensions of many decisions, it is very difficult to systemize a "best" strategy when striving to make a quality decision. Whenever a manager or supervisor chooses a course of action, except only in the simplest of situations, his plan will involve a number of variables, obvious and subtle. Consequently, some of his aspirations and objectives will be reached; others will fall short of the mark. As long as the resultant assets outweigh the liabilities to an acceptable degree, the decision is considered to be a good one.

How can a person make a quality decision? Behavioral scientists have studied this question at length, and from a number of these studies, Janis and Mann (*Decision Making*) have outlined seven steps, which if followed increases one's chances of making a quality decision. Although the development of these criteria was somewhat removed from creativity research, such a guideline seems most compatible with the spirit of this chapter.

The major premise concerning this guideline is that if a decision-maker were to carefully address each of the seven items, in effect he would increase the probability of attaining his important goals. Or stated in a negative fashion, disregard for any step would amount (in proportion) to a defect in the decision-making process.

However stated, the decision-maker must give weighty consideration to each of the following criteria:

1. Generate a wide range of alternatives.
2. Identify the spectrum of objectives along with the corresponding values.
3. Compare the consequences, pro and con, of each alternative.
4. Explore for additional information concerning each alternative.
5. Assimilate this additional information, whether negative or positive, into the existing reservoir of knowledge.
6. Re-appraise each alternative; weigh the consequential risks and rewards before deciding on the final choice.
7. Implement the chosen course of action; however in conjunction develop contingency plans in case unacceptable risks come to materialize.

Perhaps in the above outline, the reader can identify the several problem-solving phases as extended by Dewey.

C. The Synectics Process

As with any creative problem-solving system, the synectics process follows the basic pattern of problem definition, development of ideas, and verification. The innovative approach, as described by William J. J. Gordon in *Synectics—The Development of Creative Capacity*, is especially applicable for group brainstorming.

For the purpose of this discussion, only the Synectics method (somewhat modified) for generating ideas will be discussed, because the problem definition and verification phases are similar to those previously explained. Through the years, every individual develops his own unique habitual method of dealing with difficulties. A major premise in Gordon's methodology is to "make the familiar strange." By premeditated distortion, inversion, reversal, substitution, temporary self-deception, etc., the innovator is forced to break his "mental set." As a result he alters his normal judicial and analytical way of looking at ideas, people, and things. As with the Osborn method, the synectics processes call for flexible minds and deferred judgment until all alternatives are brought to roost. Somewhat analogous to Osborn's "quantity breeds quality." Gordon offers the following equation applicable to groups:

$$\text{Elegance of a solution} = \frac{\text{Number and diversity of the group}}{\text{Simplicity of the solution}}$$

For an individual this equation could be modified to read:

$$\text{Best decision} = \frac{\text{Number and diversity of alternatives}}{\text{Simplicity of the solution}}$$

One very promising technique of compiling ideas, whether in an individual or a group setting, originates with the concept of viewing a problem from a number of uncommon angles. For example, Brunel, as he watched the shipworms tunneling through wood, and building "caissons," certainly must have adapted a different viewpoint—a direct analogy that yielded an ingenious underwater construction method. Closer to home, if all spec writers and designers would wear the "shoes" of the estimator and the contractor (and know the problems that face them in the real world of bidding and constructing a building), there would be fewer troubles in the construction phase: "as shown" but not shown; "hooks up" and not spelled out; hazy or general limits, such as "zero tolerance," "shall not be noisy," or of "suitable" quality. The same could be said for owners wearing the contractor's and designer's shoes, and vice versa in various combinations.

Note that active pursuit of "strangeness" is not a haphazard attempt to achieve the bizarre, nor a request to join Bohemia. Instead, it is a deliberate, developed, and proven method to gain new perspectives about people, problems, things, ideas, and concepts. Two such mechanisms commonly used to spur mental gymnastics are: (1) personal analogy; and (2) direct analogy.

1. Personal Analogy

This mechanism calls for the individual to identify himself with the problem intimately. Faraday saw himself as an atom under pressure. While doing research on the benzene molecule, Kekule imagined that he was a snake swallowing his tail, thereby thinking of the molecule in terms of a ring as opposed to a chain of carbon atoms. A resourceful inventor of plastic machinery imagined himself to be the plastic being compressed, heated, processed, and formed through the various channels and chambers of the machinery, thus leading to a number of profitable improvements. When faced with a leaky roof or foundation, could not some innovative solutions result from imagining yourself to be a water molecule seeking the path of least resistance? Or pretend to be a beam under load, or a tractor excavating a hole—could you perform the task better or improve upon the function?

Ridiculous! Sure, it is ridiculous *on the judicial and analytical planes*, but *not on the creative level*. "But people will laugh at me! Call me a crackpot!" Well, if that bothers you, then keep the techniques to yourself, but continue to solve problems creatively publicly. Through the ages, many creative people have been labeled eccentric (da Vinci, Copernicus, and Newton, to name a few).

Bear in mind that the task is to solve a problem, and in creativity the end justifies the means. Personal analogy is a potent means to that end. If one thinks about it, the construction site overflows with commonplace personal analogies:

Thumb and forefinger—pliers or wrench
Hand—vise or fastener or rake
Fingernail—screwdriver
Teeth—saw
Jaw—pulverizer
Arm—lever
Arm & fist—hammer
Heart—pump
Stomach—mixer
Lungs—fan and filter
Veins—pipes
Eyes, ears, fingers—automatic control system
Brain—computer

The list could go on and on. Sometime, somewhere, some ingenious soul (out of necessity or possibly laziness) drew a personal analogy, and invented one of the above tools. Howe, observing his wife sew, thought and thought about how a machine could reproduce the motions of her hand. Finally he hit upon the idea of using two threads, and making stitches with the help of a shuttle.

Such questions as "If I were the . . . (problem, machine, leak), how might I "see" the situation?", or a rephrasing of Osborn's questions in terms of "I" will yield uncommon ideas and alternatives. Drawing personal analogies is not restricted to technical areas; it applies to interpersonal relations as well. In fact, the Biblical quote "Do unto others as you would have others do unto you" is an example of putting yourself in another's position. Every disagreement has at least two sides; personal analogy attempts to force an individual to recognize other points of view. From such insights may result unique ideas to bring to the verification phase, where they can be judged on their own merits.

2. Direct Analogy

Brunel's shipworm-caisson development is a case of direct analogy and exemplifies comparing parallel facts, concepts, and technologies. Irrespective of creativity methods, direct analogies are used throughout the scientific and technical fields as a matter of course. Scientists and engineers commonly borrow knowledge gleaned from one field and apply the similarities with very powerful results. The analog computer solves mechanical, hydrodynamics, and vibration problems because of the similarity between the governing equations and physical electric circuitry involved. Actual currents and voltages are measured to solve difficult analytical equations, In fact, throughout mathematics and physics, a few general equations describe a multitude of systems. Therefore, various intersystem analogies can be drawn, from, say, an electrical system to answer an acoustic question. In basic physics, a student is presented with a direct comparison between the flow of water and the flow of electricity, as shown in the sketch.

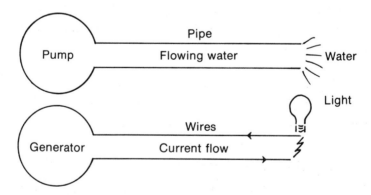

Such comparisons prove extremely insightful, and sometimes prove essential.

In structures (see Timoshenko, *Strength of Materials*) certain complicated stress problems are investigated by direct analogy. For example, there is an analogy between the stress distribution in a twisted shaft and the distribution of electric current in a plate which can be experimentally measured. Another case relates to complex situations in which the form of the deflection surface of a membrane cannot be easily obtained analytically. Therefore, this surface can be investigated experimentally by using a soap film for the uniformly stretched membrane, and measuring its surface slope by optical methods. In medical and biological research, it is common practice to experiment with animals, and judiciously transfer the findings to human health and welfare.

This interchange of knowledge from one field to another underscores the potential of brainstorming, especially when the group consists of members with diverse, even seemingly unrelated, areas of expertise. Quantity plus quality breeds better quality.

As with personal analogy, direct analogy is also a very potent technique to develop creative ideas. By drawing comparisons from nature and animal life, one can find a rich source of new viewpoints. Da Vinci wrote (1511) "A bird is an instrument working according to mathematical law . . . it is within the capacity of man to reproduce all its movements." It appeared easy enough to accomplish, simply build a pair of wings, flap them energetically, and leap from the rooftop—which is exactly what many fifteenth century daredevils did, often with fatal results. Three hundred years later, a brilliant Englishman, Sir George Cayley, who, by studying birds, developed some basic dynamic principles, notably that rushing air had something to do with lifting the bird.

For centuries man has adapted from animal behavior to suit his own needs. With little stretch of the imagination, one can recognize similar analogies:

Birds—aircraft
Shipworms—caissons
Bats—radar
Chameleons—camouflage
Moles—tunneling
Turtles—tanks
Spiders—netting
Beavers—dams

But how, one may argue, does this tie into practical construction problems? The answer is that drawing resemblances from nature may yield innovative solutions. For instance, a Synectics group drew an ingenious comparison between a flounder and a roof. Confronted with a problem of how to invent a new kind of roof, more durable than the traditional one, they began to investigate the economic advantage of having a roof white in the summer (to reflect heat and save on air conditioning costs) and black in winter (to absorb the sun's rays and save on heating costs). One of the group with a knowledge of zoology explained that a flounder turns white if lying on white sand, and dark if on mud. From this the group proceeded to conceive of the idea of a black roofing material with small white plastic balls buried in the material. In hot weather, as the heat rises, the white balls expand until they pop through the black substance. Consequently, the roof turns white, reflecting the rays, and rendering the house cooler. A remarkable concept indeed!

Like gems ready to be mined, similar relationships, abound all around us, just waiting to be observed by the acute eye. In fact, novelists and writers borrow extensively from animal life, metaphorically—sly as a fox, built like a bear, a snake in the grass, light as a feather, and a thousand other concrete descriptions to help us create vivid images.

In his excellent article, "Tree of Life: Bionics," Victor Papanek* asserts that nature provides an immense and, for the most part, unexplored wealth of biological prototypes that can be utilized in the design of man-made systems.

> With more and more emphasis on buildings being placed on dollar-per cubic-foot cost, the role of the architect has been neatly reduced to one of a jigsaw puzzle assembler. With 26 volumes of "Sweet's Catalogue" at his elbow, the contemporary architectural designer fits together a puzzle called "house" or "school"; he plugs in components (designed, for the most part, by industrial designers and conveniently listed among the 10,000 entries in "Sweet's"), substituting aluminum sandwich panels filled with polystyrene for the marble fasciae used by his predecessors . . .
>
> . . . The use of a handbook to meet and solve problems is not new. Mankind has always used one—the handbook of nature, but this one has the advantage over "Sweet's" of never going out of style. Nature also accommodates far more than 10,000 entries. Here, in the totality of biological and biochemical systems, man has found (and optimally at that) relevant, ever-new, aesthetic answers of applications to his needs . . .
>
> Arteries and Arteries: Consider next the characteristics of a leaf. D'Arcy Thompson quotes Roux as formulating the following empirical rules for the branching of arteries and leaf venation:
>
> 1. If an artery bifurcates into two equal branches, these branches come off at equal angles to the stem.

---

*Bionics is the creative process whereby biological prototypes are utilized in the design of human systems. See S. Parnes, R. Noller, and A. Biondi, *Guide to Creative Action*, New York: Scribner's, 1977. Reprinted with permission from *The Journal of Creative Behavior*, 1969, Vol. 3 (1), published by The Creative Educational Foundation, Buffalo, New York.

2. If one of the branches be smaller than the other, then the main branch or continuation of the original artery makes the latter a smaller angle than does the smaller or lateral branch.

3. All branches which are so small that they scarcely seem to weaken or diminish the main stem come off from it at a large angle, from seventy to ninety degrees.

Greater London, with a population exceeding that of Greater New York by some 2 million people, has an unbelievably primitive and leaky water conduit system; and yet it uses only 1/7 of the water consumed in New York. Why? The conduits were laid out according to the above biological rules and, in spite of marginal losses, represent a far more stable system.

. . .

One might argue, of course, that the "average" industrial designer or design engineer concerned with research and development lacks sufficient educational background to utilize biology as a consistent inspirational source of ideas. This might be true (although correctible through a reorganization of current educational curricula) . . . nature contains an inexhaustible supply of primitive structures that have never been properly investigated, exploited or adapted by designers; and these biological schemes are accessible to anyone, free for the observation during a Sunday afternoon's walk.

D. Miscellaneous Techniques

The book, *Guide to Creative Action*, contains a number of articles dealing with concrete techniques to trigger ideas. Two such articles are discussed here: "Functional Visualization," by Don Taylor; and "Idea-Stimulation Techniques," by Sydney Parnes.

1. Functional Visualization

Similar to synectics' analogies, functional visualization tends to break the habitual pattern of response by first emphasizing the performance of the needed function. When confronted with a problem, define the goal or function, preferably with only two words: a verb and a noun. Although primarily geared toward design, it can be modified to suit many situations. For instance, suppose a contractor required a hole to be cut in a wall (a trench to be dug, etc.); instead of emphasizing that a coring machine is the obvious solution, it may prove more fruitful to emphasize the goal or function, such as "cut hole." Even though the rephrasing superficially appears subtle, there is a great difference in that the former represents only one solution, while the latter "cut hole" shifts the emphasis to various ways to cut a hole. This technique forces the individual to think of other ways to reach the goal or function.

Once the function is succinctly defined, a sketch is made in the end form without the necessary hardware (means). Gradually the necessary hardware is added until the final solution emerges. This is somewhat similar to Osborn's reversal questions. Instead of developing a design or goal from the beginning, the sequence is changed: begin with the final form and work backward.

As a simplistic design example, suppose one were faced with a pipe penetrating a foundation wall in the presence of a high water table. The most obvious approach would be to rummage through handbooks or catalogs for a standard design, although, in doing so, one might overlook an important consideration, such as the consequences of pipe settlement. Functional visualization would define the problem as "seal hole." First the designer would picture (as if by magic) the pipe and the hole with no supports or packing.

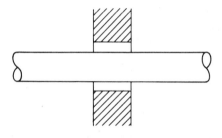

Obviously the problem is to prevent leakage. Upon inspecting the sketch one may ask: what about pipe settlement? pipe expansion and contraction? sleeving? size of core? Standard details exist in books, but possibly a better design exists functionally or economically. Work the design backward, introducing the necessary hardware and components via descriptive sketches, until all the details have been finished. The beauty of this approach is that it pinpoints the function to be performed and offers an opportunity to provide a number of varied solutions.

Taylor also illustrates how this technique can be adapted to esthetic subjects, say to design a lounge chair. "Support person." Begin with a sketch of a person in a reclining position without support.

Next, determine the surface points of the body that require support.

The next step is to connect the support surfaces for average body measurements, and to relate the structure to the floor.

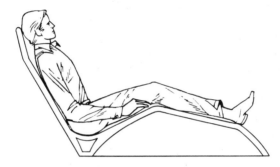

As a finale, add the comfort paraphernalia: arm, foot, and head rests, cushions, adjustment devices—the completed design.

A pipe designer could envision a nonsupported pipe (say in a trench) and work the design backward through the support system, backfill, etc. A contractor (estimator, purchaser, or scheduler) could begin with the imaginary finished structure and dismantle all the components step by step. Such reversals sometimes provide valuable insights, as well as preventive measures against oversights and malice of forethought.

2. Idea-Stimulation Techniques

The techniques focus on four key methods that initiate the development of ideas. Each method (as with Osborn's checklist, Synectics' "make the familiar strange," and Taylor's functional visualization) attempts to compel the innovator to depart from the traditional approaches commonly used in problem-solving, especially the convergent kind. Each method tends to jolt one's memory storage kaleidoscope somewhat, so that new patterns and outlooks and combinations emerge. This forces the inventor to associate this new information with the problem currently being investigated. The four methods are: (1) checklists, (2) forced relationships, (3) attribute listing, and (4) matrix construction.

a. Checklists.   Osborn's use of manipulative verbs in question form (other uses? adapt? modify? magnify? minify? substitute? rearrange? reverse? combine?) provides one of the most useful and potent checklists available for creative problem-solving. Not only do such questions stimulate a fresh viewpoint, but they invariably trigger new thoughts that may prove more applicable. Therefore, when trying to spur ideas, run through a checklist, either Osborn's or your own.

b. Forced Relationships.   Somewhat alien to one's normal approach to problem solving, the forced relationship tries to associate with the problem anything in a person's awareness, such as sight, smell, sound, fantasy, etc. For example, suppose a manager were trying to improve on estimating procedures. First he could concentrate on some object, say, look out the window at a telephone pole or cloud (or smell a fragrance, or touch a desk pad). Next he would attempt to associate whatever he focused on (say, the telephone pole) to the problem, say, improving the estimating procedures. Although uncommon to one's nature of comparing only apples to apples, this technique of forcing a relationship between two superficially unrelated things, is extremely effective in twisting and shaking the kaleidoscope. A normal reaction to forced relationships is, "What has A (a telephone pole) got to do with B (estimating)? It's bizarre!"

Strange?—yes; effective?—very. For instance, looking at a telephone pole, a manager's train of thought might go as follows:

Observed	Stimulated Idea
Top looks like a grid of wires	The tabular form to systemize data
Steps on pole	Devise a step-by-step procedure for everyone to follow, easier to check.
Steps like a ladder to top—electricity at top—electricity—computer	Use computers to store and update new data
Telephone lines at top—how can I improve telephone quotes?	Punch out vendor's telephone number on cards used by blind people. Save time and fingers.
Pole is round	Instead of square file cabinets, have elongated circular files for easy access.

And so on and so on. Just as effectively, a manager could have tried to relate a safari or a ghost to spark ideas. The beauty of forced relationships is that if one association fails, you can try another. The potential is limited only by the borders of one's imagination and the realization that, from the jungle of ideas, only the most promising options must be plucked for verification.

As an illustration of the effectiveness of this method, recall the flounder-roof association found by synectics. Now the reader should appreciate why open-mindedness and flexibility are traits conducive to creativity.

c. Attribute-Listing.   Because many problems are too broad or ill-defined in scope, one is often required to limit his focus to only one specific aspect of the trouble. For example, a construction manager may well ask, "In what ways can costs be cut?" Within a short time he could write a list longer than his arm, because the question covers an area too broad. By restricting his attention to one, maybe troublesome, area, he may increase his chances of success. For example, "In what ways can material be stored on site to optimize efficiency?" is more limited and certainly more manageable. Therefore, using this method a person identifies a number of important characteristics associated with the problem or situation, and selects one or a few for examination. Checklists and forced relationships can then be applied to produce ideas and alternatives. As an illustration of this method, suppose the owner, a government agency, were very interested in curtailing change orders on future projects. The agency assigned a project engineer to develop some preventative measures. In what ways could he approach the task? One way is to list those factors that contribute to change orders. In Chapter 2, the more frequent causes (in this case attributes) for change orders were:

1. Request
2. Differing site conditions
3. Inadequate plans and specifications
4. Delays
5. Inspection and acceptance
6. Suspension of work

Each of these causes could be selected for analysis, say, differing site conditions. The engineer could explore ideas by asking "In what ways can change orders originating with differing sites be reduced or eliminated?" Checklists, forced relationships, and analogies would yield a number of options.

The engineer could break down the one attribute into subclassifications, and construct a column of site conditions (ledge; water; hidden utilities—underground and behind walls . . .) and choose one of these to investigate via the creativity process.

Similar to attribute lists, but on a more visual plane, a general contractor could use blocks, pieces of cardboard, site plans and CPM (or bar graph) schedules to identify bottlenecks and to entertain possible solutions.

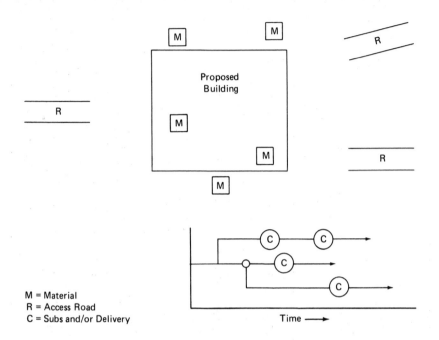

M = Material
R = Access Road
C = Subs and/or Delivery

Time ⟶

d. Matrix Construction. This fourth, and final, technique involves the construction of a matrix of attributes, and relies upon forced choices to break fixations and mental set. For example, suppose a building had three attributes: height, shape, and material. A table could be constructed such as:

MATERIAL		HEIGHT		SHAPE	
A	B	A	B	A	B
W	C	T	L	S	R
O	O	A	O	Q	O
O	N	L	W	U	U
D	C	L		A	N
	R			R	D
	E			E	
	T				
	E				

For each attribute of the building select either A or B across the line.

There are eight (2^3) possible combinations, two of which would be AAA and BAB, respectively, a wooden (A), tall (A), square (A) building, and a concrete (B), tall (A), round (B) building. Each combination conjures up

Box 7.4. BUILDING DESIGN MATRIX

Attributes → I	II	III	IV Width/Height	V Height/Length	VI	VII	VIII	IX	X
Items ↓ Function	Plan view	Elevation	Width/Height	Height/Length	Window area	Exterior materials	Color	Site features	Special features
1 Office bldg.	Round or semicircular	10% flat	10%	10%	0% (no windows)	Red brick	White	Reflecting pool	Enclosed garden
2 Hospital	Rectangular	Round	25%	25%	25%	Finished panels	Black	Modern art sculpture	Roof garden or hanging garden
3 School	Triangular	Hyperbolic	50%	50%	50% or round windows	Finished concrete	Silver	Large, open surrounding spaces	Surrounding garden (park)
4 Library	Polygonal (pentagonal, trapezoidal)	Sawtooth	75%	75%	75%	Exposed aggregate	Rust or orange	Limited, restricted spaces	Floating garden
5 Apartment building	Spoked or star-shaped	Arched	90% tall and thin	90%	90%	Unfinished concrete	Gray	Surrounding wall	No shrubs

To develop options for a building design, use the table as follows:

Choose ten numbers at random, ranging from 1–5, one from each column. Then *sketch* your "building." For example, "3 2 3 4 1 5 3 1 3 4" would result in a building with the following characteristics:

School (I-3): Rectangular shape (II-2); Hyperbolic elevation (III-3); Width/height ratio—75% (IV-4); Height/length ratio—10% (V-1); % Window area—90% (VI-5); Finished concrete (VII-3); White (VIII-1); Large open surroundings (IX-3); Floating garden (X-4).

Repeat the procedure until the final design is chosen.

a different building with the likelihood that newer, better ideas will be found. Forced relationships or checklists and characteristics can all be combined into a similar table, chart, or matrix to explode a number of thoughts in geometric progression.

One such prolific device is to form a matrix of attributes as column headings and list underneath relevant subattributes or characteristics. For instance, every designer could construct a table like that in Box 7.4. The beauty of this method is that it breaks the habitual pattern of response that an individual develops in problem-solving. If, for example, a designer were looking for various designs for a new school, he could follow the procedure shown. By selecting a random series of numbers, and sketching the resultant buildings, he could not possibly fail to discover new concepts. With such a technique no designer needs to be at a loss for ideas to stimulate his imagination. In fact, whether owner, contractor, or designer, tables such as that in Box 7.4 provide a wealth of options—literally in the millions. Many of these options may well prove useless; others may require major surgery; others may lead to dead ends. Those are the gambles one must take along the road—a fork here, a new path there. None of the foregoing techniques and systems guarantees ultimate solutions and neatly packaged choices. Through considerable study and research, however, all prove to be instrumental in nurturing fresh outlooks, and in providing arrays of alternatives that, in the end, must be pruned to survive the rigors of test. In the world of creativity, the end justifies the means.

E. Final Comment

With respect to brainstorming (collective problem-solving), many of these techniques apply equally well to a group. However, because, on an individual basis, creativity involves a risk in traveling along uncharted paths, in a group setting, the risk is amplified. Everyone sets up defense mechanisms: "I'll say nothing because I don't wish to appear stupid or different." Because of this a number of brainstorming strategies have been developed by psychologists. This text chooses those rules employed by Osborn, which call for strict adherence by all members.

1. No criticism is allowed.
2. Freewheeling is encouraged.
3. Quantity is desirable.
4. Revisions are welcome.

Rule 1. No Criticism is Allowed

Criticism and judgment are prohibited *until* the evaluation stage. It is imperative that all members understand the rationale behind creativity techniques, when they should be applied, and the necessity of solid group cohesion. Because of the nature of the construction industry and the legal and psychological relationships between the owner, architect, and general contractor, it appears doubtful if a brainstorming session, in the true sense of the word, would work effectively in a *team* setting, which consists of three groups, each with its goals and values. Each group could, and should, brainstorm in-house. For example, any group could attempt to identify and solve an in-house question "In what ways can we improve. . . ?" For optimum results a climate conducive to trust and openness must be established. Often this means that authority figures and designated leaders are best removed from the group—because of the defenses they may create in their subordinates. For example, if one were afraid to look foolish in front of one's peers, he would be even more afraid in front of his boss. This task ultimately falls not only on the membership but upon the "leader," whose job is to educate all the membership to the ways of creativity.

Rule 2. Freewheeling is Encouraged

An atmosphere must be established so that all participants can feel free to offer ideas ranging from the sublime to the ridiculous. It is important to realize that one man's "wild" ideas may trigger an ingenious solution in another's head. That is why there must be an unrestricted deluge of data. A secretary can record these ideas for future review and revision.

Rule 3. Quantity is Desirable

In line with Osborn's premise and quality decision making strategies, the more options and alternatives, the more probable a good solution or decision.

Rule 4. Revisions are Welcome

There is seldom *one final* answer. Improvement is always a possibility. As long as one does not become entrapped in a law of diminishing returns, one should always seek a better way, a more genuine innovation.

Box 7.5. CREATIVITY CHECKLIST

The following are pointers to aid you in jogging your creative potential. Again, we stress that you must let the ideas flow no matter how stupid or illogical or seemingly unrelated. Just take pencil and paper and write as fast and as furious as the ideas flow.
1. Problem Definition Phase
  a. State the problem, using an action verb and a noun; change verb repeatedly.

    b. List all parameters and attributes.

    c. Write as many questions with respect to the problem that you think of. Ask "Why?" Ask open-ended questions.

    d. List all special features. List objectives.

    e. List similar problems. List all solutions.

    f. List developments of problem. Establish cause and effect.

    g. State problem concisely.

2. *Hypotheses Phase*

    A. *Viewpoint change. Look at the problem from the following viewpoints:*

        a. Owner

        b. Architect

        c. Contractor

        d. Recipient of the idea

        e. Child

        f. Animal

        g. Artist

        h. Layman

        i. Instrument

    B. *Force Relationships. Concentrate on how the following relate to the problem:*

        a. Eyes

        b. Nose

        c. Ears

        d. Touch

        e. Imagination

    C. *Matrix. List general attributes and specific characteristics. Construct a matrix, and force various combinations by random selections.*

    D. *Analogies. List all the analogies from:*

        a. Your body

        b. Animal life

        c. Music

        d. Art

        e. Sports

        f. Philosophy

        g. Religion

    E. *Checklists*

        a. Lists all the effects of removing parts, reassembly, adding parts, etc.

        b. List all simplifications and improvements.

> c. List all the effects of time, space, and changing dimensions and properties. Go to extremes.
>
> d. Apply Osborn's checklist: Other uses? Adapt? Modify? Magnify? Minify? Substitute? Rearrange? Reverse? Combine?
>
> 3. Final Evaluation Phase
>
> a. List the ideas most suited to solve the problem and the least suited; also, the simplest and most complex solutions.
>
> b. List most practical, and effective ideas.
>
> c. List new applications and offshoots.
>
> d. List all tests, experiments, and behavior, necessary to verify the most promising alternatives.
>
> e. Consider carefully consequences of all decisions and implementations.
>
> f. Review the seven steps in the decision making process: 1) survey alternatives; 2) survey objectives; 3) examine risks; 4) research information; 5) assimilate information; 6) re-appraise alternatives; 7) implement final choice but develop contingency plans.

POSTSCRIPT

New ideas can be good or bad, just the same as old ones

Franklin D. Roosevelt

Bibliography

Brown, A. E., and H. A. Jeffcott. *Absolutely Mad Inventions.* New York: Dover Publications, Inc., 1970.

Goldenson, Robert M. *The Encyclopedia of Human Behavior,* Vols. 1 and 2. New York: Doubleday and Co., Inc., 1970.

Good, Paul, and the editors of Time-Life Books. *Human Behavior—The Individual.* New York: Time, Inc., 1974.

Goodpasture, Bruce. *Creative Thinking: A Commonsense Approach.* Small Marketers Aids, No. 92. Washington, D.C.: Small Business Administration, 1963.

Gordon, William J. *Synectics.* New York: Collier Books, 1961.

Janis, Irving L., Leon Mann. *Decision Making.* New York: Macmillan Publishing Co., Inc., 1977.

Kidder, Frank E. *The Architect's and Builder's Pocket-Book,* 15 ed. New York: John Wiley & Sons, 1908.

Kneller, George F. *The Art and Science of Creativity.* New York: Holt, Rinehart and Winston, Inc., 1965.

Meyer, Jerome S. *Great Inventions.* New York: Pocket Books, Inc., 1956.

Osborn, A. *Applied Imagination*, 3 ed. New York: Charles Scribner's Sons, 1963.

Parnes, Sydney J., Ruth B. Noller, and Angelo M. Biondi. *Guide to Creative Action*. New York: Charles Scribner's Sons, 1977.

Parnes, Sidney J. *Creativity Behavior Workbook*. New York: Charles Scribner's Sons, 1967.

Those Inventive Americans. The National Geographic Society, 1971.

Timoshenko, S. *Strength of Materials*, part 2, 3 ed. New York: D. Van Nostrand Co., Inc., 1956.

Vernon, P. E., ed. *Creativity*. Baltimore: Penguin Books, Inc., 1970.

Wheeler, Ladd, Robert A. Goodale, and James Deese. *General Psychology*. Boston: Allyn and Bacon, Inc., 1975.

Editors. *Building Construction Cost Data*. Duxbury, Mass: R. Means Co., Inc., 1977.

Appendix I

AIA Contracts

1. AIA General Conditions of the Contract for Construction
2. AIA Standard Form of Agreement Between Owner and Architect

THE AMERICAN INSTITUTE OF ARCHITECTS

AIA Document A201

General Conditions of the Contract for Construction

THIS DOCUMENT HAS IMPORTANT LEGAL CONSEQUENCES; CONSULTATION WITH AN ATTORNEY IS ENCOURAGED WITH RESPECT TO ITS MODIFICATION

1976 EDITION
TABLE OF ARTICLES

This document has been approved and endorsed by The Associated General Contractors of America.

AIA DOCUMENT A201 • GENERAL CONDITIONS OF THE CONTRACT FOR CONSTRUCTION • THIRTEENTH EDITION • AUGUST 1976
AIA® • © 1976 • THE AMERICAN INSTITUTE OF ARCHITECTS, 1735 NEW YORK AVENUE, N.W., WASHINGTON, D.C. 20006   **A201-1976**

This document has been reproduced with the permission of The American Institute of Architects under application number 78105. Further reproduction, in part or in whole, is not authorized.

INDEX

GENERAL CONDITIONS OF THE CONTRACT FOR CONSTRUCTION

ARTICLE 1

CONTRACT DOCUMENTS

1.1   DEFINITIONS

1.1.1   THE CONTRACT DOCUMENTS

The Contract Documents consist of the Owner-Contractor Agreement, the Conditions of the Contract (General, Supplementary and other Conditions), the Drawings, the Specifications, and all Addenda issued prior to and all Modifications issued after execution of the Contract. A Modification is (1) a written amendment to the Contract signed by both parties, (2) a Change Order, (3) a written interpretation issued by the Architect pursuant to Subparagraph 2.2.8, or (4) a written order for a minor change in the Work issued by the Architect pursuant to Paragraph 12.4. The Contract Documents do not include Bidding Documents such as the Advertisement or Invitation to Bid, the Instructions to Bidders, sample forms, the Contractor's Bid or portions of Addenda relating to any of these, or any other documents, unless specifically enumerated in the Owner-Contractor Agreement.

1.1.2   THE CONTRACT

The Contract Documents form the Contract for Construction. This Contract represents the entire and integrated agreement between the parties hereto and supersedes all prior negotiations, representations, or agreements, either written or oral. The Contract may be amended or modified only by a Modification as defined in Subparagraph 1.1.1. The Contract Documents shall not be construed to create any contractual relationship of any kind between the Architect and the Contractor, but the Architect shall be entitled to performance of obligations intended for his benefit, and to enforcement thereof. Nothing contained in the Contract Documents shall create any contractual relationship between the Owner or the Architect and any Subcontractor or Sub-subcontractor.

1.1.3   THE WORK

The Work comprises the completed construction required by the Contract Documents and includes all labor necessary to produce such construction, and all materials and equipment incorporated or to be incorporated in such construction.

1.1.4   THE PROJECT

The Project is the total construction of which the Work performed under the Contract Documents may be the whole or a part.

1.2   EXECUTION, CORRELATION AND INTENT

1.2.1 The Contract Documents shall be signed in not less than triplicate by the Owner and Contractor. If either the Owner or the Contractor or both do not sign the Conditions of the Contract, Drawings, Specifications, or any of the other Contract Documents, the Architect shall identify such Documents.

1.2.2 By executing the Contract, the Contractor represents that he has visited the site, familiarized himself with the local conditions under which the Work is to be performed, and correlated his observations with the requirements of the Contract Documents.

1.2.3 The intent of the Contract Documents is to include all items necessary for the proper execution and completion of the Work. The Contract Documents are complementary, and what is required by any one shall be as binding as if required by all. Work not covered in the Contract Documents will not be required unless it is consistent therewith and is reasonably inferable therefrom as being necessary to produce the intended results. Words and abbreviations which have well-known technical or trade meanings are used in the Contract Documents in accordance with such recognized meanings.

1.2.4 The organization of the Specifications into divisions, sections and articles, and the arrangement of Drawings shall not control the Contractor in dividing the Work among Subcontractors or in establishing the extent of Work to be performed by any trade.

1.3   OWNERSHIP AND USE OF DOCUMENTS

1.3.1 All Drawings, Specifications and copies thereof furnished by the Architect are and shall remain his property. They are to be used only with respect to this Project and are not to be used on any other project. With the exception of one contract set for each party to the Contract, such documents are to be returned or suitably accounted for to the Architect on request at the completion of the Work. Submission or distribution to meet official regulatory requirements or for other purposes in connection with the Project is not to be construed as publication in derogation of the Architect's common law copyright or other reserved rights.

ARTICLE 2

ARCHITECT

2.1   DEFINITION

2.1.1 The Architect is the person lawfully licensed to practice architecture, or an entity lawfully practicing architecture identified as such in the Owner-Contractor Agreement, and is referred to throughout the Contract Documents as if singular in number and masculine in gender. The term Architect means the Architect or his authorized representative.

2.2   ADMINISTRATION OF THE CONTRACT

2.2.1 The Architect will provide administration of the Contract as hereinafter described.

2.2.2 The Architect will be the Owner's representative during construction and until final payment is due. The Architect will advise and consult with the Owner. The Owner's instructions to the Contractor shall be forwarded through the Architect. The Architect will have authority to act on behalf of the Owner only to the extent provided in the Contract Documents, unless otherwise modified by written instrument in accordance with Subparagraph 2.2.18.

2.2.3 The Architect will visit the site at intervals appropriate to the stage of construction to familiarize himself generally with the progress and quality of the Work and to determine in general if the Work is proceeding in accordance with the Contract Documents. However, the Architect will not be required to make exhaustive or continuous on-site inspections to check the quality or quantity of the Work. On the basis of his on-site observations as an architect, he will keep the Owner informed of the progress of the Work, and will endeavor to guard the Owner against defects and deficiencies in the Work of the Contractor.

2.2.4 The Architect will not be responsible for and will not have control or charge of construction means, methods, techniques, sequences or procedures, or for safety precautions and programs in connection with the Work, and he will not be responsible for the Contractor's failure to carry out the Work in accordance with the Contract Documents. The Architect will not be responsible for or have control or charge over the acts or omissions of the Contractor, Subcontractors, or any of their agents or employees, or any other persons performing any of the Work.

2.2.5 The Architect shall at all times have access to the Work wherever it is in preparation and progress. The Contractor shall provide facilities for such access so the Architect may perform his functions under the Contract Documents.

2.2.6 Based on the Architect's observations and an evaluation of the Contractor's Applications for Payment, the Architect will determine the amounts owing to the Contractor and will issue Certificates for Payment in such amounts, as provided in Paragraph 9.4.

2.2.7 The Architect will be the interpreter of the requirements of the Contract Documents and the judge of the performance thereunder by both the Owner and Contractor.

2.2.8 The Architect will render interpretations necessary for the proper execution or progress of the Work, with reasonable promptness and in accordance with any time limit agreed upon. Either party to the Contract may make written request to the Architect for such interpretations.

2.2.9 Claims, disputes and other matters in question between the Contractor and the Owner relating to the execution or progress of the Work or the interpretation of the Contract Documents shall be referred initially to the Architect for decision which he will render in writing within a reasonable time.

2.2.10 All interpretations and decisions of the Architect shall be consistent with the intent of and reasonably inferable from the Contract Documents and will be in writing or in the form of drawings. In his capacity as interpreter and judge, he will endeavor to secure faithful performance by both the Owner and the Contractor, will not show partiality to either, and will not be liable for the result of any interpretation or decision rendered in good faith in such capacity.

2.2.11 The Architect's decisions in matters relating to artistic effect will be final if consistent with the intent of the Contract Documents.

2.2.12 Any claim, dispute or other matter in question between the Contractor and the Owner referred to the Architect, except those relating to artistic effect as provided in Subparagraph 2.2.11 and except those which have been waived by the making or acceptance of final payment as provided in Subparagraphs 9.9.4 and 9.9.5, shall be subject to arbitration upon the written demand of either party. However, no demand for arbitration of any such claim, dispute or other matter may be made until the earlier of (1) the date on which the Architect has rendered a written decision, or (2) the tenth day after the parties have presented their evidence to the Architect or have been given a reasonable opportunity to do so, if the Architect has not rendered his written decision by that date. When such a written decision of the Architect states (1) that the decision is final but subject to appeal, and (2) that any demand for arbitration of a claim, dispute or other matter covered by such decision must be made within thirty days after the date on which the party making the demand receives the written decision, failure to demand arbitration within said thirty days' period will result in the Architect's decision becoming final and binding upon the Owner and the Contractor. If the Architect renders a decision after arbitration proceedings have been initiated, such decision may be entered as evidence but will not supersede any arbitration proceedings unless the decision is acceptable to all parties concerned.

2.2.13 The Architect will have authority to reject Work which does not conform to the Contract Documents. Whenever, in his opinion, he considers it necessary or advisable for the implementation of the intent of the Contract Documents, he will have authority to require special inspection or testing of the Work in accordance with Subparagraph 7.7.2 whether or not such Work be then fabricated, installed or completed. However, neither the Architect's authority to act under this Subparagraph 2.2.13, nor any decision made by him in good faith either to exercise or not to exercise such authority, shall give rise to any duty or responsibility of the Architect to the Contractor, any Subcontractor, any of their agents or employees, or any other person performing any of the Work.

2.2.14 The Architect will review and approve or take other appropriate action upon Contractor's submittals such as Shop Drawings, Product Data and Samples, but only for conformance with the design concept of the Work and with the information given in the Contract Documents. Such action shall be taken with reasonable promptness so as to cause no delay. The Architect's approval of a specific item shall not indicate approval of an assembly of which the item is a component.

2.2.15 The Architect will prepare Change Orders in accordance with Article 12, and will have authority to order minor changes in the Work as provided in Subparagraph 12.4.1.

2.2.16 The Architect will conduct inspections to determine the dates of Substantial Completion and final completion, will receive and forward to the Owner for the Owner's review written warranties and related documents required by the Contract and assembled by the Contractor, and will issue a final Certificate for Payment upon compliance with the requirements of Paragraph 9.9.

2.2.17 If the Owner and Architect agree, the Architect will provide one or more Project Representatives to assist the Architect in carrying out his responsibilities at the site. The duties, responsibilities and limitations of authority of any such Project Representative shall be as set forth in an exhibit to be incorporated in the Contract Documents.

2.2.18 The duties, responsibilities and limitations of authority of the Architect as the Owner's representative during construction as set forth in the Contract Documents will not be modified or extended without written consent of the Owner, the Contractor and the Architect.

2.2.19 In case of the termination of the employment of the Architect, the Owner shall appoint an architect against whom the Contractor makes no reasonable objection whose status under the Contract Documents shall be that of the former architect. Any dispute in connection with such appointment shall be subject to arbitration.

ARTICLE 3

OWNER

3.1 DEFINITION

3.1.1 The Owner is the person or entity identified as such in the Owner-Contractor Agreement and is referred to throughout the Contract Documents as if singular in number and masculine in gender. The term Owner means the Owner or his authorized representative.

3.2 INFORMATION AND SERVICES REQUIRED OF THE OWNER

3.2.1 The Owner shall, at the request of the Contractor, at the time of execution of the Owner-Contractor Agreement, furnish to the Contractor reasonable evidence that he has made financial arrangements to fulfill his obligations under the Contract. Unless such reasonable evidence is furnished, the Contractor is not required to execute the Owner-Contractor Agreement or to commence the Work.

3.2.2 The Owner shall furnish all surveys describing the physical characteristics, legal limitations and utility locations for the site of the Project, and a legal description of the site.

3.2.3 Except as provided in Subparagraph 4.7.1, the Owner shall secure and pay for necessary approvals, easements, assessments and charges required for the construction, use or occupancy of permanent structures or for permanent changes in existing facilities.

3.2.4 Information or services under the Owner's control shall be furnished by the Owner with reasonable promptness to avoid delay in the orderly progress of the Work.

3.2.5 Unless otherwise provided in the Contract Documents, the Contractor will be furnished, free of charge, all copies of Drawings and Specifications reasonably necessary for the execution of the Work.

3.2.6 The Owner shall forward all instructions to the Contractor through the Architect.

3.2.7 The foregoing are in addition to other duties and responsibilities of the Owner enumerated herein and especially those in respect to Work by Owner or by Separate Contractors, Payments and Completion, and Insurance in Articles 6, 9 and 11 respectively.

3.3 OWNER'S RIGHT TO STOP THE WORK

3.3.1 If the Contractor fails to correct defective Work as required by Paragraph 13.2 or persistently fails to carry out the Work in accordance with the Contract Documents, the Owner, by a written order signed personally or by an agent specifically so empowered by the Owner in writing, may order the Contractor to stop the Work, or any portion thereof, until the cause for such order has been eliminated; however, this right of the Owner to stop the Work shall not give rise to any duty on the part of the Owner to exercise this right for the benefit of the Contractor or any other person or entity, except to the extent required by Subparagraph 6.1.3.

3.4 OWNER'S RIGHT TO CARRY OUT THE WORK

3.4.1 If the Contractor defaults or neglects to carry out the Work in accordance with the Contract Documents and fails within seven days after receipt of written notice from the Owner to commence and continue correction of such default or neglect with diligence and promptness, the Owner may, after seven days following receipt by the Contractor of an additional written notice and without prejudice to any other remedy he may have, make good such deficiencies. In such case an appropriate Change Order shall be issued deducting from the payments then or thereafter due the Contractor the cost of correcting such deficiencies, including compensation for the Architect's additional services made necessary by such default, neglect or failure. Such action by the Owner and the amount charged to the Contractor are both subject to the prior approval of the Architect. If the payments then or thereafter due the Contractor are not sufficient to cover such amount, the Contractor shall pay the difference to the Owner.

ARTICLE 4

CONTRACTOR

4.1 DEFINITION

4.1.1 The Contractor is the person or entity identified as such in the Owner-Contractor Agreement and is referred to throughout the Contract Documents as if singular in number and masculine in gender. The term Contractor means the Contractor or his authorized representative.

4.2 REVIEW OF CONTRACT DOCUMENTS

4.2.1 The Contractor shall carefully study and compare the Contract Documents and shall at once report to the Architect any error, inconsistency or omission he may discover. The Contractor shall not be liable to the Owner or the Architect for any damage resulting from any such errors, inconsistencies or omissions in the Contract Documents. The Contractor shall perform no portion of the Work at any time without Contract Documents or, where required, approved Shop Drawings, Product Data or Samples for such portion of the Work.

4.3 SUPERVISION AND CONSTRUCTION PROCEDURES

4.3.1 The Contractor shall supervise and direct the Work, using his best skill and attention. He shall be solely responsible for all construction means, methods, techniques, sequences and procedures and for coordinating all portions of the Work under the Contract.

4.3.2 The Contractor shall be responsible to the Owner for the acts and omissions of his employees, Subcontractors and their agents and employees, and other persons performing any of the Work under a contract with the Contractor.

4.3.3 The Contractor shall not be relieved from his obligations to perform the Work in accordance with the Contract Documents either by the activities or duties of the Architect in his administration of the Contract, or by inspections, tests or approvals required or performed under Paragraph 7.7 by persons other than the Contractor.

4.4 LABOR AND MATERIALS

4.4.1 Unless otherwise provided in the Contract Documents, the Contractor shall provide and pay for all labor, materials, equipment, tools, construction equipment and machinery, water, heat, utilities, transportation, and other facilities and services necessary for the proper execution and completion of the Work, whether temporary or permanent and whether or not incorporated or to be incorporated in the Work.

4.4.2 The Contractor shall at all times enforce strict discipline and good order among his employees and shall not employ on the Work any unfit person or anyone not skilled in the task assigned to him.

4.5 WARRANTY

4.5.1 The Contractor warrants to the Owner and the Architect that all materials and equipment furnished under this Contract will be new unless otherwise specified, and that all Work will be of good quality, free from faults and defects and in conformance with the Contract Documents. All Work not conforming to these requirements, including substitutions not properly approved and authorized, may be considered defective. If required by the Architect, the Contractor shall furnish satisfactory evidence as to the kind and quality of materials and equipment. This warranty is not limited by the provisions of Paragraph 13.2.

4.6 TAXES

4.6.1 The Contractor shall pay all sales, consumer, use and other similar taxes for the Work or portions.thereof provided by the Contractor which are legally enacted at the time bids are received, whether or not yet effective.

4.7 PERMITS, FEES AND NOTICES

4.7.1 Unless otherwise provided in the Contract Documents, the Contractor shall secure and pay for the building permit and for all other permits and governmental fees, licenses and inspections necessary for the proper execution and completion of the Work which are customarily secured after execution of the Contract and which are legally required at the time the bids are received.

4.7.2 The Contractor shall give all notices and comply with all laws, ordinances, rules, regulations and lawful orders of any public authority bearing on the performance of the Work.

4.7.3 It is not the responsibility of the Contractor to make certain that the Contract Documents are in accordance with applicable laws, statutes, building codes and

regulations. If the Contractor observes that any of the Contract Documents are at variance therewith in any respect, he shall promptly notify the Architect in writing, and any necessary changes shall be accomplished by appropriate Modification.

4.7.4 If the Contractor performs any Work knowing it to be contrary to such laws, ordinances, rules and regulations, and without such notice to the Architect, he shall assume full responsibility therefor and shall bear all costs attributable thereto.

4.8 ALLOWANCES

4.8.1 The Contractor shall include in the Contract Sum all allowances stated in the Contract Documents. Items covered by these allowances shall be supplied for such amounts and by such persons as the Owner may direct, but the Contractor will not be required to employ persons against whom he makes a reasonable objection.

4.8.2 Unless otherwise provided in the Contract Documents:

  .1 these allowances shall cover the cost to the Contractor, less any applicable trade discount, of the materials and equipment required by the allowance delivered at the site, and all applicable taxes;

  .2 the Contractor's costs for unloading and handling on the site, labor, installation costs, overhead, profit and other expenses contemplated for the original allowance shall be included in the Contract Sum and not in the allowance;

  .3 whenever the cost is more than or less than the allowance, the Contract Sum shall be adjusted accordingly by Change Order, the amount of which will recognize changes, if any, in handling costs on the site, labor, installation costs, overhead, profit and other expenses.

4.9 SUPERINTENDENT

4.9.1 The Contractor shall employ a competent superintendent and necessary assistants who shall be in attendance at the Project site during the progress of the Work. The superintendent shall represent the Contractor and all communications given to the superintendent shall be as binding as if given to the Contractor. Important communications shall be confirmed in writing. Other communications shall be so confirmed on written request in each case.

4.10 PROGRESS SCHEDULE

4.10.1 The Contractor, immediately after being awarded the Contract, shall prepare and submit for the Owner's and Architect's information an estimated progress schedule for the Work. The progress schedule shall be related to the entire Project to the extent required by the Contract Documents, and shall provide for expeditious and practicable execution of the Work.

4.11 DOCUMENTS AND SAMPLES AT THE SITE

4.11.1 The Contractor shall maintain at the site for the Owner one record copy of all Drawings, Specifications, Addenda, Change Orders and other Modifications, in good order and marked currently to record all changes made during construction, and approved Shop Drawings, Product Data and Samples. These shall be available to the Architect and shall be delivered to him for the Owner upon completion of the Work.

4.12 SHOP DRAWINGS, PRODUCT DATA AND SAMPLES

4.12.1 Shop Drawings are drawings, diagrams, schedules and other data specially prepared for the Work by the Contractor or any Subcontractor, manufacturer, supplier or distributor to illustrate some portion of the Work.

4.12.2 Product Data are illustrations, standard schedules, performance charts, instructions, brochures, diagrams and other information furnished by the Contractor to illustrate a material, product or system for some portion of the Work.

4.12.3 Samples are physical examples which illustrate materials, equipment or workmanship and establish standards by which the Work will be judged.

4.12.4 The Contractor shall review, approve and submit, with reasonable promptness and in such sequence as to cause no delay in the Work or in the work of the Owner or any separate contractor, all Shop Drawings, Product Data and Samples required by the Contract Documents.

4.12.5 By approving and submitting Shop Drawings, Product Data and Samples, the Contractor represents that he has determined and verified all materials, field measurements, and field construction criteria related thereto, or will do so, and that he has checked and coordinated the information contained within such submittals with the requirements of the Work and of the Contract Documents.

4.12.6 The Contractor shall not be relieved of responsibility for any deviation from the requirements of the Contract Documents by the Architect's approval of Shop Drawings, Product Data or Samples under Subparagraph 2.2.14 unless the Contractor has specifically informed the Architect in writing of such deviation at the time of submission and the Architect has given written approval to the specific deviation. The Contractor shall not be relieved from responsibility for errors or omissions in the Shop Drawings, Product Data or Samples by the Architect's approval thereof.

4.12.7 The Contractor shall direct specific attention, in writing or on resubmitted Shop Drawings, Product Data or Samples, to revisions other than those requested by the Architect on previous submittals.

4.12.8 No portion of the Work requiring submission of a Shop Drawing, Product Data or Sample shall be commenced until the submittal has been approved by the Architect as provided in Subparagraph 2.2.14. All such portions of the Work shall be in accordance with approved submittals.

4.13 USE OF SITE

4.13.1 The Contractor shall confine operations at the site to areas permitted by law, ordinances, permits and the Contract Documents and shall not unreasonably encumber the site with any materials or equipment.

4.14 CUTTING AND PATCHING OF WORK

4.14.1 The Contractor shall be responsible for all cutting, fitting or patching that may be required to complete the Work or to make its several parts fit together properly.

4.14.2 The Contractor shall not damage or endanger any portion of the Work or the work of the Owner or any separate contractors by cutting, patching or otherwise altering any work, or by excavation. The Contractor shall not cut or otherwise alter the work of the Owner or any separate contractor except with the written consent of the Owner and of such separate contractor. The Contractor shall not unreasonably withhold from the Owner or any separate contractor his consent to cutting or otherwise altering the Work.

4.15 CLEANING UP

4.15.1 The Contractor at all times shall keep the premises free from accumulation of waste materials or rubbish caused by his operations. At the completion of the Work he shall remove all his waste materials and rubbish from

and about the Project as well as all his tools, construction equipment, machinery and surplus materials.

4.15.2 If the Contractor fails to clean up at the completion of the Work, the Owner may do so as provided in Paragraph 3.4 and the cost thereof shall be charged to the Contractor.

4.16 COMMUNICATIONS

4.16.1 The Contractor shall forward all communications to the Owner through the Architect.

4.17 ROYALTIES AND PATENTS

4.17.1 The Contractor shall pay all royalties and license fees. He shall defend all suits or claims for infringement of any patent rights and shall save the Owner harmless from loss on account thereof, except that the Owner shall be responsible for all such loss when a particular design, process or the product of a particular manufacturer or manufacturers is specified, but if the Contractor has reason to believe that the design, process or product specified is an infringement of a patent, he shall be responsible for such loss unless he promptly gives such information to the Architect.

4.18 INDEMNIFICATION

4.18.1 To the fullest extent permitted by law, the Contractor shall indemnify and hold harmless the Owner and the Architect and their agents and employees from and against all claims, damages, losses and expenses, including but not limited to attorneys' fees, arising out of or resulting from the performance of the Work, provided that any such claim, damage, loss or expense (1) is attributable to bodily injury, sickness, disease or death, or to injury to or destruction of tangible property (other than the Work itself) including the loss of use resulting therefrom, and (2) is caused in whole or in part by any negligent act or omission of the Contractor, any Subcontractor, anyone directly or indirectly employed by any of them or anyone for whose acts any of them may be liable, regardless of whether or not it is caused in part by a party indemnified hereunder. Such obligation shall not be construed to negate, abridge, or otherwise reduce any other right or obligation of indemnity which would otherwise exist as to any party or person described in this Paragraph 4.18.

4.18.2 In any and all claims against the Owner or the Architect or any of their agents or employees by any employee of the Contractor, any Subcontractor, anyone directly or indirectly employed by any of them or anyone for whose acts any of them may be liable, the indemnification obligation under this Paragraph 4.18 shall not be limited in any way by any limitation on the amount or type of damages, compensation or benefits payable by or for the Contractor or any Subcontractor under workers' or workmen's compensation acts, disability benefit acts or other employee benefit acts.

4.18.3 The obligations of the Contractor under this Paragraph 4.18 shall not extend to the liability of the Architect, his agents or employees, arising out of (1) the preparation or approval of maps, drawings, opinions, reports, surveys, change orders, designs or specifications, or (2) the giving of or the failure to give directions or instructions by the Architect, his agents or employees provided such giving or failure to give is the primary cause of the injury or damage.

ARTICLE 5

SUBCONTRACTORS

5.1 DEFINITION

5.1.1 A Subcontractor is a person or entity who has a direct contract with the Contractor to perform any of the Work at the site. The term Subcontractor is referred to throughout the Contract Documents as if singular in number and masculine in gender and means a Subcontractor or his authorized representative. The term Subcontractor does not include any separate contractor or his subcontractors.

5.1.2 A Sub-subcontractor is a person or entity who has a direct or indirect contract with a Subcontractor to perform any of the Work at the site. The term Sub-subcontractor is referred to throughout the Contract Documents as if singular in number and masculine in gender and means a Sub-subcontractor or an authorized representative thereof.

5.2 AWARD OF SUBCONTRACTS AND OTHER CONTRACTS FOR PORTIONS OF THE WORK

5.2.1 Unless otherwise required by the Contract Documents or the Bidding Documents, the Contractor, as soon as practicable after the award of the Contract, shall furnish to the Owner and the Architect in writing the names of the persons or entities (including those who are to furnish materials or equipment fabricated to a special design) proposed for each of the principal portions of the Work. The Architect will promptly reply to the Contractor in writing stating whether or not the Owner or the Architect, after due investigation, has reasonable objection to any such proposed person or entity. Failure of the Owner or Architect to reply promptly shall constitute notice of no reasonable objection.

5.2.2 The Contractor shall not contract with any such proposed person or entity to whom the Owner or the Architect has made reasonable objection under the provisions of Subparagraph 5.2.1. The Contractor shall not be required to contract with anyone to whom he has a reasonable objection.

5.2.3 If the Owner or the Architect has reasonable objection to any such proposed person or entity, the Contractor shall submit a substitute to whom the Owner or the Architect has no reasonable objection, and the Contract Sum shall be increased or decreased by the difference in cost occasioned by such substitution and an appropriate Change Order shall be issued; however, no increase in the Contract Sum shall be allowed for any such substitution unless the Contractor has acted promptly and responsively in submitting names as required by Subparagraph 5.2.1.

5.2.4 The Contractor shall make no substitution for any Subcontractor, person or entity previously selected if the Owner or Architect makes reasonable objection to such substitution.

5.3 SUBCONTRACTUAL RELATIONS

5.3.1 By an appropriate agreement, written where legally required for validity, the Contractor shall require each Subcontractor, to the extent of the Work to be performed by the Subcontractor, to be bound to the Contractor by the terms of the Contract Documents, and to assume toward the Contractor all the obligations and responsibilities which the Contractor, by these Documents, assumes toward the Owner and the Architect. Said agreement shall preserve and protect the rights of the Owner and the Architect under the Contract Documents with respect to the Work to be performed by the Subcontractor so that the subcontracting thereof will not prejudice such rights, and shall allow to the Subcontractor, unless specifically provided otherwise in the Contractor-Subcontractor agreement, the benefit of all rights, remedies and redress against the Contractor that the Contractor, by these Documents, has against the Owner. Where appropriate, the Contractor shall require each Subcontractor to enter into similar agreements with his Sub-subcontractors. The Contractor shall make available to each proposed Subcontractor, prior to the execution of the Subcontract, copies

of the Contract Documents to which the Subcontractor will be bound by this Paragraph 5.3, and identify to the Subcontractor any terms and conditions of the proposed Subcontract which may be at variance with the Contract Documents. Each Subcontractor shall similarly make copies of such Documents available to his Sub-subcontractors.

ARTICLE 6

WORK BY OWNER OR BY SEPARATE CONTRACTORS

6.1 OWNER'S RIGHT TO PERFORM WORK AND TO AWARD SEPARATE CONTRACTS

6.1.1 The Owner reserves the right to perform work related to the Project with his own forces, and to award separate contracts in connection with other portions of the Project or other work on the site under these or similar Conditions of the Contract. If the Contractor claims that delay or additional cost is involved because of such action by the Owner, he shall make such claim as provided elsewhere in the Contract Documents.

6.1.2 When separate contracts are awarded for different portions of the Project or other work on the site, the term Contractor in the Contract Documents in each case shall mean the Contractor who executes each separate Owner-Contractor Agreement.

6.1.3 The Owner will provide for the coordination of the work of his own forces and of each separate contractor with the Work of the Contractor, who shall cooperate therewith as provided in Paragraph 6.2.

6.2 MUTUAL RESPONSIBILITY

6.2.1 The Contractor shall afford the Owner and separate contractors reasonable opportunity for the introduction and storage of their materials and equipment and the execution of their work, and shall connect and coordinate his Work with theirs as required by the Contract Documents.

6.2.2 If any part of the Contractor's Work depends for proper execution or results upon the work of the Owner or any separate contractor, the Contractor shall, prior to proceeding with the Work, promptly report to the Architect any apparent discrepancies or defects in such other work that render it unsuitable for such proper execution and results. Failure of the Contractor so to report shall constitute an acceptance of the Owner's or separate contractors' work as fit and proper to receive his Work, except as to defects which may subsequently become apparent in such work by others.

6.2.3 Any costs caused by defective or ill-timed work shall be borne by the party responsible therefor.

6.2.4 Should the Contractor wrongfully cause damage to the work or property of the Owner, or to other work on the site, the Contractor shall promptly remedy such damage as provided in Subparagraph 10.2.5.

6.2.5 Should the Contractor wrongfully cause damage to the work or property of any separate contractor, the Contractor shall upon due notice promptly attempt to settle with such other contractor by agreement, or otherwise to resolve the dispute. If such separate contractor sues or initiates an arbitration proceeding against the Owner on account of any damage alleged to have been caused by the Contractor, the Owner shall notify the Contractor who shall defend such proceedings at the Owner's expense, and if any judgment or award against the Owner arises therefrom the Contractor shall pay or satisfy it and shall reimburse the Owner for all attorneys' fees and court or arbitration costs which the Owner has incurred.

6.3 OWNER'S RIGHT TO CLEAN UP

6.3.1 If a dispute arises between the Contractor and separate contractors as to their responsibility for cleaning up as required by Paragraph 4.15, the Owner may clean up and charge the cost thereof to the contractors responsible therefor as the Architect shall determine to be just.

ARTICLE 7

MISCELLANEOUS PROVISIONS

7.1 GOVERNING LAW

7.1.1 The Contract shall be governed by the law of the place where the Project is located.

7.2 SUCCESSORS AND ASSIGNS

7.2.1 The Owner and the Contractor each binds himself, his partners, successors, assigns and legal representatives to the other party hereto and to the partners, successors, assigns and legal representatives of such other party in respect to all covenants, agreements and obligations contained in the Contract Documents. Neither party to the Contract shall assign the Contract or sublet it as a whole without the written consent of the other, nor shall the Contractor assign any moneys due or to become due to him hereunder, without the previous written consent of the Owner.

7.3 WRITTEN NOTICE

7.3.1 Written notice shall be deemed to have been duly served if delivered in person to the individual or member of the firm or entity or to an officer of the corporation for whom it was intended, or if delivered at or sent by registered or certified mail to the last business address known to him who gives the notice.

7.4 CLAIMS FOR DAMAGES

7.4.1 Should either party to the Contract suffer injury or damage to person or property because of any act or omission of the other party or of any of his employees, agents or others for whose acts he is legally liable, claim shall be made in writing to such other party within a reasonable time after the first observance of such injury or damage.

7.5 PERFORMANCE BOND AND LABOR AND MATERIAL PAYMENT BOND

7.5.1 The Owner shall have the right to require the Contractor to furnish bonds covering the faithful performance of the Contract and the payment of all obligations arising thereunder if and as required in the Bidding Documents or in the Contract Documents.

7.6 RIGHTS AND REMEDIES

7.6.1 The duties and obligations imposed by the Contract Documents and the rights and remedies available thereunder shall be in addition to and not a limitation of any duties, obligations, rights and remedies otherwise imposed or available by law.

7.6.2 No action or failure to act by the Owner, Architect or Contractor shall constitute a waiver of any right or duty afforded any of them under the Contract, nor shall any such action or failure to act constitute an approval of or acquiescence in any breach thereunder, except as may be specifically agreed in writing.

7.7 TESTS

7.7.1 If the Contract Documents, laws, ordinances, rules, regulations or orders of any public authority having jurisdiction require any portion of the Work to be inspected,

tested or approved, the Contractor shall give the Architect timely notice of its readiness so the Architect may observe such inspection, testing or approval. The Contractor shall bear all costs of such inspections, tests or approvals conducted by public authorities. Unless otherwise provided, the Owner shall bear all costs of other inspections, tests or approvals.

7.7.2 If the Architect determines that any Work requires special inspection, testing, or approval which Subparagraph 7.7.1 does not include, he will, upon written authorization from the Owner, instruct the Contractor to order such special inspection, testing or approval, and the Contractor shall give notice as provided in Subparagraph 7.7.1. If such special inspection or testing reveals a failure of the Work to comply with the requirements of the Contract Documents, the Contractor shall bear all costs thereof, including compensation for the Architect's additional services made necessary by such failure; otherwise the Owner shall bear such costs, and an appropriate Change Order shall be issued.

7.7.3 Required certificates of inspection, testing or approval shall be secured by the Contractor and promptly delivered by him to the Architect.

7.7.4 If the Architect is to observe the inspections, tests or approvals required by the Contract Documents, he will do so promptly and, where practicable, at the source of supply.

7.8 INTEREST

7.8.1 Payments due and unpaid under the Contract Documents shall bear interest from the date payment is due at such rate as the parties may agree upon in writing or, in the absence thereof, at the legal rate prevailing at the place of the Project.

7.9 ARBITRATION

7.9.1 All claims, disputes and other matters in question between the Contractor and the Owner arising out of, or relating to, the Contract Documents or the breach thereof, except as provided in Subparagraph 2.2.11 with respect to the Architect's decisions on matters relating to artistic effect, and except for claims which have been waived by the making or acceptance of final payment as provided by Subparagraphs 9.9.4 and 9.9.5, shall be decided by arbitration in accordance with the Construction Industry Arbitration Rules of the American Arbitration Association then obtaining unless the parties mutually agree otherwise. No arbitration arising out of or relating to the Contract Documents shall include, by consolidation, joinder or in any other manner, the Architect, his employees or consultants except by written consent containing a specific reference to the Owner-Contractor Agreement and signed by the Architect, the Owner, the Contractor and any other person sought to be joined. No arbitration shall include by consolidation, joinder or in any other manner, parties other than the Owner, the Contractor and any other persons substantially involved in a common question of fact or law, whose presence is required if complete relief is to be accorded in the arbitration. No person other than the Owner or Contractor shall be included as an original third party or additional third party to an arbitration whose interest or responsibility is insubstantial. Any consent to arbitration involving an additional person or persons shall not constitute consent to arbitration of any dispute not described therein or with any person not named or described therein. The foregoing agreement to arbitrate and any other agreement to arbitrate with an additional person or persons duly consented to by the parties to the Owner-Contractor Agreement shall be specifically enforceable under the prevailing arbitration law. The award rendered by the arbitrators shall be final, and judgment may be entered upon it in accordance with applicable law in any court having jurisdiction thereof.

7.9.2 Notice of the demand for arbitration shall be filed in writing with the other party to the Owner-Contractor Agreement and with the American Arbitration Association, and a copy shall be filed with the Architect. The demand for arbitration shall be made within the time limits specified in Subparagraph 2.2.12 where applicable, and in all other cases within a reasonable time after the claim, dispute or other matter in question has arisen, and in no event shall it be made after the date when institution of legal or equitable proceedings based on such claim, dispute or other matter in question would be barred by the applicable statute of limitations.

7.9.3 Unless otherwise agreed in writing, the Contractor shall carry on the Work and maintain its progress during any arbitration proceedings, and the Owner shall continue to make payments to the Contractor in accordance with the Contract Documents.

ARTICLE 8

TIME

8.1 DEFINITIONS

8.1.1 Unless otherwise provided, the Contract Time is the period of time allotted in the Contract Documents for Substantial Completion of the Work as defined in Subparagraph 8.1.3, including authorized adjustments thereto.

8.1.2 The date of commencement of the Work is the date established in a notice to proceed. If there is no notice to proceed, it shall be the date of the Owner-Contractor Agreement or such other date as may be established therein.

8.1.3 The Date of Substantial Completion of the Work or designated portion thereof is the Date certified by the Architect when construction is sufficiently complete, in accordance with the Contract Documents, so the Owner can occupy or utilize the Work or designated portion thereof for the use for which it is intended.

8.1.4 The term day as used in the Contract Documents shall mean calendar day unless otherwise specifically designated.

8.2 PROGRESS AND COMPLETION

8.2.1 All time limits stated in the Contract Documents are of the essence of the Contract.

8.2.2 The Contractor shall begin the Work on the date of commencement as defined in Subparagraph 8.1.2. He shall carry the Work forward expeditiously with adequate forces and shall achieve Substantial Completion within the Contract Time.

8.3 DELAYS AND EXTENSIONS OF TIME

8.3.1 If the Contractor is delayed at any time in the progress of the Work by any act or neglect of the Owner or the Architect, or by any employee of either, or by any separate contractor employed by the Owner, or by changes ordered in the Work, or by labor disputes, fire, unusual delay in transportation, adverse weather conditions not reasonably anticipatable, unavoidable casualties, or any causes beyond the Contractor's control, or by delay authorized by the Owner pending arbitration, or by any other cause which the Architect determines may justify the delay, then the Contract Time shall be extended by Change Order for such reasonable time as the Architect may determine.

8.3.2 Any claim for extension of time shall be made in writing to the Architect not more than twenty days after the commencement of the delay; otherwise it shall be waived. In the case of a continuing delay only one claim is necessary. The Contractor shall provide an estimate of the probable effect of such delay on the progress of the Work.

8.3.3 If no agreement is made stating the dates upon which interpretations as provided in Subparagraph 2.2.8 shall be furnished, then no claim for delay shall be allowed on account of failure to furnish such interpretations until fifteen days after written request is made for them, and not then unless such claim is reasonable.

8.3.4 This Paragraph 8.3 does not exclude the recovery of damages for delay by either party under other provisions of the Contract Documents.

ARTICLE 9

PAYMENTS AND COMPLETION

9.1 CONTRACT SUM

9.1.1 The Contract Sum is stated in the Owner-Contractor Agreement and, including authorized adjustments thereto, is the total amount payable by the Owner to the Contractor for the performance of the Work under the Contract Documents.

9.2 SCHEDULE OF VALUES

9.2.1 Before the first Application for Payment, the Contractor shall submit to the Architect a schedule of values allocated to the various portions of the Work, prepared in such form and supported by such data to substantiate its accuracy as the Architect may require. This schedule, unless objected to by the Architect, shall be used only as a basis for the Contractor's Applications for Payment.

9.3 APPLICATIONS FOR PAYMENT

9.3.1 At least ten days before the date for each progress payment established in the Owner-Contractor Agreement, the Contractor shall submit to the Architect an itemized Application for Payment, notarized if required, supported by such data substantiating the Contractor's right to payment as the Owner or the Architect may require, and reflecting retainage, if any, as provided elsewhere in the Contract Documents.

9.3.2 Unless otherwise provided in the Contract Documents, payments will be made on account of materials or equipment not incorporated in the Work but delivered and suitably stored at the site and, if approved in advance by the Owner, payments may similarly be made for materials or equipment suitably stored at some other location agreed upon in writing. Payments for materials or equipment stored on or off the site shall be conditioned upon submission by the Contractor of bills of sale or such other procedures satisfactory to the Owner to establish the Owner's title to such materials or equipment or otherwise protect the Owner's interest, including applicable insurance and transportation to the site for those materials and equipment stored off the site.

9.3.3 The Contractor warrants that title to all Work, materials and equipment covered by an Application for Payment will pass to the Owner either by incorporation in the construction or upon the receipt of payment by the Contractor, whichever occurs first, free and clear of all liens, claims, security interests or encumbrances, hereinafter referred to in this Article 9 as "liens"; and that no Work, materials or equipment covered by an Application for Payment will have been acquired by the Contractor, or by any other person performing Work at the site or furnishing materials and equipment for the Project, subject to an agreement under which an interest therein or an encumbrance thereon is retained by the seller or otherwise imposed by the Contractor or such other person.

9.4   CERTIFICATES FOR PAYMENT

9.4.1 The Architect will, within seven days after the receipt of the Contractor's Application for Payment, either issue a Certificate for Payment to the Owner, with a copy to the Contractor, for such amount as the Architect determines is properly due, or notify the Contractor in writing his reasons for withholding a Certificate as provided in Subparagraph 9.6.1.

9.4.2 The issuance of a Certificate for Payment will constitute a representation by the Architect to the Owner, based on his observations at the site as provided in Subparagraph 2.2.3 and the data comprising the Application for Payment, that the Work has progressed to the point indicated; that, to the best of his knowledge, information and belief, the quality of the Work is in accordance with the Contract Documents (subject to an evaluation of the Work for conformance with the Contract Documents upon Substantial Completion, to the results of any subsequent tests required by or performed under the Contract Documents, to minor deviations from the Contract Documents correctable prior to completion, and to any specific qualifications stated in his Certificate); and that the Contractor is entitled to payment in the amount certified. However, by issuing a Certificate for Payment, the Architect shall not thereby be deemed to represent that he has made exhaustive or continuous on-site inspections to check the quality or quantity of the Work or that he has reviewed the construction means, methods, techniques, sequences or procedures, or that he has made any examination to ascertain how or for what purpose the Contractor has used the moneys previously paid on account of the Contract Sum.

9.5   PROGRESS PAYMENTS

9.5.1 After the Architect has issued a Certificate for Payment, the Owner shall make payment in the manner and within the time provided in the Contract Documents.

9.5.2 The Contractor shall promptly pay each Subcontractor, upon receipt of payment from the Owner, out of the amount paid to the Contractor on account of such Subcontractor's Work, the amount to which said Subcontractor is entitled, reflecting the percentage actually retained, if any, from payments to the Contractor on account of such Subcontractor's Work. The Contractor shall, by an appropriate agreement with each Subcontractor, require each Subcontractor to make payments to his Subsubcontractors in similar manner.

9.5.3 The Architect may, on request and at his discretion, furnish to any Subcontractor, if practicable, information regarding the percentages of completion or the amounts applied for by the Contractor and the action taken thereon by the Architect on account of Work done by such Subcontractor.

9.5.4 Neither the Owner nor the Architect shall have any obligation to pay or to see to the payment of any moneys to any Subcontractor except as may otherwise be required by law.

9.5.5 No Certificate for a progress payment, nor any progress payment, nor any partial or entire use or occupancy of the Project by the Owner, shall constitute an acceptance of any Work not in accordance with the Contract Documents.

9.6   PAYMENTS WITHHELD

9.6.1 The Architect may decline to certify payment and may withhold his Certificate in whole or in part, to the extent necessary reasonably to protect the Owner, if in his opinion he is unable to make representations to the Owner as provided in Subparagraph 9.4.2. If the Architect is unable to make representations to the Owner as provided in Subparagraph 9.4.2 and to certify payment in the amount of the Application, he will notify the Contractor as provided in Subparagraph 9.4.1. If the Contractor and the Architect cannot agree on a revised amount, the Architect will promptly issue a Certificate for Payment for the amount for which he is able to make such representations to the Owner. The Architect may also decline to certify payment or, because of subsequently discovered evidence or subsequent observations, he may nullify the whole or any part of any Certificate for Payment previously issued, to such extent as may be necessary in his opinion to protect the Owner from loss because of:

  .1 defective work not remedied,

  .2 third party claims filed or reasonable evidence indicating probable filing of such claims,

  .3 failure of the Contractor to make payments properly to Subcontractors or for labor, materials or equipment,

  .4 reasonable evidence that the Work cannot be completed for the unpaid balance of the Contract Sum,

  .5 damage to the Owner or another contractor,

  .6 reasonable evidence that the Work will not be completed within the Contract Time, or

  .7 persistent failure to carry out the Work in accordance with the Contract Documents.

9.6.2 When the above grounds in Subparagraph 9.6.1 are removed, payment shall be made for amounts withheld because of them.

9.7   FAILURE OF PAYMENT

9.7.1 If the Architect does not issue a Certificate for Payment, through no fault of the Contractor, within seven days after receipt of the Contractor's Application for Payment, or if the Owner does not pay the Contractor within seven days after the date established in the Contract Documents any amount certified by the Architect or awarded by arbitration, then the Contractor may, upon seven additional days' written notice to the Owner and the Architect, stop the Work until payment of the amount owing has been received. The Contract Sum shall be increased by the amount of the Contractor's reasonable costs of shut-down, delay and start-up, which shall be effected by appropriate Change Order in accordance with Paragraph 12.3.

9.8   SUBSTANTIAL COMPLETION

9.8.1 When the Contractor considers that the Work, or a designated portion thereof which is acceptable to the Owner, is substantially complete as defined in Subparagraph 8.1.3, the Contractor shall prepare for submission to the Architect a list of items to be completed or corrected. The failure to include any items on such list does not alter the responsibility of the Contractor to complete all Work in accordance with the Contract Documents. When the Architect on the basis of an inspection determines that the Work or designated portion thereof is substantially complete, he will then prepare a Certificate of Substantial Completion which shall establish the Date of Substantial Completion, shall state the responsibilities of the Owner and the Contractor for security, maintenance, heat, utilities, damage to the Work, and insurance, and shall fix the time within which the Contractor shall complete the items listed therein. Warranties required by the Contract Documents shall commence on the Date of Substantial Completion of the Work or designated portion thereof unless otherwise provided in the Certificate of Substantial Completion. The Certificate of Substantial Completion shall be submitted to the Owner and the Contractor for their written acceptance of the responsibilities assigned to them in such Certificate.

9.8.2 Upon Substantial Completion of the Work or designated portion thereof and upon application by the Contractor and certification by the Architect, the Owner shall make payment, reflecting adjustment in retainage, if any, for such Work or portion thereof, as provided in the Contract Documents.

9.9   FINAL COMPLETION AND FINAL PAYMENT

9.9.1 Upon receipt of written notice that the Work is ready for final inspection and acceptance and upon receipt of a final Application for Payment, the Architect will promptly make such inspection and, when he finds the Work acceptable under the Contract Documents and the Contract fully performed, he will promptly issue a final Certificate for Payment stating that to the best of his knowledge, information and belief, and on the basis of his observations and inspections, the Work has been completed in accordance with the terms and conditions of the Contract Documents and that the entire balance found to be due the Contractor, and noted in said final Certificate, is due and payable. The Architect's final Certificate for Payment will constitute a further representation that the conditions precedent to the Contractor's being entitled to final payment as set forth in Subparagraph 9.9.2 have been fulfilled.

9.9.2 Neither the final payment nor the remaining retained percentage shall become due until the Contractor submits to the Architect (1) an affidavit that all payrolls, bills for materials and equipment, and other indebtedness connected with the Work for which the Owner or his property might in any way be responsible, have been paid or otherwise satisfied, (2) consent of surety, if any, to final payment and (3), if required by the Owner, other data establishing payment or satisfaction of all such obligations, such as receipts, releases and waivers of liens arising out of the Contract, to the extent and in such form as may be designated by the Owner. If any Subcontractor refuses to furnish a release or waiver required by the Owner, the Contractor may furnish a bond satisfactory to the Owner to indemnify him against any such lien. If any such lien remains unsatisfied after all payments are made, the Contractor shall refund to the Owner all moneys that the latter may be compelled to pay in discharging such lien, including all costs and reasonable attorneys' fees.

9.9.3 If, after Substantial Completion of the Work, final completion thereof is materially delayed through no fault of the Contractor or by the issuance of Change Orders affecting final completion, and the Architect so confirms, the Owner shall, upon application by the Contractor and certification by the Architect, and without terminating the Contract, make payment of the balance due for that portion of the Work fully completed and accepted. If the remaining balance for Work not fully completed or corrected is less than the retainage stipulated in the Contract Documents, and if bonds have been furnished as provided in Paragraph 7.5, the written consent of the surety to the payment of the balance due for that portion of the Work fully completed and accepted shall be submitted by the Contractor to the Architect prior to certification of such payment. Such payment shall be made under the terms and conditions governing final payment, except that it shall not constitute a waiver of claims.

9.9.4 The making of final payment shall constitute a waiver of all claims by the Owner except those arising from:

.1 unsettled liens,

.2 faulty or defective Work appearing after Substantial Completion,

.3 failure of the Work to comply with the requirements of the Contract Documents, or

.4 terms of any special warranties required by the Contract Documents.

9.9.5 The acceptance of final payment shall constitute a waiver of all claims by the Contractor except those previously made in writing and identified by the Contractor as unsettled at the time of the final Application for Payment.

ARTICLE 10

PROTECTION OF PERSONS AND PROPERTY

10.1   SAFETY PRECAUTIONS AND PROGRAMS

10.1.1 The Contractor shall be responsible for initiating, maintaining and supervising all safety precautions and programs in connection with the Work.

10.2   SAFETY OF PERSONS AND PROPERTY

10.2.1 The Contractor shall take all reasonable precautions for the safety of, and shall provide all reasonable protection to prevent damage, injury or loss to:

.1 all employees on the Work and all other persons who may be affected thereby;

.2 all the Work and all materials and equipment to be incorporated therein, whether in storage on or off the site, under the care, custody or control of the Contractor or any of his Subcontractors or Sub-subcontractors; and

.3 other property at the site or adjacent thereto, including trees, shrubs, lawns, walks, pavements, roadways, structures and utilities not designated for removal, relocation or replacement in the course of construction.

10.2.2 The Contractor shall give all notices and comply with all applicable laws, ordinances, rules, regulations and lawful orders of any public authority bearing on the safety of persons or property or their protection from damage, injury or loss.

10.2.3 The Contractor shall erect and maintain, as required by existing conditions and progress of the Work, all reasonable safeguards for safety and protection, including posting danger signs and other warnings against hazards, promulgating safety regulations and notifying owners and users of adjacent utilities.

10.2.4 When the use or storage of explosives or other hazardous materials or equipment is necessary for the execution of the Work, the Contractor shall exercise the utmost care and shall carry on such activities under the supervision of properly qualified personnel.

10.2.5 The Contractor shall promptly remedy all damage or loss (other than damage or loss insured under Paragraph 11.3) to any property referred to in Clauses 10.2.1.2 and 10.2.1.3 caused in whole or in part by the Contractor, any Subcontractor, any Sub-subcontractor, or anyone directly or indirectly employed by any of them, or by anyone for whose acts any of them may be liable and for which the Contractor is responsible under Clauses 10.2.1.2 and 10.2.1.3, except damage or loss attributable to the acts or omissions of the Owner or Architect or anyone directly or indirectly employed by either of them, or by anyone for whose acts either of them may be liable, and not attributable to the fault or negligence of the Contractor. The foregoing obligations of the Contractor are in addition to his obligations under Paragraph 4.18.

10.2.6 The Contractor shall designate a responsible member of his organization at the site whose duty shall be the prevention of accidents. This person shall be the Contractor's superintendent unless otherwise designated by the Contractor in writing to the Owner and the Architect.

10.2.7 The Contractor shall not load or permit any part of the Work to be loaded so as to endanger its safety.

10.3 EMERGENCIES

10.3.1 In any emergency affecting the safety of persons or property, the Contractor shall act, at his discretion, to prevent threatened damage, injury or loss. Any additional compensation or extension of time claimed by the Contractor on account of emergency work shall be determined as provided in Article 12 for Changes in the Work.

ARTICLE 11

INSURANCE

11.1 CONTRACTOR'S LIABILITY INSURANCE

11.1.1 The Contractor shall purchase and maintain such insurance as will protect him from claims set forth below which may arise out of or result from the Contractor's operations under the Contract, whether such operations be by himself or by any Subcontractor or by anyone directly or indirectly employed by any of them, or by anyone for whose acts any of them may be liable:

.1 claims under workers' or workmen's compensation, disability benefit and other similar employee benefit acts;

.2 claims for damages because of bodily injury, occupational sickness or disease, or death of his employees;

.3 claims for damages because of bodily injury, sickness or disease, or death of any person other than his employees;

.4 claims for damages insured by usual personal injury liability coverage which are sustained (1) by any person as a result of an offense directly or indirectly related to the employment of such person by the Contractor, or (2) by any other person;

.5 claims for damages, other than to the Work itself, because of injury to or destruction of tangible property, including loss of use resulting therefrom; and

.6 claims for damages because of bodily injury or death of any person or property damage arising out of the ownership, maintenance or use of any motor vehicle.

11.1.2 The insurance required by Subparagraph 11.1.1 shall be written for not less than any limits of liability specified in the Contract Documents, or required by law, whichever is greater.

11.1.3 The insurance required by Subparagraph 11.1.1 shall include contractual liability insurance applicable to the Contractor's obligations under Paragraph 4.18.

11.1.4 Certificates of Insurance acceptable to the Owner shall be filed with the Owner prior to commencement of the Work. These Certificates shall contain a provision that coverages afforded under the policies will not be cancelled until at least thirty days' prior written notice has been given to the Owner.

11.2 OWNER'S LIABILITY INSURANCE

11.2.1 The Owner shall be responsible for purchasing and maintaining his own liability insurance and, at his option, may purchase and maintain such insurance as will protect him against claims which may arise from operations under the Contract.

11.3 PROPERTY INSURANCE

11.3.1 Unless otherwise provided, the Owner shall purchase and maintain property insurance upon the entire Work at the site to the full insurable value thereof. This insurance shall include the interests of the Owner, the Contractor, Subcontractors and Sub-subcontractors in the Work and shall insure against the perils of fire and extended coverage and shall include "all risk" insurance for physical loss or damage including, without duplication of coverage, theft, vandalism and malicious mischief. If the Owner does not intend to purchase such insurance for the full insurable value of the entire Work, he shall inform the Contractor in writing prior to commencement of the Work. The Contractor may then effect insurance which will protect the interests of himself, his Subcontractors and his Sub-subcontractors in the Work, and by appropriate Change Order the cost thereof shall be charged to the Owner. If the Contractor is damaged by failure of the Owner to purchase or maintain such insurance and to so notify the Contractor, then the Owner shall bear all reasonable costs properly attributable thereto. If not covered under the all risk insurance or otherwise provided in the Contract Documents, the Contractor shall effect and maintain similar property insurance on portions of the Work stored off the site or in transit when such portions of the Work are to be included in an Application for Payment under Subparagraph 9.3.2.

11.3.2 The Owner shall purchase and maintain such boiler and machinery insurance as may be required by the Contract Documents or by law. This insurance shall include the interests of the Owner, the Contractor, Subcontractors and Sub-subcontractors in the Work.

11.3.3 Any loss insured under Subparagraph 11.3.1 is to be adjusted with the Owner and made payable to the Owner as trustee for the insureds, as their interests may appear, subject to the requirements of any applicable mortgagee clause and of Subparagraph 11.3.8. The Contractor shall pay each Subcontractor a just share of any insurance moneys received by the Contractor, and by appropriate agreement, written where legally required for validity, shall require each Subcontractor to make payments to his Sub-subcontractors in similar manner.

11.3.4 The Owner shall file a copy of all policies with the Contractor before an exposure to loss may occur.

11.3.5 If the Contractor requests in writing that insurance for risks other than those described in Subparagraphs 11.3.1 and 11.3.2 or other special hazards be included in the property insurance policy, the Owner shall, if possible, include such insurance, and the cost thereof shall be charged to the Contractor by appropriate Change Order.

11.3.6 The Owner and Contractor waive all rights against (1) each other and the Subcontractors, Sub-subcontractors, agents and employees each of the other, and (2) the Architect and separate contractors, if any, and their subcontractors, sub-subcontractors, agents and employees, for damages caused by fire or other perils to the extent covered by insurance obtained pursuant to this Paragraph 11.3 or any other property insurance applicable to the Work, except such rights as they may have to the proceeds of such insurance held by the Owner as trustee. The foregoing waiver afforded the Architect, his agents and employees shall not extend to the liability imposed by Subparagraph 4.18.3. The Owner or the Contractor, as appropriate, shall require of the Architect, separate contractors, Subcontractors and Sub-subcontractors by appropriate agreements, written where legally required for validity, similar waivers each in favor of all other parties enumerated in this Subparagraph 11.3.6.

11.3.7 If required in writing by any party in interest, the Owner as trustee shall, upon the occurrence of an insured loss, give bond for the proper performance of his duties. He shall deposit in a separate account any money so received, and he shall distribute it in accordance with such agreement as the parties in interest may reach, or in accordance with an award by arbitration in which case the procedure shall be as provided in Paragraph 7.9. If after such loss no other special agreement is made, replacement of damaged work shall be covered by an appropriate Change Order.

11.3.8 The Owner as trustee shall have power to adjust and settle any loss with the insurers unless one of the parties in interest shall object in writing within five days after the occurrence of loss to the Owner's exercise of this power, and if such objection be made, arbitrators shall be chosen as provided in Paragraph 7.9. The Owner as trustee shall, in that case, make settlement with the insurers in accordance with the directions of such arbitrators. If distribution of the insurance proceeds by arbitration is required, the arbitrators will direct such distribution.

11.3.9 If the Owner finds it necessary to occupy or use a portion or portions of the Work prior to Substantial Completion thereof, such occupancy or use shall not commence prior to a time mutually agreed to by the Owner and Contractor and to which the insurance company or companies providing the property insurance have consented by endorsement to the policy or policies. This insurance shall not be cancelled or lapsed on account of such partial occupancy or use. Consent of the Contractor and of the insurance company or companies to such occupancy or use shall not be unreasonably withheld.

11.4 LOSS OF USE INSURANCE

11.4.1 The Owner, at his option, may purchase and maintain such insurance as will insure him against loss of use of his property due to fire or other hazards, however caused. The Owner waives all rights of action against the Contractor for loss of use of his property, including consequential losses due to fire or other hazards however caused, to the extent covered by insurance under this Paragraph 11.4.

ARTICLE 12

CHANGES IN THE WORK

12.1 CHANGE ORDERS

12.1.1 A Change Order is a written order to the Contractor signed by the Owner and the Architect, issued after execution of the Contract, authorizing a change in the Work or an adjustment in the Contract Sum or the Contract Time. The Contract Sum and the Contract Time may be changed only by Change Order. A Change Order signed by the Contractor indicates his agreement therewith, including the adjustment in the Contract Sum or the Contract Time.

12.1.2 The Owner, without invalidating the Contract, may order changes in the Work within the general scope of the Contract consisting of additions, deletions or other revisions, the Contract Sum and the Contract Time being

adjusted accordingly. All such changes in the Work shall be authorized by Change Order, and shall be performed under the applicable conditions of the Contract Documents.

12.1.3 The cost or credit to the Owner resulting from a change in the Work shall be determined in one or more of the following ways:

.1 by mutual acceptance of a lump sum properly itemized and supported by sufficient substantiating data to permit evaluation;

.2 by unit prices stated in the Contract Documents or subsequently agreed upon;

.3 by cost to be determined in a manner agreed upon by the parties and a mutually acceptable fixed or percentage fee; or

.4 by the method provided in Subparagraph 12.1.4.

12.1.4 If none of the methods set forth in Clauses 12.1.3.1, 12.1.3.2 or 12.1.3.3 is agreed upon, the Contractor, provided he receives a written order signed by the Owner, shall promptly proceed with the Work involved. The cost of such Work shall then be determined by the Architect on the basis of the reasonable expenditures and savings of those performing the Work attributable to the change, including, in the case of an increase in the Contract Sum, a reasonable allowance for overhead and profit. In such case, and also under Clauses 12.1.3.3 and 12.1.3.4 above, the Contractor shall keep and present, in such form as the Architect may prescribe, an itemized accounting together with appropriate supporting data for inclusion in a Change Order. Unless otherwise provided in the Contract Documents, cost shall be limited to the following: cost of materials, including sales tax and cost of delivery; cost of labor, including social security, old age and unemployment insurance, and fringe benefits required by agreement or custom; workers' or workmen's compensation insurance; bond premiums; rental value of equipment and machinery; and the additional costs of supervision and field office personnel directly attributable to the change. Pending final determination of cost to the Owner, payments on account shall be made on the Architect's Certificate for Payment. The amount of credit to be allowed by the Contractor to the Owner for any deletion or change which results in a net decrease in the Contract Sum will be the amount of the actual net cost as confirmed by the Architect. When both additions and credits covering related Work or substitutions are involved in any one change, the allowance for overhead and profit shall be figured on the basis of the net increase, if any, with respect to that change.

12.1.5 If unit prices are stated in the Contract Documents or subsequently agreed upon, and if the quantities originally contemplated are so changed in a proposed Change Order that application of the agreed unit prices to the quantities of Work proposed will cause substantial inequity to the Owner or the Contractor, the applicable unit prices shall be equitably adjusted.

12.2 CONCEALED CONDITIONS

12.2.1 Should concealed conditions encountered in the performance of the Work below the surface of the ground or should concealed or unknown conditions in an existing structure be at variance with the conditions indicated by the Contract Documents, or should unknown physical conditions below the surface of the ground or should concealed or unknown conditions in an existing structure of an unusual nature, differing materially from those ordinarily encountered and generally recognized as inherent in work of the character provided for in this Contract, be encountered, the Contract Sum shall be equitably adjusted by Change Order upon claim by either party made within twenty days after the first observance of the conditions.

12.3   CLAIMS FOR ADDITIONAL COST

12.3.1 If the Contractor wishes to make a claim for an increase in the Contract Sum, he shall give the Architect written notice thereof within twenty days after the occurrence of the event giving rise to such claim. This notice shall be given by the Contractor before proceeding to execute the Work, except in an emergency endangering life or property in which case the Contractor shall proceed in accordance with Paragraph 10.3. No such claim shall be valid unless so made. If the Owner and the Contractor cannot agree on the amount of the adjustment in the Contract Sum, it shall be determined by the Architect. Any change in the Contract Sum resulting from such claim shall be authorized by Change Order.

12.3.2 If the Contractor claims that additional cost is involved because of, but not limited to, (1) any written interpretation pursuant to Subparagraph 2.2.8, (2) any order by the Owner to stop the Work pursuant to Paragraph 3.3 where the Contractor was not at fault, (3) any written order for a minor change in the Work issued pursuant to Paragraph 12.4, or (4) failure of payment by the Owner pursuant to Paragraph 9.7, the Contractor shall make such claim as provided in Subparagraph 12.3.1.

12.4   MINOR CHANGES IN THE WORK

12.4.1 The Architect will have authority to order minor changes in the Work not involving an adjustment in the Contract Sum or an extension of the Contract Time and not inconsistent with the intent of the Contract Documents. Such changes shall be effected by written order, and shall be binding on the Owner and the Contractor. The Contractor shall carry out such written orders promptly.

ARTICLE 13

UNCOVERING AND CORRECTION OF WORK

13.1   UNCOVERING OF WORK

13.1.1 If any portion of the Work should be covered contrary to the request of the Architect or to requirements specifically expressed in the Contract Documents, it must, if required in writing by the Architect, be uncovered for his observation and shall be replaced at the Contractor's expense.

13.1.2 If any other portion of the Work has been covered which the Architect has not specifically requested to observe prior to being covered, the Architect may request to see such Work and it shall be uncovered by the Contractor. If such Work be found in accordance with the Contract Documents, the cost of uncovering and replacement shall, by appropriate Change Order, be charged to the Owner. If such Work be found not in accordance with the Contract Documents, the Contractor shall pay such costs unless it be found that this condition was caused by the Owner or a separate contractor as provided in Article 6, in which event the Owner shall be responsible for the payment of such costs.

13.2   CORRECTION OF WORK

13.2.1 The Contractor shall promptly correct all Work rejected by the Architect as defective or as failing to conform to the Contract Documents whether observed before or after Substantial Completion and whether or not fabricated, installed or completed. The Contractor shall bear all costs of correcting such rejected Work, including

compensation for the Architect's additional services made necessary thereby.

13.2.2 If, within one year after the Date of Substantial Completion of the Work or designated portion thereof or within one year after acceptance by the Owner of designated equipment or within such longer period of time as may be prescribed by law or by the terms of any applicable special warranty required by the Contract Documents, any of the Work is found to be defective or not in accordance with the Contract Documents, the Contractor shall correct it promptly after receipt of a written notice from the Owner to do so unless the Owner has previously given the Contractor a written acceptance of such condition. This obligation shall survive termination of the Contract. The Owner shall give such notice promptly after discovery of the condition.

13.2.3 The Contractor shall remove from the site all portions of the Work which are defective or non-conforming and which have not been corrected under Subparagraphs 4.5.1, 13.2.1 and 13.2.2, unless removal is waived by the Owner.

13.2.4 If the Contractor fails to correct defective or non-conforming Work as provided in Subparagraphs 4.5.1, 13.2.1 and 13.2.2, the Owner may correct it in accordance with Paragraph 3.4.

13.2.5 If the Contractor does not proceed with the correction of such defective or non-conforming Work within a reasonable time fixed by written notice from the Architect, the Owner may remove it and may store the materials or equipment at the expense of the Contractor. If the Contractor does not pay the cost of such removal and storage within ten days thereafter, the Owner may upon ten additional days' written notice sell such Work at auction or at private sale and shall account for the net proceeds thereof, after deducting all the costs that should have been borne by the Contractor, including compensation for the Architect's additional services made necessary thereby. If such proceeds of sale do not cover all costs which the Contractor should have borne, the difference shall be charged to the Contractor and an appropriate Change Order shall be issued. If the payments then or thereafter due the Contractor are not sufficient to cover such amount, the Contractor shall pay the difference to the Owner.

13.2.6 The Contractor shall bear the cost of making good all work of the Owner or separate contractors destroyed or damaged by such correction or removal.

13.2.7 Nothing contained in this Paragraph 13.2 shall be construed to establish a period of limitation with respect to any other obligation which the Contractor might have under the Contract Documents, including Paragraph 4.5 hereof. The establishment of the time period of one year after the Date of Substantial Completion or such longer period of time as may be prescribed by law or by the terms of any warranty required by the Contract Documents relates only to the specific obligation of the Contractor to correct the Work, and has no relationship to the time within which his obligation to comply with the Contract Documents may be sought to be enforced, nor to the time within which proceedings may be commenced to establish the Contractor's liability with respect to his obligations other than specifically to correct the Work.

13.3   ACCEPTANCE OF DEFECTIVE OR NON-CONFORMING WORK

13.3.1 If the Owner prefers to accept defective or non-conforming Work, he may do so instead of requiring its removal and correction, in which case a Change Order will be issued to reflect a reduction in the Contract Sum where appropriate and equitable. Such adjustment shall be effected whether or not final payment has been made.

ARTICLE 14

TERMINATION OF THE CONTRACT

14.1   TERMINATION BY THE CONTRACTOR

14.1.1 If the Work is stopped for a period of thirty days under an order of any court or other public authority having jurisdiction, or as a result of an act of government, such as a declaration of a national emergency making materials unavailable, through no act or fault of the Contractor or a Subcontractor or their agents or employees or any other persons performing any of the Work under a contract with the Contractor, or if the Work should be stopped for a period of thirty days by the Contractor because the Architect has not issued a Certificate for Payment as provided in Paragraph 9.7 or because the Owner has not made payment thereon as provided in Paragraph 9.7, then the Contractor may, upon seven additional days' written notice to the Owner and the Architect, terminate the Contract and recover from the Owner payment for all Work executed and for any proven loss sustained upon any materials, equipment, tools, construction equipment and machinery, including reasonable profit and damages.

14.2   TERMINATION BY THE OWNER

14.2.1 If the Contractor is adjudged a bankrupt, or if he makes a general assignment for the benefit of his creditors, or if a receiver is appointed on account of his insolvency, or if he persistently or repeatedly refuses or fails, except in cases for which extension of time is provided, to supply enough properly skilled workmen or proper materials, or if he fails to make prompt payment to Subcontractors or for materials or labor, or persistently disregards laws, ordinances, rules, regulations or orders of any public authority having jurisdiction, or otherwise is guilty of a substantial violation of a provision of the Contract Documents, then the Owner, upon certification by the Architect that sufficient cause exists to justify such action, may, without prejudice to any right or remedy and after giving the Contractor and his surety, if any, seven days' written notice, terminate the employment of the Contractor and take possession of the site and of all materials, equipment, tools, construction equipment and machinery thereon owned by the Contractor and may finish the Work by whatever method he may deem expedient. In such case the Contractor shall not be entitled to receive any further payment until the Work is finished.

14.2.2 If the unpaid balance of the Contract Sum exceeds the costs of finishing the Work, including compensation for the Architect's additional services made necessary thereby, such excess shall be paid to the Contractor. If such costs exceed the unpaid balance, the Contractor shall pay the difference to the Owner. The amount to be paid to the Contractor or to the Owner, as the case may be, shall be certified by the Architect, upon application, in the manner provided in Paragraph 9.4, and this obligation for payment shall survive the termination of the Contract.

8/76 200M

RPC 12/76 200M

AIA DOCUMENT A201 • GENERAL CONDITIONS OF THE CONTRACT FOR CONSTRUCTION • THIRTEENTH EDITION • AUGUST 1976
AIA® • © 1976 • THE AMERICAN INSTITUTE OF ARCHITECTS, 1735 NEW YORK AVENUE, N.W., WASHINGTON, D.C. 20006   **A201-1976**

THE AMERICAN INSTITUTE OF ARCHITECTS

AIA Document B141

Standard Form of Agreement Between Owner and Architect

1977 EDITION

*THIS DOCUMENT HAS IMPORTANT LEGAL CONSEQUENCES; CONSULTATION WITH
AN ATTORNEY IS ENCOURAGED WITH RESPECT TO ITS COMPLETION OR MODIFICATION*

AGREEMENT

made as of the   day of   in the year of Nineteen
Hundred and

BETWEEN the Owner:

and the Architect:

For the following Project:
(Include detailed description of Project location and scope.)

The Owner and the Architect agree as set forth below.

AIA DOCUMENT B141 • OWNER-ARCHITECT AGREEMENT • THIRTEENTH EDITION • JULY 1977 • AIA® • © 1977
THE AMERICAN INSTITUTE OF ARCHITECTS, 1735 NEW YORK AVENUE, N.W., WASHINGTON, D.C. 20006   **B141-1977**

TERMS AND CONDITIONS OF AGREEMENT BETWEEN OWNER AND ARCHITECT

ARTICLE 1

ARCHITECT'S SERVICES AND RESPONSIBILITIES

BASIC SERVICES

The Architect's Basic Services consist of the five phases described in Paragraphs 1.1 through 1.5 and include normal structural, mechanical and electrical engineering services and any other services included in Article 15 as part of Basic Services.

1.1   SCHEMATIC DESIGN PHASE

1.1.1   The Architect shall review the program furnished by the Owner to ascertain the requirements of the Project and shall review the understanding of such requirements with the Owner.

1.1.2   The Architect shall provide a preliminary evaluation of the program and the Project budget requirements, each in terms of the other, subject to the limitations set forth in Subparagraph 3.2.1.

1.1.3   The Architect shall review with the Owner alternative approaches to design and construction of the Project.

1.1.4   Based on the mutually agreed upon program and Project budget requirements, the Architect shall prepare, for approval by the Owner, Schematic Design Documents consisting of drawings and other documents illustrating the scale and relationship of Project components.

1.1.5   The Architect shall submit to the Owner a Statement of Probable Construction Cost based on current area, volume or other unit costs.

1.2   DESIGN DEVELOPMENT PHASE

1.2.1   Based on the approved Schematic Design Documents and any adjustments authorized by the Owner in the program or Project budget, the Architect shall prepare, for approval by the Owner, Design Development Documents consisting of drawings and other documents to fix and describe the size and character of the entire Project as to architectural, structural, mechanical and electrical systems, materials and such other elements as may be appropriate.

1.2.2   The Architect shall submit to the Owner a further Statement of Probable Construction Cost.

1.3   CONSTRUCTION DOCUMENTS PHASE

1.3.1   Based on the approved Design Development Documents and any further adjustments in the scope or quality of the Project or in the Project budget authorized by the Owner, the Architect shall prepare, for approval by the Owner, Construction Documents consisting of Drawings and Specifications setting forth in detail the requirements for the construction of the Project.

1.3.2   The Architect shall assist the Owner in the preparation of the necessary bidding information, bidding forms, the Conditions of the Contract, and the form of Agreement between the Owner and the Contractor.

1.3.3   The Architect shall advise the Owner of any adjustments to previous Statements of Probable Construction Cost indicated by changes in requirements or general market conditions.

1.3.4   The Architect shall assist the Owner in connection with the Owner's responsibility for filing documents required for the approval of governmental authorities having jurisdiction over the Project.

1.4   BIDDING OR NEGOTIATION PHASE

1.4.1   The Architect, following the Owner's approval of the Construction Documents and of the latest Statement of Probable Construction Cost, shall assist the Owner in obtaining bids or negotiated proposals, and assist in awarding and preparing contracts for construction.

1.5   CONSTRUCTION PHASE—ADMINISTRATION OF THE CONSTRUCTION CONTRACT

1.5.1   The Construction Phase will commence with the award of the Contract for Construction and, together with the Architect's obligation to provide Basic Services under this Agreement, will terminate when final payment to the Contractor is due, or in the absence of a final Certificate for Payment or of such due date, sixty days after the Date of Substantial Completion of the Work, whichever occurs first.

1.5.2   Unless otherwise provided in this Agreement and incorporated in the Contract Documents, the Architect shall provide administration of the Contract for Construction as set forth below and in the edition of AIA Document A201, General Conditions of the Contract for Construction, current as of the date of this Agreement.

1.5.3   The Architect shall be a representative of the Owner during the Construction Phase, and shall advise and consult with the Owner. Instructions to the Contractor shall be forwarded through the Architect. The Architect shall have authority to act on behalf of the Owner only to the extent provided in the Contract Documents unless otherwise modified by written instrument in accordance with Subparagraph 1.5.16.

1.5.4   The Architect shall visit the site at intervals appropriate to the stage of construction or as otherwise agreed by the Architect in writing to become generally familiar with the progress and quality of the Work and to determine in general if the Work is proceeding in accordance with the Contract Documents. However, the Architect shall not be required to make exhaustive or continuous on-site inspections to check the quality or quantity of the Work. On the basis of such on-site observations as an architect, the Architect shall keep the Owner informed of the progress and quality of the Work, and shall endeavor to guard the Owner against defects and deficiencies in the Work of the Contractor.

1.5.5   The Architect shall not have control or charge of and shall not be responsible for construction means, methods, techniques, sequences or procedures, or for safety precautions and programs in connection with the Work, for the acts or omissions of the Contractor. Subcontractors or any other persons performing any of the Work, or for the failure of any of them to carry out the Work in accordance with the Contract Documents.

1.5.6   The Architect shall at all times have access to the Work wherever it is in preparation or progress.

1.5.7   The Architect shall determine the amounts owing to the Contractor based on observations at the site and on evaluations of the Contractor's Applications for Payment, and shall issue Certificates for Payment in such amounts, as provided in the Contract Documents.

1.5.8   The issuance of a Certificate for Payment shall constitute a representation by the Architect to the Owner, based on the Architect's observations at the site as provided in Subparagraph 1.5.4 and on the data comprising the Contractor's Application for Payment, that the Work has progressed to the point indicated; that, to the best of

AIA DOCUMENT B141 • OWNER-ARCHITECT AGREEMENT • THIRTEENTH EDITION • JULY 1977 • AIA® • © 1977
THE AMERICAN INSTITUTE OF ARCHITECTS, 1735 NEW YORK AVENUE, N.W., WASHINGTON, D.C. 20006

the Architect's knowledge, information and belief, the quality of the Work is in accordance with the Contract Documents (subject to an evaluation of the Work for conformance with the Contract Documents upon Substantial Completion, to the results of any subsequent tests required by or performed under the Contract Documents, to minor deviations from the Contract Documents correctable prior to completion, and to any specific qualifications stated in the Certificate for Payment); and that the Contractor is entitled to payment in the amount certified. However, the issuance of a Certificate for Payment shall not be a representation that the Architect has made any examination to ascertain how and for what purpose the Contractor has used the moneys paid on account of the Contract Sum.

1.5.9 The Architect shall be the interpreter of the requirements of the Contract Documents and the judge of the performance thereunder by both the Owner and Contractor. The Architect shall render interpretations necessary for the proper execution or progress of the Work with reasonable promptness on written request of either the Owner or the Contractor, and shall render written decisions, within a reasonable time, on all claims, disputes and other matters in question between the Owner and the Contractor relating to the execution or progress of the Work or the interpretation of the Contract Documents.

1.5.10 Interpretations and decisions of the Architect shall be consistent with the intent of and reasonably inferable from the Contract Documents and shall be in written or graphic form. In the capacity of interpreter and judge, the Architect shall endeavor to secure faithful performance by both the Owner and the Contractor, shall not show partiality to either, and shall not be liable for the result of any interpretation or decision rendered in good faith in such capacity.

1.5.11 The Architect's decisions in matters relating to artistic effect shall be final if consistent with the intent of the Contract Documents. The Architect's decisions on any other claims, disputes or other matters, including those in question between the Owner and the Contractor, shall be subject to arbitration as provided in this Agreement and in the Contract Documents.

1.5.12 The Architect shall have authority to reject Work which does not conform to the Contract Documents. Whenever, in the Architect's reasonable opinion, it is necessary or advisable for the implementation of the intent of the Contract Documents, the Architect will have authority to require special inspection or testing of the Work in accordance with the provisions of the Contract Documents, whether or not such Work be then fabricated, installed or completed.

1.5.13 The Architect shall review and approve or take other appropriate action upon the Contractor's submittals such as Shop Drawings, Product Data and Samples, but only for conformance with the design concept of the Work and with the information given in the Contract Documents. Such action shall be taken with reasonable promptness so as to cause no delay. The Architect's approval of a specific item shall not indicate approval of an assembly of which the item is a component.

1.5.14 The Architect shall prepare Change Orders for the Owner's approval and execution in accordance with the Contract Documents, and shall have authority to order minor changes in the Work not involving an adjustment in the Contract Sum or an extension of the Contract Time which are not inconsistent with the intent of the Contract Documents.

1.5.15 The Architect shall conduct inspections to determine the Dates of Substantial Completion and final completion, shall receive and forward to the Owner for the Owner's review written warranties and related documents required by the Contract Documents and assembled by the Contractor, and shall issue a final Certificate for Payment.

1.5.16 The extent of the duties, responsibilities and limitations of authority of the Architect as the Owner's representative during construction shall not be modified or extended without written consent of the Owner, the Contractor and the Architect.

1.6 PROJECT REPRESENTATION BEYOND BASIC SERVICES

1.6.1 If the Owner and Architect agree that more extensive representation at the site than is described in Paragraph 1.5 shall be provided, the Architect shall provide one or more Project Representatives to assist the Architect in carrying out such responsibilities at the site.

1.6.2 Such Project Representatives shall be selected, employed and directed by the Architect, and the Architect shall be compensated therefor as mutually agreed between the Owner and the Architect as set forth in an exhibit appended to this Agreement, which shall describe the duties, responsibilities and limitations of authority of such Project Representatives.

1.6.3 Through the observations by such Project Representatives, the Architect shall endeavor to provide further protection for the Owner against defects and deficiencies in the Work, but the furnishing of such project representation shall not modify the rights, responsibilities or obligations of the Architect as described in Paragraph 1.5.

1.7 ADDITIONAL SERVICES

The following Services are not included in Basic Services unless so identified in Article 15. They shall be provided if authorized or confirmed in writing by the Owner, and they shall be paid for by the Owner as provided in this Agreement, in addition to the compensation for Basic Services.

1.7.1 Providing analyses of the Owner's needs, and programming the requirements of the Project.

1.7.2 Providing financial feasibility or other special studies.

1.7.3 Providing planning surveys, site evaluations, environmental studies or comparative studies of prospective sites, and preparing special surveys, studies and submissions required for approvals of governmental authorities or others having jurisdiction over the Project.

1.7.4 Providing services relative to future facilities, systems and equipment which are not intended to be constructed during the Construction Phase.

1.7.5 Providing services to investigate existing conditions or facilities or to make measured drawings thereof, or to verify the accuracy of drawings or other information furnished by the Owner.

1.7.6 Preparing documents of alternate, separate or sequential bids or providing extra services in connection with bidding, negotiation or construction prior to the completion of the Construction Documents Phase, when requested by the Owner.

1.7.7 Providing coordination of Work performed by separate contractors or by the Owner's own forces.

1.7.8 Providing services in connection with the work of a construction manager or separate consultants retained by the Owner.

1.7.9 Providing Detailed Estimates of Construction Cost, analyses of owning and operating costs, or detailed quantity surveys or inventories of material, equipment and labor.

1.7.10 Providing interior design and other similar services required for or in connection with the selection, procurement or installation of furniture, furnishings and related equipment.

1.7.11 Providing services for planning tenant or rental spaces.

1.7.12 Making revisions in Drawings, Specifications or other documents when such revisions are inconsistent with written approvals or instructions previously given, are required by the enactment or revision of codes, laws or regulations subsequent to the preparation of such documents or are due to other causes not solely within the control of the Architect.

1.7.13 Preparing Drawings, Specifications and supporting data and providing other services in connection with Change Orders to the extent that the adjustment in the Basic Compensation resulting from the adjusted Construction Cost is not commensurate with the services required of the Architect, provided such Change Orders are required by causes not solely within the control of the Architect.

1.7.14 Making investigations, surveys, valuations, inventories or detailed appraisals of existing facilities, and services required in connection with construction performed by the Owner.

1.7.15 Providing consultation concerning replacement of any Work damaged by fire or other cause during construction, and furnishing services as may be required in connection with the replacement of such Work.

1.7.16 Providing services made necessary by the default of the Contractor, or by major defects or deficiencies in the Work of the Contractor, or by failure of performance of either the Owner or Contractor under the Contract for Construction.

1.7.17 Preparing a set of reproducible record drawings showing significant changes in the Work made during construction based on marked-up prints, drawings and other data furnished by the Contractor to the Architect.

1.7.18 Providing extensive assistance in the utilization of any equipment or system such as initial start-up or testing, adjusting and balancing, preparation of operation and maintenance manuals, training personnel for operation and maintenance, and consultation during operation.

1.7.19 Providing services after issuance to the Owner of the final Certificate for Payment, or in the absence of a final Certificate for Payment, more than sixty days after the Date of Substantial Completion of the Work.

1.7.20 Preparing to serve or serving as an expert witness in connection with any public hearing, arbitration proceeding or legal proceeding.

1.7.21 Providing services of consultants for other than the normal architectural, structural, mechanical and electrical engineering services for the Project.

1.7.22 Providing any other services not otherwise included in this Agreement or not customarily furnished in accordance with generally accepted architectural practice.

1.8 TIME

1.8.1 The Architect shall perform Basic and Additional Services as expeditiously as is consistent with professional skill and care and the orderly progress of the Work. Upon request of the Owner, the Architect shall submit for the Owner's approval, a schedule for the performance of the Architect's services which shall be adjusted as required as the Project proceeds, and shall include allowances for periods of time required for the Owner's review and approval of submissions and for approvals of authorities having

jurisdiction over the Project. This schedule, when approved by the Owner, shall not, except for reasonable cause, be exceeded by the Architect.

ARTICLE 2

THE OWNER'S RESPONSIBILITIES

2.1 The Owner shall provide full information regarding requirements for the Project including a program, which shall set forth the Owner's design objectives, constraints and criteria, including space requirements and relationships, flexibility and expandability, special equipment and systems and site requirements.

2.2 If the Owner provides a budget for the Project it shall include contingencies for bidding, changes in the Work during construction, and other costs which are the responsibility of the Owner, including those described in this Article 2 and in Subparagraph 3.1.2. The Owner shall, at the request of the Architect, provide a statement of funds available for the Project, and their source.

2.3 The Owner shall designate, when necessary, a representative authorized to act in the Owner's behalf with respect to the Project. The Owner or such authorized representative shall examine the documents submitted by the Architect and shall render decisions pertaining thereto promptly, to avoid unreasonable delay in the progress of the Architect's services.

2.4 The Owner shall furnish a legal description and a certified land survey of the site, giving, as applicable, grades and lines of streets, alleys, pavements and adjoining property; rights-of-way, restrictions, easements, encroachments, zoning, deed restrictions, boundaries and contours of the site; locations, dimensions and complete data pertaining to existing buildings, other improvements and trees; and full information concerning available service and utility lines both public and private, above and below grade, including inverts and depths.

2.5 The Owner shall furnish the services of soil engineers or other consultants when such services are deemed necessary by the Architect. Such services shall include test borings, test pits, soil bearing values, percolation tests, air and water pollution tests, ground corrosion and resistivity tests, including necessary operations for determining subsoil, air and water conditions, with reports and appropriate professional recommendations.

2.6 The Owner shall furnish structural, mechanical, chemical and other laboratory tests, inspections and reports as required by law or the Contract Documents.

2.7 The Owner shall furnish all legal, accounting and insurance counseling services as may be necessary at any time for the Project, including such auditing services as the Owner may require to verify the Contractor's Applications for Payment or to ascertain how or for what purposes the Contractor uses the moneys paid by or on behalf of the Owner.

2.8 The services, information, surveys and reports required by Paragraphs 2.4 through 2.7 inclusive shall be furnished at the Owner's expense, and the Architect shall be entitled to rely upon the accuracy and completeness thereof.

2.9 If the Owner observes or otherwise becomes aware of any fault or defect in the Project or nonconformance with the Contract Documents, prompt written notice thereof shall be given by the Owner to the Architect.

2.10 The Owner shall furnish required information and services and shall render approvals and decisions as expeditiously as necessary for the orderly progress of the Architect's services and of the Work.

AIA DOCUMENT B141 • OWNER-ARCHITECT AGREEMENT • THIRTEENTH EDITION • JULY 1977 • AIA® • © 1977
THE AMERICAN INSTITUTE OF ARCHITECTS, 1735 NEW YORK AVENUE, N.W., WASHINGTON, D.C. 20006

ARTICLE 3

CONSTRUCTION COST

3.1 DEFINITION

3.1.1 The Construction Cost shall be the total cost or estimated cost to the Owner of all elements of the Project designed or specified by the Architect.

3.1.2 The Construction Cost shall include at current market rates, including a reasonable allowance for overhead and profit, the cost of labor and materials furnished by the Owner and any equipment which has been designed, specified, selected or specially provided for by the Architect.

3.1.3 Construction Cost does not include the compensation of the Architect and the Architect's consultants, the cost of the land, rights-of-way, or other costs which are the responsibility of the Owner as provided in Article 2.

3.2 RESPONSIBILITY FOR CONSTRUCTION COST

3.2.1 Evaluations of the Owner's Project budget, Statements of Probable Construction Cost and Detailed Estimates of Construction Cost, if any, prepared by the Architect, represent the Architect's best judgment as a design professional familiar with the construction industry. It is recognized, however, that neither the Architect nor the Owner has control over the cost of labor, materials or equipment, over the Contractor's methods of determining bid prices, or over competitive bidding, market or negotiating conditions. Accordingly, the Architect cannot and does not warrant or represent that bids or negotiated prices will not vary from the Project budget proposed, established or approved by the Owner, if any, or from any Statement of Probable Construction Cost or other cost estimate or evaluation prepared by the Architect.

3.2.2 No fixed limit of Construction Cost shall be established as a condition of this Agreement by the furnishing, proposal or establishment of a Project budget under Subparagraph 1.1.2 or Paragraph 2.2 or otherwise, unless such fixed limit has been agreed upon in writing and signed by the parties hereto. If such a fixed limit has been established, the Architect shall be permitted to include contingencies for design, bidding and price escalation, to determine what materials, equipment, component systems and types of construction are to be included in the Contract Documents, to make reasonable adjustments in the scope of the Project and to include in the Contract Documents alternate bids to adjust the Construction Cost to the fixed limit. Any such fixed limit shall be increased in the amount of any increase in the Contract Sum occurring after execution of the Contract for Construction.

3.2.3 If the Bidding or Negotiation Phase has not commenced within three months after the Architect submits the Construction Documents to the Owner, any Project budget or fixed limit of Construction Cost shall be adjusted to reflect any change in the general level of prices in the construction industry between the date of submission of the Construction Documents to the Owner and the date on which proposals are sought.

3.2.4 If a Project budget or fixed limit of Construction Cost (adjusted as provided in Subparagraph 3.2.3) is exceeded by the lowest bona fide bid or negotiated proposal, the Owner shall (1) give written approval of an increase in such fixed limit, (2) authorize rebidding or renegotiating of the Project within a reasonable time, (3) if the Project is abandoned, terminate in accordance with Paragraph 10.2, or (4) cooperate in revising the Project scope and quality as required to reduce the Construction Cost. In the case of (4), provided a fixed limit of Construc-

tion Cost has been established as a condition of this Agreement, the Architect, without additional charge, shall modify the Drawings and Specifications as necessary to comply with the fixed limit. The providing of such service shall be the limit of the Architect's responsibility arising from the establishment of such fixed limit, and having done so, the Architect shall be entitled to compensation for all services performed, in accordance with this Agreement, whether or not the Construction Phase is commenced.

ARTICLE 4

DIRECT PERSONNEL EXPENSE

4.1 Direct Personnel Expense is defined as the direct salaries of all the Architect's personnel engaged on the Project, and the portion of the cost of their mandatory and customary contributions and benefits related thereto, such as employment taxes and other statutory employee benefits, insurance, sick leave, holidays, vacations, pensions and similar contributions and benefits.

ARTICLE 5

REIMBURSABLE EXPENSES

5.1 Reimbursable Expenses are in addition to the Compensation for Basic and Additional Services and include actual expenditures made by the Architect and the Architect's employees and consultants in the interest of the Project for the expenses listed in the following Subparagraphs:

5.1.1 Expense of transportation in connection with the Project; living expenses in connection with out-of-town travel; long distance communications; and fees paid for securing approval of authorities having jurisdiction over the Project.

5.1.2 Expense of reproductions, postage and handling of Drawings, Specifications and other documents, excluding reproductions for the office use of the Architect and the Architect's consultants.

5.1.3 Expense of data processing and photographic production techniques when used in connection with Additional Services.

5.1.4 If authorized in advance by the Owner, expense of overtime work requiring higher than regular rates.

5.1.5 Expense of renderings, models and mock-ups requested by the Owner.

5.1.6 Expense of any additional insurance coverage or limits, including professional liability insurance, requested by the Owner in excess of that normally carried by the Architect and the Architect's consultants.

ARTICLE 6

PAYMENTS TO THE ARCHITECT

6.1 PAYMENTS ON ACCOUNT OF BASIC SERVICES

6.1.1 An initial payment as set forth in Paragraph 14.1 is the minimum payment under this Agreement.

6.1.2 Subsequent payments for Basic Services shall be made monthly and shall be in proportion to services performed within each Phase of services, on the basis set forth in Article 14.

6.1.3 If and to the extent that the Contract Time initially established in the Contract for Construction is exceeded or extended through no fault of the Architect, compensation for any Basic Services required for such extended period of Administration of the Construction Contract shall be computed as set forth in Paragraph 14.4 for Additional Services.

AIA DOCUMENT B141 • OWNER-ARCHITECT AGREEMENT • THIRTEENTH EDITION • JULY 1977 • AIA® • © 1977
THE AMERICAN INSTITUTE OF ARCHITECTS, 1735 NEW YORK AVENUE, N.W., WASHINGTON, D.C. 20006

6.1.4 When compensation is based on a percentage of Construction Cost, and any portions of the Project are deleted or otherwise not constructed, compensation for such portions of the Project shall be payable to the extent services are performed on such portions, in accordance with the schedule set forth in Subparagraph 14.2.2, based on (1) the lowest bona fide bid or negotiated proposal or, (2) if no such bid or proposal is received, the most recent Statement of Probable Construction Cost or Detailed Estimate of Construction Cost for such portions of the Project.

6.2 PAYMENTS ON ACCOUNT OF ADDITIONAL SERVICES

6.2.1 Payments on account of the Architect's Additional Services as defined in Paragraph 1.7 and for Reimbursable Expenses as defined in Article 5 shall be made monthly upon presentation of the Architect's statement of services rendered or expenses incurred.

6.3 PAYMENTS WITHHELD

6.3.1 No deductions shall be made from the Architect's compensation on account of penalty, liquidated damages or other sums withheld from payments to contractors, or on account of the cost of changes in the Work other than those for which the Architect is held legally liable.

6.4 PROJECT SUSPENSION OR TERMINATION

6.4.1 If the Project is suspended or abandoned in whole or in part for more than three months, the Architect shall be compensated for all services performed prior to receipt of written notice from the Owner of such suspension or abandonment, together with Reimbursable Expenses then due and all Termination Expenses as defined in Paragraph 10.4. If the Project is resumed after being suspended for more than three months, the Architect's compensation shall be equitably adjusted.

ARTICLE 7

ARCHITECT'S ACCOUNTING RECORDS

7.1 Records of Reimbursable Expenses and expenses pertaining to Additional Services and services performed on the basis of a Multiple of Direct Personnel Expense shall be kept on the basis of generally accepted accounting principles and shall be available to the Owner or the Owner's authorized representative at mutually convenient times.

ARTICLE 8

OWNERSHIP AND USE OF DOCUMENTS

8.1 Drawings and Specifications as instruments of service are and shall remain the property of the Architect whether the Project for which they are made is executed or not. The Owner shall be permitted to retain copies, including reproducible copies, of Drawings and Specifications for information and reference in connection with the Owner's use and occupancy of the Project. The Drawings and Specifications shall not be used by the Owner on other projects, for additions to this Project, or for completion of this Project by others provided the Architect is not in default under this Agreement, except by agreement in writing and with appropriate compensation to the Architect.

8.2 Submission or distribution to meet official regulatory requirements or for other purposes in connection with the Project is not to be construed as publication in derogation of the Architect's rights.

ARTICLE 9

ARBITRATION

9.1 All claims, disputes and other matters in question between the parties to this Agreement, arising out of or relating to this Agreement or the breach thereof, shall be decided by arbitration in accordance with the Construction Industry Arbitration Rules of the American Arbitration Association then obtaining unless the parties mutually agree otherwise. No arbitration, arising out of or relating to this Agreement, shall include, by consolidation, joinder or in any other manner, any additional person not a party to this Agreement except by written consent containing a specific reference to this Agreement and signed by the Architect, the Owner, and any other person sought to be joined. Any consent to arbitration involving an additional person or persons shall not constitute consent to arbitration of any dispute not described therein or with any person not named or described therein. This Agreement to arbitrate and any agreement to arbitrate with an additional person or persons duly consented to by the parties to this Agreement shall be specifically enforceable under the prevailing arbitration law.

9.2 Notice of the demand for arbitration shall be filed in writing with the other party to this Agreement and with the American Arbitration Association. The demand shall be made within a reasonable time after the claim, dispute or other matter in question has arisen. In no event shall the demand for arbitration be made after the date when institution of legal or equitable proceedings based on such claim, dispute or other matter in question would be barred by the applicable statute of limitations.

9.3 The award rendered by the arbitrators shall be final, and judgment may be entered upon it in accordance with applicable law in any court having jurisdiction thereof.

ARTICLE 10

TERMINATION OF AGREEMENT

10.1 This Agreement may be terminated by either party upon seven days' written notice should the other party fail substantially to perform in accordance with its terms through no fault of the party initiating the termination.

10.2 This Agreement may be terminated by the Owner upon at least seven days' written notice to the Architect in the event that the Project is permanently abandoned.

10.3 In the event of termination not the fault of the Architect, the Architect shall be compensated for all services performed to termination date, together with Reimbursable Expenses then due and all Termination Expenses as defined in Paragraph 10.4.

10.4 Termination Expenses include expenses directly attributable to termination for which the Architect is not otherwise compensated, plus an amount computed as a percentage of the total Basic and Additional Compensation earned to the time of termination, as follows:

   .1 20 percent if termination occurs during the Schematic Design Phase; or

   .2 10 percent if termination occurs during the Design Development Phase; or

   .3 5 percent if termination occurs during any subsequent phase.

ARTICLE 11

MISCELLANEOUS PROVISIONS

11.1 Unless otherwise specified, this Agreement shall be governed by the law of the principal place of business of the Architect.

11.2 Terms in this Agreement shall have the same meaning as those in AIA Document A201, General Conditions of the Contract for Construction, current as of the date of this Agreement.

11.3 As between the parties to this Agreement: as to all acts or failures to act by either party to this Agreement, any applicable statute of limitations shall commence to run and any alleged cause of action shall be deemed to have accrued in any and all events not later than the relevant Date of Substantial Completion of the Work, and as to any acts or failures to act occurring after the relevant Date of Substantial Completion, not later than the date of issuance of the final Certificate for Payment.

11.4 The Owner and the Architect waive all rights against each other and against the contractors, consultants, agents and employees of the other for damages covered by any property insurance during construction as set forth in the edition of AIA Document A201, General Conditions, current as of the date of this Agreement. The Owner and the Architect each shall require appropriate similar waivers from their contractors, consultants and agents.

ARTICLE 12

SUCCESSORS AND ASSIGNS

12.1 The Owner and the Architect, respectively, bind themselves, their partners, successors, assigns and legal representatives to the other party to this Agreement and to the partners, successors, assigns and legal representatives of such other party with respect to all covenants of this Agreement. Neither the Owner nor the Architect shall assign, sublet or transfer any interest in this Agreement without the written consent of the other.

ARTICLE 13

EXTENT OF AGREEMENT

13.1 This Agreement represents the entire and integrated agreement between the Owner and the Architect and supersedes all prior negotiations, representations or agreements, either written or oral. This Agreement may be amended only by written instrument signed by both Owner and Architect.

ARTICLE 14

BASIS OF COMPENSATION

The Owner shall compensate the Architect for the Scope of Services provided, in accordance with Article 6, Payments to the Architect, and the other Terms and Conditions of this Agreement, as follows:

14.1   AN INITIAL PAYMENT of   dollars ($)

shall be made upon execution of this Agreement and credited to the Owner's account as follows:

14.2   BASIC COMPENSATION

14.2.1   FOR BASIC SERVICES, as described in Paragraphs 1.1 through 1.5, and any other services included in Article 15 as part of Basic Services, Basic Compensation shall be computed as follows:

(Here insert basis of compensation, including fixed amounts, multiples or percentages, and identify Phases to which particular methods of compensation apply, if necessary.)

14.2.2 Where compensation is based on a Stipulated Sum or Percentage of Construction Cost, payments for Basic Services shall be made as provided in Subparagraph 6.1.2, so that Basic Compensation for each Phase shall equal the following percentages of the total Basic Compensation payable:

(Include any additional Phases as appropriate.)

Schematic Design Phase:	percent (%)
Design Development Phase:	percent (%)
Construction Documents Phase:	percent (%)
Bidding or Negotiation Phase:	percent (%)
Construction Phase:	percent (%)

14.3 FOR PROJECT REPRESENTATION BEYOND BASIC SERVICES, as described in Paragraph 1.6, Compensation shall be computed separately in accordance with Subparagraph 1.6.2.

14.4 COMPENSATION FOR ADDITIONAL SERVICES

14.4.1 FOR ADDITIONAL SERVICES OF THE ARCHITECT, as described in Paragraph 1.7, and any other services included in Article 15 as part of Additional Services, but excluding Additional Services of consultants, Compensation shall be computed as follows:

(Here insert basis of compensation, including rates and/or multiples of Direct Personnel Expense for Principals and employees, and identify Principals and classify employees, if required. Identify specific services to which particular methods of compensation apply, if necessary.)

14.4.2 FOR ADDITIONAL SERVICES OF CONSULTANTS, including additional structural, mechanical and electrical engineering services and those provided under Subparagraph 1.7.21 or identified in Article 15 as part of Additional Services, a multiple of (   ) times the amounts billed to the Architect for such services.

(Identify specific types of consultants in Article 15, if required.)

14.5 FOR REIMBURSABLE EXPENSES, as described in Article 5, and any other items included in Article 15 as Reimbursable Expenses, a multiple of (   ) times the amounts expended by the Architect, the Architect's employees and consultants in the interest of the Project.

14.6 Payments due the Architect and unpaid under this Agreement shall bear interest from the date payment is due at the rate entered below, or in the absence thereof, at the legal rate prevailing at the principal place of business of the Architect.

(Here insert any rate of interest agreed upon.)

(Usury laws and requirements under the Federal Truth in Lending Act, similar state and local consumer credit laws and other regulations at the Owner's and Architect's principal places of business, the location of the Project and elsewhere may affect the validity of this provision. Specific legal advice should be obtained with respect to deletion, modification, or other requirements such as written disclosures or waivers.)

14.7 The Owner and the Architect agree in accordance with the Terms and Conditions of this Agreement that:

14.7.1 IF THE SCOPE of the Project or of the Architect's Services is changed materially, the amounts of compensation shall be equitably adjusted.

14.7.2 IF THE SERVICES covered by this Agreement have not been completed within

( ) months of the date hereof, through no fault of the Architect, the amounts of compensation, rates and multiples set forth herein shall be equitably adjusted.

ARTICLE 15

OTHER CONDITIONS OR SERVICES

This Agreement entered into as of the day and year first written above.

OWNER _____ ARCHITECT _____

_____ _____

_____ _____

_____ _____

BY _____ BY _____

AIA DOCUMENT B141 • OWNER-ARCHITECT AGREEMENT • THIRTEENTH EDITION • JULY 1977 • AIA® • © 1977
THE AMERICAN INSTITUTE OF ARCHITECTS, 1735 NEW YORK AVENUE, N.W., WASHINGTON, D.C. 20006   **B141-1977**

Appendix II

Memory Techniques

In Chapter 3, a few learning techniques were analyzed in detail with little mention of remembering or retaining material so essential to learning. Obviously, in order to carry out jobs or functions, even on the most basic levels, an individual must retain in his memory certain facts and figures, policies, and procedures. Therefore, in this appendix, basic mnemonic strategies are offered, along with proven techniques to improve the memory. We emphasize that, because much data in our lives demand sheer rote learning, mnemonic techniques often fall short of the mark of practical (and appropriate) application. Like all suggestions, a person will judge for himself the compatibility of such techniques to his particular situation. If a certain strategy appears confusing or not worth the time and effort, one should discard it in favor of the basic learning principles. Although much of the following investigations originally related to a formal school setting, one may easily modify the results to suit construction situations.

A. How to Improve Memory

Psychologists find three basic techniques useful for improving the retention of learned material.

1) Overlearning

When an individual desires to learn a new task (say, memorize an important list or learn a new critical procedure or analyze a design detail), practice makes perfect. Generally, if he can recall the material without error, he reasonably assumes that his task is completed, so he stops studying. Nevertheless, a number of experiments strongly indicate that additional practice (overlearning) dramatically improves one's retention of the material, notably at a later date. Usually overlearning applies to academic settings. A student rereads the text until the material becomes part of his memory; this principle applies equally to construction, especially when one considers job experience. The more projects a manager completes, the more meetings he attends, the more conflicts he resolves, the more intensely he overlearns, or, stated another way, the more experience he has gained. With respect to overlearning, psychologists find that motivation is a crucial ingredient—the desire to excel.

2) Review

Another basic technique utilized to improve retention concerns periodic review of the subject. In the mastery of any task, or skill (say learning a specific topic), an individual, after initially absorbing the total contents, gains considerably more retention at a later date by periodically reviewing the subject matter. In fact, with each review, he requires less and less practice time to solidly commit the material to memory (the material becomes second nature). This concept lends support to the arguments for periodic professional examinations to test competence (and obsolescence). By and large, most professional personnel update themselves on technological innovations by taking refresher courses, reading trade journals, attending seminars, or even in buzz sessions with coworkers. With respect to construction management, a supervisor may well profit by periodically scanning project progress reports and correspondence (for anticipation of conflicts), latest cost records (for estimating), innovative building methods or processes (for future application), and notable technical difficulties (for preventive measures).

3) Active Participation

When an individual masters a task, psychological tests show that he more effectively retains the material when he actively participates in the learning process (by writing, reading aloud, or paraphrasing the material). Therefore, when reading correspondence, examining plans and specs, or taking off a job, one must constantly check attentiveness. Too often one's eyes read the words, although his heart and mind lie 10 light years away. Participate actively and forcefully. Construction management should, as standard policy, require independent (say, by printed checklists) review by colleagues for bid proposals, design details, etc.—too often errors are committed because of mental sets and malice of forethought, and, of course, the pressures imposed by schedules. A new face provides a fresh approach, which may in itself catch errors and oversights.

B. Mnemonic Strategies

Although many scientists question the value of memory-training techniques, others argue that some mnemonic devices indeed work. Operationally, these devices utilize old knowledge as anchor points to which new knowledge is linked. Two common strategies are: (1) increase the meaningfulness of material to be remembered, and (2) create visual images that relate to the material to be remembered. Of utmost importance, the appropriate procedure depends on the type of material (lists, subject content, or names) to be learned and the type of remembering that is required (short-term or lasting).

1. Increase the Meaningfulness

Generally, coordinated material is more readily recalled than reams of unrelated data. The following example illustrates this point neatly. Read the following sequential groups (chunks) of letters once and try to repeat them from memory.

TH-EDO-GSA-WTH-ECA-T

Probably, you find the groups difficult to remember. [Psychologists find the limits of short-term memory to range from five to nine chunks (numbers of organizational units) for once-presented material.] If, however, the letters are regrouped in the same sequence:

THE DOG SAW THE CAT

This is very easy to recall.

Studies suggest that capacity for retention of chunks increases sevenfold by combining letters into words, and, with words into sentences, capacity increases accordingly.

Therefore, a few suggestions are offered:

1. Encode the material in such a way that the quantity to be retained is reduced. For example: "ROY G BIV" aids in recalling the order of spectral colors—*R*ed, *O*range, *Y*ellow. . . .
2. Arrange the items in a list so the initial letter spells a familar word. For example, "HOMES" helps one to remember the Great Lakes—*H*uron, *O*ntario, *M*ichigan, *E*rie, *S*uperior. "GAPS" provides the contract documents—*G*eneral Conditions, *A*greement, *P*lans, *S*pecifications.
3. When confronted with word or item lists, incorporate the words into a meaningful sentence, or use the initial letters to construct a sentence. As a simple illustration using the material above (GAPS) two sentences are constructed: (1) The *G*eneral *a*grees to *p*lan the *s*pecifications; (2) *G*ood *A*rchitects *P*lan *S*pontaneously.

2. Create Visual Images

When small groups of meaningful items must be retained, connect these items by way of vivid interrelating pictures. Usually the more ridiculous or bizarre the image, the increased likelihood it will be remembered. Again using our contract document example, visualize first an army general (General Conditions) smiling and shaking hands (Agreement). Next associate the plans and specs. Applying the exaggeration, distortion, expansion concepts learned in creativity, imagine the general with a book on his head, and shaking hands, not with a person, but with a set of plans. This visual image leads to recall of the list. Visual association yields powerful results; however, some scientists question whether the time and effort justify the results. Again the decision is appealed to the judgment of the user and the specifics of the situation. A powerful application of visual techniques worth noting pertains to remembering names. In social interactions, one constantly meets new people, and, whether because of inner tension or distraction during the introduction, frequently one fails to give his full attention, and consequently he forgets the name. In accord with Maslow's hierarchy, normal healthy adults possess self-esteem needs; consequently, a conscious attempt should be given to correct this inattention. To forget a person's name may be construed as a nonverbal message that you wish to ignore another person, or that you consider that individual not worth the effort of retention. Therefore, upon introduction stop, look, listen, and repeat:

a. Stop and listen carefully to the name, repeating it out loud.
b. Look squarely at the person to get a graphic picture.

c. In the course of conversation, repeat the name several times to refresh your memory.

If these basic steps fail, one can opt for the strategy of linking the name (a verbal expression) with a face or body (a pictorial expression) as explained below:

a. Name.   Listen to the name carefully; attach the name to a related and concrete object. For example, connect the name with a celebrity (Lincoln—Abe Lincoln; Smith—Smith brothers; Tom—Tom Thumb); or relate to an object of similar meaning (Light—lightbulb; Bill—a bill; Dennis—den of ice). Or associate the name with words spelled similarly or sound-alikes (Paul—tall; Churchill—Church on a hill; Crosby—cross covered with bees). Change the name into something tangible—exaggerate, amplify—create the concrete image that sticks out in your mind.

b. Person.   Observe the person, tactfully but intently. Study the face and build for prominent, distinctive details. Note attentively the eyes, nose, teeth, complexion, hair, blemishes or peculiarities, shape, mannerisms, voice, and expressions. Mentally manipulate the most noticeable features—not necessarily on a complimentary basis, but necessarily clear and concrete (wide eyes—boiled eggs; large teeth—a horse; bull neck—a walrus; animal analogies supply a wealth of images). As explained in brainstorm techniques, subdue the normal impulse to consider this approach ridiculous—this tip aids in remembering!

c. Tie the Person to the Name.   With the image of the name, the prominent feature, blend the two together. Suppose the name is Bush; then imagine a large bush. If the person possesses large bushy eyebrows, mentally place two bushes over the person's eyes. This mind's picture will aid in recall.

NAME	PROMINENT FEATURE	IMAGE
Snow	White hair	Snow-capped mountain on head
Starsky	Bald head	Star skiing down bald head
Ball	Fat	Man inside a ball
Cushman	Bushman	An aborigine
George Hill	Gorge-hill	Hill rising over a gorge

d. Overlearn.   Last, but not least, repeat the name (overlearn) in the ensuing conversation until the strategy is no longer required. Although this technique may appear artificial, it succeeds repeatedly. Indirectly sometimes, in the attempt to create images, active participation often improves memory simply by virtue of paying attention to the name.

Appendix III

Written Communication and Documentation

Throughout history man has excelled in perpetrating harm and hardships via the spoken word. The same could be attributed to the written word, except that, in this case, we have a permanent record. Somewhat analogous to the speaking and listening dilemma, people often assume that because they understand what they have written, the reader will likewise comprehend the message. Unfortunately, this proves to be a dangerous assumption, as witnessed in many disagreements between contractors and designers over a specification. "But it's clear to me," says the spec writer. "Well, I don't see it that way!" asserts the foreman. In other cases, minutes of meetings, written "understandings," letters, and reports commonly provoke controversy because of imprecise wording and fuzzy concepts.

In construction, the importance of accurate and detailed documentation can seldom be overemphasized, especially from the contractor's vantage. Countless tragedies, needless business failures, and lost (but valid) claims owe their origin to the lack of a single letter, possibly even a poorly stated or ambiguous phrase. Probably most could have been prevented had an astute job captain, inspector, project manager, or super properly recorded the facts—"For want of a nail, a kingdom was lost." Therefore this appendix briefly covers two vital components of the written word: (1) written communication, and (2) documentation. The former covers the more general terms, whereas the latter, extracted from *The Handbook of Construction Management and Organization*, stands, as is, essentially the last word on the subject of construction documentation.

A. Written Communication

To illustrate the difference between good and bad writing, Eric Blair, an English journalist, in an essay on jargon and obscurity in contemporary English usage,* translated a well-known biblical verse from Ecclesiastes into jargon of the worst sort.

Ecclesiastes: "I returned and saw under the sun, that the race is not to the swift, nor the battle to the strong, neither yet bread to the wise, nor yet riches to men of understanding, nor yet favor to men of skill; but time and chance happeneth to them all."

---

*See George Orwell, *Shooting an Elephant and Other Essays;* Copyright, 1950, by Sonia Orwell. Reprinted by permission of Harcourt Brace Jovanovich, Inc.

Modern jargon: "Objective consideration of contemporary phenomena compels the conclusion that success or failure in competitive activities exhibits no tendency to be commensurate with innate capacity, but that a considerable element of the unpredictable must invariably be taken into account."

Which passage rings clearly and specifically? The reader may well ask, "What's this got to do with construction?" Everything! A slab on grade cracks and settles shortly after the project has been completed. A two-year old report reads that on the day the slab was placed ". . . weather was inclement . . ." or, in verbose fashion, "objective consideration of questionable suitability of environment compels the conclusion that potentiality of future problem exists somewhat."

Such obscurities and imprecision beg for trouble. Was the slab placed in a light drizzle or amidst a roaring blizzard with a wind chill factor of −42°F? Although not quite as dramatic, much of the writing in construction suffers from the same deficiencies, as well as from a legion of others. Therefore, we offer a few comments as a constructive beginning:

1. In speaking, a person must consciously work to express himself clearly and succinctly, so that the listener will fully understand. Otherwise, why communicate in the first place? This commitment to clarity is all the more critical in writing because the reader usually cannot ask the writer what he meant. At best, the reader must guess at the meaning, or try to read "between the lines."

In addition, it is well to remember that, in face-to-face communication, words are often flavored by nonverbal cues: tone, gestures, facial movements—all of which are absent from written communiques. The written word must carry the message by itself. Thus, in every sentence, the writer should ask himself at least three questions:

1. What am I trying to say?
2. What words will best express the message in accurate detail?
3. Can it be said more tersely?

The writer should be alert, not only to the precise meanings of words, but to their possible interpretation and to the connotations they may carry. As discussed in regard to propaganda techniques, certain words are loaded with emotion. To express that a piece of equipment is inexpensive may be relatively factual, but to write that it is "cheap" may invite litigation from the manufacturer.

2. Generally short sentences consisting of simple, concrete words make reading easier and, all other factors held constant, less susceptible to misunderstanding. Long-winded phrases and awkward grammatical constructions are first cousins to confusion. Therefore be brief, but never to the point of sacrificing accuracy and readability. This is not to imply that correspondence need be written with a drone of consecutive subject–verb–object statements, like a preschool primer: "Dick sees Sally." Yet, neither should it be impregnated with abstractions, so that it is as abstruse as the Rosetta Stone.

To guide the writer, Blair suggested a number of useful rules that can specifically apply to construction correspondence.

1. Never use a long word where a short one will do.
2. If a word can be deleted, then always cut it out.

3. Preferably use the active voice instead of the passive voice (except in writing letters about trouble—author's note).
4. Never use a foreign phrase or a jargon word if an everyday English equivalent is available.
5. Break any of these rules sooner than say anything outright insulting or injurious.

So much for the general rules for writing. We now look at some of the interpersonal aspects of letter writing. Not only is the content important, so are the means and methods—the timing, the phraseology, and the judicious use of passive verbs. It is well to bear in mind that any correspondence inundated with misspellings, incorrect grammar, erasures, and coffee stains presents a poor image, which reflects on the total organization. Even though unjust and prejudicial, and actually unrelated to technical capability, it is, nevertheless, a fact of life. Proofread *everything*.

Letters

In construction meetings, especially in the heat of frustration and clashing viewpoints, angry individuals vocally express themselves rather forcefully, directly, and sometimes profanely. But usually two weeks later, with tempers cooled, all is forgiven and forgotten. Whenever a subtle insult or damaging innuendo is written, however, the situation takes on an entirely different complexion. Seldom, if ever, is the matter forgotten or forgiven. Therefore, never in written correspondence be brutally frank, even if the facts support your position. If at all possible, take the edge off the sword. An enemy created is never an asset. Above and beyond the legal implications, a few basic psychological points should be considered when writing letters especially those dealing with troubles.

1. Unless given no other alternative, try to write only favorable (or at worst neutral) remarks about individuals and organizations. Try to protect their good names. If the situation demands that you tell an unfavorable truth, consider first a telephone call. Explain your concern and intentions. Possibly the situation can be ironed out. If not, what have you lost? At least you will be reputed to be above board, and you will have lessened the shock of an unexpected trouble letter. Remember that, in a society of Xerox machines, a letter lives forever.

2. Especially when embroiled in a highly emotional problem, keep a tight rein on your anger, fear, revenge, etc. Such charged correspondence breeds reprisal, direct and insidious. Stick to the facts, and avoid insult and innuendo.

3. In writing about trouble, state the facts in such a way that unpleasant insinuations or connotations are softened. Avoid those phrases that may intimate an infuriated, desk-banging attitude—"Your complete failure . . . ", "Your unsupported claim . . .", "Frankly speaking", the "we-versus-you" attitude. Instead, soften the tone by using passive verbs, which are usually more impersonal (and more face-saving in that they avoid spotlighting any particular person). For example, compare the difference between the following sentences:

Active: "You failed to provide the necessary manpower."
Passive: "The necessary manpower has not been provided."
Active: "You committed an error."
Passive: "An error has been committed."

All these statements convey the facts, but the passive voice, intentionally vague, is more tactful and psychologically more suitable.

4. Since timing is a nonverbal form of communication, address problems and answer letters of complaint promptly. Reflect your concern. If time is required to review and research, then state when a final response will be forthcoming.

5. With respect to the mechanics and format, try to open your letter on a friendly note. Establish rapport by expressing your concern or appreciation of his position. (For example: "We appreciate your request . . .", "We acknowledge your . . .", or "We have reviewed . . .".) Explain what action you have taken to handle the matter, in sufficient detail to show that the matter has not been entombed in the inactivity file or hook-shotted into the waste basket. If your position differs from that of others, give specific factual reasons, such as: "In specification 24.5.1 it states. . . ." Whenever possible, offer suggestions and alternative solutions. Finally close with a goodwill statement.

B. Documentation

Possibly the reader can identify with the following unfortunate situations.

1. In haste, a designer verbally requests the contractor to perform an "extra," promising that the paperwork will come through later. Being a "nice guy," the contractor does the work without proper authorization from the owner. Later, for a number of reasons (e.g., the designer forgot, personnel were transferred, etc.), the contractor is denied payment.

2. On the basis of verbal priorities, the architect designs the job. In the working plan stage, he finds the priorities completely switched around, rendering the present design useless. A "nice guy," he loses time and money.

3. A costly disagreement brings the owner to court in a suit against the general contractor. The owner's lawyer carries to the docket three neatly bound volumes of the clerk of the work's reports, inspection reports, and considerable correspondence to substantiate his claim. On the other side, the contractor (say, for illustrative purposes, the innocent party) can provide for evidence only a single partially legible carbon copy of a note scribbled by a hurried super. Ultimately, the contractor unjustly loses the case.

Box III.1. SAMPLE AGENDA

There is no one best way to prepare an agenda or to take notes. One technique is to prepare an agenda concentrating on issues that you feel are important to you. Leave adequate space between each item, or in the margin, to write your notes. During the meeting, listen for key words and ideas, instead of trying to capture every word. Develop your own code and shorthand to ease the task. Very importantly, at the end of the meeting, review the highlights to ensure that everyone agrees with the decisions and issues.

An agenda used for a preconstruction meeting follows:

THOMAS M. MELVIN
Professional Engineer

92 TAXIERA ROAD
STOUGHTON, MASSACHUSETTS
617 - 344 - 7729

STATE UNIVERSITY

PROJECT NUMBER
UB76-6 Cont. #1

H & C #1
MODIFICATIONS TO 010
BUILDING

PRE-CONSTRUCTION MEETING

I. General Comments
1. Introduction of parties.
2. When will project begin? Any long lead items which could cause delay? Time is critical.
3. 120 calendar days from contract signing to complete job. The G.C. must submit to Designer a progress schedule within 10 days.

Note: Progress schedule must be coordinated with the University. Because of school situations, all necessary shutdowns must be scheduled with the school.

Which areas are the most critical to be completed? Which areas are the least critical?

Any potential problems? With existing systems? With utility companies?
4. Has office space or trailer been arranged? parking spaces? telephones required? photographs? necessary data?
Where will storage area be designated? Protect Equipment.
5. No accumulation of debris. Maximize protection of students. Protect equipment from vandalism and/or theft.
6. G.C. super must be on job every day to supervise construction.

II. Administrative Comments
1. Project number and title of all correspondence. Copies to all parties.
2. Early shop drawing submittals. 7 copies required.
3. Submit schedule for delivery of equipment.
4. G.C. to maintain updated record drawings as work progresses. *Very important.*
5. Payments. Form 55.
(a) Periodic payment requests shall be submitted on the first of the month.
(b) Prior to this date, the designer, the clerk of works and contractor shall decide on percentage of work completed.

III. Change Orders—Form #13
1. *No* deviations from plans and specs.
2. The designer will decide on all questions regarding interpretation of plans and specs.
3. Review change order format.

Thomas Melvin

THOMAS MELVIN, P.E.

TM/sj

Box III.2.

PROJECT NO. ....

CONTRACT NO. ....

SHEET .... OF ....

DAILY PROGRESS REPORT

.... 19.............

Project Title ....   Weather ....
Institution ....   Temperature ....
Contractor ....   A.M.   Noon   P.M.
Superintendent ....

1. What work of general contractor was in progress today? Give location and approximate quantities.
2. Same for work of subcontractors.   3. What items of work subcontracts or extra started today?
4. What completed today? 5. What is delaying or threatening to delay progress? 6. What serious accidents occurred? 7. What visitors; who and why? 8. What variations from plans and specifications were suggested by whom; action taken? If contractor is performing any work on which he intends to seek extra compensation describe work in detail on a separate sheet and itemize man hours and material employed on such work. See Art. XVII of contract. 9. What else occurred that should be recorded? 10. (Report on separate sheet) What material and equipment for installation in job was received; did it meet specifications?

USE PARAGRAPHS AS NUMBERED ABOVE IN MAKING REPORT

No. of Carpenters	Helpers	Foremen	Subcon.	For	No. Men	Helpers
" " Masons	Tenders	"				
" " Ironworkers		"				
" " Reinf. Steel Men		"				
" " Finishers		"				
" " Other Trades	Helpers	"				
" " Laborers						
" " Office Force	Watchmen					

Total Gen. Constr. Men _____   Total Subcontractors Men _____
Copies to _____

Signed_____
Clerk of Works

Box III.3.

INSPECTOR'S DAILY REPORT

Project No. .... Contract No. .... Date ....

Project Title & Location ....

To: Mr. .... Project Engineer   From: Mr. .... Inspector

NOTE: Information in this report must be accurate and concise.

PERSONS CONTACTED:

JOB PROGRESS:

EQUIPMENT WORKING ON JOB:

NON-COMPLIANCES:

ANTICIPATED CHANGES:

DISPUTES:

REMARKS:

....
Inspector's Signature

CONCURRED BY: .... DATE: ....

CHECKED BY PROJECT ENGINEER: .... DATE: ....

4. The minutes of a progress meeting contain erroneous statements, or statements contrary to the project manager's understanding of the decisions. Being a "nice guy," he fails to respond to the inaccuracies. He rationalizes—why hassle the designer. A year later, that one document returns to haunt the contractor.

In the words of many caustic observers, "Nice guys finish last." Lesson to be learned: whenever a potential conflict or "extra work" or a decision is made, document the facts. Obtain proper authorization—always! Even in the most congenial professional settings, people honestly forget (and sometimes conveniently); personnel transfer or leave; misunderstandings develop; and psychological conditions change, as each group seeks its own goals and values.

Detailed, accurate records are the arteries on which successful companies depend. They not only document past events, but pave the way for future bidding estimates and identify strengths and weaknesses within the organization. Additionally, many such records are required by bankers, surety companies, insurance companies, and, of course, tax collectors.

To many individuals (i.e., construction workers would rather work with their hands) documentation is an evil in league with the plague—but a *necessary* evil. Admittedly, daily and weekly reports can be trying, but, in times of trouble, an obscure, dusty letter may become a precious document. Suffice it to say that, within reason, success, as well as protection, in the construction field calls for accurate, detailed records.

For informational purposes, some typical report formats are included (pp. 364–367), as well as an excellent presentation, written by O. P. Easterwood, Chapter 27, *Handbook of Construction Management and Organization.*

27 LEGAL AND CONTRACTUAL PROBLEMS*

O. P. EASTERWOOD, JR.

Partner
McNutt, Dudley, Easterwood and Losch
Washington, D.C. 20006

27-3. Documents and Records

Today is a day of mechanization of records. We have payrolls and other computations in computers; we have Xerox and other copying machines that turn out volumes of reproductions; and government, state, and large private corporations have multicopy forms with instructions in fine print that challenge the most ingenious to fill them out properly. *Further, the owner always has an abundance of inspection personnel to ensure compliance with every detail of the contract and specifications that is favorable to him. These inspectors generally have certain prescribed duties and daily inspection reports to fill out and turn over to the owner. These become the "official records" of an owner and will be accepted as such by any appeal board or court.*

---

*Reference: *Handbook of Construction Management and Organization*, J. Bonny and J. Frien, New York: Van Nostrand Reinhold Co., 1973. Italics by author.

A. The Daily Diary *In addition, the inspectors are generally instructed to and do keep a "daily diary." In these neatly bound volumes are found the opinions and self-serving declarations of the individuals who daily observe the activities of a contractor. It must be remembered that the owner has only three basic obligations under a contract: (1) to inspect the work as it progresses to ensure that it meets all the terms and conditions of the contract; (2) to enforce the progress schedule to see that the work is performed within the time limits; and (3) to pay the contractor for the percentage of satisfactory work in place. These responsibilities leave ample time for meticulous record keeping on the part of the owner, and an ominous burden to meet on the part of a successful contractor. Therefore, like it or not, it is incumbent upon a contractor to keep sufficient records to equalize or offset the documents accumulated by the owner as the "official record."*

B. Job Photographs It has almost become standard practice for all owners to take and retain "progressive photos" to record and document each stage of the work. This, in turn, requires a prudent contractor to have periodic job progress photographs, *taken at the angle and from the location* the contractor selects. For this purpose, the camera should be as important a piece of equipment as the first typewriters and adding machines that are shipped to the job office!

C. Serial Letters But first things first. In starting a job, it is strongly recommended that a series of "serial numbered" letters be inaugurated so that all correspondence can be properly logged and located throughout the period of the work. It is also recommended that Serial Letter No. 1 set up the organization on the work site that you, as the contractor, propose to utilize and, most important, that it delineate the authority of your personnel. In other words, do you want to give your project engineer authority to sign change orders? Do you want your office manager committing the organization for all subcontracts and purchase orders? Under good management and organization contained in other chapters herein, a determination will be made as to organization.

The emphasis here is that the duties and responsibilities be definitely determined and delegated and properly described in this first letter. By doing this for your personnel, you have every right and you should demand that the owner furnish to you in writing the authority that has been delegated to his representatives on the job. This may save many arguments and misunderstandings as the job progresses. It may also save many hours in conferences with personnel who have no authority to act on matters where you must have a decision to proceed with your work.

D. Document Events in Writing *Having a mutual understanding as to the duties and responsibilities of personnel on the job, it is next suggested that you , as contractor, relate to the owner's representatives on the job that it is customary on your work (and required by your board of directors, senior partners, or corporate officers) that you document various events that transpire on the job so that they will be in a better position to review all details of the job. In other words, there will be numerous occasions when "field changes" or "problem areas" are temporarily solved, but the owner's representative is reluctant to, or actually refuses, to reduce his verbal decision to writing. This is a situation where you must immediately write a letter* *confirming the oral decision—who made it and when—so that,* if necessary, *it can be used later to support your position.*

Contentions based upon oral conversations frequently turn out to be just allegations, whereas a letter that should have and did document the happening on the occasion turns out to be the statement of accepted fact. *To repeat, when any decision is made by an owner's representative that may cause a change in your work or in your schedule of work sequence, it should be documented immediately. It may never be used, but if it should become critical later in a matter of proof, it will be worth its weight in gold! So long as the owner's representatives are given to understand,* in advance, *that you intend to document in writing the various events that occur, it will cause much less friction than if you wait until your collections on estimates vs. expenditures show a deficit and you suddenly pour in reams of correspondence attempting to establish claims!*

E. Allocation of Work on Time Cards   Once these preliminary matters are out of the way, what do you tell your office manager to set up in the way of files and records? Whether you follow the Dewey decimal system, an alphabetical system, or a numbered system, you must be able to allocate in some manner *categories of work to items of cost.* This is the basic key to costing out any contract recovery you may ultimately receive under the contract.

Perhaps the most reliable method is by the proper use of time cards for individual workmen engaged upon a specific item of work. For example, suppose you are building room X and when you are halfway through with your rough carpentry, the owner issues a change order to you to make a 45° angle and jut one wall out 3 feet from elevation 6 feet to the eave of the roof elevation 10 feet. Although this sounds like a simple change at this stage of the work, in order to estimate its cost initially and then to be able actually to price it out ultimately, it will necessitate the consideration of numerous trades and supplies.

Suppose that in attempting to negotiate out a contract change on an estimated basis the owner is either slow in accepting or does not like your estimating basis. You cannot stop the job while the paper work is being done, but you can start immediately to keep time cards on this particular segment of the work so that you will ultimately know what it has cost to perform.

You would start with your carpenters assigned to put in the changed arrangement of studs. They would probably have to put in additional bracing and blocking because of the change in weight-bearing timbers. If the owner does not furnish you a detailed drawing as to load-bearing timbers, you may have to allocate engineering time, or stop all work until an appropriate design is furnished.

Once the rough timbers are in, you may have a plastering subcontractor or a sheetrock installer from whom you will need a detailed quotation for the small added quantities of his work and an allocation of time of his workmen on the changed work vs. what the unchanged work was priced out on their estimate.

Further, this may have changed your electrical installation, your heating and cooling system and your painter's work. It may have changed the planned sequence of your operations. All of the time of any workman who worked upon this changed installation should be carefully allocated to it and all of these data placed in one file so that they can be quickly referred to. You may have to order more lumber, more plaster or sheetrock, and more cable or wiring. These added materials costs should also be included in this file.

If the alteration has changed the sequence of your operations (i.e., a delay in receipt of materials, or an argument over bearing timbers) and it occasions moving in and out of scaffolding, a crane, or other equipment, this should be included in the file. If you were delayed in this operation for any reason (other than your own fault or negligence), a notation to this effect should be contained in the file and a time extension sought in connection with your pricing of the item.

In other words, each and every item that is requested by the owner that varies in any respect from what is shown in your contract plans and specifications should be the subject of a separate file with time of labor and materials allocated to it. This same procedure should be followed by your subcontractors and vendors and their data promptly submitted to you.

Admittedly, this makes the cost and time records more voluminous and more difficult to keep, but it is absolutely essential if you expect to receive for yourself, your vendors, and subcontractors a complete recovery for additional work performed under the contract. You may say, "I have good cost records. I can account for every penny spent on the job." This may be quite true on a *total cost* basis, but can you state how much each change order cost you—how much each request for what you claim is additional work under your contract cost you? Probably not, and this is most important.

27-4. Total Cost Less Bid Price

The contracting officers, the Courts, and the Contract Appeals Boards are most reluctant to accept as a pricing basis the difference between a contractor's estimate and his actual costs as the measure of payment for the work item. To quote from the headnote of a recent Court of Claims decision along this line: (*Turnbull, Inc.* v. *United States*, 180 Ct. Cl. 1010, 389 F. 2d 1007 (1967):

"The total cost theory of computing the amount due a contractor under a cause of action against the Government, i.e., the difference between the contractor's bid price and the actual cost of performing the entire contract as changed by order of the Government as distinguished from computing damages on the basis of the increased costs relative to specific or separate items, is not the most satisfactory method since it assumes that the contractor's costs were reasonable and that the contractor was not responsible for any of the increases in costs, and it also assumes that the contractor's bid was accurately computed which is not always the case. Accordingly, this means of computing damages is only used where other and better proof is lacking. *F. H. McGraw & Co.* v. *United States*, 131 Ct. Cl. 501, 511, 130 F. Supp. 394, 400 (1955)."

Thus, it is much better to have available a realistic estimate, and ultimately a file that contains completely detailed costs specifically allocated to this item. Estimates can generally be optimistic to forestall possible contingencies, but after-the-fact pricing must be supported by records; otherwise, an owner-audit might prove most embarrassing.

27-5. Record of Negotiations and Schedules

The files must also contain all negotiations or "understandings" with vendors and subcontractors from the initial contact with them through all stages of the work and up to the time that all matters are settled and a final release is obtained. As protection for all concerned, all work schedules, all job changes, all owner caused delays that affect the vendor and subcontractor must be immediately communicated to him and such reference included in the file.

Much litigation is created by the failure of a prime contractor to currently advise a subcontractor, on an accurate progress schedule, just when his portion of the work is expected. If he is not on an accurate schedule, and he is forced to mobilize without proper notice, he may have a justifiable acceleration claim. By the same token, if the contractor is unduly delayed because of failure to furnish the subcontractor with proper scheduling, he may well claim a delay and rescheduling of his work, which increases his costs of performance. This means that the "scheduling file" must be constantly revised to meet changing conditions, and notice of all changes promptly communicated to all interested parties with appropriate notation in the files that this has been done.

Further the simple transmission of a schedule change by the owner to the contractor and thence to the subcontractor and vendor is not sufficient. The contractor must ascertain whether the schedule change affects the work of his subcontractors or vendors and, if so, accumulate all of this material and appropriately advise the owner of the increase in costs and/or time extensions, or both, if such is the case. To save some correspondence back and forth, when these matters are submitted to subcontractors or vendors, a phrase might well be included in the letter along these lines:

"Unless a written notice is received from you within _____ days it will be presumed that the attached _____ does not affect your price or time for performance and that you release _____ from any claim or demand for increases therein."

Although admittedly this is a self-serving type of communication, it nevertheless tends to crystallize problem areas before they become too serious and end up in litigation toward the end of the job. When a party decides to file a claim or a suit in court, he generally picks up every trifling matter he has, and this can prolong and increase the expenses of litigation.

27-6. Daily Chronology of Progress

Last but not least, a contractor's project manager (or superintendent) should keep and maintain an accurate daily diary, setting forth in succinct terms the progress of work and the routine and unusual happenings of each day. All job conferences with owner's representatives should be covered, as well as any meeting with subcontractors and vendors. Problems of the job should be written up in sufficient detail to later form the basis of correspondence, if needed. Weather details and working conditions can be covered briefly, and equipment performance or problems covered in brief fashion.

Many times an owner will claim that equipment is not in good working condition and that excessive downtime is charged into a contractor's costs. If feasible, the diary should be reviewed by one other member of the contractor's personnel, such as the project engineer, the quality control representative, or the labor-relations officer to assure its completeness and to eliminate careless statements that might later reflect upon the contractor's good workmanship and ingenuity. With the current day discovery proceedings now in vogue with appeal boards and courts, you can expect your complete set of files and records to be examined and copied by the owner's personnel if you become engaged in an adversary proceeding of any nature. Therefore, it behooves you to keep them orderly and with content that reflects upon your good qualities and capabilities for performance.

Since many of a prime contractor's claims are in part based upon actions and activities of his subcontractors, they should likewise keep similar records. Further, it should be remembered that if the subcontract has a "disputes clause through the owner" the subcontractor's files should not reflect contentions against the prime— they should be primarily directed toward adverse actions of the owner affecting the subcontractor through the prime. If, after the disputes procedure is pursued against the owner, their remain issues between the prime and subcontractor, these can then be considered.

Appendix IV

Worker Trait Components

The following job descriptions and worker trait components have been reproduced from *Dictionary of Occupational Titles*, vol. 2, 3rd ed., Washington, D.C.: U.S. Department of Labor, Manpower Administration, 1965. It describes the following jobs:

1. Administration (Owner)
2. Managerial Work (Project Manager)
3. Supervisory Work (Foreman, Subs)
4. Supervisory Work (Superintendent)
5. Craftsmanship and Related Work (Tradesmen)
6. Engineering Research and Design (Designers)
7. Engineering, Scientific and Technical Coordination (Designers)
8. Engineering and Related Work (Designers)

In order to provide an explanation to the codes and keys used in the qualification profile, Appendix A and B are included for reference.

DICTIONARY

OF

OCCUPATIONAL TITLES

1965

Volume II

OCCUPATIONAL CLASSIFICATION

AND INDUSTRY INDEX

Third Edition

U.S. DEPARTMENT OF LABOR
W. Willard Wirtz, Secretary
MANPOWER ADMINISTRATION

Bureau of Employment Security
Robert C. Goodwin, Administrator

For sale by the Superintendent of Documents
U.S. Government Printing Office, Washington, D.C. 20402

ADMINISTRATION
.118; .168

Work Performed

Work activities in this group primarily involve formulating and carrying out administrative principles, practices, and techniques in an organization or establishment. These activities typically entail program planning, allocation of responsibilities to organizational components, monitoring the internal activities of these components, and coordinating their achievements in a manner that will insure success of the overall objective.

Worker Requirements

An occupationally significant combination of: Organizational ability to plan, formulate, and execute policies and programs; capacity to acquire knowledge of various administrative concepts and practices and successfully apply them to different organizational environments; verbal facility to deal effectively with persons at all levels; facility with numbers to prepare and review various financial and materiel reports; ability to relate to people in a manner to win their confidence and establish rapport; flexibility to adjust to changing conditions; and an analytical mind to solve complex problems.

Clues for Relating Applicants and Requirements

Successful achievement and advancement in lower level jobs in similar or related fields.

Educational background that includes business or governmental administration coursework.

Extracurricular or leisure-time activities and positions held that have afforded opportunities to acquire organizational skills, such as serving as community chairman of charity drives and production manager of amateur plays.

Training and Methods of Entry

Entry into this type of work may be accomplished in a variety of ways. Applicants frequently enter after years of experience, working up from lower level positions in which they have become familiar with the policies and operations of an organization or activity and have impressed with their efficiency, initiative, judgment, and organizational ability.

Many organizations have established administrative training programs. They hire promising college graduates, usually those with a degree in business administration, and funnel them through a training program designed to familiarize them with the functions of all phases of the organizational network and thereby prepare them to step into administrative positions.

RELATED CLASSIFICATIONS

Accounting, Auditing, and Related
  Work (.188; .288) p. 252
Business Training (.228) p. 241
Consultative and Business Services (.168;
  .268) p. 248
Contract Negotiating and Related Work
  (.118; .168) p. 239
Managerial Work (.168) p. 245

QUALIFICATIONS PROFILE

GED: 5 6
SVP: 8 9

Apt:	GVN	SPQ	KFM	EC
	1 1 2	4 4 4	4 4 4	5 5
	2 2 3	3 3 3		4

Int: 5 2 6
Temp: 4 5 1 9
Phys. Dem: S L 5

MANAGERIAL WORK
.168

Work Performed
Work activities in this group primarily involve organizing and coordinating the functions of a unit, department, or branch of an organization or establishment. Certain activities are concerned with the managing of one organization that is part of a larger chain or of an establishment of limited size and diversification. Also included is the planning and coordination of a singular program, project, or other organized endeavor, either public or private, originated for a specific purpose.

Worker Requirements
An occupationally significant combination of: Ability to plan, initiate, and execute programs; ability to understand, interpret, and apply procedures and directives; numerical facility to analyze and use statistics and maintain production and inventory controls and records; leadership qualities; verbal facility; and the ability to relate to people in order to motivate and direct employees and to maintain good employer-employee and customer relationships.

Clues for Relating Applicants and Requirements
Successful experience in applicable work field at lower levels.

Academic preparation in pertinent coursework, such as business management.

Leadership qualities as indicated by elective offices held in academic or community environment.

Expressed interest in assuming management responsibilities.

Training and Methods of Entry
Promotion from within is the most common method employed for filling positions in this group. In some cases, however, employers desire new ideas, new techniques, new procedures, and new personalities, and recruit from outside the organization.

Most of the larger employers consider only those individuals who are recent college graduates. They look for an educational background consisting of appropriate personnel, vocational, business, merchandising, or similar coursework, and then provide their new employees with management-trainee programs which usually entail a combination of special training seminars and actual on-the-job training.

RELATED CLASSIFICATIONS

Administration (.118; .168) p. 237

Consultative and Business Services (.168; .268) p. 248

Supervisory Work (Clerical, Sales, and Related Activities) (.138) p. 243

Engineering, Scientific, and Technical Coordination (.168) p. 375

QUALIFICATIONS PROFILE

GED: 4 5

SVP: 6 7 8

Apt: **GVN SPQ KFM EC**
     2 2 3 4 4 2 4 4 4 5 5
     1 1 2

Int: 5 2   3

Temp: 1 4 5 9 0

Phys. Dem: S L

SUPERVISORY WORK (Farming, Logging, Manufacturing, Processing, Construction, Transportation, and Related Activities) .130; .131; .132; .133; .134; .137

Work Performed

Work activities in this group primarily involve supervising and coordinating the activities of workers in such fields as manufacturing, processing, construction, and transportation. Skill in the particular field of work and in the use of materials, tools, and machines involved is essential because workers are frequently required to participate in the work of their subordinates.

Worker Requirements

An occupationally significant combination of: Ability to understand, learn, and apply the techniques appropriate to the field of work supervised; ability to communicate this knowledge to the persons supervised; ability to demonstrate efficient technical "know-how" or work along with subordinates in difficult phases of a job; initiative and drive; and ability to maintain harmony in working relationships and among workers.

Clues for Relating Applicants and Requirements

Good physical condition.
Success as worker in applicable trade or craft.
Vocational training in school.
Desire for recognition.
Leadership in school, organization, or community activities.

Training and Methods of Entry

Individuals usually enter into supervisory work of this type from the worker ranks since skill in the appropriate trade or craft and mastery of its tools and machines is of paramount importance. Training may be finished by the employer either on the job or in formalized courses. It also may be procured by the employee on his own initiative in technical or other appropriate schools.

RELATED CLASSIFICATIONS

Supervisory Work (Services and Related Activities) (.138) p. 461
Supervisory Work (Farming, Logging, Manufacturing, Processing, Construction, Transportation, and Related Activities) (.138) p. 305

QUALIFICATIONS PROFILE

GED: 4
SVP: 8 7

Apt: GVN   SPQ   KFM   EC
    3 3 3   3 3 4   3 3 3   5 4
          2 2   2 2   3 5

Int: 9 5
Temp: 1 4 5
Phys. Dem: L M H 2 3 4 5 6

SUPERVISORY WORK (Farming, Logging, Manufacturing, Processing, Construction, Transportation, and Related Activities)
.138

Work Performed

Work activities in this group primarily involve supervising and coordinating the activities of groups of workers representing different occupations in such fields as manufacturing, farming, logging, processing, construction, and transportation. Planning and supervision are the primary concerns, and the ability to perform the work of subordinates is not essential.

Worker Requirements

An occupationally significant combination of: Ability to understand and apply techniques appropriate to the type of work supervised; organizational ability to plan and assign duties to subordinates; and ability to maintain harmony in working relationships and among workers.

Clues for Applicants and Requirements

Interest in work of industrial nature.
Demonstrated success in nonsupervisory jobs.
Vocational training in school.
Leadership in school or organizations.

Training and Methods of Entry

Entrants into this type of work are commonly selected from outstanding personnel in the pertinent field of work. Experience in more than one facet of the work involved and completion of appropriate technical courses enhance entry prospects.

RELATED CLASSIFICATIONS

Administration (.118; .168) p. 237
Managerial Work (.168) p. 245
Supervisory Work (Farming, Logging, Manufacturing, Processing, Construction, Transportation, and Related Activities) (.130; .131; .132; .133; .134; .137) p. 299

QUALIFICATIONS PROFILE

GED: 4 5
SVP: 8 7 6
Apt: **GVN** SPQ KFM EC
     3 3 3 3 3 4 4 4 4 5 5
     2 2 4 4 4 3   3 4 4

Int: 5 9
Temp: 4 5 1
Phys. Dem: S L 5 6

CRAFTSMANSHIP AND RELATED WORK
.281; .381

Work Performed

Work activities in this group primarily involve fabricating, processing, inspecting, or repairing materials, products, or structural units. Activities in this group are characterized by the emphasis placed upon manual skills, and the application of an organized body of knowledge related to materials, tools, and principles associated with various crafts.

Worker Requirements

An occupationally significant combination of: Ability to learn and apply craft techniques, processes, and principles; ability to use independent judgment in planning sequence of operations and in selecting proper tools and materials; ability to assume responsibility for attainment of prescribed qualitative standards; ability to apply shop mathematics to practical problems, such as computing dimensions and locating reference points from specifications data when laying out work; spatial perception to visualize arrangement and relationships of static or moving parts and assemblies represented in blueprints and diagrams; form perception as required in such activities as inspecting work to verify acceptability of surface finish; and some combination of finger and manual dexterity and eye-hand coordination to use handtools and manually controlled power tools when executing work to close tolerances.

Clues for Relating Applicants and Requirements

Hobbies, such as model building or ceramics, which involve hand craftsmanship.
Successful completion of high school industrial arts or vocational education courses.
Military training and experience in craft-related activities.
Preference for work activities offering tangible productive satisfaction.

Training and Methods of Entry

Apprenticeships providing 2 to 6 years of on-the-job training and trade instruction are generally accepted as the best methods of entry into craft work. Many firms have established on-the-job training programs in which entry workers are placed under the supervision of a journeyman or a foreman and are advanced from elementary tasks to progressively more difficult work as they demonstrate increased proficiency in the skills of the craft. Training received in vocational, trade, or technical schools or the armed services enhance entry and advancement prospects, and may shorten training periods in some crafts. Craftsmen who become thoroughly familiar with all aspects of their trade through apprenticeship training generally stand the best chance for advancement to supervisory positions.

RELATED CLASSIFICATIONS

Drafting and Related Work (.181; .281)
  p. 377
Manipulating (.884) p. 322
Cooking and Related Work (.281; .381)
  p. 310
Precision Working (.781) p. 319

QUALIFICATIONS PROFILE

GED: 4 3
SVP: 7 6 8

Apt:	GVN	SPQ	KFM	EC
	3 3 3	2 3 4	3 3 3	5 5
	2 4 4	3 4 2	2 2 2	4
	2	2 3		3
				2

Int: 1 9 0
Temp: 0 Y
Phys. Dem: L M H 2 3 4 6

ENGINEERING RESEARCH AND DESIGN
.081

Work Performed

Work activities in this group primarily involve using and adapting earth substances, properties of matter, natural sources of power, and physical forces to satisfy human needs and desires. Typically, workers are engaged in conducting analyses and experiments of materials and systems by application of known laws and relationships; in conceiving and designing new structures, machines, tools, precision instruments, and other devices; in devising and constructing cooling, heating, lighting, communication, transportation, and other productive systems; in developing the most practical forms of new techniques, processes, and products; in performing structural, functional, and compositional tests of materials and parts; and in preparing technical reports of investigations.

Worker Requirements

An occupationally significant combination of: Ability to learn and apply basic engineering principles and methods; good visual acuity with respect to graphic representations; creative talent or imagination; ability to perceive or visualize spatial relationships of plane and solid objects; logical mind; organizational ability; and facility in mathematics.

Clues for Relating Applicants and Requirements

Level of attainment in language and mathematics as indicated by scores on aptitude tests and grades in educational courses.

Previous drawings or sketches produced, either freehand or mechanical.

Kind of literature read (whether scientifically or technically oriented).

Clear, coherent verbal expression.

Interest in scientific and technological developments.

Training and Methods of Entry

A bachelor's degree in engineering is usually the minimum educational requirement for entrance into this field. However, some draftsmen and engineering technicians having extensive experience together with some college-level training may qualify for entry.

Most employers require either advanced graduate degrees or significant experience on the basic engineering level for entry into research work.

Students interested in engineering should acquire a strong background in mathematics and the physical sciences.

RELATED CLASSIFICATIONS

Sales Engineering (.151) p. 373
Engineering, Scientific, and Technical
   Coordination (.168) p. 375
Engineering and Related Work (.187) p. 381
Technical Work, Engineering and Related Fields (.181; .281) p. 379
Industrial Engineering and Related
   Work (.188; .288) p. 383
Drafting and Related Work (.181; .281)
   p. 377

QUALIFICATIONS PROFILE

GED: 6
SVP: 8 7

Apt:	GVN	SPQ	KFM	EC
	1 1 1	1 2 4	3 3 3	5 4
	2 2	2 3		

Int: 7 8
Temp: 4 0 Y
Phys. Dem: S L 4 6

ENGINEERING, SCIENTIFIC, AND TECHNICAL COORDINATION
.168

Work Performed
Work activities in this group primarily involve planning and coordinating engineering, scientific, and technical programs and activities. Typically, work occurs in a scientific or industrial environment and involves formulating policies and standards, planning and directing projects and programs, and monitoring personnel.

Work Requirements
An occupationally significant combination of: Intellectual capacity to comprehend and apply engineering, scientific, or technical principles and methods; organizational ability to plan, formulate, and carry out programs and policies; verbal facility to deal effectively with personnel; and mathematical ability.

Clues for Relating Applicants and Requirements
Successful background in appropriate field.
Expressed desire to work with people.
Clear, coherent, verbal expression.
Interest in scientific and technological developments.

Training and Methods of Entry
The minimum of a bachelor's degree in the occupational specialty is usually required for entry, with many employers requiring education at the graduate level. The worker usually enters the job by virtue of successful performance, length of experience, and demonstrated ability to organize complex activities and deal with people.

RELATED CLASSIFICATIONS

Technical Work, Engineering and Related Fields (.181; 281) p. 379

Engineering and Related Work (.187) p. 381

Industrial Engineering and Related Work (.188; .288) p. 383

Engineering Research and Design (.081) p. 371

Administration (.118; .168) p. 237

Mathematics, Physical Sciences, and Related Research (.088; .188) p. 468

QUALIFICATIONS PROFILE

GED: 5 6
SVP: 7 8 9
Apt: GVN   SPQ   KFM   EC
      2 2 2   2 2 3   4 4 4   5 5
      1 1 1   3 3 4   3 3 3   4 4

Int: 7 6 5
Temp: 1 4 5 9 0 Y
Phys. Dem: S L M H 3 4 5 6

ENGINEERING AND RELATED WORK
.187

Work Performed
Work activities in this group primarily involve the application of engineering knowledge to the planning, direction, and installation of projects and systems. Typi-

cally, workers are concerned with a specific field of engineering, such as civil engineering, mechanical engineering, and electrical engineering.

Workers Requirements

An occupationally significant combination of: Organizational ability; clear verbal expression; ability to learn and apply engineering principles and methods; spatial and form perception; and facility with mathematics.

Clues for Relating Applicants and Requirements

Expressed interest in industrial developments.

Success in pertinent academic subjects, such as mathematics.

Subscriptions to engineering and technical magazines.

Training and Methods of Entry

A bachelor's degree in engineering is usually the minimum educational requirement for entrance into this field, and many employers are now requiring a graduate degree in engineering.

RELATED CLASSIFICATIONS

Industrial Engineering and Related Work (.188; .288) p. 383

Engineering Research and Design (.081) p. 371

Technical Work, Engineering and Related Fields (.181; .281) p. 379

Engineering, Scientific, and Technical Coordination (.168) p. 375

Technical Writing and Related Work (.188; .288) p. 387

Drafting and Related Work (.181; .281) p. 377

QUALIFICATIONS PROFILE

GED: 6 5

SVP: 8 7

Apt: **GVN   SPQ   KFM   EC**
     1 1 1   2 2 4   4 4 4   5 5
     2 2 2   3 3

Int: 1 7 9

Temp: 4 0 Y

Phys. Dem: S L 6

APPENDIX A

Explanation of Relationships Within Data, People, Things Hierarchies

Much of the information in this edition of the Dictionary is based on the premise that every job requires a worker to function in relation to Data, People, and Things, in varying degrees. These relationships are identified and explained below. They appear in the form of three hierarchies arranged in each instance from the relatively simple to the complex in such a manner that each successive relationship includes those that are simpler and excludes the more complex.[1] The identifications attached to these relationships are referred to as worker functions, and provide standard terminology for use in summarizing exactly what a worker does on the job by means of one or more meaningful verbs.

[1]As each of the relationships to People represents a wide range of complexity, resulting in considerable overlap among occupations, their arrangement is somewhat arbitrary and can be considered a hierarchy only in the most general sense.

A job's relationship to Data, People, and Things can be expressed in terms of the highest appropriate function in each hierarchy to which the worker has an occupationally significant relationship, and these functions taken together indicate the total level of complexity at which he must perform. The last three digits of the occupational code numbers in the Dictionary reflect significant relationships to Data, People, and Things, respectively.[2] These last three digits express a job's relationship to Data, People, and Things by identifying the highest appropriate function in each hierarchy to which the job requires the worker to have a significant relationship, as reflected by the following table:

DATA (4th digit)	PEOPLE (5th digit)	THINGS (6th digit)
0 Synthesizing	0 Mentoring	0 Setting-Up
1 Coordinating	1 Negotiating	1 Precision Working
2 Analyzing	2 Instructing	2 Operating-Controlling
3 Compiling	3 Supervising	3 Driving-Operating
4 Computing	4 Diverting	4 Manipulating
5 Copying	5 Persuading	5 Tending
6 Comparing	6 Speaking-Signaling	6 Feeding-Offbearing
7 } No significant relationship	7 Serving	7 Handling
8	8 No significant relationship	8 No significant relationship

DATA: Information, knowledge, and conceptions, related to data, people, or things, obtained by observation, investigation, interpretation, visualization, mental creation; incapable of being touched; written data take the form of numbers, words, symbols; other data are ideas, concepts, oral verbalization.

0 **Synthesizing:** Integrating analyses of data to discover facts and/or develop knowledge concepts of interpretations.

1 **Coordinating:** Determining time, place, and sequence of operations or action to be taken on the basis of analysis of data; executing determinations and/or reporting on events.

2 **Analyzing:** Examining and evaluating data. Presenting alternative actions in relation to the evaluation is frequently involved.

3 **Compiling:** Gathering, collating, or classifying information about data, people, or things. Reporting and/or carrying out a prescribed action in relation to the information is frequently involved.

4 **Computing:** Performing arithmetic operations and reporting on and/or carrying out a prescribed action in relation to them. Does not include counting.

5 **Copying:** Transcribing, entering, or posting data.

---

[2]Only those relationshps which are occupationally significant in terms of the requirements of the job are reflected in the code numbers. The incidental relationships which every worker has to Data, People, and Things, but which do not seriously affect successful performance of the essential duties of the job, are not reflected.

6 **Comparing:** Judging the readily observable functional, structural, or compositional characteristics (whether similar to or divergent from obvious standards) of data, people, or things.

PEOPLE: Human beings; also animals dealt with on an individual basis as if they were human.

0 **Mentoring:** Dealing with individuals in terms of their total personality in order to advise, counsel, and/or guide them with regard to problems that may be resolved by legal, scientific, clinical, spiritual, and/or other professional principles.

1 **Negotiating:** Exchanging ideas, information, and opinions with others to formulate policies and programs and/or arrive jointly at decisions, conclusions, or solutions.

2 **Instructing:** Teaching subject matter to others, or training others (including animals) through explanation, demonstration, and supervised practice; or making recommendations on the basis of technical disciplines.

3 **Supervising:** Determining or interpreting work procedures for a group of workers, assigning specific duties to them, maintaining harmonious relations among them, and promoting efficiency.

4 **Diverting:** Amusing others.

5 **Persuading:** Influencing others in favor of a product, service, or point of view.

6 **Speaking-Signaling:** Talking with and/or signaling people to convey or exchange information. Includes giving assignments and/or directions to helpers or assistants.

7 **Serving:** Attending to the needs or requests of people or animals or the expressed or implicit wishes of people. Immediate response is involved.

THINGS: Inanimate objects as distinguished from human beings; substances or materials; machines, tools, equipment; products. A thing is tangible and has shape, form, and other physical characteristics.

0 **Setting Up:** Adjusting machines or equipment by replacing or altering tools, jigs, fixtures, and attachments to prepare them to perform their functions, change their performance, or restore their proper functioning if they break down. Workers who set up one or a number of machines for other workers or who set up and personally operate a variety of machines are included here.

1 **Precision Working:** Using body members and/or tools or work aids to work, move, guide, or place objects or materials in situations where ultimate responsibility for the attainment of standards occurs and selection of appropriate tools, objects, or materials, and the adjustment of the tool to the task require exercise of considerable judgment.

2 **Operating-Controlling:** Starting, stopping, controlling, and adjusting the progress of machines or equipment designed to fabricate and/or process objects or materials. Operating machines involves setting up the machine and adjusting

the machine or material as the work progresses. Controlling equipment involves observing gages, dials, etc., and turning valves and other devices to control such factors as temperature, pressure, flow of liquids, speed of pumps, and reactions of materials. Setup involves several variables and adjustment is more frequent than in tending.

3 **Driving-Operating:** Starting, stopping, and controlling the actions of machines or equipment for which a course must be steered, or which must be guided, in order to fabricate, process, and/or move things or people. Involves such activities as observing gages and dials; estimating distances and determining speed and direction of other objects; turning cranks and wheels; pushing clutches or brakes; and pushing or pulling gear lifts or levers. Includes such machines as cranes, conveyor systems, tractors, furnace charging machines, paving machines and hoisting machines. Excludes manually powered machines, such as hand-trucks and dollies, and power assisted machines, such as electric wheelbarrows and handtrucks.

4 **Manipulating:** Using body members, tools, or special devices to work, move, guide, or place objects or materials. Involves some latitude for judgment with regard to precision attained and selecting appropriate tool, object, or material, although this is readily manifest.

5 **Tending:** Starting, stopping, and observing the functioning of machines and equipment. Involves adjusting materials or controls of the machine, such as changing guides, adjusting timers and temperature gages, turning valves to allow flow of materials, and flipping switches in response to lights. Little judgment is involved in making these adjustments.

6 **Feeding-Offbearing:** Inserting, throwing, dumping, or placing materials in or removing them from machines or equipment which are automatic or tended or operated by other workers.

7 **Handling:** Using body members, handtools, and/or special devices to work, move, or carry objects or materials. Involves little or no latitude for judgment with regard to attainment of standards or in selecting appropriate tool, object, or material.

NOTE: Included in the concept of Feeding-Offbearing, Tending, Operating-Controlling, and Setting Up, is the situation in which the worker is actually part of the setup of the machine, either as the holder and guider of the material or holder and guider of the tool.

APPENDIX B

Explanation of Worker Trait Components

Those abilities, personal traits, and individual characteristics required of a worker in order to achieve average successful job performance are referred to as worker traits. Occupational information presented in volumes I and II is based in part on analysis of required worker traits in terms of the six distinct worker trait components described in this appendix. These six components have been selected for this purpose because they provide the broadest and yet most comprehensive framework for the effective presentation of worker trait information. Within this framework the user will find data concerning the requirements of jobs for: (1) The amount of general educational development and specific vocational preparation a worker must have, (2) the specific capacities and abilities required of him in order to learn or perform certain tasks or duties, (3) preferences for certain types of work activities or experiences considered necessary for job success, (4) types of occupational situations to which an individual must adjust, (5) physical activities required in work situations, and (6) physical surroundings prevalent in jobs.

Information reflecting significant worker trait requirements is contained, explicitly or by implication, in the job definitions in volume I. In the Worker Traits Arrangement in volume II, the qualifications profile for each worker trait group shows the range of required traits and/or levels of traits for the first five of these components. Numbers or letters are used to identify each specific trait and level. In this appendix, these identifying numbers and letters appear in italics.

The worker trait components are:

I. Training time (general educational development, specific vocational preparation)
II. Aptitudes
III. Interests
IV. Temperaments
V. Physical Demands
VI. Working conditions[1]

I. Training Time

The amount of general educational development and specific vocational preparation required for a worker to acquire the knowledge and abilities necessary for average performance in a particular job.

General Educational Development: This embraces those aspects of education (formal and informal) which contribute to the worker's (a) reasoning development and ability to follow instructions, and (b) acquisition of "tool" knowledges, such as language and mathematical skills. It is education of a general nature which does not have a recognized, fairly specific, occupational objective. Ordinarily such education is obtained in elementary school, high school, or college. It also derives from experience and individual study.

(The table on pp. 390–391 explains the various levels of general educational development.—*Author's Note.*)

---

[1]Working conditions were recorded as part of each job analysis, and are reflected, when appropriate, in job definitions in volume I. However, because they did not contribute to the homogeneity of worker trait groups, they do not appear as a component in the Worker Traits Arrangement.

GENERAL EDUCATIONAL DEVELOPMENT

LEVEL	REASONING DEVELOPMENT	MATHEMATICAL DEVELOPMENT	LANGUAGE DEVELOPMENT
6	Apply principles of logical or scientific thinking to a wide range of intellectual and practical problems. Deal with nonverbal symbolism (formulas, scientific equations, graphs, musical notes, etc.) in its most difficult phases. Deal with a variety of abstract and concrete variables. Apprehend the most abstruse classes of concepts.	Apply knowledge of advanced mathematical and statistical techniques such as differential and integral calculus, factor analysis, and probability determination, or work with a wide variety of theoretical mathematical concepts and make original applications of mathematical procedures, as in empirical and differential equations.	Comprehension and expression of a level to —Report, write, or edit articles for such publications as newspapers, magazines, and technical or scientific journals. Prepare and draw up deeds, leases, wills, mortgages, and contracts. —Prepare and deliver lectures on politics, economics, education, or science. —Interview, counsel, or advise such people as students, clients, or patients, in such matters as welfare eligibility, vocational rehabilitation, mental hygiene, or marital relations. —Evaluate engineering technical data to design buildings and bridges.
5	Apply principles of logical or scientific thinking to define problems, collect data, establish facts, and draw valid conclusions. Interpret an extensive variety of technical instructions, in books, manuals, and mathematical or diagrammatic form. Deal with several abstract and concrete variables.		
4	Apply principles of rational systems[1] to solve practical problems and deal with a variety of concrete variables in situations where only limited standardization exists. Interpret a variety of instructions, furnished in written, oral, diagrammatic, or schedule form.	Perform ordinary arithmetic, algebraic, and geometric procedures in standard, practical applications.	Comprehension and expression of a level to —Transcribe dictation, make appointments for executive and handle his personal mail, interview and screen people wishing to speak to him, and write routine correspondence on own initiative. —Interview job applicants to determine work best suited for their abilities and experience, and contact employers to interest them in services of agency.

	Reasoning	Mathematics	Language
3	Apply common sense understanding to carry out instructions furnished in written, oral, or diagrammatic form. Deal with problems involving several concrete variables in or from standardized situations.	Make arithmetic calculations involving fractions, decimals and percentages.	Interpret technical manuals as well as drawings and specifications, such as layouts, blueprints, and schematics. Comprehension and expression of a level to— —File, post, and mail such materials as forms, checks, receipts, and bills. —Copy data from one record to another, fill in report forms, and type all work from rough draft or corrected copy. —Interview members of household to obtain such information as age, occupation, and number of children, to be used, as data for surveys, or economic studies. —Guide people on tours through historical or public buildings, describing such features as size, value, and points of interest.
2	Apply common sense understanding to carry out detailed but uninvolved written or oral instructions. Deal with problems involving a few concrete variables in or from standardized situations.	Use arithmetic to add, subtract, multiply, and divide whole numbers.	Comprehension and expression of a level to— —Learn job duties from oral instructions or demonstration. —Write identifying information, such as name and address of customer, weight, number, or type of product, on tags, or slips. —Request orally, or in writing, such supplies as linen, soap, or work materials.
1	Apply common sense understanding to carry out simple one- or two-step instructions. Deal with standardized situations with occasional or no variables in or from these situations encountered on the job.	Perform simple addition and subtraction, reading and copying of figures, or counting and recording.	

[1]Examples of "principles of rational systems" are: Bookkeeping, internal combustion engines, electric wiring systems, house building, nursing, farm management, ship sailing.

Specific Vocational Preparation: The amount of time required to learn the techniques, acquire information, and develop the facility needed for average performance in a specific job-worker situation. This training may be acquired in a school, work, military, institutional, or avocational environment. It does not include orientation training required of even every fully qualified worker to become accustomed to the special conditions of any new job. Specific vocational training includes training given in any of the following circumstances:

a. Vocational education (such as high school commercial or shop training, technical school, art school, and that part of college training which is organized around a specific vocational objective);

b. Apprentice training (for apprenticeable jobs only);

c. In-plant training (given by an employer in the form of organized classroom study);

d. On-the-job training (serving as learner or trainee on the job under the instruction of a qualified worker);

e. Essential experience in other jobs (serving in less responsible jobs which lead to the higher grade job or serving in other jobs which qualify).

The following is an explanation of the various levels of specific vocational preparation.

Level	Time	Level	Time
1	Short demonstration only.	5	Over 6 months up to and including 1 year.
2	Anything beyond short demonstration up and including 30 days.	6	Over 1 year up to and including 2 years.
3	Over 30 days up to and including 3 months.	7	Over 2 years up to and including 4 years.
4	Over 3 months up to and including 6 months.	8	Over 4 years up to and including 10 years.
		9	Over 10 years.

II. APTITUDES

Specific capacities and abilities required of an individual in order to learn or perform adequately a task or job duty.

G INTELLIGENCE: General learning ability. The ability to "catch on" or understand instructions and underlying principles. Abilty to reason and make judgments. Closely related to doing well in school.

V VERBAL: Ability to understand meanings of words and ideas associated with them, and to use them effectively. To comprehend language, to understand relationships between words, and to understand meanings of whole sentences and paragraphs. To present information or ideas clearly.

N NUMERICAL: Ability to perform arithmetic operations quickly and accurately.

S SPATIAL: Ability to comprehend forms in space and understand relationships of plane and solid objects. May be used in such tasks as blueprint reading and in solving geometry problems. Frequently described as the ability to "visualize" objects of two or three dimensions, or to think visually of geometric forms.

P FORM PERCEPTION: Ability to perceive pertinent detail in objects or in pictorial or graphic material; To make visual comparisons and discriminations and see slight differences in shapes and shadings of figures and widths and lengths of lines.

Q CLERICAL PERCEPTION: Ability to perceive pertinent detail in verbal or tabular material. To observe differences in copy, to proofread words and numbers, and to avoid perceptual errors in arithmetic computation.

K MOTOR COORDINATION: Ability to coordinate eyes and hands or fingers rapidly and accurately in making precise movements with speed. Ability to make a movement response accurately and quickly.

F FINGER DEXTERITY: Ability to move fingers and manipulate small objects with the fingers rapidly or accurately.

M MANUAL DEXTERITY: Ability to move the hands easily and skillfully. To work with the hands in placing and turning motions.

E EYE-HAND-FOOT COORDINATION: Ability to move the hand and foot coordinately with each other in accordance with visual stimuli.

C COLOR DISCRIMINATION: Ability to perceive or recognize similarities or differences in colors, or in shades or other values of the same color; to identify a particular color, or to recognize harmonious or contrasting color combinations, or to match colors accurately.

Explanation of Levels

The digits indicate how much of each aptitude the job requires for satisfactory (average) performance. The average requirements, rather than maximum or minimum, are cited. The amount required is expressed in terms of equivalent amounts possessed by segments of the general working population.

The following scale is used:

1 The top 10 percent of the population. This segment of the population possesses an extremely high degree of the aptitude.

2 The highest third exclusive of the top 10 percent of the population. This segment of the population possesses an above average or high degree of the aptitude.

3 The middle third of the population. This segment of the population possesses a medium degree of the aptitude, ranging from slightly below to slightly above average.

4 The lowest third exclusive of the bottom 10 percent of the population. This segment of the population possesses a below average or low degree of the aptitude.

5 The lowest 10 percent of the population. This segment of the population possesses a negligible degree of the aptitude.

Significant Aptitudes

Certain aptitudes appear in boldface type on the qualifications profiles for the worker trait groups. These aptitudes are considered to be occupationally significant for the specific group; i.e., essential for average successful job performance. All boldface aptitudes are not necessarily required for a worker for each individual job within a worker trait group, but some combination of them is essential in every case.

III. INTERESTS

Preferenes for certain types of work activities or experiences, with accompanying rejection of contrary types of activities or experiences. Five pairs of interest factors are provided so that a positive preference for one factor of a pair also implies rejection of the other factor of that pair.

1 Situations involving a preference for activities dealing with things and objects.

vs. *6* Situations involving a preference for activities concerned with people and the communication of ideas.

2 Situations involving a preference for activities involving business contact with people.

vs. *7* Situations involving a preference for activities of a scientific and technical nature.

3 Situations involving a preference for activities of a routine, concrete, organized nature.

vs. *8* Situations involving a preference for activities of an abstract and creative nature.

4 Situations involving a preference for working for people for their presumed good, as in the social welfare sense, or for dealing with people and language in social situations.

vs. *9* Situations involving a preference for activities that are nonsocial in nature, and are carried on in relation to processes, machines, and techniques.

5 Situations involving a preference for activities resulting in prestige or the esteem of others.

vs. *0* Situations involving a preference for activities resulting in tangible, productive satisfaction.

IV. TEMPERAMENTS

Different types of occupational situations to which workers must adjust.

1 Situations involving a variety of duties often characterized by frequent change.

2 Situations involving repetitive or short cycle operations carried out according to set procedures or sequences.

3 Situations involving doing things only under specific instruction, allowing little or no room for independent action or judgment in working out job problems.

4 Situations involving the direction, control, and planning of an entire activity or the activities of others.

5 Situations involving the necessity of dealing with people in actual job duties beyond giving and receiving instructions.

6 Situations involving working alone and apart in physical isolation from others, although the activity may be integrated with that of others.

7 Situations involving influencing people in their opinions, attitudes, or judgments about ideas or things.

8 Situations involving performing adequately under stress when confronted with the critical or unexpected or when taking risks.

9 Situations involving the evaluation (arriving at generalizations, judgments, or decisions) of information against sensory or judgmental criteria.

O Situations involving the evaluation (arriving at generalizations, judgments, or decisions) of information against measurable or verifiable criteria.

X Situations involving the interpretation of feelings, ideas, or facts in terms of personal viewpoint.

Y Situations involving the precise attainment of set limits, tolerances, or standards.

V. PHYSICAL DEMANDS

Physical demands are those physical activities required of a worker in a job.

The physical demands referred to in this Dictionary serve as a means of expressing both the physical requirements of the job and the physical capacities (specific physical traits) a worker must have to meet the requirements. For example, "seeing" is the name of a physical demand required by many jobs (perceiving by the sense of vision), and also the name of a specific capacity possessed by many people (having the power of sight). The worker must possess physical capacities at least in an amount equal to the physical demands made by the job.

The Factors

1 **Lifting, Carrying, Pushing, and/or Pulling (Strength).** These are the primary "strength" physical requirements, and generally speaking, a person who engages in one of these activities can engage in all.

Specifically, each of these activities can be described as:

(1) Lifting: Raising or lowering an object from one level to another (includes upward pulling).

(2) Carrying: Transporting an object, usually holding it in the hands or arms or on the shoulder.

(3) Pushing: Exerting force upon an object so that the object moves away from the force (includes slapping, striking, kicking, and treadle actions).

(4) Pulling: Exerting force upon an object so that the object moves toward the force (includes jerking).

The five degrees of Physical Demands Factor No. 1 (Lifting, Carrying, Pushing, and/or Pulling), are as follows:

S Sedentary Work

Lifting 10 lbs. maximum and occasionally lifting and/or carrying such articles as dockets, ledgers, and small tools. Although a sedentary job is defined as one which involves sitting, a certain amount of walking and standing is often necessary in carrying out job duties. Jobs are sedentary if walking and standing are required only occasionally and other sedentary criteria are met.

L Light Work

Lifting 20 lbs. maximum with frequent lifting and/or carrying of objects weighing up to 10 lbs. Even though the weight lifted may be only a negligible amount, a job is in this category when it requires walking or standing to a significant degree, or when it involves sitting most of the time with a degree of pushing and pulling of arm and/or leg controls.

M   Medium Work

Lifting 50 lbs. maximum with frequent lifting and/or carrying of objects weighing up to 25 lbs.

H   Heavy Work

Lifting 100 lbs. maximum with frequent lifting and/or carrying of objects weighing up to 50 lbs.

V   Very Heavy Work

Lifting objects in excess of 100 lbs. with frequent lifting and/or carrying of objects weighing 50 lbs. or more.

2 **Climbing and/or Balancing:**
   (1) Climbing: Ascending or descending ladders, stairs, scaffolding, ramps, poles, ropes, and the like, using the feet and legs and/or hands and arms.
   (2) Balancing: Maintaining body equilibrium to prevent falling when walking, standing, crouching, or running on narrow, slippery, or erratically moving surfaces; or maintaining body equilibrium when performing gymnastic feats.

3 **Stooping, Kneeling, Crouching, and/or Crawling:**
   (1) Stooping: Bending the body downward and forward by bending the spine at the waist.
   (2) Kneeling: Bending the legs at the knees to come to rest on the knee or knees.
   (3) Crouching: Bending the body downward and forward by bending the legs and spine.
   (4) Crawling: Moving about on the hands and knees or hands and feet.

4 **Reaching, Handling, Fingering, and/or Feeling:**
   (1) Reaching: Extending the hands and arms in any direction.
   (2) Handling: Seizing, holding, grasping, turning, or otherwise working with the hand or hands (fingering not involved).
   (3) Fingering: Picking, pinching, or otherwise working with the fingers primarily (rather than with the whole hand or arm as in handling).
   (4) Feeling: Perceiving such attributes of objects and materials as size, shape, temperature, or texture, by means of receptors in the skin, particularly those of the finger tips.

5 **Talking and/or Hearing:**
   (1) Talking: Expressing or exchanging ideas by means of the spoken word.
   (2) Hearing: Perceiving the nature of sounds by the ear.

6 **Seeing:**
Obtaining impressions through the eyes of the shape, size, distance, motion, color, or other characteristics of objects. The major visual functions are: (1) acuity, far and near, (2) depth perception, (3) field of vision, (4) accommodation, (5) color vision. The functions are defined as follows:
   (1) Acuity, far—clarity of vision at 20 feet or more.
   Acuity, near—clarity of vision at 20 inches or less.

(2) Depth perception—three dimensional vision. The ability to judge distance and space relationships so as to see objects where and as they actually are.

(3) Field of vision—the area that can be seen up and down or to the right or left while the eyes are fixed on a given point.

(4) Accommodation—adjustment of the lens of the eye to bring an object into sharp focus. This item is especially important when doing near-point work at varying distances from the eye.

(5) Color vision—the ability to identify and distinguish colors.

VI. WORKING CONDITIONS

Working conditions are the physical surroundings of a worker in a specific job.

1 Inside, Outside, or Both:

I   Inside: Protection from weather conditions but not necessarily from temperature changes.

O   Outside: No effective protection from weather.

B   Both: Inside and outside.

A job is considered "inside" if the worker spends approximately 75 per cent or more of his time inside, and "outside" if he spends approximately 75 per cent or more of his time outside. A job is considered "both" if the activities occur inside or outside in approximately equal amounts.

2 Extremes of Cold Plus Temperature Changes:

(1) Extremes of Cold: Temperature sufficiently low to cause marked bodily discomfort unless the worker is provided with exceptional protection.

(2) Temperature Changes: Variations in temperature which are sufficiently marked and abrupt to cause noticeable bodily reactions.

3 Extremes of Heat Plus Temperature Changes:

(1) Extremes of Heat: Temperature sufficiently high to cause marked bodily discomfort unless the worker is provided with exceptional protection.

(2) Temperature Changes: Same as **2** (2).

4 Wet and Humid:

(1) Wet: Contact with water or other liquids.

(2) Humid: Atmospheric condition with moisture content sufficiently high to cause marked bodily discomfort.

5 Noise and Vibration:

Sufficient noise, either constant or intermittent, to cause marked distraction or possible injury to the sense of hearing and/or sufficient vibration (production of an oscillating movement or strain on the body or its extremities from repeated motion or shock) to cause bodily harm if endured day after day.

6 Hazards:

Situations in which the individual is exposed to the definite risk of bodily injury.

7 Fumes, Odors, Toxic Conditions, Dust, and Poor Ventilation:

(1) Fumes: Smoky or vaporous exhalations, usually odorous, thrown off as the result of combustion or chemical reaction.

(2) Odors: Noxious smells, either toxic or nontoxic.

(3) Toxic Conditions: Exposure to toxic dust, fumes, gases, vapors, mists, or liquids which cause general or localized disabling conditions as a result of inhalation or action on the skin.

(4) Dust: Air filled with small particles of any kind, such as textile dust, flour, wood, leather, feathers, etc., and inorganic dust, including silica and asbestos, which make the workplace unpleasant or are the source of occupational diseases.

(5) Poor Ventilation: Insufficient movement of air causing a feeling of suffocation; or exposure to drafts.

Index

Date Due
